LA VIE D'EDOUARD LE CONFESSEUR,

BY A NUN OF BARKING ABBEY

EXETER MEDIEVAL TEXTS AND STUDIES

Series Editors: Vincent Gillespie and Richard Dance

Founded by M. J. Swanton
and later co-edited by Marion Glasscoe

La Vie d'Edouard le Confesseur,

by a Nun of Barking Abbey

Jane Bliss

LIVERPOOL UNIVERSITY PRESS

First published in 2014 by
Liverpool University Press
4 Cambridge Street
Liverpool
L69 7ZU

Copyright © 2014 Jane Bliss

The right of Jane Bliss to be identified as author of this book has been asserted by her in accordance with the Copyright, Designs and Patents Act 1988.

All rights reserved. No part of this book may be reproduced, stored in a retrieval system, or transmitted, in any form or by any means, electronic, mechanical, photocopying, recording, or otherwise, without the prior written permission of the publisher.

British Library Cataloguing-in-Publication data
A British Library CIP record is available

ISBN 978-1-84631-951-8 (cased)

Typeset in URW Garamond by Quentin Miller using LaTeX and LyX.

Printed and bound by BooksFactory.co.uk

Contents

Acknowledgements	vii
Abbreviations	vii

Introduction

Edward the Confessor	1
The Poem's Themes	3
Sources	12
The Nun and her World	33
Translation and Presentation	52

The Life of Edward the Confessor

Prologue (1–10)	55
The Introduction to Edward (11–68)	57
1 Of his Lineage (69–142)	59
2 Edward is chosen King (143–266)	61
3 The young Edward (267–354)	64
4 Brihtwald's Vision (355–510)	68
5 Exile and Return (511–850)	71
6 Description of Edward (851–978)	77
7 Edward's Treasure (979–1080)	80
8 Edward and Edith (1081–462)	83
9 The Vision of the Ships (1463–640)	90
10 Edward's Pilgrimage (1641–2018)	94
11 Pope Leo's Letter (2019–108)	100
12 Saint Peter and the Hermit (2109–284)	102
13 Gille Michel the Cripple (2285–480)	105
14 Mellit and the Fisherman (2481–696)	110

15	A Visit to Pope Nicholas (2697–960)	114
16	Edward and Lievrich (2961–3074)	119
17	The King's Evil (3075–256)	122
18	A Blind Man sees Edward's Beard (3257–438)	126
19	The Blind Man of Lincoln (3439–500)	129
20	The Blinded Woodcutter (3501–628)	131
21	Seven Blind Eyes (3629–92)	134
22	The Fate of Godwin's Sons (3693–766)	136
23	The Fate of Godwin (3767–932)	138
24	The Seven Sleepers (3933–4164)	142
25	King Edward and the Ring (4165–476)	146
26	Edward's Last Illness (4477–638)	153
27	The Vision of the Tree (4639–912)	156
28	The Tree Explained (4913–5016)	163
29	Edward's Death (5017–295)	165
30	Of the Nun Herself (5296–335)	170
31	Ralph the Norman Cured (5336–453)	172
32	Thirteen Blind Eyes (5454–501)	174
33	The Prophecy about Harold Fulfilled (5502–601)	175
34	The Bell-ringer (5602–69)	177
35	Saint Ulstan (5670–949)	179
36	The Saint's Body Uncorrupted (5950–6071)	184
37	The Sewing-Girl (6072–243)	187
38	Osbert's Fever (6244–371)	191
39	Gerins Cured Likewise (6372–441)	194
40	A Nun of Barking Healed (6442–545)	196
41	A Triple Cure (6546–685)	199

Appendix
  Dream and Prophecy   203

Glossary   207

Bibliography
  Primary Texts   213
  Secondary Texts   218

Indexes
  Bible References   231
  Proper Names in Text   233
  General Index   235

Acknowledgements

My first and greatest debt is to Henrietta Leyser, who introduced me to the poem and has given unfailing support in many aspects of my work. I would especially like to thank librarians in the following Oxford libraries: Duke Humfrey, the History Faculty Library, St John's College, and the Taylor Institution. I also thank Cardiff Public Library for supplying me with a copy of part of its MS 1.381. I am grateful to the editorial teams of both Exeter and Liverpool University Press, especially Vincent Gillespie, and to the publishers of my own work cited in the following pages.

Friends and colleagues whose help and support I gratefully acknowledge are as follows: Ilya Afanasyev, Marianne Ailes, Laura Ashe, Mark Atherton, Diane Auslander, Anne Bailey, Terri Barnes, David Bates, Paul Brand, Daphne Briggs, Clive Brooks, Dauvit Broun, Jennifer Brown, Jane Burkowski, John Burrows, Donna Bussell, Mary Carruthers, Michael Clanchy, Stephen Clarke, Judith Collard, Victoria Condie, Helen Cooper, Roger Dalrymple, Jennifer Deepold, Hugh Doherty, Marsha Dutton, Graham Edwards, Mark Faulkner, Jennifer Fellows, Thelma Fenster, Peter Garrard, Linda Gowans, Douglas Gray, Ruth Harvey, Eliza Hoyer-Millar, David Howlett, Richard Ingham, Peter Jackson, Matthew Kilburn, Anne Lawrence-Mathers, Francesco Marzella, Ruth Morse, Marco Nievergelt, Emily O'Brien, Thomas O'Donnell, Bernard and Heather O'Donoghue, Nicholas Orme, Monika Otter, Malcolm Parkes, Carl Phelpstead, Laurie Postlewaite, Jackie Pritchard, A. G. Rigg, Natasha Romanova, Maggie Ross, Winfried Rudolf, Kate Russell, Delbert Russell, Richard Sharpe, Eric Stanley, Jacqueline Tasioulas, Elizabeth Tyler, David Trotter, Benedicta Ward, Diane Watt, Judith Weiss, Frances White, Jocelyn Wogan-Browne.

Finally I thank my partner, best friend and best typesetter, Quentin Miller.

Abbreviations

In addition to short forms for core-texts frequently cited, the following abbreviations are used:

Vie — The Nun's Anglo-Norman *Vie* (*La Vie d'Edouard* ed. Södergård); alternatively entitled *Edouard*, when more appropriate

Vita — Aelred's Latin *Vita* ('Vita S. Edwardi Regis et Confessoris', Aelred of Rielvaulx, ed. Migne)

Life — Aelred's *Life* of Edward (modern English translation, in Aelred of Rievaulx, *The Historical Works* ed. Dutton)

Estoire — The thirteenth-century Anglo-Norman *Estoire*, attributed to Matthew Paris (*La Estoire de Seint Aedward le Rei* ed. Wallace)

History — The thirteenth-century *Estoire* in modern English translation (*The History of Saint Edward* tr. Fenster and Wogan-Browne)

MS P	the Paris manuscript of the *Vie*; readings cited *passim* in Södergård's footnotes.
MS V	the Vatican manuscript, Södergård's base for his edition
MS W	the Welbeck (now Campsey) manuscript
Anon	The Anonymous Life of Edward (*The Life of King Edward* ed. and tr. Barlow)
Catherine	Clemence's *Life* (Clemence of Barking, *The Life of St Catherine* ed. MacBain)
Genealogy	Aelred's *Genealogy* in modern English translation (in Aelred of Rievaulx, *The Historical Works* ed. Dutton)
Osbert	Osbert of Clare's Life of Edward ('La Vie par Osbert' ed. Bloch)
AV	Authorized Version of the Bible (King James Bible)
LV	Latin Vulgate Bible
OT	Old Testament
NT	New Testament
AND	*Anglo-Norman Dictionary*; I use the online version (www.anglo-norman.net), last accessed 7.9.2013
ANTS	Anglo-Norman Text Society
ASC	*The Anglo-Saxon Chronicle* tr. Garmonsway
EETS	Early English Text Society
GL	*Golden Legend*, Jacobus de Voragine, tr. Ryan
IPN	Index of Proper Names (or Table des Noms Propres)
MP	Author of the *Estoire*, which has been attributed to Matthew Paris
Morawski	Morawski, ed., *Proverbes Français*
ODNB	*Oxford Dictionary of National Biography*. Available online; web-address and access-dates shown in notes for individual entries
ODS	*Oxford Dictionary of Saints*, Farmer
OED	Oxford English Dictionary
PL	*Patrologia Latina*

Bible Books

Asterisks denote books in *AV* Apocrypha; names of corresponding books in *LV* added in brackets. Psalm numbers are indexed according to their *AV* numbers

Acts	Acts of the Apostles
II Chr.	II Chronicles (Paralipomenon)
I Cor.	First Epistle to the Corinthians
II Cor.	Second Epistle to the Corinthians
Dan.	Daniel
Ecclus.	Ecclesiasticus*
Ex.	Exodus
Gen.	Genesis
Heb.	Epistle to the Hebrews
Is.	Isaiah
Jer.	Jeremiah
Lam.	Lamentations
Matt.	Matthew's Gospel
Num.	Numbers
Ps.	Psalms
Prov.	Proverbs
Rev.	Revelation (Apocalypse)
I Sam.	First Book of Samuel (I Reg.)
II Sam.	Second Book of Samuel (II Reg.)
Song	Song of Solomon (Canticum Canticorum)
Tob.	Tobit*

Introduction

Edward the Confessor

La Vie d'Edouard[1]

The twelfth-century Life of King Edward the Confessor, in Anglo-Norman verse, is here presented in modern English for the first time. Its author, an anonymous Nun of Barking Abbey, offers a many-faceted and absorbing portrait of the celebrated king and saint, together with legendary material found in no other version of this hagiographic narrative. In addition, there is a wealth of detail about Edward's times as well as about the twelfth-century context in which the Nun was writing. The poem is thus of the greatest interest not only for literary scholars but also for historians. It is among the earliest texts in French known to be by a woman,[2] and so will be of value to scholars investigating medieval female authorship. Long neglected, perhaps because mistakenly deemed a mere translation of Aelred of Rievaulx's *Vita* in Latin, it proves on examination to be remarkably independent of its main source and raises questions about the freedom and originality of medieval 'transposition'.[3]

The only conventional edition of the *Vie*, by Södergård, is out of print, but copies are available in university and college libraries around Britain. Further, there is an easily-accessible and fully-searchable online edition of all three manuscript versions: the Campsey Collection (margot.uwaterloo.ca). This covers all the Lives in the Campsey, previously the Welbeck, manuscript. Not only does it give the Campsey version of the *Vie d'Edouard* but also the other two versions of it (see Manuscripts, below). The compilers are still working on these, so readers are advised to consult them directly.

The poem is in two parts: the Life and Death of Edward, and then a collection of posthumous Miracles. As explained below, I retain the divisions that appear in the manuscripts. They are retained in the edition, and they broadly follow divisions in the *Vita*. Because I have named the chapters, the structure of the book may be seen at a glance in the Table of Contents.

---

[1] Dean and Boulton, *Anglo-Norman Literature*, number 523. For context and date, see esp. Mitchell, 'Patrons and Politics'; Legge's account remains valuable: *Background*, pp. 60–66.
[2] See Short, *Manual*, p. 32; the probable date of the work is discussed below.
[3] Short, '*Verbatim and Literatim*', prefers this word for such translations (p. 160).

2   *Introduction*

The first part of the book begins with the background to Edward's life, and an account of how he became king. His saintly qualities are stressed from the outset, and miraculous happenings reinforce the hagiographical nature of the work. The adventure of his life combines historical events with legendary material, some of the latter taken from earlier accounts. His death is politicized, with discussion of the future state of the realm. After a short linking chapter, in which the Nun writes of herself, the second part of the book recounts a number of miracles including one reported to have taken place at Barking Abbey. Miraculous happenings include events based ultimately, though somewhat loosely, on historical occurences: the Battle of Stamford Bridge, the story of Ulstan's Staff, and the opening of Edward's tomb. The present Introduction explores many of these topics in order to give a comprehensive account of the Nun and her work.

The Three Principal Manuscripts

V: Vatican, MS Reg. Lat. 489, is base manuscript for Södergård's edition of the *Vie*. Its 5222 lines (fols 1a–35b) comprise sections 9–41, vv. 1463–6885. It lacks the account of Edward's early life and marriage, but it continues after the other two manuscripts end and is alone in recounting the miracles. This manuscript may be from Barking.[4] It also contains a Latin verse Life based on Aelred's (see *Estoire*, pp. xii–iii). Södergård bases his edition on this Vatican version because it is older (twelfth century, see his p. 48), and less is missing from it, than the others. However, because it lacks vv. 11–1462 these lines are supplied from the Campsey version (MS W).[5]

W: London, BL MS Additional 70513, formerly Welbeck Abbey Coll. Duke of Portland I.C.1. In the fourteenth century it belonged to Campsey Ash Priory, and is widely known as the Campsey manuscript. Södergård calls it MS W; therefore it appears as 'MS W' in the present work, in case readers wish to check the edition. It contains 4239 lines (fols 55c–85c), and provides sections 0–8 (vv. 11–1462) of the printed edition.[6] It provides the Introduction to Edward, without the Prologue (which exists in one fragmentary copy). It stops very much *in medias res* at v. 4240: in chapter 25, part-way through a passage about Edward's love for the saints Peter and John. It therefore lacks anything to connect the poem with Barking Abbey, viz. chapters 30 and 40, although the cut is in such an arbitrary place that it can hardly be a deliberate effort to delocalize the text. Without V, we should have no evidence that the poem was written at Barking, nor by a nun. The Campsey *Catherine* likewise lacks evidence of authorship.

P: Paris, BnF fonds fr. 1416. This thirteenth-century manuscript, copied by a native of Northern France, has recently been studied not only for the version of *Edouard* it

---

[4]   Hoste, *Bibliotheca*, p. 131.
[5]   See pp. 90 & 201 below.
[6]   See pp. 57 & 89 below.

contains but also as a version of *Brut*.[7] Although condensed, it is unmistakably a copy of the Nun's *Vie*, because of consistent similarity to the other versions throughout in spite of its variants. In terms of the story, it is the most complete of the three extant versions of the text. The later French prose version, described below, is in this sense more 'complete' than the verse copies. P comprises only 3879 lines, corresponding to vv. 69–4482. The main structure is retained, but some episodes are omitted. These will be signalled, together with other variants, in footnotes below. It begins 'In the days of good Englishmen' (chapter 1) and ends with Edward's death.[8] Its importance has been, until recently, mainly and only as evidence that the Nun's work travelled beyond the Channel. This version is inserted into a copy of Wace's *Brut*, the redactor here replacing a passage of twelve lines with *Edouard*. The P-text,[9] then, reads: 'Athelstan was ... the first to be crowned. In the days of good Englishmen ...'. It ends with Edward's death and burial, continuing immediately with the next section of *Brut*. Södergård's footnote to v. 4482 (p. 245) describes the end of the P copy. *Brut* in this Paris manuscript continues: 'Chadwalader wanted to return and rule his land ...'.[10] The dates, needless to say, are inconsistent. Wace's *Brut* is cut at a description of Edward the Elder;[11] the copyist saw fit to insert the Confessor here. Södergård complains that the abbreviations make this version hard to read: 'This MS is executed with a certain negligence.' Arnold similarly remarks on additions made, in this manuscript, to *Brut*: he calls them 'useless'.[12] Södergård provides a count of lines omitted (525) and added (73), but does not apparently notice that the 'negligent' copyist makes alterations with a pattern in mind. Having examined the variations provided in Södergård's notes, I found interesting differences in the scribes' treatment. Differences between W and V are usually slight, whereas the P scribe has a detectably different way of going to work; variants are noted below as they occur.

The Poem's Themes

A number of details and shorter passages of interest will be examined later; this section looks at some broad themes of the Nun's work.

Edward: Holy Warrior, Royal Saint

For the poem as hagiography, see first Hill, for differing types of saint's life within the genre. The 'art *vita*' especially, not designed for liturgical or mealtime reading, was not constrained as to length.[13] Legge characterizes it as ambitious and important.

---

[7] *Vie*, p. 48; *Wace's Brut* ed. and tr. Weiss, pp. 370–71; and Bliss and Weiss, 'The "J" Manuscript'.
[8] See pp. 59 & 153 below.
[9] MS J in *Wace's Brut* ed. and tr. Weiss.
[10] ed. and tr. Weiss, pp. 370–71.
[11] Athelstan r. 924–40. See William of Malmesbury, *Kings* tr. Stephenson, §126, pp. 109–10 (and note 7 on p. 109), for William's account of Athelstan's birth.
[12] Introduction to *Le Roman de Brut* ed. Arnold.
[13] 'Imago Dei', p. 37.

Based on Aelred, it has nevertheless a personal interest: its propaganda of a different kind from the monastic, its object 'more political than pious'. The prologue and epilogue form, likewise based on Aelred, is new in hagiography.[14] The Nun's version of Edward's Life can, like Aelred's, claim to be historical biography. That a copy without miracles (MS P) appears in Wace's *Brut* indicates it was read also as history. It is factual compared to much current hagiography.[15] Legge also points to another Anglo-Norman translation from Aelred, now lost.[16] For Edward's canonization, see Kemp;[17] Pope Alexander III agreed to canonize him to please Henry II, who sided with this pope over the papal schism. For an overview of the circumstances, historical and political, see especially Scholz: Aelred's *Vita* was written after the 1161 canonization, so Osbert's efforts were not in vain.[18]

The Nun, not wishing us to forget Edward as holy warrior, yet prefers to stress his qualities as royal saint. He was royal because it was his lot to be king, and not because he showed typical kingly qualities (for her concept of 'valur', see Glossary). Both Edward and Edith are characterized as wise even when young.[19] However, the Nun makes no suggestion that Edward is a 'holy innocent' (see note to v. 4554, in chapter 26), in spite of her insistence on his virtuous simplicity.[20] The Nun's apparent citation from *The Battle of Maldon*, if that is what it is, could be a way of referring to Edward as a saintly warrior. A not dissimilar phrase appears in Edith's prayer (in chapter 8).

William of Malmesbury insists Edward's healing 'virtue' was personal rather than inherited: 'people wrongly assert that the cure [of the King's Evil] proceeded not from personal sanctity but from hereditary virtue in the royal blood'. That is, the cure proceeds from personal sanctity and not from inherited regality. In any case, William had no great admiration for Edward's father.[21] William may have been 'replying' to accounts of French kings who had achieved such cures, and to the suggestion that English kings were incapable of doing so. His main source for Edward is the (earliest) anonymous Life. He would have known a complete text, perhaps an "improved" copy containing legendary material. Several details, such as Edward's moderation in taxation, are thought to be from oral sources.[22]

Edward as prophet, of his own as well as others' destiny, is crucial to his saintliness. Those who become saints are predestined: Edward shares with Saint Modwenna the

---

[14] *Background*, pp. 246–7.
[15] Thiry-Stassin, 'L'hagiographie', p. 413, note 21; Legge, *Background*, p. 305.
[16] Mason, 'St Wulfstan's Staff', cites Legge.
[17] *Canonization*, pp. 76–8 & 82–3.
[18] 'Canonization of Edward', pp. 49–50; Osbert's own miracle is noted at p. 50. See also John, 'Celibate Life'.
[19] Laurent, *Plaire et édifier* (p. 423): Edward, and St Audrey, are *puer senex* types (see Curtius, *European Literature*, pp. 98–101). At pp. 422–4 she discusses interchangeable saints and a 'model of sanctity'.
[20] Carpenter, 'Origins', on his simplicity, discusses 'sacral kingship' (esp. p. 879).
[21] *Gesta Regum*, vol. I, p. 303.
[22] Ibid. vol. II, p. 206ff.; Edward's personal sanctity in vol. I, bk. ii, 222 (pp. 406–9). See also Nelson, 'Royal Saints': sacrality, in the blood, is not to be confused with sacredness.

gift of dreaming the date of his own death.[23] Edward does not really dream this: the information is brought him miraculously via somebody else's vision (chapter 25; and Appendix, on Dreams). For the related theme of Edward's chastity, see my section on his marriage.

A distinctive aspect of the Nun's portrayal is the way she aligns Edward, tacitly and explicitly, with Christ: there are several passages. Aelred adapts earlier stories, enhancing Edward's compassion and piety (*Historical Works*, Introduction, pp. 22–3); the Nun extends the *imitatio Christi*. The first is in the description of young Edward (chapter 3).[24] The child finds his way to church, to talk to the men who belong there, in a manner reminiscent of the young Jesus in the temple (Luke 2:42–7). Our first view of the adult Edward is not in the flesh but in Brihtwald's vision (chapter 4), not named until the Nun's comment after the dream has ended. 'It seemed to him that he saw a bright-faced figure'. At first sight this could be Jesus himself, until his consecration by Saint Peter shows the figure to be a future earthly king. In an extended comparison (chapter 5), the Nun prays that God, in whose likeness Edward delivered his people, may save us; that Christ may give us our own, as Edward did for his people. She goes on, that Jesus freed Holy Church, and so did Edward all his life. In this passage Christ is called 'King Jesus' three times, strengthening the parallel with King Edward. In chapter 6, the Nun uses the phrase 'nun disable' for Edward's goodness. A similar negative is used in *Catherine*, where three out of four times it refers to God, but it should be noted that "inexpressibility", or a negative expression, is conventional for talking of God (in modern English: ineffable, invisible, infinite, immortal, unknowable, boundless, incomprehensible ... inexpressible). The rarity of 'nun disable', used by both Clemence and the Nun, has been offered as evidence they were the same person. But both must have been taught this kind of language.[25] In chapter 8 Edward prays his marriage may be like that of God with the Virgin Mary, while protesting that he hardly dares make the comparison. He calls himself 'thy servant, and the son of thine handmaid'. This is a citation: Ps. 116:16 (115 in *LV*), although it looks like a reference either to his own mother, Emma, or indeed to Mary. His wife Edith is also aligned with Mary (see notes *passim*). It may be significant that his first vision (in chapter 9) happens at Pentecost. In any case, his receiving enlightenment through the Holy Ghost identifies him rather with the apostles than with God. In the next chapter Edward seeks a Viceroy to look after his realm while he goes to Rome: a notable parallel between two holy kings. Edward is a type of Christ later in the same chapter: there was such grieving in the land as had never been seen for a mere mortal man ('Pur un seul hume', v. 1952). At the beginning of Edward's letter to the Pope (chapter 15), 'maintenir' occurs three times. God takes care of the Church, Edward takes care of the English, God takes care of the world (vv. 2753–61). At the end of chapter 16, after King Edward swears Lievrich to secrecy, as Jesus did his

---

[23] Laurent, *Plaire et édifier*, p. 415.
[24] This chapter also includes a reference about Jesus which is not in Aelred (John 14:10–11).
[25] See John of Salisbury, *The Metalogicon*, p. 271. Russell, 'Notes on Style', is cited below; see p. 42.

disciples after the Transfiguration, the Nun looks forward to the day when the secret will be disclosed by the will of King Jesus.

Most saints' lives contain accounts of miracles, and Jesus performed miracles in the Gospels, but this is not enough to show any saint as a type of Christ unless the narrator makes a point of saying so. In chapter 17 the Nun describes people's reaction to Edward's cure of the scrofulous woman. They marvel how a mortal man can do heavenly deeds (vv. 3235–6). Her focus is different from Aelred's, where they marvel at such holiness under the purple, and such power in the sceptred hands (*Life*, p. 180). The next miracle is explicitly compared, by Aelred, to one in John's Gospel (*Life*, p. 182). Although the Nun omits reference to the Pool of Siloam, many details match, even to the cured man's friends being unsure of his identity. As Edward's death approaches the Nun adds a reference to John's Gospel: he was going away whence he had come – as Jesus said, and did (v. 4647, in chapter 27). In chapter 29 he says he is going to his Father (John 14:28). Before his death Edith mourns as Mary did at the Crucifixion. Most of the posthumous miracles are without explicit Gospel parallels, except the cure of the Barking nun. This resembles one performed by Jesus (Matt. 8:8) and indeed cites the supplicant's speech: 'say the word, and [thy] servant shall be healed' (cf. vv. 6520–21). These passages, slight in themselves, add up to a certainty that the Nun, both following and adding to her source, characterizes Edward as *imitatio Christi*.

Historical and Legendary Women

All the female figures in the poem are enhanced to a greater or lesser extent. Emma, Edward's mother, is made rather more noble and virtuous than in Aelred's account.[26] Also, the Nun adds a reference to 'Matilda the Good'. At the end of chapter 28 she adds a prayer for England's heirs, and their father and mother. This prayer, with its mention of Eleanor, is not in Aelred. His dedication to the king does not mention the queen, either. An exception is Godiva, where Aelred's passage is simplified. A variant in the ω version studied by Marzella,[27] and used by the Nun, is not copied by the latter; she appears to remain independent of Aelred in many places.

Non-historical female figures are given extra descriptive treatment, as noted in certain episodes. These include the woman healed of scrofula, the helpful woman in the woodcutter's story, the sewing-girl's mistress, the sick nun of Barking. Although such details, taken together, do not add up to an argument that the Nun's is a feminist text, they do show her paying attention to the women in her story (including an added villainess: Ethelred's mother Aelfthryth).[28] Other details of interest include her comment about the gender of the shadowy advisor in the sewing-girl story, and her addition of 'holy virgins' to a list of saintly figures in chapter 36. It is not surprising

---

[26] See, for example, references in Mason, *House of Godwine*, for her reputation.
[27] See p. 14, below.
[28] See also Brown, 'Body, Gender and Nation'.

that a female writer should pay extra attention to female characters, and this further shows the Nun's capacity for independent thinking.

Edward's queen deserves a chapter to herself, had not previous critics already celebrated her special role.[29] The most notable feature of Edith's characterization, unique to the Nun, is that she has a passage in direct speech: a voice of her own. She expresses desire for wedded chastity, so that the agreement reached by the couple is mutual; this is additionally enhanced in the later Egerton version.[30] Apart from this, her accomplishments are considerable, though not untypical for a noblewoman. Embroidery in particular was considered an acceptable occupation for elite women, and English embroidery widely celebrated. Fine sewing was often associated with holy women; the Nun may have enjoyed expanding the description of this one. But a reputation among nuns for such work may be why readers of *Ancrene Wisse* were warned they must do only the plainest of useful sewing, and no fancy stuff, so as not to be tempted by the world's flattery.[31] In medieval legend Mary is noted for her skill in weaving and sewing.[32] It is possible that Edith is aligned with the holiest of women, especially in view of the passage about her being a rose among thorns (see also *History*, notes to vv. 1159–66 and 1175–6). It is notable that in chapter 37 the Nun lays great emphasis on the piety of the sewing-girl's mistress, who is a wonderfully skilled textile artist. Further, Edith's mourning at Edward's death evokes Mary's tears at the foot of the Cross.

Edith, after the marriage scene in chapter 8, disappears until the end of Edward's life (chapters 26–9). Named only once and never again, she is 'the queen', capable of taking over responsibility from Edward in his last illness, and tending him devoutly on his death-bed. His dying wishes are for her, and his last words on earth are for her comfort.

Chaste Marriage

Saint Magnus, Earl of Orkney, and his wife lived without any 'stain of lechery' upon either of them.[33] Magnus died *c.* 1116–17; his legend, written around 1200, may have been influenced by that of Edward and others. For the topic of the virgin wife, see for example de Gaiffier's article (although neither Magnus nor Edward is mentioned). Discussion includes even Saint Alexis, and one wonders whether any real-life couples were inspired by these legends, even to practising wedded chastity.[34] Saint Cecilia, whose story circulated in pre-Conquest England, was probably a closer model for Christina of Markyate than the Norman Alexis. Alexis was never popular in England,

---

[29] See, *inter al.* esp. Wogan-Browne, 'Wreaths of Thyme', p. 54; *eadem*, 'Clerc u lai', pp. 68–73; Fenster, 'Equal Chastity'.
[30] See Russell, 'Cultural Context'.
[31] See *Christina* ed. Fanous and Leyser, p. 71 and note on p. 96 (and p. xxv: her embroidery was sent to Pope Adrian IV); see *Ancrene Wisse* ed. Tolkien, pp. 215–16, and *The Ancrene Riwle* tr. Salu, p. 187.
[32] For example 'Young Mary', in *Cher Alme* ed. Hunt.
[33] *Orkneyinga Saga* tr. Pálsson and Edwards, pp. 89–90.
[34] 'Intactam Sponsam'.

'today there is not a single church dedicated to him ...', though this Life was copied here more than once.[35] But Christina must have known of Alexis because of the chapel dedicated to him at St Alban's. Cecilia, like Edward, persuaded her spouse to live chastely with her; like Edward (and unlike Alexis) there was no running away. The chapel was made by Ranulf Flambard, Christina's would-be seducer and her aunt's lover, c. 1115–19 (the oldest version of *Alexis* is found there).[36] Alexis appears in *GL* but not the English *Gilte Legende*; however, a legend of Saint Malchus and his chaste marriage is in the latter.[37] Alexis is mentioned in Osbert's *Life*, in context of Edward's chaste marriage.[38] There are parallels with *Edouard* in the Middle English *Alexius*, probably coincidental: both saints' youthful vow to go on pilgrimage, and the hiding of 'his book of gode paraile' so that none might see it until after his death (cf. the Nun's chapter 16).[39]

The legend of Magnus and his chastity was widespread. On the Hymn for St Magnus (probably late thirteenth century), the editor notes '... this may say more about the attitudes of the author than about the saint. At least this story would prevent anyone making a claim to be the rightful earl of half of Orkney as Magnus's descendant.'[40] The notion of virtuous and chaste wedlock was a commonplace. Gregory the Great tells of a priest who, as soon as he was ordained, loved his wife as a sister: *nam ut semper ab inlicitis longe sint, a se plerumque etiam licita abscidunt* [to avoid the illicit, he would not allow himself even the licit].[41] Laurent reads the emphasis on Edward's chastity as evidence the *Vie* was for an audience of nuns vowed to chastity.[42] This is of course no evidence, because all versions of his Life (that is, versions *not* made by a nun among nuns) make much of it.

Virtuous chastity, rather than infertility, may be proposed by story-tellers to explain any couple's childlessness. In Edward's case it was also thought he wanted no children with a woman of Godwin's house. That he agreed to marry Edith was merely to placate his counsellors (children would arrive as a matter of course). It may have been rumoured in some circles that he was homosexual and therefore disinclined for marital relations. The Nun's elaborate defence against any such 'vice' leads one to suspect she had heard something of the sort (see chapter 3).[43] Several historians suspected William Rufus of homosexuality; Orderic Vitalis points especially to Normandy as a place of wickedness. The Nun could have known rumours such as these, including Henry of Huntingdon's hint that young William's drowning in the White Ship was

---

[35] Legge, *Background*, p. 243.
[36] *Christina* ed. Fanous and Leyser, p. 11 & note pp. 90–91; also pp. xxi–ii.
[37] *GL*, I:94 (pp. 371–4) for Alexis; *Gilte Legende* ed. Hamer and Russell, I:66 (pp. 347–55) for Malchus.
[38] Osbert, p. 75 and note 1; but see Barlow, *Edward the Confessor*, p. 83.
[39] See 'The Life of St Alexius' ed. Furnivall, pp. 30 (MS Cotton) & 56 (MS Laud 622).
[40] *Triumph Tree* ed. Clancy et al., pp. 292–4.
[41] *Dialogues* ed. de Vogüé, IV:12:1–2.
[42] *Plaire et édifier*, pp. 235–7.
[43] See also Barlow, *William Rufus*, pp. 102–4.

a punishment for the vice of sodomy.[44] The Introduction to *Anon* says there may have been 'some report about the youth's behaviour' (p. lxxv). This is the closest anybody has come, as far as I can discover, to suggesting that Edward was thought not to like women. William of Malmesbury declares himself unable to discover the reason for Edward's action (or, non-action). He goes on 'it is *notoriously* affirmed, that he never violated his purity by connexion *with any woman*' (my emphasis);[45] if this is a hint, it may be among Barlow's 'evidence'. His biography of Edward also suggests something of the kind, but again fails to indicate where such a story could have originated. He remarks 'we are completely without reliable evidence' about the questionable behaviour of young Edward and his companions, but gives no reference to any *unreliable* evidence causing his remark; he also mentions Edward's possible visit to the French royal court.[46] Barlow discusses Edward's apparent lack of interest in women; religious scruples are unlikely to be the explanation. Little was known about sex, including impotence and infertility: 'homosexuality was common and acknowledged, but discussed only in connexion with sin'. Edward was described as 'claene' [clean-living]. However, Aelred's remark that he was free of *luxuria* seems no more than conventional praise.[47] *History* does not discuss chaste marriage as typical in saints' lives: a note to vv. 1267–8 merely remarks on the advantages of Edward's remaining childless. MP (and indeed Aelred, and the Nun) followed hagiographic tradition in the matter of this vow of chastity (*Estoire*, p. xxix). For Edward's own feelings about the succession, as far as they may be guessed, see Barlow, *Edward the Confessor*, *passim*.[48]

A link between certain saints and a desire for virginity is found in some aspects of twelfth-century theology: the humanity of God (a vision of the baby Jesus), and new emphasis on friendship (cf. spiritual friendship between Edward and Edith, emphasized by the Nun). Christina, who successfully resisted marriage and certainly knew the story of Alexis, may have known of Edward's reputed chastity in marriage.[49]

The Nun as a Mystical Writer

This topic has already been explored by Leyser and Legge among others.[50] Laurent discusses mystical qualities in *Edouard*; her observations are noted *passim* in the text below.[51] She remarks a dominant theme of fearing and loving God in several saints' lives: in *Edouard*, and *Saint Osith*: 'a clearly didactic thread throughout the

---

[44] Partner, *Serious Entertainments*, p. 219 and note; Barlow, *William I*, pp. 11–12.
[45] *Kings* tr. Stephenson, §197, p. 186.
[46] *Edward the Confessor*, pp. 40–41; and see my note to v. 319.
[47] Ibid. pp. 81–4, 129, & 133.
[48] For example, a 'God will provide' attitude, and evocation of Dan. 2:21 & 4:25, and Matt. 19:26 (pp. 219–20).
[49] *Christina* ed. Fanous and Leyser (p. xviii); see, further, Huntington, 'Edward the Celibate'; Elliott, *Spiritual Marriage*; and Wogan-Browne, 'How to Marry'.
[50] Leyser, 'Texts'; Legge remarks on the *Vie*'s mystical passages: *Background*, p. 233.
[51] *Plaire et édifier*.

hagiographic texture' (p. 199). She draws parallels between Edward and other saints (pp. 201–4). In our text, she says, juxtaposition of Edward and Ulstan shows that the narrative is not intended to be about a particular individual, but that any God-fearing person will receive grace in answer to prayer (see esp. pp. 202–3, and vv. 5670–83). Edward's body is beautiful, not because of any worldly beauty but because his soul mirrors the beauty of God (pp. 427–8). For the miracle of the Ring, see introduction to chapter 25, and note to v. 4445ff. Macbain also remarks on the extraordinary qualities of this part of the narrative.[52]

The source for this mystical quality in the Nun's writing is uncertain. Elements are already in Aelred's text, but the Nun develops them to create and express a distinct and deeply-felt personal devotion to her chosen saint, and to God. Anselm's writings may have influenced Aelred (whether they influenced the Barking nuns directly or not), but Anselm did not invent personal and private prayer. The tradition of prayer to Christ revived and developed in the eleventh century. It was a mental climate rather than a source which formed Anselm's life and prayer, and so could equally have formed the lives, prayers, and writings of others such as our nuns.[53] Passages among Anselm's prayers correspond broadly to paradoxical and mystical passages in the Nun's narrative of Edward. In his prayer to Saint Stephen (ed. Ward, p. 181) appears the image of 'always drinking, always fulfilled', and in the *Proslogion* (p. 243) to 'seek by desiring, desire by seeking'. Ward has confirmed the unlikelihood of his direct influence at Barking (pers. comm). The relative novelty of Anselm's arguments have been much debated.[54] Anselm's prayer for friends is unlikely to be a direct source for the Nun's preoccupation with friendship.

For the idea of holy drunkenness (see Glossary, saüler), it is notable that Osbert of Clare uses the Latin words for this kind of intoxication quite frequently in his letters.[55] It may have been a common topos among clerical writers of the day.

From Latin to Medieval French

It has been said that before 1200 verse was considered proper to convey historical truth. After this it was overtaken by prose, having suffered from association with the licentious fictions of romance.[56] The Nun translates Aelred's prose into verse; the change of medium necessitates, as does the change of language, alterations of diction and vocabulary. It also allows the author freedom to add poetic figures such as word-play, paradox, and antithesis. She develops this very literary diction with apparent relish, and makes it her personal contribution. Too numerous to list here,

---

[52] 'Vocabulary'.
[53] *Preces Privates* in *Prayers and Meditations* tr. Ward, pp. 35–43: parallels at pp. 94, 120, & 285 (appendix). Bestul, 'Antecedents', gives useful background.
[54] Fulton, *Judgment to Passion*, esp. pp. 145–8.
[55] *The Letters* ed. Williamson, pp. 92, 139, 167 (*passim*).
[56] Robertson, *The Medieval Saints' Lives*, p. 23 (given the Nun's celebrated and early use of the term 'fin' amur', there is a nice irony to this statement). But see Gowans, 'What Did Robert Write?', esp. pp. 15–16.

some of the most attractive examples will be set out in footnotes, with Aelred's text for comparison.

She does not, as many medieval writers do, play with names and place-names. An outstanding example is Wace, who shows off his English in this fashion, although his knowledge of English topography is not extensive.[57] In chapter 16, Aelred plays on Godiva's name; the Nun omits the name-play, without reducing her description of Godiva's goodness.[58]

A distinctive trait is her handling of supernatural characters: the way these creatures take their leave. Later medieval examples include Bertilak's departure, at the end of *Sir Gawain and the Green Knight*. The phrase 'whiderwarde-so-ever he wolde' suggests that this mysterious character, now known to be a shape-shifter, is vanishing into a different world.[59] The enchanted werewolf in *William of Palerne* often departs 'wherever he wished'. Ordinary humans go somewhere specific, unless they simply "take their leave" without any added phrase.[60] Further, a messenger in the Middle English *Brendan* vanishes so the travellers do not know what has become of him, which signals he is from heaven: 'we nuste whar he bi-com'.[61] The account of Christina's visitor is comparable: the pilgrim 'announces *by way of his mysterious disappearance* his identity as Christ.'[62] Christina lived earlier in the twelfth century, and the Nun may have known her Life, or perhaps this was a common way of describing such apparitions in twelfth-century narrative. *Edouard* contains several such departures. In chapter 12 Saint Peter appears to a hermit to deliver a message, after which 'Si s'en ala, si cum li plout' [he went away where it pleased him to go]. Aelred writes simply *desparuit* (cf. *Estoire* v. 1814). Something vague about his departure makes one suspect, as if one didn't know, that this is no human visitor. Another is in chapter 25, where Edward gives his ring to a beggar. Some time later, benighted pilgrims meet a marvellous being who shelters them and sets them on their way next morning, saying: 'Here, take this ring to Edward. I am Saint John, whom he generously gave it to the other day ...', and charges them with further messages. It is curious that the beggar, before we know who he was, had disappeared rather oddly: 'Si s'en ala u esvani' [he went away or vanished]. I do not claim there is a particular standard form of words for this situation, but certainly such pointed vagueness about a character's departure indicates that he or she is supernatural. The proliferation of dreams and visions in Edward means that other-worldly creatures, mostly saints, intrude into everyday reality with considerable facility.

Overall, the Nun's style is distinctly more personal than Aelred's, and she repeatedly addresses her audience, using first- and second-person forms as well as expressions

---

[57] *Wace's Brut* ed. and tr. Weiss, p. xx.
[58] For etymology in medieval thought, see Curtius, *European Literature*, appendix xiv.
[59] Numerous in *Of Arthour and of Merlin* ed. Macrae-Gibson: the demon (64), a dragon (114–15), Merlin (124–5, 144–6, 219, 333), and Gawain (249; his magical strength is explained elsewhere in the text).
[60] ed. Skeat, during the protagonists' adventures in disguise, *passim*.
[61] *The Early South-English Legendary* ed. Horstmann, pp. 220–40, at 222.
[62] ed. Fanous and Leyser, pp. xiv–v (my emphasis).

conveying dramatic immediacy. Södergård discusses the Nun's style in his Introduction (esp. p. 34 and note). Laurent further notes her use of poetic techniques: intensifying doublets (chasté/chaste), phonic associations (quer/cor), anaphoric oppositions (ou les vieux/ou les vallez), rhyme (mal faire/bien atreire).[63] These techniques, perhaps owing to differences between French and Latin, have the advantage of clarifying representation of the saint's fine qualities. Words and ideas usually associated with "romantic" love are signalled in footnotes and/or in the Glossary. The Nun's is the earliest known insular use of 'fin' amur'. It is an innovative reworking of Aelred, with a range of relationships (God for humanity, Edward for Saint John, people for one another, Edward and Edith). '*Pace* its use in courtly poetry ... *fin' amor* in the Anglo-Norman High Middle Ages can be the very opposite of private romantic transgressive love.'[64]

Sources

> 'Have a bucher's at that little lot. That's a picture of how it will look when it's finished.' 'Oh yeah? And you designed this all by yourself?' 'Well, not exactly; it was my idea to tear it out of the book.'[65]
>
> Translations generally only gain firm purchase in literary history when they somehow manage to surpass their source and to function as 'autonomous' expressions.[66]

Warren's article contains provocative insights on the status of texts labelled, or self-labelled, as translations. They invite investigation into their relations to texts that are not, in fact, their sources (and that may be written in any language). The term *translatio* encompasses translation as well as transfer (including travel); the latter ought to take precedence more often. Further, anything monolingual, by drawing attention to its language (as the Nun's does), will remind us that a different choice could have been made. Finally, the translated text is as much an original as the source. That every text is an original, or that every text is a translation, amounts to the same thing (pp. 52, 58–9, 65). My own translation of the Nun's text examines her treatment of its source(s), and her use of language, in the light of these remarks.

Earlier Lives of Edward[67]

The Nun's *Vie* is based on Aelred's *Vita* (1161–63). Aelred, Abbot of Rievaulx, died in 1167, therefore the *Vita* was written late in his life. Further, he preached a sermon for Edward's translation in 1163.[68] The Nun, given her reverence for Edward, may have

---

[63] *Plaire et édifier*, pp. 423–4.
[64] Wogan-Browne, 'How to Marry', pp. 139–40.
[65] Hancock's Half Hour: *A House on the Cliff* (January 1955); Ray Galton & Alan Simpson, writers.
[66] Warren, 'Translation', p. 51.
[67] For the historical Edward, see the indispensable Barlow, *Edward the Confessor*.
[68] 'In translacione' ed. Jackson; and *The Life of Aelred*, Walter Daniel, p. xlviii.

gone to Westminster and perhaps obtained her copy of the *Vita* then (see p. 32, below). Although there has been doubt about Aelred's actual presence at the translation, in spite of Jackson's evidence, it is probable that he worked on the *Vita* in London. He may have started it as early as 1161, the date of Edward's canonization.[69] Marzella points to evidence that he witnessed a document there early in 1163.[70] Marzella argues that the ω version of the text was probably not made by Aelred himself, but shows it must have been made very soon after the 'publication' of his *Vita* and certainly before 1170 (his pp. 367–9).

This in its turn is based on Osbert's (*Osbert*, 1138), which uses material from the earliest Life (*Anon*).[71] The Nun makes no mention of any previous Lives except Aelred's, which she is following. By contrast Clemence of Barking, the Nun's contemporary, refers to earlier Lives of Catherine which she is 'correcting'. Although the Nun never names Aelred, it is unmistakably his text that she has before her as she writes.

Other and later Lives of Edward will be described below. None is a straight translation of any other: each rewrites and adapts its exemplar.[72] The Introduction to *History* (*inter al.*) gives much useful information about the historical Edward and his Lives. References to them will appear in footnotes to my text wherever interesting parallels or differences appear.[73]

Rewriting Aelred

The Nun makes so many alterations and additions to her main source that an account of them is appropriate here. Once these have been set out, other possible sources can be examined.

Aelred was commissioned to write his *Vita*, and he mentions his sources rather more explicitly than the Nun does. His 'additions' are from reliable chronicles, or sure and reliable accounts of the ancients (*Life*, p. 129). The Nun says nothing about having been commissioned, and almost nothing about her sources. Her address to her audience is very striking. Personal comments are added, together with extra details, themes, motifs. Her chapters are marked off by such comments, and were perhaps intended to be read or heard separately from one another. The Nun bases the structure of her poem on Aelred, whose text divides up clearly into chapters. However, Aelred's narrative is noticeably less padded-out with his own comments. More of his episodes

---

[69] Pezzini, *Translation*, pp. 333–72 (ch. 14) for Aelred's *Vita*: its Genealogy and Posterity.
[70] 'La tradizione', p. 369, note 88. I thank the author for supplying me with an e-copy of his article, and for corresponding with me about it (noting, *inter al.*, two passages where his Greek sigla have become garbled). I also thank Linda Gowans and Marco Nievergelt for help with the Italian. See also Ashe, *Fiction and History*, pp. 31–3.
[71] Grassi, 'The Hagiographer', challenges Barlow on the unreliability of *Anon* (without mentioning later Lives).
[72] *Anon*, Introduction; *Lives of Edward* ed. Luard; *Estoire*, Introduction.
[73] See, further: Rigg, *Anglo-Latin Literature*, pp. 12–14 and *passim* for Latin lives; the Cult of Edward in, for example, Binski, 'Reflections' (which does not, however, mention the Nun's *Vie*), and *Anon*. Other important studies include Leyser, *Medieval Women*; Campbell, *Medieval Saints' Lives*; Thomas, 'Lay Piety'.

14   Introduction

begin by going straight into the story, likewise the endings to each. The Nun often adds a sentence or two at beginning or end, and although Aelred provides some links between episodes, referring forwards or backwards, the Nun provides more links of this kind overall. Aelred's discourse is less personal than the Nun's. He rarely if ever addresses an audience directly (second-person discourse), although he sometimes uses first-person (singular or plural) as narrative pointers ('as we shall learn', 'let us return to our account', 'as I believe ...').

Some of the Nun's differences from the *PL* text of the *Vita* have recently been explained. Marzella's work demonstrates beyond reasonable doubt that the Nun must have used a manuscript belonging to the second of two families that he identifies.[74] He names the first family ϱ (rho), and the second ω (omega). The latter are mostly of Southern provenance, and the archetype was probably made at Westminster very soon after Aelred had written the copy that corresponds to the first family, which is mostly of Northern provenance. Marzella believes the *PL* version to have been based on the manuscript known as TCD 172, and not on Stowe 104 as previously thought. A preliminary examination of variants in manuscripts of the omega family, or at least those printed by Marzella, would suggest that the Nun might have known the copy witnessed in his MS S, from Bern. Its editor remarks on the English characteristics of the script. Originally a separate item, it is the oldest in the volume, probably dating from the 1160s.[75] All the other witnesses contain interpolations that she does not follow. For example, it can be seen that she does not copy one of the omega variants discussed by Marzella (Godiva's name, in chapter 16). But there remain a number of passages where she does not follow Aelred's original text, as far as we can establish what it was. Even when we have Marzella's forthcoming critical edition, it is unlikely we shall be able to pronounce for certain; the Nun may have used a manuscript that is now lost. However, it is clear even without this valuable study that the Nun used a version different from the only one so far edited.

The Nun's treatment of Aelred's Bible references is noticeable. She often rewords or deletes these, raising the question of why she should do so. The answer is partly to do with the change of language and form: translation from Latin prose into French verse immediately alters the pace and tone of the narrative. Aelred follows the Vulgate closely, for example in the Description of Edward (*Life*, pp. 142–3). He quotes II Corinthians 9:7, God loves a cheerful giver [*hilarem datorem*]. Edward is a cheerful giver [*dator hilaris*].[76] But one can quote directly from the Vulgate if writing Latin prose; not so in French verse. The Nun is constrained by language, metre, and rhyme: 'de suen doner est joius' [overjoyed to give of his own belongings] (v. 900), reproduces the same idea without reproducing the Bible words. For this reason many direct verbal parallels may get lost, even if the spirit and meaning remain close. In such

---

[74] 'La tradizione'.
[75] *The Historia regum Britannie* ed. Wright, Introduction pp. xxv–xlv, for discussion of the *Vita* in this MS.
[76] Barlow, *Edward the Confessor*, p. 159, for Edward's 1044 charter in which he cites this phrase.

cases, where Aelred does not say he is citing Corinthians, he may be using the phrase out of habit, as we might say 'with the skin of my teeth', or 'a whited sepulchre' without necessarily knowing where the saying is to be found.[77] Aelred often quotes apparently from memory. Heinzer remarks: 'most medieval theological writings are literally paved with allusions to the Psalter', not with 'quotations', but rather as a kind of 'almost unconscious intertextual dialogue ...';[78] because clerical writers (including the Nun) knew many Bible books almost by heart. The Nun seems to prefer not breaking the narrative to explain a biblical source, even if she knows it, and there is no reason to suppose she does not. Writers throughout the Middle Ages drew inspiration from Scriptures and the liturgy, in such a way that direct quotation is well-nigh impossible to pinpoint and is in any case more instinctive than deliberate. This can be noticed among well-read people of today, whose conversation is littered with cultural references.[79] In other cases, where Aelred does say what he is citing, for example, earlier in the section just mentioned he says that Edward pondered on a saying of Wisdom,[80] the Nun's reasons are a little further to seek. The answer may have something to do with her intended audience, because if they were layfolk they might not know the Bible so well (see Audience). Jackson says 'Aelred's writing, like that of most monastic authors, is suffused with biblical quotations and reminiscences, often, no doubt, mediated through the daily recitation of the liturgy.'[81] A rough count of Aelred's biblical quotations and reminiscences yields a total of some two hundred references. Just over half are from Gospels and Psalms, which almost all religious must have known almost by heart. Many others are from books that were also very familiar: Epistles, Revelation, Genesis, Solomon's books (including Proverbs), and so on. One would expect the Nun (and her fellow-nuns) to know these as well as anybody, and yet she deletes or paraphrases a large proportion of them, Gospels and Psalms included. A preliminary count of biblical references in the poem yielded approximately fifty-five examples. Further examination has come up with a somewhat larger number; the Nun's references are harder to identify than Aelred's. Curiously, just *under* half are from Gospels and Psalms; as opposed to Aelred's, which are just over half. This gives the lie to any notion that nuns would know only those parts of the Bible familiar from the liturgy. There are fewer identifiable quotations in her work, but references certainly occur. Could she be simply translating – writing straight through – without noticing whether any passage refers to the Bible? Unlikely, because if so more of them would be identifiable. Where she is translating line by line, it can be seen how she often departs from her exemplar in order to paraphrase a reference, yet she often retains a central idea that is still in keeping with the scriptural text. It might be true

---

[77] Aelred of Rielvaulx, *De Institutione*, p. 132 (note to 749).
[78] 'Holy Text?', p. 45.
[79] For example, Gillespie, 'Vernacular Theology', pp. 403–4; and Holsinger, 'Liturgy', on the literariness of liturgy.
[80] Ecclus. 32:1 (*Life*, p. 142).
[81] 'In translacione', p. 55; the same goes for the Nun (cf. *Osbert*, p. 53 note 1).

to say that Aelred's references jog her memory, but untrue to say she did not enjoy a familiarity with the Bible comparable to his.

Next, the Nun's treatment of dreaming may be contrasted with Aelred's, which conforms to the Macrobian pattern accepted in the Middle Ages. Gregory discusses six types of dream; a saint is capable of distinguishing between good ones and evil.[82] Aelred uses *somnium* and *visio* for dreams needing interpretation (or sometimes *oraculum*, in which an authority-figure speaks to the dreamer). The first, *somnium*, is enigmatic because the most neutral, and most challenging for an interpreter. It is unclear, in any sentence, when *in somnium* means 'in a dream' or simply 'in sleep'. The word *phantasma* denotes a dream not to be believed because due to natural causes (such as indigestion). Aelred uses it once in this way (*Vita*, 762C; *Life*, p. 181): Edward says the dreamer has been deceived by *phantasmatibus*, and is reluctant to believe the message.

The Nun tackles the matter of dreaming differently, although the narratives are the same (see Appendix). Overall she is more concerned about the content of any dream than its type, often saying simply 'what he saw' and the like. Examples are, lines: 422 'cele chose', 1615 'par la grace Deu icest vi', 2241 'ceste demunstrance', 2985 (and 3073) 'miracle', 3012 'glorie' (in these passages the emphasis, *passim*, is on 'what they saw'), 3299 'en dormand', 3996 'merveilles', 4727–9 'quant jo fui endormiz ... vindrent a mei', 4849 'icest', 5576 'l'afaire'. She sometimes uses 'sunge', notably in the passage where the dreamer is said to have been deceived. Edward says the dreamer has been 'par le sunge enfantomez', and it is pointed out to him that in the Bible many 'sunges' are true and reliable. She uses one word, 'sunge', in both bad and good senses. Otherwise she uses 'avisïun' sparingly, among the many dream passages: Brihtwald's vision (403 and 477), the woman cured of scrofula (3196), Edward's vision of the tree (4708), the young man who saw Edward leave his tomb (5651 and 5661). This is but a handful, against Aelred's fifteen or more examples of the parallel word *visio*. In the story of the Seven Sleepers, Aelred uses the word *omen* (the Nun has 'signe', 4052 and 4058). When Edward is elected king before he is even born, Aelred mentions *indiciis*, but the Nun avoids using any such word for what everybody knows God to have pre-ordained (see notes in chapter 2, esp. to v. 240).

The Nun's description of Edward's qualities differs from that of Aelred.[83] These (humility, justice, chastity) conform to ideals of kingship as set forth in his other writing. They are, approximately according to how often mentioned in *Vita*: general goodness, justice with humility and sanctity, simplicity and chastity, finally moderation together with lack of avarice and a wisdom beyond his years when young. The Nun's list is harder to quantify. Her language is stronger, emphasizing God's part in all this virtue. A notable addition is the description of Edward, in chapter 5, as a deliverer comparable to God and Jesus (discussed in Themes, p. 5 above). A passage about moderation, in chapter 6, is expanded from Aelred's remark that nobody ever

---

[82] *Dialogues* ed. de Vogüé, IV:50. In Brantley, 'Vision', dream-theory outlined p. 327.
[83] 'In translacione' ed. Jackson, p. 59.

saw Edward over-indulge himself. What comes across most strongly is her celebration of Edward's chastity and 'mesure', and added stress on his gifts of friendship. The Introduction to *Historical Works* notes that Aelred's *Genealogy* (as well as his *Vita*) was intended as a mirror for Henry (pp. 10–12). Aelred, and/or the Nun, may have been familiar with eleventh-century collections such as Cambridge, CCC MS 201, recently described as a kind of Mirror for Princes;[84] Barlow's biography gives texts that could have been plundered, on the subject of royal power and its problems.[85]

Broadly the Nun follows Aelred for Edward's virtues, although she often expands, adding more than she (sometimes) condenses.[86] To the epithet 'blessed', she adds that Edward was loved by everybody. She adds humility and gratitude to Edward's acknowledgement of God's goodness. She does not mention Aelred's quotation from Wisdom (noted above, in discussion of Bible references), but to the list of groups to whom Edward behaves with equality she adds friends in first place. Likewise, she does not cite Psalm 68:5 (*LV*, 67:6) directly, as Aelred does. She mentions Edward as father to orphans but, instead of his being judge to widows, she says he was devoted to all in need. Outward signs of his inner holiness are extended '... as though he had been brought up in the cloisters' (v. 910). Similarly, the Nun adds, to his style of speech, the way he talked to the foolish. Where Aelred says he was never seen to be proud, angry, or gluttonous, the Nun expands lack of gluttony into moderation in all things. Finally she inserts a passage about his chastity, among remarks about his scorn of money, which in both writers conclude one section and lead into the next. Differences in treatment overall look more like the writers' personal approaches than that they used different sources for lists of virtues, bearing in mind that saints are presumed to possess all virtues anyway.[87]

By comparison with Aelred, the Nun makes more of Emma's family. His mention of 'dual holiness' (*Life*, pp. 131–2) is expanded to include 'William the noble Bastard' [Gillame li franz bastarz] (v. 124). As far as I can discover, the Nun is the only writer to use exactly this name for him: noble, as well as bastard. Her vocabulary and rhetoric are also more expressive. Her model may be further to seek than Aelred.[88] Henry II was present at the translation of the dukes Richard II and Robert in Fécamp in 1162. This is important context for the Nun's representation of the family. Next, her assessment of Ethelred's marriage is positive. She says 'King Ethelred did wisely when he took a wife of such lineage: his heirs were able to take after her, in loving God and doing good. For it often happens, that whoever is born from the good

---

[84] Atherton discussed this MS at Oxford Medieval English Seminar, May 2010, and kindly corresponded with me about it. See his 'Mirror for Kings?', forthcoming.
[85] *Edward the Confessor*, p. 158.
[86] Robertson, *The Medieval Saints' Lives*, p. 260: translators boldly invent how a saint might have felt.
[87] Bliss, 'Who Wrote?', p. 81, for the 'Contrary Virtues'.
[88] For what follows, I thank Ilya Afanasyev for much historical information. His forthcoming article, 'Saint lignage', discusses the Nun's possible sources in detail (concluding that none can be positively identified); I am grateful for an e-copy of his draft (June 2012). See also Aurell, *Plantagenet Empire*, pp. 136–8, on the Nun's ideology.

may easily achieve good' (vv. 131-6). This is different from Aelred's '... that from the dual holiness of the two peoples an even holier child might be produced' (*Life*, p. 131). But Aelred's *rex strenuissimus* [vigorous] looks ironic (*Life*, p. 131), considering Ethelred's reputation. William of Malmesbury calls him 'strenuous and well-built for slumber'. The Nun's first sentence (quoted above) looks like polemic against views of the marriage as a catastrophe. Such views are in William's *Gesta Regum* and Henry of Huntingdon's *Historia Anglorum*. *Gesta Regum* was well disseminated, and the Nun probably knew Aelred's *Genealogy* (dated 1153). The passage above resembles Aelred's dedication in *Genealogy*, which contains similar reasoning about dual noble origin, especially: 'And for bad fruit to spring from good stock is contrary to nature' (p. 71). The Nun may be rephrasing just this passage, if she knew both *Genealogy* and *Vita* (see note to vv. 559-72 for further evidence she knew *Genealogy*). Aelred hints at the sanctity of Henry's forbears in *Genealogy*, but not extravagantly, as the Nun does. However, rather than undermining Aelred's praise of the king, perhaps she is stressing that his mother's forbears, too, were admirable.

Turgot of Durham's Life of St Margaret discusses Matilda's genealogy.[89] As with other Lives, lineage is treated in the second chapter. Her uncle Edward the Confessor is another Solomon (see vv. 837-42). This is thanks to his pious ancestors: King Edgar, and Duke Richard (Emma's father). A passage on Richard's piety may be the earliest version of our passage in question. Aelred knew Turgot (*Genealogy*, p. 116 and note). Osbert of Clare's chapter, *De sancti regis generositate et sanctitate parentum eius*, names Edward's parents and praises his lineage. When he turns to the maternal line, from 'the kings of the French and the dukes of the Normans', he describes Richard and Robert. His narrative is more about nobility and piety than about sanctity, but does contain basic material for development of the topic. Aelred, following Osbert, is rather straightforward in his vocabulary. The Nun, however, uses warmer language and especially adds William. Her other references to William match Aelred's throughout except in the story of Ulstan (chapter 35), where she adds more praise of him. So far there is no evidence the Nun drew on Osbert's *Life*, although she could have known it: he corresponded with Barking nuns, and visited there. Wace's *Roman de Rou*, c. 1160-74, was commissioned by Henry, who was keen to improve William's image (or, authors thought he was). The Nun may have known of Wace's work even if she never read it. Significantly, *Rou* was probably copied in monasteries and abbeys as history and not as fiction. However, there is nothing about the dukes' sanctity in *Rou*; piety is not the same thing. Wace's account of William's death, though a good Christian one, contains negative details. His regret for taking England wrongfully does not make him a saint, but rather an ambivalent ruler.

However, it is known that William made a visit to Barking during his first winter in England. He confirmed the abbey's rights while staying there, so may have had a special place in the memory and prayers of the community, hence perhaps the Nun's

---

[89] 1104-07; it is addressed to Henry I's wife.

exaggerated depiction of him.[90] Her desire to sanctify the dukes suggests independent-minded piety: as if she felt free to add, in a spirit of respect, exemplary characteristics to the subjects of her writings. Just such a sense of intellectual freedom enabled Robert de Boron to imagine dialogue featuring Jesus and Joseph of Arimathea. Although the genre is different, this contributes to a picture of writers confidently adding an extra dimension to the depiction of their subject, in a world where familiarity bred not contempt but reverence.[91]

Other differences of fact or detail are noted below as they occur. Some are because the Nun was using a different manuscript from the *PL* version we have today. But this could not account for all or even most of the differences. Any notion that hers is a straight translation from the Latin must be revised, above all because of the additions, sometimes quite small, that transform the Life of Edward into a vivid, chatty, dramatic, and intensely pious – intensely personal – work of Anglo-Norman literature.

The Nun and English Literature

It is possible that the Nun used English sources. One of her departures from Aelred is of considerable interest, as I have described elsewhere.[92] The passage (vv. 4167–8), where she says Edward's spirit became stronger as his body became weaker, suggests that perhaps she was familiar with sentiments expressed in *The Battle of Maldon*, and may therefore have known other Old English literature.[93] The closest proverb I have been able to find, to this "broken body / brave spirit" topos, is a Latin version of 'the spirit is willing, but the flesh is weak' (logically the inverse). The device in question may be 'words in apposition of some kind'.[94] In Edward's time the battle was comparatively recent. The idealized and poetic account must have been known to many. It was reported in *ASC* for 991.[95] The question of how much English was used and understood, in and among the French and Latin of the twelfth century, is an ongoing subject for research and cannot be explored fully here. Naturally our only evidence is written texts, from which spoken usage must be guessed.[96] Among texts investigated, for the proverb under discussion, is the Proverbs of Alfred. Although no parallel is found among them, I note that Aelred is said to have known them.[97] The Nun did not copy the sentence in question from Aelred, but it is significant nevertheless that Aelred, and perhaps the Nun too, knew Old English material of

---

[90] www.tudorplace.com.ar/Documents/barking_abbey.htm and monasticmatrix.usc.edu/monasticon/index.php?function=detail&id=918 and www.british-history.ac.uk/report.aspx?compid=39832&strquery=Barking%20abbey accessed 1.11.2011. See also Wogan-Browne, 'Afterword'.
[91] I thank Linda Gowans for this insight.
[92] Bliss, 'Old English *Gnome*', and introduction to ch. 25.
[93] Hill, 'Eliensis and Maldon', esp. p. 9.
[94] Ruth Morse (grammar.about.com/od/rhetorictoolkit/); I thank Judith Weiss for help with this.
[95] Robinson, 'Artistry', discusses a later date for the poem.
[96] Schendl and Wright, eds, *Code-Switching*, contains useful articles. Its introduction, and the first article (by the editors) on historical background and issues to be explored, provide a valuable starting-point. See also Jefferson and Putter, eds, *Multilingualism in Medieval Britain*.
[97] ed. Arngart, p. 5.

this kind. Gray's anthology contains a range of texts with useful introductions. He reminds readers that the 'revival' of English, later in the Middle Ages, is no such thing. For instance, it is known that Old English manuscripts continued to be read and copied centuries after the Conquest.[98] O'Donoghue has pointed out that Middle English lyrics may contain themes or phrases reminiscent of, perhaps influenced by, Old English poetry. Lines 33–4 of 'Alison', 'Betere is tholien while sore Then mournen evermore', resemble lines 1384–5 of *Beowulf*: 'Ne sorga ... Sēlre bið æghwæm / þæt hē his frēond wreke, þonne hē fela murne' [... do not grieve. It is better for a man to avenge his friend than to mourn him long].[99] It may be no coincidence that there is a passage in Aelred's *Life* (p. 202 and note) which recalls *Beowulf*. Old English literature was read and enjoyed more widely in later centuries than might be immediately evident.

Legge points out that Anglo-Norman was regarded as no different from other dialects much before the end of the twelfth century. The Nun's comment is the first mention of it as a dialect at all. Legge opines that within a generation of the Conquest most people were bilingual, and discusses the community of tastes that obtained among Normans and English even before the Conquest.[100] The Nun makes a point of explaining that the Pope's letter was translated into the common tongue. Södergård assumes she means 'into French' (his note to v. 2016), but of course it would have been 'into English' at the time of the story. Södergård notes a number of anglicisms.[101] They could mean she knew English *or* that her Anglo-Norman contained the construction (here, a form expressing the future); the same goes for the word 'west' (vv. 2166 and 2506.).

Short argues that by the mid-twelfth century 'Anglo-Normans' would have had both passive and active command of English.[102] Most were bilingual by the time the Nun was writing, although some readers might have had difficulty with Old English. Of such earlier material, hagiography was thought more worth preserving than epic literature.[103] It is a tantalizing notion that the manuscript containing *Maldon*, although not collated until the seventeenth century, contains saints' lives as well as this poem about a hero widely regarded as saintly. *Maldon* was indeed preserved, as though considered hagiographical. Greenfield discusses the repetition of formulas linking Byrhtnoth and Byrhtwold, as if both are heroes. He calls the sentence mentioned in connection with the Nun's description of Edward a 'collocation', conceptualizing epigrammatically the point of the narrative.[104] There is no real evidence that *Maldon*

---

[98] Gray, ed., *Norman Conquest*, pp. 169–70 & 521. See also Cameron, 'ME in OE MSS'.
[99] 'How European Was the Medieval English Love-Lyric?'; citing *Medieval English Lyrics* ed. Davies, no. 13.
[100] *Background*, pp. 366, 370 & 371; see also Leyser, 'Texts', and Hayward, 'Translation-Narratives', for Goscelin and Anglo-Saxon culture.
[101] His note to v. 2477 refers also to vv. 5017, 5018, 5553.
[102] 'Patrons and Polyglots', p. 246.
[103] Thomas, *English and Normans*, esp. ch. 23.
[104] *Interpretation*, pp. 56–7 & 52.

was known at Barking Abbey. Ashdown, however, suggests that, since the manuscript contained lives of saints connected with Barking, and Byrhtnoth's wife was a patron of Barking, perhaps this was its original home.[105]

Many important twelfth-century figures were bilingual, as well as literate in Latin. It is not known whether Thomas Becket preached, at Christmas 1170, in French or English.[106] A number of those writing in Anglo-Norman or Latin were of English parentage.[107] William of Malmesbury, like Orderic Vitalis, was of mixed parentage; he used English sources. See, for example, Gray's anthology for native English writers, writers of mixed parentage, or those known to have read and understood English. Introductions to many of his selections, from Anglo-Latin or Anglo-Norman, sketch what is known about each text and its author.[108] Well-to-do francophone families employed English-speaking servants; children learned from their nurses. Many writers in Anglo-Norman and Latin used English sources. The author of *Waldef* may have had English source(s) as well as French, some originally Celtic.[109] *Waldef* was probably an Old English saga story (p. 148). For one main English source see p. 154, where the author reports episodes plainly not to his taste.[110] Thomas of Kent, writing *c*. 1180, thinks of himself as an English speaker first. Of the constellation 'we call Charles' Wain ...', he goes on 'The French call it the Chariot ...'. He complains that translation is difficult, and his editor says this is no proof French was not his mother tongue. However, the remark about the Plough suggests he is a near-bilingual anglophone.[111] On the subject of general knowledge of English as well as French, it is notable that teachers' books were glossed in English and French, as if teachers and pupils knew either language, or both.[112]

The Anglo-Norman Geffrei Gaimar, working in Hampshire and Lincolnshire, read English: *ASC* is a major source for his *Estoire* (*c*. 1140). Gaimar was a cleric, but probably not an ecclesiastic. His patrons founded, or donated to, several monastic houses. A chaplain, Gaimar liked court life and also was interested in Anglo-Saxon saints. If not native, he must have lived here long enough to learn English well (Gaimar is not an insular name). *ASC* is a series of chronicles, written in various parts of England: Winchester, Canterbury, Abingdon, Worcester, Ripon, Peterborough.

---

[105] *Documents*, p. 4, note 1. See Ker, *Catalogue of Manuscripts*, items 171 (charms added to the last leaves of Asser's text), and 172 (*Maldon* was 'possibly bound with 171 already in medieval times'). Introduction, p. xlviii: many MSS show sign of having been read in c11 and c12 ... they were valued and consulted until end of c12, at the earliest. See also Lerer, 'Old English and its afterlife', for a useful overview.
[106] Barlow, *Thomas Becket*, p. 233. See Faulkner, 'Gerald and Old English', for writers' recognition of English dialects.
[107] Le Saux, *Companion*, p. 2.
[108] *Norman Conquest*.
[109] Legge, *Background*, pp. 143–56.
[110] See also Legge, 'Précocité'.
[111] *The Anglo-Norman* Alexander: for the Plough, see vv. 4674–5; for difficulty with translation, v. 4662 and note.
[112] See Hunt, *Teaching*; and Ingham, ed., *Anglo-Norman* (esp. Introduction). McWilliams, ed., *Saints and Scholars*: essays by Swan, and Treharne, discuss the vital activity of reading and writing (Old) English well into c13. See also Treharne, 'The Life of English'.

Introduction

Begun in the late fifth century, it continued until the mid-twelfth. Thus it indicates a wide temporal and geographical range of writers reading and read in English. Gaimar's sources include at least one other English book: 'de Wassingburc un livere Engleis'. This is unknown to us, but it swells the list of English texts known to have been used by Anglo-Norman writers. Post-Conquest Latin historians who used the chronicles include Henry of Huntingdon (c. 1084–1105),[113] Florence of Worcester (fl. 1100), Hugh Candidus, the Annalist of St Neot, and others. The Peterborough *ASC* continued until 1154–55; English entries continued in a Winchester chronicle until 1183.[114]

Christina of Markyate was from an English family; her biographer writes that her protector, Roger, spoke to her in English.[115] Stein calls her 'obviously anglophone'; however, the St Albans Psalter made for her contains no English.[116] One would guess, from French and English names in the text, that Christina conversed in both languages (unless they all spoke Latin together).[117] Osbert of Clare may have been able to read Old English. Clare is a village in Suffolk, so English was perhaps his native language.[118] William of Malmesbury used English sources. William's, and Osbert's, disdain for 'barbaric' English names is no indication they could not read English (*Osbert*, note 1 pp. 49–50 and 53–4; note 1 p. 54). Aelred was a native English speaker (*Historical Works*, Introduction, p. 8). On his deathbed he begs the angels in Latin and English to come quickly for him.[119] According to his biographer, that language [English] is in some ways sweeter to hear. Baswell continues: 'Yet at this liminal moment, when a dying holy man witnesses agents of divinity, the brief appearance of English also has an authenticating force absent from most of Walter's Latin.' It is an apt coincidence that the stricken Edward is characterized by a passage, added by the Nun to her source, which is reminiscent of a passage from an Old English poem.

Whether readers had trouble with Old English sources or not, writers clearly could and did use them. Further examination, for example whether writers known to have used English sources were connected in any way with Barking (Adgar is an example, mentioned below), could help us to estimate what the nuns might have read.[120]

Other Sources

If the Nun's ability to read Old English remains open to question, the nature of her other sources (written or oral) could also be hard to establish. Södergård's declaration

---

[113] Rigg, *Anglo-Latin Literature*, pp. 36–40. See Partner, *Serious Entertainments*, p. 185, for Henry's translation of Anglo-Saxon poetry into Latin.
[114] Introduction to *Early Middle English Verse and Prose* ed. Bennett and Smithers, p. xii. See Faulkner, 'Anglo-Saxon Manuscripts'; Trotter, 'Intra-Textual'; and Short, *Manual* (Introduction), for overview of bilingualism, trilingualism, and cultural borrowing during the period; also Chibnall, *Anglo-Norman England* (final chapter).
[115] *Christina* ed. Fanous and Leyser, p. 42; & note p. 93.
[116] 'Multilingualism', pp. 32–3.
[117] See also Millett, 'No Man's Land', pp. 91–3, for her English background and her ability to speak French.
[118] See Leyser, 'Texts'.
[119] Baswell, 'Multilingualism', p. 40.
[120] See, for example, O'Donnell, 'The ladies'.

(p. 27), that the *Vie* is wholly based on the *Vita*, must be qualified. Wallace calls it 'a translation from start to finish' (*Estoire*, pp. xxiii–iv). But it has already been shown the Nun makes additions that are clearly her own. The following are the most intriguing, and suggestive of her cultural environment. It remains possible that there are variants in the ω version of Aelred's *Vita* not printed in Marzella's recent study. We need his full critical edition before we can be certain what the Nun might or might not have copied from it.

A story not in Aelred, but known from elsewhere, is the passage about Edward the Martyr in chapter 37. It will be demonstrated, below, that she must have known his Life; here follows general discussion of the story and its circulation. It is her addition to blame the stepmother for his murder; Aelred mention this neither here (*Life*, p. 229) nor in *Genealogy*. A footnote in the latter says Edward is thought to have been murdered by Ethelred and his mother.[121] The Nun's detail demonstrates that she had sources other than Aelred. It appears in a manuscript known to have been at Barking (see Barking's Books, the Cardiff MS). This version of the story was current elsewhere, for example in William of Malmesbury's account. The Nun blames the woman, without mentioning any involvement of her hero's father. William, by contrast, takes a very poor view of Ethelred. William's account adds this story to his source (see Edward's entry in *ODS*). *ASC* says, in 978 'Edward was murdered in the evening, at Corfe "passage": he was buried at Wareham with no royal honours.' The lady commits further wickedness in *Liber Eliensis* (II:56). The story appears in Gaimar's *Estoire*, too. Such anecdotes were probably common knowledge.[122] The Barking community must have known of intrigues involving an abbess and Edward's stepmother (see below for Wulfhilda, and her entry in *ODS*). William may have heard the story from nuns at Shaftesbury, where he visited.[123] Oral material (hearsay, gossip) circulated among such communities, much finding its way into the writings of visitors and residents. For example, see p. 25 below; and Saint Dunstan in chapter 27. A note in *Life* (p. 229) comments that the Sewing-Girl story may originally have belonged to Edward the Martyr (r. 975–79, feast 18th March), but there is no mention of it in English legendaries,[124] and the Nun gives no date for the feast that so worried the lady in the story. The miracle appears in a Middle English version of Edward's Life, with no suggestion that any other than the Confessor was to be celebrated that day.[125] It is poetically appropriate that the girl should confuse the two Edwards, but, given the absence of any trace of the story in the earlier Edward's legend, one need not assume it originated there. See also *Anon*, p. 124, note 4: one manuscript of *Osbert* ignores

---

[121] p. 104; see also Hayward, 'Innocent Martyrdom'.
[122] ed. Bell, pp. lxvii–lxxii.
[123] *Gesta Regum*, vol. II, pp. 143–5.
[124] See for example *The Early South-English Legendary* ed. Horstmann, pp. 47–53; *The South English Legendary* ed. D'Evelyn and Mill, I:110–18 (the Martyr is not in *GL*).
[125] *The Middle English Edward* ed. Moore, pp. 102–3 (in the Prose life).

both the prior (who appears in Aelred's version) and confusion with the Martyr (see *Osbert*, where neither detail appears).

Several details, where the Nun does not copy Aelred closely, appear early in the poem. One is her expansion of Aelred's account of the Norman dukes, making them into saintly figures (chapter 1, and see above, p. 18). Another is her remark that the unborn Edward knew 'only the secrets of his mother's womb, and felt its oppression' (vv. 232–4). This is not in Aelred. The question of Anselm's influence is examined in my section Barking's Books. The possibility that nuns and other writers knew earlier authorities via *florilegia*, rather than their actual texts, is a real one. *Prayers and Meditations* (tr. Ward) gives additional contextual information. The idea of virgins, both male and female, as spouse of Christ is a commonplace (p. 225). Anselm's prayer for friends is a detail corresponding to Edward's care for friends, but is unlikely to be a direct source (see pp. 212–15). Friendship was a key twelfth-century topic;[126] the Nun's treatment is independent of Aelred's, and probably of Anselm's. Legge compares the Nun's Prologue (see below) to that of Gregory of Tours' book of Holy Confessors. Other sources must have been oral: learned conversation, and gossip (in French, English, or Latin). Further differences from Aelred are as follows:

The hint about young Edward's vice (in chapter 3) must be hearsay or gossip,[127] unless a source for the idea can be found. There is mention of foreigners as guilty of unnatural practices in *Vie de Saint Clement*. Its editor notes that in the source the phrase *apud Gallos* [among the French] occurs, replaced in *Clement* by 'un autre pais'. There are numerous manuscripts of *Recognitiones*, fifth century to fourteenth, part of the corpus of Pseudo-Clementine literature.[128] If Aelred knew any such rumour, perhaps he omitted it as inappropriate. 'The question of whether Edward may have been homosexual is not raised in any of the sources'.[129] The Nun's is the only mention, as I have noticed (see p. 8, above).

In 'Exile and Return' the Nun's details are more elaborate than Aelred's, as if she knew a different "history book" (here, perhaps his *Genealogy*). Aelred does not mention treachery in the matter of Ironside's death, nor the Danish destination of the princes. She expands on how Cnut was thinking, although this could be invention. Her account of the murder of Alfred differs from Aelred's: 'After some time had elapsed, Alfred ... was carried over to England at his mother's behest and put to death ... by his enemies and countrymen alike' (*Life*, p. 139). She alters the motivation for Alfred's journey, perhaps to remove any hint of blame for Emma, and spells out that the enemies were Danes and the countrymen English. She mentions her sources but not what these were.

---

[126] Barlow, *Thomas Becket*, p. 49.
[127] '... women's gossip, unlike male gossip, is nearly always erotic' (Lochrie, 'Between Women', pp. 71–4).
[128] ed. Burrows, vol. II, vv. 9225–37; in vol. III, see notes to these lines, and Introduction, pp. 40–41 & 51–2.
[129] Mason, *House of Godwine*, p. 47 & note 90 (p. 216).

There is an added reference to the Fall of Man in chapter 8; this could be drawn from everyday knowledge of the Bible and liturgical texts. Her portrait of Edith is expanded, and the young woman's difference from her father underlined.

In the Vision of the Ships, the Nun adds detail to her scene. The Danish king approaches a larger ship in a small boat, and slips while jumping from one to the other. In Aelred the king appears to be jumping up and down, 'in his great pride', on the flagship of the fleet. This is accounted for by a variant in the manuscript used by the Nun (see my introduction to chapter 9).

There is discrepancy between Aelred's account and the Nun's about what will become of Tostig and Harald Hardrada, but Aelred's is corrected in the prediction's later fulfilment, where the two accounts match. We now know for certain that the Nun was using a version of Aelred's text different from the *PL* copy, thanks to Marzella's study; this shows variants here and elsewhere (see my introduction to chapter 22). They could account for several slight differences, but it is also likely the Nun knew other versions of some of the events she 'translates'.

Introducing the Ring story, there is an added passage which looks proverbial.[130] When narrating the Green Tree prophecy, the Nun talks of knowing things from 'other people' (v. 4918); though perhaps this is simply a reference to Aelred. But in the Explanation of this prophecy, she remarks that she has heard Matilda called 'Matilda the Good' (v. 4978); this is not in *Life* (p. 208). She may be referring to *Genealogy*, where Matilda is described in glowing terms. For example: 'another Esther in our own time' (p. 119; also p. 72 and footnote, for 'Good Queen Maud'). The Nun is thus complimenting a lady who was Barking's abbess for a time. Esther, heroine and saviour of her race, originally had another name (as Matilda was Edith before her marriage to Henry I).[131]

It is unlikely that the 'escrit', mentioned in the Nun's (but not Aelred's) chapter about Dunstan's prophecy, can be a reference to *Genealogy*. She says the people knew nothing of Dunstan's prophecy, or of his promise, not having seen the writing (see chapter 27; and *Genealogy* p. 104, about Ethelred, for the prophecy). Perhaps she means some much earlier 'escrit', that people ought to have known at the time of Edward's death. This suggests she knew a life of Dunstan, or some other record of his utterances. Another possibility is that she means Aelred's own 'escrit', rather anachronistically (to us). Naturally the people would not have seen this writing.[132] Aelred is the first to add, to Dunstan's prophecy of disasters, the promise of an end to them. He probably knew William of Malmesbury's version and adapted it. Reading a promise back into Dunstan's prophecy makes very good sense in this context: matching Edward's vision with Dunstan's, stressing Edward's saintliness by pairing

---

[130] See above, and Bliss, 'Old English *Gnome*'.
[131] For Hadassah, see Esther 2:7.
[132] I thank Ilya Afanasyev for this interesting suggestion. See, further, Otter, *Inventiones*, for twelfth-century texts and their referentiality (esp. Introduction, and for example p. 153 of e-copy).

him with Saint Dunstan, expressing a hope for the future which flatters the present king.[133]

In addition to details about Edward the Martyr, the Nun's account of the sewing-girl miracle differs from Aelred's in the matter of the prior, mentioned by Aelred, who could have been Osbert himself (*Anon*, p. 125). The Nun mentions only an abbot, although in the chapter following Osbert's cure she says he is a prior (where Aelred says 'a brother'). She may have known some of the material from Osbert as well.

The cure of the sick nun of Barking, among the last miracles in our text, presents another puzzle. Aelred speaks of her as though she has died, but the Nun claims to know her: 'she is here to this day'. She mentions that 'he who made the life' told of it before, and it is possible that either (or both) invented the detail of the woman's being alive (or not), even if the whole story was not an invention of Aelred's taken up eagerly by the Nun.

There remains her reference to the Rule of Benedict (not in Aelred) in the last miracle of all: a reminder that one is not allowed to run about shouting in a Benedictine house, even if one has just been miraculously cured.

All these are noted in the text below as they occur. Each is rather slight, and many could be invention, or based on hearsay. One can imagine the Nun doing her best to follow Aelred's text, but being unable to resist slipping in details from other things she had read or heard. After all, she allowed herself plenty of leeway in the matter of personal and homiletic comment. One previously unnoticed extra source has been definitively located, that is, the Life of Edward the Martyr known to have been at Barking (see next section). Taken all together, these items add up to strong evidence that the Nun had several sources.

Barking Abbey's Books[134]

In order to arrive at an estimate of sources the Nun had access to, an account of what is known (or may be conjectured) about Barking's library is given here. In the mid-eleventh century a book, the El Escorial *Boethius*, was given to Horton Abbey in Dorset by one Aelfgyth, perhaps the abbess of Barking.[135] The dates of her abbacy are obscure, but she must have been in office until at least 1086 (depending upon when Goscelin was writing at her request).[136] Perhaps Barking had a spare *Boethius*. Only from hints like this can we guess what books the abbey possessed, and what books the Nun might have known. Links between Barking and other foundations

---

[133] For Dunstan's prophecies, and William's oral sources, see Keynes, 'Declining reputation', pp. 236–40. See also Ashe, *Fiction and History*, p. 77, on Aelred's (and, by extension, the Nun's) alterations to this passage: 'the past is comprehended only, and rightly, in terms of the present ...'.
[134] See also Bussell, 'Cicero, Aelred and Guernes'; and Blanton et al., eds, *Nuns' Literacies* (essays by Hollis and Blanton for general background, although the collection contains nothing about nuns of Barking in c12).
[135] I thank Mark Faulkner for this information (see his 'Anglo-Saxon Manuscripts', pp. 62–3).
[136] See, for example, Mitchell, 'Patrons and Politics', pp. 349–50; O'Donovan, *Charters*, pp. lviii–lxi; Hayward, 'Translation-Narratives', pp. 81–3; Hollis, 'Monastic School' pp. 49–50.

include the endowment by Edgar to Wulfhilda, of West Country properties including Horton. Hollis mentions that a wealthy vowess (Aethelgifu, d. late tenth century), who may have been educated at Barking, donated a book to monks of Bury.[137] In the late twelfth century Henry II's daughter was abbess of Barking and his half-sister Mary abbess of Shaftesbury. There must have been royal, as well as clerical, comings and goings between these houses. Visiting (religious, lay, noble) was a prime vehicle for news, gossip, and of course books. Chroniclers most often had only the common talk of the day on which to rely for knowledge of public affairs. There is some evidence that newsletters circulated between monasteries.[138] Treatises were written and passed around to argue particular points of interest. The extent of pamphlet circulation is difficult to gauge, as is any assessment of their reception in houses where they may have arrived unbidden.[139] O'Donnell discusses the writers, out-of-house authors, whose careers were shaped by the nuns' patronage, and argues that the court was not the most important point of reference in a wide exchange of literary context and influence.[140]

See Ker, ed., *Medieval Libraries*, p. 6, for what is known about manuscripts at Barking in the twelfth century. These are: Oxford, Bodleian Library, MS Bodleian 155, *Evangelia*, tenth or eleventh century;[141] Oxford, Bodleian Library, MS Laud lat. 19, *Cantica*, etc., twelfth century; and, significantly, a manuscript of saints' lives: Cardiff, Central Public Library, MS 1.381. Other manuscripts listed as from Barking are too late for our Nun to have known. Altogether, Ker lists fourteen or fifteen known manuscripts, dating from the tenth century to the fifteenth. Also listed are 'rejected' manuscripts – perhaps rejected simply because not proved to have been there.[142]

Ker, *Medieval Manuscripts*, pp. 347–9, describes Cardiff 1.381, dating it early to mid-twelfth century. On fols 1–80 is a life of Winwallus; fols 81–146 contain the seven saints' Lives listed below.[143] They were written in England; 1 and 2 (Goscelin's Ethelburga, and Lections for Hildelitha) probably at or for Barking, 1–7 probably annotated and foliated there later. For Edward the Martyr (item 3, fols 97–102) see Fell's edition.[144] Nothing in Ker's description suggests the Nun could *not* have known this Life, perhaps written for Barking, and indeed by Goscelin.[145]

---

[137] 'Monastic School', p. 45.
[138] Barber, 'Eleanor and the Media', pp. 15 & 20.
[139] Sharpe, 'Symeon as Pamphleteer'.
[140] 'The ladies', esp. his p. 94 (and *passim*).
[141] The nuns copied records into this MS (Faulkner, 'Anglo-Saxon Manuscripts', p. 159).
[142] Ker, ed., *Medieval Libraries*, and Ker, *Medieval Manuscripts*.
[143] Colker, 'Texts', p. 394; *Edward King and Martyr* ed. Fell, pp. v–vi.
[144] *Edward King and Martyr* ed. Fell; the 1898–1901 *Bibliotheca Hagiographica Latina* entry (2418) predates this.
[145] See Tyler, 'From Old English to Old French', p. 175 (citing Fell's Introduction); and Fell, 'Hagiographic Tradition' (Keynes, 'Declining reputation', p. 237, endorses this view).

Bell describes the Cardiff manuscript, dating it early twelfth to thirteenth century. He gives its seven Lives as follows:[146] Goscelin's Ethelburga, Hildelitha, Edward the Martyr, Goscelin's Edith, Ricemarch's David, Hildebert's Mary of Egypt, Ebrulfus. Bell's later study adds little:[147] he judges that the Nun was writing in the 1160s; he does not think she was Clemence nor, it would seem, that Marie of Ely was Marie de France (p. 123). He concludes that the intellectual attainments of later medieval religious women have been underrated; the study is not mainly focused on the twelfth century.

Ethelburga, Hildelith, and Erkenwald[148] form a group in the remoter past; the Life of Wulfhilda may have contained more recent, anecdotal, material which the Nun could draw upon. It is also possible the Nun knew Osbert's *Life* of Edward. Many of Goscelin's works were only attributed to him.[149] However, mention of Wulfhilda and others is found in William of Malmesbury;[150] the Nun may have known his work, among others. If Goscelin's Lives were for, and at, Barking, then some details they contain would be known by the Nun and not by Aelred. Whether by Goscelin or not, the Cardiff Life of Edward the Martyr was certainly at Barking and may have been used for mealtime reading.[151] It contains a detail that indicates it as a hitherto unnoticed source for the Nun: the mention of the stepmother's involvement in Edward's murder.

This library is likely to have contained more books, that cannot now be identified. Millett points to the formal educational provision for nuns, resulting in a high level of literacy and Latinity among recluses who were formerly nuns.[152] Barking nuns in particular taught (as well as being taught) Latin.[153] Bell discusses nuns' literary environment.[154] Barking was among the five richest religious houses (p. 10); it later possessed many texts in French (p. 37). The desire for or imposition of anonymity may have caused untold loss of male (p. 91) as well as of female authors (pp. 70–71). The statutory number of nuns was thirty-seven. Therefore, the library would have contained some forty volumes at that time (p. 42), because each was to read one book per year.[155] The Benedictine Rule states that each brother (or sister) must take a book, in Lent, to read for the year.[156] Monks are commanded to read silently during rest-periods so as not to disturb their brothers – an interesting comment upon the question

---

[146] Bell, *What Nuns Read*, p. 108, 'Barking 3'.
[147] 'What Nuns Read: The State of the Question'.
[148] Erkenwald's Life was probably not by Goscelin, but is listed in the ill-fated Cotton MS (which also contained *Maldon*).
[149] Rigg, *Anglo-Latin Literature*, pp. 20–21 (he does not list these Barking lives).
[150] *De gestis pontificum* ed. Hamilton, p. 143.
[151] Bussell and Brown, 'Introduction', pp. 13–14.
[152] 'No Man's Land', pp. 88 & 90.
[153] Stevenson, 'Anglo-Latin Women Poets'; and see note on p. 33, above.
[154] *What Nuns Read*.
[155] Introduction to Anselm, *Proslogion* ed. and tr. Charlesworth, p. 15: a rule made by Lanfranc (cited in *Monastic Constitutions* ed. and tr. Knowles, p. 19); also noted, the large libraries of most Benedictine houses.
[156] *The Rule of St Benedict* ed. Dean and Legge, ch. 48.

whether reading was silent in medieval times.[157] If this was the case at Barking in the twelfth century, then we could estimate some three dozen more books than the few we know of; Barking had the largest number of Latin books, among women's communities.[158] More nuns than we realise may have been taught Latin, and our Nun was probably aristocratic; she would have learned in-house or with a private tutor (pp. 62–3).[159] She may have possessed books of her own.[160] Given the high level of book-learning recorded at Barking,[161] it is not surprising if we find at least two (if not more) highly Latinate intellectual women, capable of informed theological comment in their writings.[162]

It is not possible to ascertain whether the library possessed any works by Anselm. His influence is debatable, and it will be necessary to examine some recent scholarly opinions on the subject.[163] A theme of mystical 'plenté' is central to the Nun's poem, and no source is known for it or other possibly Anselmian ideas in the writings of both her and Clemence.[164] A treatise on the custody of the soul, in which angels gaze at God in Heaven, is found in a manuscript that may have been at Barking, but not until the thirteenth century.[165] This, Cambridge, Trinity College, MS 1133, was rejected by Ker.[166] But Wogan-Browne says 'the Cambridge manuscript that Ker and Bell are reluctant to ascribe to Barking contains hymns to Etheldreda, sermons of Sully, Anselm's *De Custodia* ...'.[167] This reference to *De Custodia* is elusive. The manuscript in question was not used for Southern and Schmitt's edition, where its only mention is in relation to something else: it appears in the Index, but not as a manuscript of *De Custodia*. In it, and in three other manuscripts, 'the first paragraph is omitted and the sermon begins with the words *Notandum est duas esse beatudines*.' This is from the Introduction relating to Dicta and Miracula (not to *De Custodia*); and this is what appears in the manuscript. Therefore *De Custodia* is in this edition of Anselm's writings, but the Cambridge manuscript described by Wogan-Browne is not.[168] Another of Anselm's editors, Charlesworth, does not list *De Custodia* among his works at all. Further, see James, 'Essex', p. 35: Cambridge Trinity MS 1133 (A.2.29 sic) O.2.29. The entry begins with a query mark, and ends with a collect for Saint Ethelburga (he calls it 'Hermas' ...). Anselm is not mentioned among the manuscript's contents. See his *Trinity, Cambridge*, pp. 122–6, for Anselm: item 4 in MS 1133 reads *Sermo uen. Anselmi ... de duabus beatitudinibus et miseriis*. The only

---

[157] See also Hunt, *Teaching*, p. 9.
[158] Green, *Women Readers*, p. 138.
[159] See also James, 'Essex'; Ker, 'Essex Monastic Libraries'.
[160] Bussell and Brown, 'Introduction', pp. 16–17.
[161] Brown and Bussell, eds, *Barking Culture, passim*.
[162] Russell, 'Identity Matters', *passim*.
[163] See also Bliss, 'Who Wrote?'.
[164] Leyser, 'Texts', pp. 52–4 & note 10; Dinzelbacher, 'Beginnings of Mysticism'.
[165] Wogan-Browne, 'Wreaths of Thyme', p. 53 & note 27.
[166] *Medieval Libraries*, p. 6; Bell does not mention MS 1133.
[167] *Saints' Lives*; she also suggests Clemence knew Anselm via *florilegia* (pp. 232–3, and note 29).
[168] *Memorials* ed. Southern and Schmitt, pp. 354–60; for the work as Pseudo-Anselm, see pp. 12 & 16.

instance of *castitatem custodias* is in item 1, where Anselm's name does not appear. The manuscript, as noted, is thirteenth century; because of the collect for Saint Ethelburga, 'the book ought to have belonged to Barking Abbey' (the Ethelburga item, at the end, is in a late fifteenth-century hand). Unless it was copied at Barking from texts already there, our nuns could not have known the material in time to be inspired by Anselm (or Pseudo-Anselm) for their Lives. Whether the item is *De Custodia* or a sermon on Beatitudes, and whether by Anselm or not, is immaterial: our nuns could not have known it from this manuscript.

A draft article by Fenster, which I am unable to cite because unpublished, also stated the influence of Anselm. Her argument, based on a perception of common themes (not including 'plenté'), I found to be imprecise because it did not indicate where to find these themes in Anselm's work.[169] Evans points to the complex of 'will, power, and necessity' in *Cur Deus Homo*,[170] but it must be noted that forms of each of these words are commonly used as auxiliary verbs, in several languages, so that instances in *Edouard* (or *Catherine*, or elsewhere) do not by themselves constitute proof of influence. Influence is possible, because of Anselm's importance, but there is no evidence for it. Russell cites Wogan-Browne on the influence of Anselm,[171] and generously sent me e-copies of this and his 'Identity Matters'.[172] He discusses Anselmian language in the two Barking lives, but gives no precise references to Anselm's work. He also cites Fenster's earlier work, but neither author explains adequately how Anselm might have influenced the Barking nuns, taking such influence for granted. Fenster's recent article refers to 'a fervent and joyous Anselmian rhythm' in the Nun's *Edouard*, but likewise gives no particulars (her p. 140). At p. 142 there is unreferenced mention of 'pöer' and 'voler' as 'Anselmian' vocabulary.[173] It is worth noting that Aelred uses the terms *potestas* and *voluntas*.[174] Perhaps the Nun uses such language because Aelred does? The fact that such language also appears, unsurprisingly, in other works than these can hardly prove that the two lives were by the same woman. I have cited some unpublished papers that I was privileged to see. They show how an idea, such as the influence of Anselm at present under discussion, may be passed around among scholars until it becomes accepted *before* the final versions appear (for example in the Barking volume cited; and see p. 46 below). In one of these unpublished papers, a case was made for a 'school style' at Barking, that could *minimize* differences between the styles of individual authors (see discussion of the Nun's identity, below). This useful observation likewise never made it into print.

Anselm may have influenced the Barking nuns indirectly, or orally. There is a tenuous connection, via Aelred, between Anselm and Barking. Gilbert Crispin

---

[169] She kindly showed me 'Queen Edith and the Nun', subsequently withdrawn because much of the material appears in a later article (see below).
[170] *Anselm*, pp. 45–7.
[171] Russell, 'Notes on Style'; and see Wogan-Browne, *Saints' Lives*.
[172] 'Identity Matters'.
[173] 'Equal Chastity'. Elsewhere Batt, 'French of the English', cites these scholars.
[174] See, for example, Brown, 'Body, Gender and Nation', p. 158.

(one of Anselm's immediate disciples) appears in the *Vita*, and in the *Vie*, among stories of what happened after Edward's death (see chapter 36). But manuscripts of Anselm's work were rare in the twelfth century: his writings had little influence immediately after his death (1109),[175] and did not begin to be taken seriously until the thirteenth century.[176] However, Osbert of Clare was a close friend of Anselm's nephew, Anselm of Bury. He talks about Anselm senior in letters,[177] and perhaps talked about him when visiting, so the Barking nuns may have known more about him than was general elsewhere. Anselm corresponded with nuns of Wilton, Shaftesbury, and Nunnaminster (though not Barking).[178] It is worth noting here, on the subject of Osbert's letters, that he corresponded with Geoffrey of St Alban's, the man who encouraged Christina 'by founding for her the house of Markyate'.[179] The wide network of acquaintance, Osbert and other "friends of the family", suggests the nuns were familiar with a considerable range of contemporary culture.[180]

Barking may have owned at least one collection of the kind known as *florilegia*, whence Clemence, and the Nun too, may have found Anselmian and other writings. *Florilegia* are elusive and valuable repositories, of which I offer a brief account here together with selected references to them.[181] They were widely used.[182] Bloch writes despairingly of 'manuels' or 'recueils', impossible now to identify, which writers plundered for citations or references (*Osbert*, p. 55). Bell mentions a Latin 'signs of judgement', also at Barking.[183] This, like the uncertain manuscript containing 'Anselm', is dated thirteenth century and so too late for us. But it is clearly part of a *florilegium*, which contains a copy of *Liber Scintillarum* (a well-known collection of brief tracts, extracts, and commonplaces). We cannot of course argue from this that Barking definitely had *florilegia* in the twelfth century, but it is evidence that *florilegia* were very common.[184] Curtius does not discuss *florilegia* as such, but describes certain kinds of anthology.[185]

---

[175] See Barlow, *Thomas Becket*, note 25 on p. 295 (citing Southern), that his cult was never more than local (cf. Bede, in Partner, *Serious Entertainments*, p. 167 and note).
[176] Anselm, *Proslogion*, pp. 4, 11, & 20–21; Sharpe, 'Anselm as Author', for the few c12 insular MSS (and William of Malmesbury's collection of his work). See Vanni Rovighi, 'L'influence', for Aelred's knowledge of Anselm.
[177] *The Letters* ed. Williamson, letter 8, for example (and p. 3 in the Introduction).
[178] Hollis, 'Monastic School', p. 53.
[179] *The Letters* ed. Williamson, letter 32, and note on p. 218; Christina's story could have been known at Barking.
[180] See, finally, McNamer, *Affective Meditation*, pp. 84–5.
[181] See for example John of Salisbury, *Historia Pontificalis*, p. 21 note 1; de Hamel, *The Book*, p. 98; Dutton, *Julian of Norwich*, pp. 15–16, 53–4, & 137; Rouse, 'Florilegia'.
[182] See further: Hussey, 'Introduction', pp. 13–14, Knight, 'Satire', p. 281; *Cher Alme* ed. Hunt, pp. 21–2.
[183] *What Nuns Read*, p. 108; see Ker, ed., *Medieval Libraries*, p. 6.
[184] See also Partner, *Serious Entertainments*, pp. 126, 151; and in Orderic Vitalis, *The Ecclesiastical History*, bk. VII:8 (p. 44, ref. to Fulgentius).
[185] *European Literature*, pp. 51 & 57–61. Further, *inter al.*, see: Thomas à Kempis, *The Imitation of Christ*, Introduction; Dronke, *Women Writers*, pp. 140–42; and Minnis, *Authorship* (pp. 141, 145 & n. 113, 156 & n. 167, 202).

We know Barking owned the three manuscripts listed by Ker and James. Further, if an abbess of Barking donated a *Boethius* to another house, she may have retained a second copy. Clemence must have had access to a Latin *Catherine*, together with the earlier translation she mentions. The abbey probably owned more than one collection of saints' lives, and other 'historical' texts, as well as other Bible, liturgy, and service books. The amount of devotional (and other) material available to women must not be underestimated.[186] For further evidence about the nuns' reading, see Osbert's letters to Barking women. Besides Bible quotations or allusions, he refers to Bede, Jerome (several to *De Nominibus Hebraeorum*), Ovid, Virgil, and Pseudo-Seneca. He also cites Lives: Audrey, Lawrence, Cecilia, and Katherine.[187] We may suppose the nuns were familiar with some or all of these texts, perhaps having copies in their library. The Nun must have owned or borrowed a copy of Aelred's *Vita*. Perhaps she was permitted to go to Westminster, or wherever Aelred's work might be found. Within the poem, the nun healed *in absentia* dreams she is travelling, as though this would not be out of order (chapter 40). Barking nuns are recorded as travelling regularly to London. Barnes gives evidence for nuns travelling in the later medieval period.[188] Thirteenth-century legislation, aimed at stricter enclosure, is indirect evidence that nuns were perceived as having been spending too much time out and about. Barking nuns were admonished in late thirteenth century for being too involved with the outside world.[189] For an earlier period, Stafford mentions nuns travelling between Barking and London.[190] This, together with records of London houses owned by the Abbey at the Conquest,[191] suggests considerable coming and going throughout the period we are dealing with. O'Donnell discusses Barking's numerous outside links, including Westminster.[192] A convenient way of travelling to London and to Westminster was by water: Barking was on a creek, and thus had access to the Thames.[193] Whether they travelled or not, the Barking nuns were certainly literate to the point of bookishness. The Nun's description of Edith is expanded to make her a woman who enjoys fine books; Aelred merely mentions her reading (chapter 8; *Life*, p. 147).

---

[186] Swan, 'Imagining a Readership', p. 147.
[187] Letters 21, 22, 40, & 42; with margin notes, and Additional Note on Seneca (p. 228).
[188] 'A Nun's Life', pp. 64–7 (I thank the author for sending me these pages).
[189] Bussell and Brown, 'Introduction', p. 10.
[190] 'Queens, Nunneries', p. 15. See also Sturman, *Barking Abbey* (qmro.qmul.ac.uk/jspui/handle/123456789/1549 accessed 7.5.2014), *passim*; the nuns, and their servants, had large estates to administer.
[191] Weston, 'The Saint-Maker'.
[192] 'The ladies', pp. 106–11; other links mentioned in Bérat, 'Authority of Diversity', p. 214.
[193] I thank Paul Brand for this observation.

The Nun and her World

Barking Abbey[194]

A brief account of Barking and its abbesses may be useful as historical background to the Nun's work.

This Benedictine abbey, dedicated to the BVM and St Ethelburga, had a long and dramatic history between Foundation and Dissolution: ghost stories associated with its early days, a Resurrection play (and trouble with locals) in its later days. Loftus and Chettle remains the standard history, and its mention of the school, where novices learned Latin from *magistrae*, is of particular interest. The feminine is significant: the Nun could have been Clemence's teacher.[195] Barking's aristocratic abbesses, as barons of the realm, held property including numerous parishes. The community was highly literate throughout the centuries;[196] for example, the Resurrection play just mentioned was probably based on an earlier one.[197] Elkins says that Barking was the only house for monks and nuns surviving from pre-Conquest 'halcyon days' of female monasticism, and that nunneries were a refuge after the Conquest;[198] though it was no longer a double house by the twelfth century.

The first abbess was Ethelburga, probably 666–75.[199] Barking is said to have been founded in 666. Ethelburga was owner as well as ruler of the abbey; her brother Erkenwald founded it, dying there in 693. Goscelin claims that Erkenwald was a pupil of Augustine's companion Mellitus.[200] Bede writes of marvels that took place before Ethelburga's death, including the cure of her friend Tortgith (d. 681). His source, the 'little book', was probably written by the nuns (Hollis, p. 35). The abbey must have had expectations of supernatural happenings from its earliest days.[201]

Hildelith died in 712, though the date of her appointment is uncertain. She was more important in Barking's development than Ethelburga, whom Hildelith had tactfully to train in her duties. Hollis gives her dates as *c.* 695–*c.* 716. Therefore, if she tutored Ethelburga, it is unclear what happened between 675 and 695. Hildelith knew Aldhelm (639–709), who dedicated his treatise on virginity to her and her nuns.

---

[194] Mitchell, 'Patrons and Politics'; and monasticmatrix.usc.edu/monasticon/index.php?function=detail&id=918 (accessed 29.8.2011); *ODS* for individual abbesses. Knowles *et al.*, eds, *Heads of Religious Houses*, Crick, 'Women's Houses', Brown and Bussell, eds, *Barking Culture*, and Sturman, *Barking Abbey*, provide further background.

[195] *A History of Barking Abbey*. See also *Osbert*, pp. 41 & 43, for in-house teaching at Wilton.

[196] de Vegvar, 'Saints and Companions', for Barking's pre-conquest history, and its advanced level of culture and latinity; and Fry, 'Bede'.

[197] Lindenbaum, 'Drama as Textual Practice', esp. pp. 392–5; Stevenson, 'Rhythmic Liturgy'; and Yardley, 'Liturgy'.

[198] *Holy Women*, pp. 1–2.

[199] Slocum, 'Goscelin and the Translation', gives *c.* 693, with no gap before Hildelith, who continued until *c.* 720.

[200] Hollis, 'Monastic School'.

[201] Bede, *History*, pp. 216–21; and for example *Medieval Ghost Stories* ed. Joynes, pp. 12–14 (from Bede pp. 219–20). See my discussion of dreams and visions (Appendix).

His language presupposes their skill in reading Latin.[202] An early royal connection for Barking was the sojourn of King Ine's sister Cuthburga, sometime wife of King Alfrid of Northumbria. William of Malmesbury says she embraced celibacy thanks to Aldhelm's book.[203] Another who admired Hildelith was Boniface; he did not spend much time in England, though Aldhelm's writing probably influenced his. Aldhelm's Old English works have not survived, but his Latin works were read throughout Europe until the eleventh century. An Anglo-Saxon drawing, of him presenting his treatise to Hildelith, survives (*ODS*, s.v. Aldhelm). The nuns' literary activity includes their letters, which he praises. William of Malmesbury mentions their enthusiastic reading of Aldhelm's treatise. He says the Abbey was 'then famous, now insignificant', but he wrote this before the Nun and Clemence produced their important Lives.[204] The name of the abbess (or abbesses) during the time of the Viking invasions, late ninth century, is unknown. Barking was refounded in early tenth century as part of contemporary Benedictine reforms.[205]

Wulfhilda was in office *c*. 959 to 996 or 1000. The following are some of the accounts consulted: Knowles puts her in or shortly before Edgar's reign (*c*. 959), that she endured a twenty-year exile (dates not indicated), and that she died after 996.[206] Bussell and Brown say that in 978, when Ethelred came to the throne, his mother Aelfthryth sent Wulfhilda back to Horton where she remained in exile for nearly twenty years. According to this, she must have returned *c*. 997, and continued as abbess until *c*. 1000.[207] *ODS* also gives her death as *c*. 1000 (appointment not dated); her twenty-year exile, ending in 993, thus began in 973. Slocum gives Wulfhild as *c*. 963–82, and 992–1000; the exile therefore being only ten years.[208] Aelfthryth took the abbacy herself during Wulfhilda's exile,[209] though Edith may have had it for part of the time (see below). Wulfhilda is said to have been given Barking by King Edgar after he renounced his vain pursuit of her. Her appointment was some time before 973: she was reinstated *c*. 993 after an interregnum of some twenty years. Farmer dates the donation to the 960s; he discusses the nuns' intrigue with the queen (their 'protector'), and Wulfhilda's exile to Horton.[210] Her *ODS* entry says Edgar re-endowed Barking with Horton, and churches in Wessex (thus connecting Barking with Dorset). The interregnum was perhaps due to an intrigue of the nuns with Aelfthryth, who was

---

[202] Watt, 'Lost Books' (I thank the author for e-copy). See also Lees and Overing, 'Women and Origins'; and Weston, 'The Saint-Maker'.
[203] *Kings* tr. Stephenson, note on pp. 28–9.
[204] *Gesta Regum* ed. and tr. Mynors *et al.*, vol. I, bk. i, 36.1; pp. 52–3.
[205] Bussell and Brown, 'Introduction', p. 4.
[206] See Pratt, 'The voice of the king', for Wulfhilda and her dates (and possible connections with *Maldon*): pp. 152, 182, 184, & 193.
[207] 'Introduction', p. 5.
[208] 'Goscelin and the Translation'.
[209] According to Foot (see below), Wulfhild died in 996, having been back in her post for seven years. If this is the case, then she was exiled (*c*. 967) before Ethelred's accession and not at it, as suggested by Bussell and Brown above.
[210] 'Monastic Revival'.

suspected of murdering Edward the Martyr. It is not known whether she was in fact complicit in the murder.[211] Connections between Edgar's family and Barking may partly explain the Nun's added detail in chapter 37, if the story was known to the nuns but not to Aelred.[212] Stafford remarks that a daughter of Ethelred's, by another wife, was called Wulfhild; she expresses surprise because this was not a family name.[213] But perhaps the daughter was named for the abbess – still in office during the reign of Ethelred – who was given Barking by Ethelred's father.

According to Knowles, (Saint) Edith may have administered the abbey at some time during Wulfhilda's exile and before her own death in 984. Foot says Edgar made Edith head of three houses, of which one was Barking; but that Aelfthryth took Barking during Wulfhild's exile (*c.* 969–89). She also says that no abbess is named between Wulfhild and Aelfgyva, in spite of Knowles' mention of Lifleda.[214] *ODS* says that although Edith was made head of several houses, she appointed superiors, so she may never have been acting abbess. The next abbess was Lifleda; Wulfhilda was not only Judith/Wulfruna's teacher, but also Lifleda's. The latter was abbess for more than thirty years after Wulfhilda.[215] Next, Hart mentions William's charter to 'Abbess A'. He reads the name as 'Aelfwynn(?)' or Aelfgyva. Since Aelfwynn is not attested elsewhere (as far as I can discover), the name may be a misreading of minims for Aelfgyva, abbess at the time of the Conquest.[216]

Aelfgyva was abbess perhaps 1066–86 or for a good deal longer.[217] The earliest date found for her appointment is 1051. This was the abbess who received William the Conqueror at Barking in late 1066. Foot reports Goscelin as saying the nuns took refuge in London at the time of the Conquest, but some must have remained with their abbess to welcome William to the abbey.[218] She was reportedly aged fifteen at her appointment, and fifty when she commissioned Goscelin's work: therefore the commission must have been between 1086 and 1101. Hollis says she became abbess in the 1050s and died *c.* 1114.[219] In the late eleventh century, on the occasion of a translation occurring there in 1087, she asked Goscelin to write lives of the Abbey's Anglo-Saxon saints: Ethelburga, Hildelith, and Wulfhilda.[220] William of Malmesbury, who mentions Goscelin by name,[221] followed a hagiographic tradition whose early practitioners included Goscelin. They aimed to support privileges, history, and

---

[211] See Dunstan's *Early Lives*, p. xli; and Barlow, *Edward the Confessor*, p. 69, for Edgar's nuns.
[212] Stafford, 'Queens, Nunneries'.
[213] 'Royal Women', note 13 on p. 219; though it is reported that Abbess Wulfhild was related to the Wessex royal family (Hollis, 'Monastic School', p. 44).
[214] *Veiled Women*, vol. ii, pp. 27–33.
[215] Knowles, p. 290; Hollis, 'Monastic School', p. 44.
[216] Hart, 'Early Charters'.
[217] See also *Rouleaux* ed. Delisle, p. 315.
[218] *Veiled Women*.
[219] 'Monastic School'.
[220] *Saints of Ely* ed. and tr. Love, p. xxi; the footnote cites Colker, 'Texts'.
[221] *Gesta Regum*, vol. I, bk. iv, 342; pp. 590–93.

traditions of religious foundations.[222] Goscelin of Canterbury, or St Bertin (c. 1035–c. 1107),[223] was among the first writers to use and defend the testimony of women as a valid historical source.[224] Given that the question of whether the Nun knew *The Battle of Maldon* (see English Literature, above) is unresolved, it is a frustrating coincidence that the manuscript containing it (Cotton Otho A xii, destroyed by fire) also contained these Lives by Goscelin. There is no evidence that the texts had any connection with one another before collation in the seventeenth century, though it has been suggested that more items than the Lives were made and/or preserved at Barking.[225] They were composed in the eleventh and twelfth centuries;[226] this part of the manuscript is in more than one twelfth-century hand. Because of the association with Barking, it has been suggested that perhaps all of the manuscript except part A (that is, including part B, which contains *Maldon*) may have been made or preserved there.[227] Goscelin may have written the anonymous Life of Edward. Barlow evaluates the claims of both Goscelin and Folcard;[228] it has also been suggested that Muriel of Wilton wrote it.[229]

Between Aelfgyva and Adelidis are three women about whose incumbency we know very little. Edith or Matilda, the first queen of Henry I, is said to have had custody in late eleventh or early twelfth century. If she was indeed abbess for a time, the Nun calling her Matilda the Good is understandable. According to Knowles, an Agnes was appointed between 1114 and 1122. A grant of custody to Stephen's queen Matilda in 1136 or 1137 suggests there may have been a vacancy about that time.

Adelidis (Alice) Fitzjohn, 1137–66, was appointed by Stephen (r. 1135–54); her brother was one of his supporters.[230] There is some confusion about this abbess, who may have been dismissed and later reinstated, unless there were two abbesses of that name. Knowles (p. 290) gives scanty detail about the doings of this lady or ladies, mentioning Ermelina (between 1152 and 1166) as 'probably between the two Alices' without further explanation. It is of some interest to this study, because any scandal or dispute, and any intervening abbess such as Ermelina, could have occurred at the time the Nun was writing. Auslander mentions an accusation against Alice;[231] Robertson mentions her dismissal in 1166.[232] If it is the case that Alice was dismissed, Ermelina perhaps had the abbey before a second Alice was appointed.

---

[222] *Saints' Lives* ed. and tr. Winterbottom and Thomson, p. xxxi.
[223] Rigg, *Anglo-Latin Literature, passim.*
[224] Slocum, 'Goscelin and the Translation', p. 81 and note 37.
[225] See *The Battle of Maldon* ed. Scragg, for contents of the MS; the last (Erkenwald, not by Goscelin) associated with Barking as the others are.
[226] Scragg, ed., *The Battle of Maldon, AD 991 (essays)*, p. 15.
[227] See also p. 21 above.
[228] *Anon*, esp. Appendix C.
[229] *Anon*, p. 97, note 3; Mason, *House of Godwine*, p. 190, & note 75 (p. 252).
[230] See Vincent, 'New Charters', for 'specific insight into Barking abbey's relations with the Crown'.
[231] 'Clemence and Catherine', p. 177.
[232] *The Medieval Saints' Lives*, note 21, pp. 74–5.

John of Salisbury, acting as secretary for Archbishop Theobald (d. 1161), wrote to an abbess who can only have been Alice. The letter, written between 1154 and 1161,[233] accused her of long-standing and notorious familiarity, and cohabitation, with Hugh the abbey's steward.[234] There is no evidence that the abbess dismissed the man as she was commanded to do, nor what her punishment (if any) may have been. The editors remark on the irony of Osbert's writing a treatise on chastity for her at this time. They also note that Hugh's administration of the abbey was in the late 1160s, so he must have remained in his post. Given the amount of delay and procrastination (and the facility with which the abbess seems to have defended herself) that occurred during a property dispute discussed in a letter of late 1160,[235] there is no reason to believe that either Alice or Hugh would have acted promptly in response to the letter of castigation. It is also possible that the matter was not followed up after Theobald's death. Be that as it may, Robertson's claim that Alice was dismissed in 1166 must be wrong (other accounts agree on the date of her death), but he may have been confused about some information concerning a dismissal earlier in Alice's administration. He cites a paper that cannot now be recovered: its author tells me her notes were lost in a fire. I have been unable to trace the matter further. My own note,[236] about John of Salisbury writing to an abbess as if this were evidence of literary correspondence, must now be qualified.

Alice, or her namesake, stayed on under Henry II until her death in 1166. Then the abbacy remained vacant, Henry appointing no successor until 1173. This was Mary (Marie), Thomas Becket's sister, who remained until late 1170s. Marie as abbess would not have allowed one of her nuns to praise the king.

In a charter of 1177–79, Henry appointed Matilda (also spelled Maud, or Mahaut), his illegitimate daughter. She is recorded as being abbess until 1195. Campbell gives 1163–89 as possible dates for the Nun's work;[237] she also mentions Barking's connections with Henry's court.[238] Mitchell thinks the Nun may have been writing after Matilda's appointment, which would put *Edouard* nearer *Catherine* in time.[239] Currently, *Catherine* is datable only by the earliest known manuscript, c. 1200. Matilda's incumbency seems to have been a period of familial concord; she may have wanted to get the nuns 'on her side' away from any anti-Henry feeling propagated by Marie. She may have realised that the Green Tree prophecy could be used to promote her family in her own time. This was probably the Mahaut to whom Adgar, possibly a Barking cleric, dedicated *Le Gracial*.[240] Guernes, another writer whose work is linked

---
[233] John of Salisbury, *Letters* ed. Millor and Butler, p. 275.
[234] Ibid. number 69 (p. 111).
[235] Ibid. number 132. There seems to be no connection between this and the affair of the steward.
[236] 'Who Wrote?', note 22.
[237] *Medieval Saints' Lives*, p. 231.
[238] See esp. p. 38, below.
[239] 'Patrons and Politics'.
[240] Adgar, *Le Gracial* ed. Kunstmann; and Thiry-Stassin, 'L'hagiographie', p. 413. Short, 'Patrons and Polyglots', thinks it unlikely. But see Bérat, 'Authority of Diversity'.

to Barking and who frequented the place, thanks Marie (the previous abbess) for a horse and clothing.[241] Baker remarks that the life of wandering friars such as Guernes resembled that of a *jongleur*; Adgar may have been another such. Tyler is certain that his Mahaut was the abbess.[242] Whether the Nun was writing earlier or later, Barking was often host to literary visitors.

The Poem's Date

The Nun probably wrote her *Vie* during the abbacy of Adelidis or soon afterwards. There is no convincing reason to revise Legge's estimate that it should be dated earlier (after 1163, when Aelred's *Vita* was written) rather than later, before Henry's death in 1189.[243] This estimate is based on the fact that the Nun's eulogy of Henry could hardly apply to the royal family as troubled as it was later in the reign. For example, Eleanor disappeared into prison after the rebellion of 1173, and did not re-emerge into public attention until after Henry's death.[244] The Nun's straightforward manner ignores not only the the rebellion of Henry's wife and sons, but also the Young King (1170–83). Praise of Henry and his family is interpolated by the Nun (vv. 105–30); Aelred does not mention the family. Later, a prayer for the heirs to the throne includes their father *and their mother* (vv. 4996–5006). Aelred mentions only the king at the corresponding point in *Vita*, so the Nun must have added the queen deliberately. Then, Marie Becket becoming abbess soon after Thomas' death, it is unlikely the Nun would be permitted to express warmth for Henry during her incumbency. Short doubts the Nun could express such warmth for Henry as early as Becket's exile in 1164,[245] but he was not yet a martyr. Barlow points out 'Thomas when alive could be treated as an ordinary human being'.[246] At this time his affairs would be no barrier to anybody wishing to praise the king. Opinions would have been mixed at Barking, as elsewhere. The nuns were probably worried about the lack of an abbess between 1166 and 1173, and more concerned with their own friends and networks than with affairs at Canterbury.[247]

Thiry-Stassin and Bell uphold a date in 1160s,[248] as does Marzella.[249] It is possible the Nun wrote before the death of Adelidis, abbess when Osbert wrote his *Life*. Aurell is convinced of the earlier date, and that any later date is difficult to establish.[250] Osbert corresponded with Barking nuns, and perhaps fostered their interest in Edward. Mitchell says he also recommended Saint Catherine to them.[251] His letters include

---

[241] See *inter al*. O'Donnell, 'The ladies'; Baker, 'Saints' Lives in Anglo-French', p. 125.
[242] 'From Old English to Old French', pp. 166–7 (and *Cloisters*, p. 123; *Background*, p. 188).
[243] *Background*, pp. 60–61.
[244] Barber, 'Eleanor and the Media', p. 16.
[245] 'Another Look', p. 47, note 38.
[246] *Thomas Becket*, p. 26.
[247] Bussell, 'Cicero, Aelred and Guernes', pp. 188–90.
[248] 'L'hagiographie', p. 413; *What Nuns Read*, p. 62.
[249] 'La tradizione', p. 370, note 90.
[250] *Plantagenet Empire*, pp. 136–7; & note 255, p. 317).
[251] 'Patrons and Politics'.

one to Adelidis and one to each of his nieces, Margaret and Cecilia, who had entered Barking. Another, to Ida, may also have been destined for Barking (Ida being under Saint Ethelburga's protection). Ida was Adeliza of Louvain's niece.[252] This shows three, perhaps four, nuns known by name reading Latin – or why not write to them in French or English? He visited Barking: he expresses thanks for kindness and entertainment. A note in the Introduction to *Letters* suggests that the lady healed by Edward, a miracle added by Aelred, was a friend of Osbert's (p. 23). The Nun says the lady is still alive, although Aelred speaks of her as though she has died. The story may have been added by Osbert.[253] Osbert and the Nun could have known each other, if *Edouard*'s date is earlier rather than later. Elkins dates his letters praising the nuns, plus a panegyric to virginity for Adelidis, to 1140s and 1150s.[254] This is a not impossible time-frame, for the Nun to be writing a life of Edward a decade or two later. Barking is important as being the source of two Campsey texts (the Nun's, and Clemence's), and patron of a third (Guernes' *Becket*). Further, the hitherto unidentified Marie, who wrote a thirteenth-century Life of Audrey of Ely, may have been a vowess or nun either at Chatteris or Barking.[255] If at Barking, and if she was not indeed Marie de France, she may have been inspired by its strong literary tradition. There was, at Barking, an environment of interest in Edward; and there was plenty of time, after 1163, for the Nun to write her *Edouard* before the events of the 1170s.

The Nun's Identity as Author of Edouard

Although we know a little about the audience of the Nun's poem (see below), we know less about its author's identity. We cannot even be certain what her native language was. If she was English, some of her sources could have been in English, as examined earlier. The Nun writes in French but could have been trilingual: *Edouard*'s Prologue, where she protests her 'faus franceis', is a mere literary topos and no evidence of incompetence. It probably means English was her first language,[256] but there are few clues in the poem. She says: 'Godwine ot nun en cel language' [He was called Godwin in this – or that – language] (v. 1253). What does 'cel' mean? Is she referring to 'our insular language', which in context (that is, pre-Conquest) must mean English? The word 'cel' is more likely to mean 'that language' than 'this' (the latter would be 'cest'), but either way the phrase is no evidence she could not understand (Old) English. She probably means the language spoken at *that* time, because recounting what happened more than a hundred years before. John of Canterbury, however, says his *Polistorie* is

---

[252] Ibid. p. 351.
[253] *The Letters* ed. Williamson, letters 21, 22, 40, & 42, and notes; *Anon*, pp. 124–6.
[254] *Holy Women*, pp. 147–8. For literary activity see also Wogan-Browne, 'Powers of Record'; and *Guidance for Women* tr. Morton.
[255] Stevenson, 'Anglo-Latin Women Poets', p. 95, for 'Marie of Barking'.
[256] Short, 'Another Look', pp. 50–53. See also Aurell, *Plantagenet Empire*, p. 74 ('... Anglophones who had to use French, such as the Nun of Barking').

in French because people generally understand 'cel langage' (that is, not 'cest' as one would expect).[257]

Two important authors are known to have been writing in the abbey at this time, and not much is known about the second of them either. Much current interest in the author of *Edouard* centres upon whether she was identical with Clemence of Barking, who names herself in her own Saint's Life translated from Latin: the *Catherine*. This is partly because named authoresses are rare in early vernacular literature, although women were probably among the authors of anonymous works.[258] In my opinion they were not the same. Mitchell has doubts: 'it is not possible to prove that the two texts were written by the same author'.[259] It is entirely likely there were two female writers at Barking; further, a woman may have written a Life of Becket, perhaps at Guernes' suggestion.[260] Even MacBain, held to be a champion of common authorship, warns that an urge to conflate authors 'may have perhaps arisen from an assumption that a proliferation of women writers in so brief a time-frame was highly unlikely', suggesting only 'the possiblility of common authorship'. After all, an abbey where women were taught to read and write Latin could easily give rise to a 'proliferation' of women writers.[261] I have previously examined differences of style and address between the poems by the Nun and Clemence;[262] here I examine their themes in more detail, and add new research.

Modern studies of writing style have noticed that lexical differences between one text another *however caused* cannot obscure underlying and distinctive personal style, which is identified by examination of prosody and syntax.[263] It follows that lexical similarities cannot identify two writers as one. Similarities of style and syntax could, but not in the case of the Nun and Clemence, as I have shown elsewhere by non-lexical analysis. Other scholars have examined the question. One cannot prove anything, even by computer analysis, with only two texts.[264] Hodgson discusses differences in (for example) word patterns in two 'similar' texts. Parallels could be common authorship *or* coincidence *or* imitation.[265] Fogel says that two works in the same genre by different authors may look more similar than two works by the same author

---

[257] Legge, *Background*, p. 291.
[258] Wogan-Browne, 'Wreaths of Thyme', p. 55.
[259] 'Patrons and Politics', p. 357, note 47; citing MacBain, 'Apprenticeship'.
[260] Wogan-Browne, 'Clerc u lai', p. 67, notes 40 & 1.
[261] 'Hagiographers', p. 235. In 'Apprenticeship', he was modestly convinced of their identity. He revised this in an unpublished paper ('Courtly Echoes', cited by both Elkins and Ferrante), saying *Edouard* is so much less sophisticated than *Catherine* they are unlikely to be by the same author. For the urge towards attribution at any cost, even in medieval times, see Gillespie, 'Fatherless Books': readers were warned against books that had no named author.
[262] 'Who Wrote?'; this also discusses the Nun's audience, and her sources (notably the Cardiff Life of Edward the Martyr).
[263] Thanks are due especially to Peter Garrard and John Burrows, who have kindly corresponded with me on this question.
[264] See Erdman and Fogel, eds, *Evidence*, esp. Schoenbaum, 'Internal Evidence'.
[265] In Erdman and Fogel, 'English Literature to 1500', p. 407; and see Schoenbaum's p. 200.

in different genres.[266] More recently, Love cites Schoenbaum (p. 200 of the article noted above). He points out the strong possibility of authors modelling themselves on a revered elder or predecessor (the Nun as Clemence's teacher, or successful elder): 'information acquired from a single [schoolmaster] ... or at a particular community of the learned ... may be the possession of a group rather than an individual' (p. 81; see esp. his chapter, 'Internal Evidence', pp. 79–97). Love further discusses the limited success of stylometry to date, including that quantitative analysis is not going to prove conclusive where the investigator has only two texts to work with.[267] A recent video documentary on stylometrics provides further evidence that the two writers in question are unlikely to be the same woman.[268]

Legge considers Clemence more 'courtly' than the Nun. If so, this is indirect evidence that they are distinct, unless the Nun was a younger Clemence writing before 'courtly' ideas reached Barking.[269] However, whether Legge's pronouncement is fair depends on what is meant by 'courtly'. In fact, *different* sets of courtly language are in question. Clemence uses words such as 'chevalerie', and 'barnilment' to mean 'noble behaviour', and refers to (for example) heavenly chivalry.[270] The Nun's 'chevalerie', at v. 4261, is no more than an assembly of nobles at a ceremony. MacBain notes Clemence's 'language of chivalry' (*Catherine*, p. xxiv), giving examples of words meaning chivalry, rather than love or courtesy. But Clemence uses 'curteisement' only once, as the manner of Katherine's speech to somebody, without particular weight (v. 1303; she is about to become heavily sarcastic).[271] The Nun uses 'curteis' or 'curteisement', with special significance, at least five times: once for the manner of saving Judith from her enemies (that is, God was 'curteis'; v. 1163). Messengers to the Pope must be wise, courteous, and righteous (v. 1888): no ordinary errand-boys, these are bishops and the like. The idea is strengthened as the Nun goes on to say they must be able to understand, and render, reason in any *court*. Other occurrences of 'curteis' are: Edgar (v. 78), Lanfranc (v. 5726), and the helpful foot in the story of Godwin's death (v. 3866).[272] The Nun's early use of the term 'fin' amur' is discussed notably by MacBain.[273] Laurent believes that common topics (riches versus poverty, and the frailty of the flesh) are no proof the two works are by the same hand, but rather due to the influence of a common spirituality at Barking and in its time.[274] This

---

[266] 'Salmons', p. 85.
[267] *Attributing Authorship*.
[268] vimeo.com/70881172, accessed 24.7.2013.
[269] *Background*, pp. 60–66: the Nun adds 'chiefly moralizations of no striking interest'. For *Catherine*, see pp. 66–72 ('nowhere else save in this text do such courtly passages occur in a saint's Life'). For Clemence's knowledge of poems about Tristan, see p. 67. See also Glossary, *s.v.* 'curteisement' & 'fin'amur'.
[270] See Owst, *Literature and Pulpit*, p. 518, for 'chevalerie of heaven'.
[271] The poem is entitled *Life of St Catherine*, but I spell the heroine Katherine (as Clemence does) for clarity.
[272] Bliss, 'Who Wrote?', p. 85 (and note 74).
[273] 'Vocabulary'.
[274] *Plaire et édifier*, p. 263; see Robertson, *The Medieval Saints' Lives*, p. 256, for the nuns' textual community.

would account for similarities of vocabulary noted by MacBain and others. Given the likelihood of similarity, for this reason, it is surprising how far the two styles diverge. Noyer states that according to his analysis the Nun's work could perhaps be attributed to Clemence, but not conclusively. However, given that his analysis likewise allows the attribution of *Guillaume d'Angleterre* to Chrétien, when critics are well-nigh unanimous in pronouncing it not to be by the master, we cannot take this analysis as useful for our two texts in question, as Noyer himself allows. Legge pointed out that *a few resemblances in vocabulary* were not enough to make a case for *Guillaume* to be by Chrétien (my emphasis, bearing in mind that resemblances in vocabulary have been claimed as proof that the Nun is Clemence).[275]

Since publication of my article, further examination suggests that although there are similarities of vocabulary, certain lexical groups are used distinctively.[276] For example, the Nun's word 'dru', meaning intimate friend or even lover. Clemence uses it once only, in a doublet: 'ses privez e ses druz' (v. 94), for the friends (inner court circle) of the Emperor. This is very different from the Nun's holy men: at v. 2116 the hermit is Saint Peter's 'dru', and at v. 4456 Saint John is God's. The context is godly, even mystical, rather than courtly. For 'blandir', usually meaning to flatter, Clemence uses it once in this bad sense: the Emperor tries to flatter Katherine into submission (v. 357). The Nun gives it a different meaning: in v. 924 Edward is said to 'flatter' fools (unlikely, of course: he coaxes them). An interesting variation comes at v. 4243, where Edward feels the need to flatter [losengier] Saint Peter so that he will let him into Heaven. Here it is better translated as 'cajole' (see my notes to these lines). The Nun uses negative language in a positive way, unlike Clemence. Edward is 'vaillant' [having value], which means either valiant or worthy. The Nun would rather stress Edward's worthiness, as king and saint, than his valour as a soldier even of God. But there are passages where either would make sense (not the case with Clemence's 'worthies'). Clemence uses it at least twice, but differently: the clerks massed against Katherine are worthy in that they are learned and competent (see Glossary for 'valur'). For the 'inexpressibilty topos', where Clemence talks of the unspeakable [nun disable] goodness of God (v. 1190; also vv. 597, 826, 1786), Russell argues that because this is a rare term, and because one example occurs in the Nun's poem (and nowhere else among the Campsey texts), therefore the two poems were written by the same person. In *Edouard*, see v. 973; Södergård's notes give other examples of 'nun' before adjective, from a range of texts outside Russell's corpus (MacBain makes no note on the term in *Catherine*).[277] But MacBain, noting Clemence's use of the rare form 'ancienè' (v. 232), points out its occurence in one manuscript of a Life of Saint Thomas. It has been suggested this, too, may have been written by a woman (see p. 40, above). So does the evidence of the word 'ancienè' therefore suggest that the woman was Clemence, as 'nun disable' is supposed to suggest that the Nun was Clemence? It is far more

---

[275] See Noyer, 'Generative Metrics', esp. pp. 155-8; and Gowans, 'Guillaume'.
[276] For the Nun's use of '(re)quere' to mean 'visit, see Glossary.
[277] 'Identity Matters'.

likely that (she or) this author, and the nuns, were employing a common vocabulary. Burrows has analysed a pair of Anglo-Norman texts:[278] the similarities he lists are far more numerous than the few identified between the Nun's work and Clemence's. Not surprisingly, he begins by pointing to the similarity to be expected between two texts of similar age and dialect copied in the same scriptorium.

Katherine's prayers, compared with Edward's, express none of that dizzying sweetness experienced by Edward. The words 'duz' or 'dulzur' (variously spelt), not frequent in Clemence's poem, are frequent in the Nun's. Edward's relationship with his dearest friends (God, Edith, favourite saints) is suffused with heavenly and very repetitive sweetness. Clemence uses it sparingly: of God's gentleness, of the saint's sweet speech and her beauty; but not in her description of the Virgin Mary, which is just where one would expect to find such an idea (vv. 1745–68). It appears in clusters of other names for God, rather than as a single special quality. There is only one cluster of 'sweetness', where Katherine comforts the queen on her approaching death. Her new 'king' is characterized with words in 'duz' five times in six lines (vv. 2291–6), perhaps as contrast with her earthly husband's violence. Much of Katherine's discourse is descriptive and narrative; she is after all attempting to convert her heathen antagonists, and the difference is partly due to the fact that she is a martyr whereas Edward is a confessor. Edward's discourse, and passages concerned with his experiences, is less about what God *does* than what God *is*. The Nun, unlike Clemence, is mystical in her language. It is unsurprising to find Katherine described as friend and handmaid of God, and God as her lover and her husband; this is standard language for female religious (and for the Virgin Mary). The Nun calls herself 'cele Deu ancele' at v. 5326. Furthermore, male religious may call God their spouse.[279] However, courtly language in Clemence's poem is more concerned with heavenly chivalry, as MacBain notes, than with 'fin' amur' as the Nun's is. An exception is the Emperor's extremely romantic lament for his wife.[280] In the Nun, the situation of Edward and his wife is predicated on friendship as well as love, without the desperate and doubtless sexual yearning of Clemence's Emperor, where at least one Tristanian rhyme occurs ('amur' with 'dulur', 2183–4; and see above, p. 41). Legge's word 'courtly' needs to be qualified. Scholars wishing to establish that the Nun and Clemence are identical have failed to note that Clemence never uses the term 'fin' amur', whatever similarities may be perceived between her vocabulary and the Nun's.[281]

The role of dreams is different in the two poems. In *Edouard*, dreams and visions are of central importance and their value discussed. In *Catherine* there is only one dream and its value is not questioned. The queen's vision of Katherine is cleverly crafted, studded with repetitions of the verb to see (and 'vis' = face, which echoes it: vv. 1535–41, within the dream-passage vv. 1529–50). But it expresses no anxiety about

---
[278] *La Vie de Seint Clement* ed. Burrows, vol. 3, pp. 59–65.
[279] See, for example, *Prayers and Meditations* tr. Ward, p. 225; also Laurent, *Plaire et édifier*, p. 460.
[280] Discussed in MacBain, 'Five Renderings'.
[281] See also Bussell, 'Cicero, Aelred and Guernes', esp. pp. 194–5.

whether dreams are true, and no miracle or prophecy is attached (see my Appendix, Dreams). Another difference is that Clemence refers to Plato and the Sybil (vv. 897, 903, and 915); this is not the sort of reference the Nun makes. On the other hand, when the Nun refers to the Three in the Furnace (chapter 8; see Dan. chapter 3) it is clear that she, in Edward's voice, is citing the Bible story. The context is protection of Edward's chastity. In Clemence, those cast into the fire are found unharmed (vv. 1173–88) but the author draws no such parallel. Her scene shows the martyrs' uncharred but undoubtedly dead bodies (vv. 1160, 1171–88, and 1238). Clemence cites the Bible less than the Nun does, even though the latter deletes or rewrites many citations from her source. Clemence's fund of proverbial saws is also less extensive than the Nun's. None of the supernatural appearances in *Catherine* is closed by a mysterious departure signalling that the apparition was from another world (as noted in *Edouard*; see Latin to Medieval French, above).

Further, I note Russell's work on analysis of the Nun's language compared with Clemence's, using the electronic Campsey. There are thirteen lives (late twelfth century to early fourteenth); seven about women, three by women. In a sample of this nature it is inevitable that similarities will be found between the only two written *by* women and *at* Barking. Whether women's language differs identifiably from men's or not, naturally writers in the same convent would show some similarities (as anybody who went to boarding-school will know) because of their habits of language and conversation; perhaps because they had the same teacher(s).[282] Given the known *magistrae* at Barking, it is quite possible that the Nun was Clemence's teacher (see note on p. 33, above). This too would account for similarities of theme and vocabulary. Russell's New York paper (2009) argued that the only barrier to our identifying the two writers as one was the Nun's poor self-image compared to Clemence. He was kind enough to show me this early version of 'Identity Matters', which cited Fenster's 'Queen Edith and the Nun' on the influence of Anselm (see p. 30, above). It is has been established for some time (see Nun's Prologue, especially note of Wogan-Browne's 1994 work) that the Nun's 'modesty' is no such thing – a point I thoroughly agree with. But this 'newly-discovered' confidence is no proof she is Clemence. Her manner betrays a confidence differing markedly from that of Clemence: her narrative voice resembles that of a bossy, chatty, and yet profoundly devout older woman. Clemence does not come across like this: her confidence shows piety, but is almost entirely unconversational. In any case Clemence (generally considered the better poet) probably copied certain turns of phrase, aspects of style, and so on, from her elder sister.[283] Clemence's scene where everybody weeps for the queen (2331ff.), may be compared with the Nun's scene of grief at Edward's death.

Clemence's special vocabulary of debate or discussion is prolific (I give the first occurrence of each): traitier (v. 30), opposer (v. 142), essample (v. 283), resnable acheisun (v. 395), pruveure (v. 428), desputer (v. 429), cuntraires (v. 810), plait (v. 2382);

---

[282] 'Notes on Style' (I thank the author for e-copy).
[283] See Howlett, *Origins*, pp. 67–9 & 73–4.

terms such as 'dialeticien', 'filosophe', 'gramaire', 'retorien' (the Nun rarely if ever betrays knowledge of such vocabulary). Furthermore, the over-riding tone of dispute includes ideas of 'sens' and 'raison' – words repeated again and again. Clemence handles oppositions with dexterity (as at vv. 1727-36), as well as the kind of descriptive list given at v. 2519ff. Notes in the edition (for example, to v. 183) point to Clemence's love of antithetical balance. However, Clemence uses certain deictic terms, common in the Nun, very rarely: but two examples of 'es vus' (vv. 406 and 2119), and none of 'oissiez' or 'veissiez'. The closest is 'oussiez errur' (v. 1182), which means merely 'you would be wrong'. Her audience is referred to as exclusively listening (not reading: vv. 34, 2693). There is much less reference, than in the Nun, to the hearing of books and the business of writing. Clemence's narrator addresses the audience from time to time, but nowhere does she nag or tease them. Her remarks are reminders about what she has read, or what has been said before, not 'if you were listening', or 'I don't know because I wasn't there!' as the Nun does. The scattered use of sarcasm, in Clemence's work, is something quite foreign to the Nun. Katherine exclaims at the nobility of the emperor's gods (v. 401). One of the wise clerks complains that the memory of victory will be a worthy one (vv. 483-4): if they win over a woman, it will be pretty feeble; if Katherine wins, it will be distinctly unworthy. The emperor's remarks about Katherine's beautiful eyes are almost sarcastic (vv. 1247-8), since he is obviously exasperated. Katherine mocks the idea of a golden statue: 'Ohi, cum ore sui boneuree...!' (1305ff.) [Ooh, what a lucky girl I am!]. Then she asks rudely what the emperor will do about birds or dogs who might soil it (vv. 1343-9). There is nothing in the Nun's story of Edward to compare with this kind of grim humour.

Clemence uses the common *contemptus mundi* topos, as the Nun does not (see esp. the speech to Porfire, v. 1666ff.), but does not refer to the past longingly as the Nun does (noted in chapter 17). Clemence gives a reason, fear, for lack of love in the past but also in the present (vv. 1041-4); a clear difference of emphasis. Nor does she invoke the 'still-there' topos to prove a story's truth, the closest to this being mention of Katherine's body still at Mount Sinai (v. 2630). Even where Katherine talks to the queen about contrasting kinds of love (v. 1633ff.), the term 'fin' amur' does not appear. The Nun's word 'per' (see Glossary) appears in Clemence to mean 'equal' only in a bad sense: no proud person can bear anybody to be his equal in goodness (vv. 461-2). This contrasts with the Nun's alignment of Edward with Christ, done most reverently (see above, p. 5), as against Clemence's parody of Saint Peter's role, in the speech where the emperor offers Katherine power to raise or cast down any of his courtiers (vv. 1275-8). Katherine occasionally betrays signs of human weakness: fear (v. 172), and desire for vengeance (v. 1944, instantly converted into the vengeance of God). Russell discusses Clemence's comments on language evolution,[284] remarking that her awareness of language is similar to that expressed in the *Edouard* (without citing

---

[284] In *Catherine*, vv. 29-50, as pointed out in O'Donnell, 'False French'; the author tells me this is still unpublished, but confirms my citation (pers. comm).

where).[285] I have not found the Nun to show any comparable sense of ephemerality as far as language is concerned. O'Donnell likewise finds it only in Clemence.[286] Although my additional remarks include several points of vocabulary (there are far more differences in vocabulary than similarities), the bulk of the argument here relates to style and theme.

The Nun's text has been scrutinized for evidence about authorship, and date. It is hard to be convinced, as Rossi is, that 'vus' in v. 9 must be singular, and feminine, and that it must refer to the current abbess. She cites 'Mais vus ki ailurs apris l'avez' [But you who have learned French elsewhere]; 'ailurs' may be taken to mean 'abroad' in this context. But it could equally well refer to a court audience, even the king (if plural, the royal family). It is clear that her apology is no more than a conventional topos, and so 'vus' could be anybody – the implied reader(s). The Nun does not dedicate the work to anybody. An apology to general readers is not a dedication to a particular reader. The work is not dedicated to Henry II merely because the Nun praises him elsewhere in the text. For example, Brown repeatedly mentions the Nun's 'dedication' of her work to Henry.[287] Broadhurst, who states that the Nun's remarks do *not* constitute a dedication, cites the following salutory comment: 'The danger of tentative conclusions growing with repetition into positive assertions is so great ...'.[288] Rossi deduces that 'vus' must be Marie Becket, and that she commissioned *Edouard*. She goes on to argue that the abbess is Marie de France (because 'you' learned French abroad). The argument appears to be that Marie felt France to be her home 'culturally and sentimentally', although Rossi admits 'she does not speak about her birth on French soil'.[289] But none of this proves the Nun wrote *Edouard* at the behest of her abbess. Rossi (pp. 175–6) cites Ferrante as saying the Nun dedicated her work 'perhaps to her abbess'; Ferrante says this twice without giving any supporting evidence.[290] Further, Rossi (p. 176) cites the Nun's apparent reluctance to undertake the translation as evidence that she was obliged to do it by her abbess; but it will be seen that the Nun declares her apparently independent desire to do the translation, and expresses reluctance just at this point because the matter is a difficult one (see note to v. 4925). Finally, it should be remembered, if that abbess was Marie Becket then the Nun would not have praised Henry and his family as she did (as has been frequently pointed out).

Controversy about the Nun's identity, and about the date of her work, has obscured a very real question, and that is to ask *why* she insists on withholding her name. Her humility in this regard may be just as much a pose as her much-debated modesty. It is unusual for any author, female or not, to declare themselves anonymous quite so distinctly. If her modesty is an authorial stance, her anonymity (although apparently

---

[285] Russell, 'Identity Matters', p. 132.
[286] See also Bliss, 'Who Wrote?', pp. 85–6.
[287] 'Translating Edward'; and 'Body, Gender and Nation'.
[288] 'Henry and Eleanor', pp. 62–3 & 84; see also Haskins, 'Henry as Patron'.
[289] www.carlarossi.info/marie.html (accessed 29.11.2011). Her *Marie et les érudits*, is cited *passim* in Brown and Bussell, eds, *Barking Culture*; I have consulted it as well as the website.
[290] *Glory of her Sex*, notes 7 & 61 (on pp. 231 & 237).

humble) may be part of the same self-construction. We can deduce that her anonymity is transparent because, her work being read aloud by and for her fellow-nuns, the whole audience knew quite well who she was. So why did she bother? Clemence gives her name regardless of any such considerations, although her audience must have been comparable. It has been suggested that Clemence's audience may initially have contained fewer visitors from outside the abbey. Therefore giving her name was not strictly necessary, for the same reason: everybody would have known her. The Nun's reluctance to put her name to a page where the saint's name appears is on a par with her playful treatment of her audience: pretended humility mingled with an authoritative story-teller's confidence. A further and similar characteristic of the Nun's authorial persona is her ambivalence about wanting to do the translation at all. The pattern is repeated, if pattern it is, in places where the Nun explains that she does not know something, even where she probably had Aelred's text in front of her. In these cases, the comments add a lively personal touch to the narrative.[291] It is noted, *passim*, that sometimes she seems to be undertaking the work because she wishes to do it, and sometimes she pleads unwillingness. Given her elaborately pretended modesty and her transparently pointless anonymity, it seems likely that this too is a pose. One is reminded of the reluctant but thoroughly competent after-dinner speaker who protests for form's sake, although quite obviously enjoying himself (or herself) enormously.

The Poem's Audience

Who were the audience for the Nun's poem? The nuns of Barking should not be envisaged as cloistered or cut off. Their audiences would include visitors both clerical and lay. *Edouard* contains 'direct political propaganda in its promotion of Henry II'; the nuns 'gained access to channels of power which were mostly denied to them in the secular world, and found new ways in which to express themselves'.[292] Some Lives were later used for mealtime reading, but this is no indication of what audience was envisaged at the outset, by either of the nuns writing at Barking in the twelfth century. The verse saint's legend (even if written by religious) was generally for lay folk, patrons and guests, for feast-day relaxation; use at Campsey for mealtimes was exceptional.[293] An important feature of the Nun's *Vie* is its 'aurality': it was clearly intended for recitation.[294] Aurality strives to free discussion of medieval texts from opposition between orality and literacy, with all its evolutionary baggage. Texts may be read, not recited from memory, to a literate audience who could read for themselves if they wished. Thus, expressions such as 'you have heard the writing' are no paradox. Coleman calls reading before an audience 'prelection' (cf. modern 'lecture'): 'saints'

---

[291] See Stempel, 'La modernité'; comments of this type in early romances, and writers teasing their audience, pp. 279 & 287–8.
[292] Mitchell, 'Patrons and Politics', pp. 362–4.
[293] Legge, *Background*, p. 275.
[294] Coleman, 'Aurality'.

lives [were] prelected probably everywhere' (p. 71). See the Nun's address at vv. 4913, 5020, 5297, and 5310. v. 5297 reads 'vus ... Ki avez oï cest rumanz'; this probably means 'the book'.[295]

Aelred's text does not show comparable evidence of aurality; he does not write as if to a listening audience. It is unlikely that he intended his *Vita* exclusively for the private (silent) reading of Laurence, its patron, although copies would have been made for, and the text perhaps read to, others interested in Edward. The preface directing the work to the king, and the preface to Laurence, state why it was written. Chapter headings, present in the *PL Vita*, may be intended to make it suitable for public reading,[296] but we have no means of knowing whether they were added by Aelred himself. We may compare authorial declarations in the two Barking poems. The Nun tells us she undertook hers for love of Edward, Clemence for love of the abbey. The Nun refers to the currently-reigning monarch, and Clemence does not. Both exhibit features of aurality, but the Nun's are more prominent.

The dramatic tone of the Nun's poem shows it was probably to be read aloud, and addresses to the audience are frequent. Södergård notes her lively additions (Introduction, pp. 28 and 34). She calls them 'Seignurs' [My lords] as if they were noblemen and women. This, given the Abbey's links with Court life,[297] seems entirely plausible, though she also uses 'seignurs' within her narrative, when 'good men' or 'monks' is meant. Barking was no longer a double house, so there was no "captive audience" of monks – even supposing them permitted to mix for social occasions. The address may be intended for clerical visitors. 'Seignurs' was a well-attested form within monastic circles,[298] by analogy with Latin *seniores* for senior religious, although the Nun uses it independently (that is, not translating *seniores*). The passages where she calls the audience 'seignurs' are additions to her source; Aelred rarely addresses anybody. After his Prologues, no audience is indicated. Most examples of the Nun's 'seignurs', when not to audience, match words in Aelred meaning 'monks' or 'brothers'. Once he has *sociis* [companions]; only once *seniores* [one of the senior monks] where the Nun has 'one of the other monks' (v. 6641, and see Glossary). 'Seignurs' meant no more (or less) than modern 'Ladies and gentlemen'.[299] Her address therefore suggests an audience that included visitors: monks and/or lay nobility. Further, her address extends to a future audience. In chapter 30 (where she introduces herself) she begs the indulgence of not only those who hear, but also those who will ever hear, her book [Ki mais orrunt cest soen rumanz]. Her reference to the abbey 'which is called Barking' (chapter 40) shows that she expects her work to travel beyond the walls within which she lives. She could hardly withhold from her fellow-nuns a name they

---

[295] Hiatt, 'Genre without System', pp. 281–4: '*romaunz* and *bok* may be used interchangeably'. See also Glossary, for 'romanz'.
[296] Cf. Eadmer, *Life of Anselm*, p. xxii.
[297] Mitchell, 'Patrons and Politics'; and Campbell, *Medieval Saints' Lives*, p. 231.
[298] Short, 'Patrons and Polyglots', p. 235; nuns as 'les dames', p. 236.
[299] Legge, *Background*, pp. 195–6, 261, 263, 271, 273.

already knew, so her deliberate anonymity would be pointless within the abbey in her own day. Perhaps the nun cured by Edward (chapter 40) was present; she, and her story in Aelred, are among possible reasons for the Nun to have written *Edouard*.[300]

A notable difference between *Vie* and *Vita* is that the latter is amply furnished with Bible references; the Nun deletes many of them. Is this because a female audience was considered to be unfamiliar with the Bible? Unlikely, given that any exclusively female audience must have been the nuns of Barking, who were as well-versed in Scripture as any other religious. Further, the Nun replaces many quotations with homiletic passages, many of them proverbial or proverb-like. She was more likely considering a mixed audience, of religious and lay. The latter would be less familiar than nuns with the Bible, but everybody can recognize proverbs. In the text below, proverbs are identified wherever possible; many sentient and homiletic sayings are not readily identifiable as proverbs. The Nun's tendency to suppress or alter Bible references is further evidence that the proposed audience included lay visitors, and also that she envisaged her work being read outside the Abbey (for further discussion of Bible references, see Rewriting Aelred).

The Campsey version was for mealtime reading, although its chapters of unequal length might not have been entirely convenient for this (divisions, closely matching Aelred's, are probably authorial). However, it was not at Campsey until the fourteenth century. A note on the last folio reads: 'Ce livre deviseie a la priorie de Kampseie de lire a mengier' [This book for the Priory of Campsey, to read at mealtimes] (*Vie*, Introduction, p. 47). It was either donated to or commissioned by the priory; if commissioned, the Lives must have been collected by whoever put the manuscript together.[301] We do not know whether it was thus used before its arrival there, nor whether it was composed with mealtime reading in mind. However, a mixed audience of visitors and residents may be envisaged, readings taking place after dinner or at other suitable times (but see p. 47, above). Further, the twelfth-century Vatican manuscript of the *Vie* also includes texts for male use.[302]

The poem is addressed not only to a present audience ('seignurs'), but also to an absent and future audience. In spite of the personal, immediate, and dramatic tone of the Nun's style, passages where Barking Abbey is named as if to outsiders are evidence that the poem was intended to travel beyond the place and time of its composition. MS P (thirteenth century) and the prose version (fourteenth century) are Continental, which suggests that the Nun's work did indeed travel. Clemence says 'De Berkinge sui nunain' (v. 2691), not 'this abbey which is called Barking' as the Nun does. *Catherine* may initially have been for an internal audience.

---

[300] See Thiry-Stassin, 'L'hagiographie', p. 413.
[301] Campbell, *Medieval Saints' Lives*, p. 183. See also Wogan-Browne, 'Powers of Record'; Legge, *Background*, p. 275, 'bequeathed by a lay-woman at Campsey'.
[302] Wogan-Browne, 'Clerc u lai', p. 62 (and note 11).

Later Lives of Edward

After the Nun's twelfth-century *Edouard*, there were a number of further Lives. Some were based, broadly, on Aelred's and some on the Nun's.

Alexander of Ashby made a Latin verse Life, not mentioned in the Introduction to *Estoire*; Alexander having died before 1215, it predates MP's Life but not the Nun's.[303] The Nun's *Vie* itself was rewritten in a later French Prose version.[304] It was also the source for at least one of the Middle English Lives.[305] Södergård (Introduction, p. 45) judges that the Nun's is source for the Middle English *Edward*, because of verbal similarities. He is mistaken in saying Moore does not consider any Old French text to be its source. The Nun's work must have been fairly well known within Britain, too.

The French Prose Life was recently re-examined by Russell.[306] He remarks particularly on its extended treatment of the scene about Edward with his wife, in which Edith's role is further enhanced. He also discusses a second miracle, reportedly from Barking, that it contains. It is clear that its editor, Meyer, knew only one manuscript of *Edouard*: Campsey (*olim* Welbeck), and speculates upon how the text would have ended. Interestingly, Meyer noticed that another nun of Barking gives her name, Clemence, in her own saint's life (the *Catherine*). But he cannot have seen this name in the Campsey manuscript because, the Campsey copy of *Catherine* being incomplete, her name does not appear in it; he does not state where he saw it. For this extra Barking miracle, the prose redactor may have known another (lost) copy of *Edouard* in which it appeared. The Nun's text ends rather abruptly immediately after the Triple Cure in the present chapter 41, and it may once have ended with a prayer as the Prose does. Alternatively, the Nun's version may initially have ended after Edward's death, where a natural break occurs, adding the miracles later (see p. 169, below). If the scribes of MSS P and W, the two of our three versions that end at or around Edward's death, were working from such a version, this would explain why they lack the miracles. It would be pleasing if the Nun's version had ended with a second Barking miracle, but unless another manuscript comes to light this must remain a matter for speculation. After the second Barking miracle in the Prose version, of a lady cured by her prayers to Edward, the redactor adds that writing all Edward's miracles would be too long a task, finishing with a short prayer that conforms closely to the standard ending of saints' lives. The Egerton redactor seems to admire the Nun's work: he (or she) neither deletes nor substantially alters what she says about herself. On the contrary, to the famous 'modesty' passage he adds a qualifier: 'ele n'est encore pas digne, *selon s'entente*, que ses nons ...' [She is not yet worthy, *in her opinion*, that her name ...], my emphasis (§57, cf. vv. 5308–11). He also writes that she is 'mie noumés', instead of 'a ore' [not at all named] thus removing a hint that the Nun might

---

[303] *History* p. 7 (note 25), and Rigg, *Anglo-Latin Literature* (pp. 14 & 131-3); it *is* in fact published, see *Liber Festiualis* ed. Dinkova-Bruun.
[304] 'Notice' ed. Meyer. See p. 199, below.
[305] *The Middle English Edward* ed. Moore, Sources (pp. lxiii–lxxi): 'It must derive from the French verse translation ... of MS Welbeck Abbey I.C.1' (p. lxviii).
[306] 'Cultural Context'.

give her name in later writings (sometimes cited as evidence that she was Clemence). Because the Nun originally cast this passage in the third person, speaking of herself, the redactor can render it exactly as 'nobody must think the worse of it because it was translated by a woman' – a significant passage to leave unedited, in an age of contempt for women's learning! He also helps the Nun's reputation when explaining his (or her) unwillingness to translate the Life: that s/he does not know enough about the story, rather than that s/he lacks 'wit and wisdom'. It is known that the author of the *Vie* is female, and the redactor of the Prose could be male; it is not clear which voice declares these sentiments. Russell discusses the manuscript's provenance: possibly commissioned, though probably not executed, by Marie de Saint-Pol, who may have visited Campsey Priory.[307] However, because the Campsey *Edouard* is incomplete, the question remains: where did the redactor find an exemplar to work from? Despite the Saint-Pol family's connections with insular culture, and despite the text's English subject-matter, even Dean makes no attempt to claim it as an Anglo-Norman text,[308] although further research may eventually pull it into the fold.

Aelred's *Vita* inspired a thirteenth-century Anglo-Norman Life: that attributed to Matthew Paris (*Estoire*). The attribution ought perhaps to remain open, given that not all scholars are fully convinced it was by Matthew.[309] Collard questions it;[310] Baswell cites another scholar who does so.[311]

The Matthew Paris *Life of St Edmund* may be consulted in this context: Edward the Confessor was the first English saint whose canonization, in 1161, can be established with certainty.[312] That hagiography was a recognized province of the medieval historiographer is noted (pp. 104–5); Matthew wrote both hagiography and history.[313] However, he was not a man of great spiritual perception (p. 116); judging by his (if he wrote it) Edward compared with that of the Nun and indeed that of Aelred.[314] There are interesting parallels between the two saints: after performing a miracle, Edmund swears his companions to secrecy (p. 136). This is similar to Edward swearing Lievrich to secrecy after the Vision of the Christ Child (vv. 3041–2, in chapter 16). A comparable story is told of Thomas Becket,[315] and no doubt of other saintly figures. Further, the ageing Edmund is described in terms reminiscent of Edward in the Nun's *Vie*: 'While his limbs grew weak, the strength of his soul increased' (p. 137, Lawrence's translation; cf. the opening of chapter 25, below). This is the more striking, given the lack of proverbial precedent for the idea;[316] it is not in Aelred's *Vita*, nor in MP's

---

[307] See also Wogan-Browne et al., eds, *French of England*, p. 236.
[308] Her *Anglo-Norman Literature* contains a number of borderline cases.
[309] Cf. Wallace's Introduction to the *Estoire*, and Vaughan, *Matthew Paris* (esp. pp. 168–81).
[310] 'A Lesson in Holy Kingship' (I thank the author for discussion, and a copy of her article).
[311] 'King Edward and the Cripple', note 3 and References (Morgan 1988).
[312] *The Life of St Edmund* tr. Lawrence, p. 92.
[313] See, however, Tyler, 'Review of *Wulfric*': that hagiography is best experienced as a kind of 'magic realism' (p. 103).
[314] See also Carpenter, 'Origins', p. 878, for treatment of Godwin in the Lives, especially MP's.
[315] Barlow, *Thomas Becket*, p. 231.
[316] See Bliss, 'Old English *Gnome*'.

Estoire of Edward. Because these passages do not appear in the *Estoire*, they cannot be construed as evidence that it was by Matthew Paris. The coincidence suggests only that Matthew may have seen the Nun's work and perhaps borrowed the ideas for his Edmund (*Estoire* predates Edmund by some years),[317] or perhaps they were unrecorded commonplaces then current elsewhere.

Translation and Presentation

> ... lest we seem violently to wrest [her] sayings according to the caprice of our own view (Gregory the Great).[318]

The present translation aims to reproduce the Nun's voice as closely as is consistent with readable modern prose. It follows Södergård's edition in the main; where the online Saints' Lives have been consulted, important differences are indicated in notes.[319] There are a few errors in the printed edition: some are silently corrected below (such as small items of punctuation); errors of vocabulary or of historical fact are noted.

Each of the Nun's chapters is prefaced by a reference to Aelred's *Vita*, together with its corresponding section in the translation (*Life*). References to *Estoire*, with page-numbers in the translation (*History*), are also given for comparison, although MP's text does not always match *Vita* or *Vie* closely. However, *Estoire* is important because, like *Vie*, it is based on Aelred's *Vita*. It is already a well-known text, and therefore comparison with the Nun's text may be of interest to readers.

I retain and translate doublets throughout. These pairs of synonyms or near-synonyms add to the richness of the text and may introduce nuances of meaning that I should be reluctant to lose, although some translators resolve them.[320] An example is where the Nun writes 'went away or vanished' (v. 4296 and note); at the corresponding point in *Estoire* the translators collapse 'went away and vanished' into 'vanished' (*History* p. 98; see From Latin to Medieval French above, for supernatural disappearances).

Some translators normalize 'wandering tenses' – narrative passages where verbs switch from past to present, for example, and it is not clear why this should be so.[321] Others follow changes in the original, presenting the narrative as more immediate; therefore it is worth attempting to reproduce a good number of these changes. 'To the modern reader, such apparent inconsistency stands out ...';[322] nevertheless it suits the Nun's conversational style. Far from being peculiar to her work, these switches are common in Old French (cf. the 'historic present' in Latin narrative). I follow

---

[317] *The Life of St Edmund* tr. Lawrence, p. 116; *Estoire* p. xxiii.
[318] Cited in Fowler, *Bible in Literature*, p. 65.
[319] (margot.uwaterloo.ca). For example, a correction to v. 5348.
[320] *History*, p. 51; but see Ruelle, 'Synonymes', for their value.
[321] See Uitti, 'The Clerkly Narrator', esp. pp. 394–6; and Fleischman, 'Philology'.
[322] See Cherewatuk and Wiethaus, eds, *Dear Sister*, p. 132 (and note 28, p. 138) for tense-switching and spoken narrative; Ménard, 'Tradition manuscrite', pp. 162–3.

them in the Nun's text as closely as seems reasonable, with a note where necessary (an example is at vv. 4129–30). Generally a present perfect form, common in the Anglo-Norman narrative, is translated into a past form in modern English ('he is/has gone' = 'he went', unless the former better fits the sense). A French present perfect form often looks, if translated literally, like an English passive. At v. 19, 'En terre est primes coruné', a translator has the choice of writing 'He is crowned first on earth' or 'He was crowned ...'. I opted for the latter in this case, because the verb in the previous line is clearly historic past [... deus feiz le coruna]. Also common is, for example, the verb 'to be' switching from 'est' in one line to 'esteit' in the next. This may be simply to arrive at the correct number of syllables, although the former could notionally be 'ert' or 'fud'. These are noted *passim*, and I normalize a few pairs that would otherwise look awkward. In broadly narrative passages, I do not usually distinguish between historic past, imperfect, and present perfect forms; the latter may sometimes be translated as present (or passive) among other present forms.[323] Owen tends to follow tense-switching in his well-respected translations of medieval romance, explaining why in his introductions.[324] *Edmund*'s modern translation does not normalize tenses: Lawrence follows the tense-switching of the original.[325] For example, on p. 157 a past is followed by a proverb in the present tense; the narrative continues in present tense. On p. 159 the tense changes without any intervening proverb.[326]

Another common problem for translators is that Old French speech often varies its second-person forms, using singular 'tu' and plural 'vous' apparently indiscriminately.[327] Unlike in Modern French, the singular (in Middle English and in Old French) is not necessarily or simply familiar, as compared to the 'you' form generally considered more formal today.[328] On the contrary, a beggar may address a king as 'thou', and a lover address his lady (even in the most intimate circumstances) as 'you'. Sometimes a speaker switches from one to the other within a speech, for no apparent reason except, conceivably, for the metre (for example, Edward's speech to God at vv. 4676–92, in chapter 27). In the conversation between Edward and the cured blind man in chapter 18 (vv. 3401–20), the two address each other as 'tu' throughout except for one speech only where the man uses 'vous'. In general, I keep 'thou' for very personal speech such as prayer to God (as in modern-day French, and traditionalist English, churches), and 'you' in other cases. Although 'thou' may sound

---

[323] Tense-switching also obtains in Old Norse (I thank Victoria Condie for her advice); I noticed this when investigating *Volsunga Saga*, for the sword that only a hero can draw (cf. the story of Saint Ulstan's staff, below). An older translation of the *Saga* follows tense-switching; a more modern one normalizes (see *Völsunga Saga* ed. Sparling, and *The Saga of the Volsungs* tr. Byock: for example, second paragraph of ch. 9 in both cases).
[324] *Chrétien Romances*, p. xxv; 'The Romance of Fergus', p. 85.
[325] *The Life of St Edmund*.
[326] See also *Fouke le Fitz Waryn* ed. Hathaway et al., p. cx.
[327] Ibid. p. cxii.
[328] See Brunot and Bruneau, *Précis de Grammaire*, pp. 281–2; Woledge, *Commentaire*, notes to vv. 326 & 6566–8; Foulet, *Petite Syntaxe*, pp. 198–201.

uncomfortably archaic to some, I want to allow both kinds of voice to be heard in the translation.

I am aware that nowadays translators have a tendency to normalize in most or all of these cases mentioned above, but it must be remembered that we cannot be sure what medieval writers intended by these habits we find so inconvenient. They may be evidence of nuances we are unable to discern, and it would be wrong to gloss over them. It is safer, and I believe more honest, to follow the original as closely as possible. Luard's translation of *Estoire*, although it has been condemned as 'archaizing', is no less readable because he respects, and follows, the variations that I discuss here.[329]

A Glossary might seem redundant in the present work, where the text is translated in its entirety. But there are a number of key words and phrases in the poem which recur again and again, often with different or debatable meanings depending on the context. I have therefore collected discussion of these terms together, at the end of the book, to save repeated explanations. Single words and phrases of particular interest, occurring only once or twice, are explained in notes to the text (these include items where Södergård's glossary has been found incorrect). The Glossary also contains some rather more common words that may be of interest to anybody wishing to compare this translation with the original; it thus acts as a supplementary Index of special terms. My Indexes are necessarily selective: it would be less than useful to index the Nun, Barking Abbey, Aelred and his *Vita*, the *Estoire*, manuscripts of the *Vie*, or Edward himself.

Divisions are presented as in the edition because they form convenient chapters (see Södergård's Analyse, pp. 1–15). Numbered and named to aid readers' navigation, they match Aelred's chapter-divisions closely (he calls them *capitulum*). I retain internal divisions, each marked off by a blank line and a larger capital in the edition: each chapter contains one or more sections, and I indicate these with a paraph-mark (¶). Other paragraphs are added as modern English style demands. They correspond, with few exceptions, to divisions marked by larger capitals in the manuscripts. Textual divisions in the *Vie* are very close to those in *Life*, which in turn follow *PL*. For the most part, they correspond to divisions in the Aelred manuscripts (Introduction to *Historical Works*, p. 37). Readers wishing to compare the translation with the edition, or with the online versions, will find them useful. Each chapter is further prefaced by a short introduction, to pick out points of interest as they occur chapter by chapter, such as important differences from Aelred or variants from the other manuscripts. The most extensive are those of MS P, which seem to reflect preference for the historical rather than the personal or mystical: some pious sentences are omitted, but explanations (sometimes rather confused) and descriptions are added.[330] Södergård's endnotes, labelled by line-number, are signalled in my footnotes so that readers can consult them if they wish.

---

[329] *Lives of Edward*, p. xiii.
[330] See Bliss and Weiss, 'The "J" Manuscript'.

The Life of Edward the Confessor

Prologue (1–10)

Introduction

This is part of a longer explanation by the author: the Prologue once comprised fifty lines, and these ten are the last of them.[1] The Nun's apology should not be taken at face value. This conventional modesty-topos in no wise indicates incompetence, and may indicate that English was her first language (cf. *Estoire*, vv. 89–96; and *History* note 18, to these lines). It is not only women who express modesty: for example, Simon of Walsingham, author of a life of Saint Faith in the Campsey manuscript, pretends diffidence about his ability to translate.[2] The Nun follows a well-trodden and classical tradition. For her Prologue, see Legge: the apology may owe something to Gregory of Tours (and not, for example, to awareness of any breakdown of the two-case declension system in Anglo-Norman).[3] Given that the reference is to Gregory's *Liber de Gloria Beatorum Confessorum*, a book about Confessors, such as Edward was, it is reasonable to suppose the Nun was familiar with it. Aelred's Prologue, about the writing of history, and Preface, to Abbot Laurence who commissioned the *Vita*, are relatively personal compared with his narrative.

Before translating what we have of the Prologue, I append the following even more fragmentary passage which precedes it:

> ... en faire ad voleir,
> ...t a sun poeir;
> ...t le blamerunt,
> ...lz fere e nel funt.
> [5] ... suffire estot,
> ... al mels qu'il pot:
> ... tot le bien fait,

---

[1] Russell, 'Campsey Collection', pp. 78–9; 'Fragment' ed. Baker.
[2] Wogan-Browne, 'Wreaths of Thyme', p. 52; Baker, 'Saints' Lives in Anglo-French', p. 126; Gransden, 'Prologues', esp. pp. 55–6; Dronke, *Women Writers*, p. 34. See, especially, Curtius, *European Literature*, pp. 83–5; and Minnis, *Authorship*, p. 165.
[3] *Background*, pp. 63–4.

> ... eiz que blasme en ait:
> ...t a sa puisance,
> [10] ...a bone voilance.
> ...e vus requise
> ... me sui mise
> ...
> ...
> ... ne grace
> ...us la parface
> ...

It would be vain to attempt a translation of this. Suffice it to say that only the word 'requise' gives any hint that the work might have been requested (it could mean a number of other things), although if so there is no guessing by whom. It is certainly no dedication. Another point that emerges from this fragment is the observation that if any Anglo-Norman writer wishes to say 'I'll do what I can' or similar, in couplets, then the rhymes 'pouvoir/vouloir', or 'puisance/volance' are likely to appear without any Anselmian influence. Robertson remarks that 'voleir' and 'poeir' are central to both Clemence's *Catherine* and Thomas' *Tristan*; he links both with Bernard of Clairvaux. Further, he finds that Clemence has more in common stylistically with several male authors than with the Nun, concluding that the two are very unlikely to be the same woman.[4]

Because the following is a fragment, there is no large capital in the edited text.

≈ ≈ ≈ ≈ ≈ ≈ ≈ ≈ ≈

... If I do not keep the order of cases, nor join part to part rightly, I certainly ought not to be reproached, for I can by no means manage it: what is nominative in Latin I shall make accusative in French. I know a false French of England, for I have not been abroad to seek it. But you, who have learned it abroad, please amend my work where necessary.[5]

---

[4] 'Textual Community'.
[5] 1–10 Legge, *Background*, translates these lines (p. 63).

The Introduction to Edward (11–68)[1]

Introduction[2]

Aelred's text begins with a Prologue which includes an address to Henry II, and then a Preface to Laurence, abbot of Westminster. His Book One begins with a discussion of Edward's generosity and sanctity, continuing with a sketch of his lineage. The Nun's Prologue is followed by immediate introduction of her subject. *Estoire*'s preface praises not the Creator but Queen Eleanor and King Henry III. It is clear that the Nun (as Laurent notes) dedicates her work to God,[3] whatever she might say later about the reigning king. In chapter 30, the Nun reiterates that she is writing for the love of Edward, with no mention of Henry. It is typical that the Nun begins this chapter with an expression of praise, ending it with a prayer. Aelred, no less typically, begins with a Bible reference.

❧ ❧ ❧ ❧ ❧ ❧ ❧ ❧ ❧

Here begins the Romance of Saint Edward, King and Confessor[4]

¶To praise the Creator and his power, I begin this work. May his power[5] now come to my aid in rewriting this Life,[6] may he be pleased to receive my work; may it also be to the Saint's liking, whom the good God loved so much that he crowned him twice: he was crowned first on earth,[7] and then in heaven for his goodness. By the terrestrial crown, he gained the celestial. He prized human riches so little, and so he won supreme abundance: the great abundance of sweetness in the Creator's presence. This is what the angels long for, and nevertheless they gaze at it endlessly.[8]

---

1 *Vita*, 739B–40D; *Life*, §1; *Estoire*, vv. 1–96; *History*, pp. 53–4.
2 In MS P, vv. 1–68 are lacking.
3 *Plaire et édifier*, p. 132.
4 Title (line unnumbered) '... rei et confessur'; MS W begins here. In this rubric, the word 'confessur' is lacking, but the copyist has effaced a word after 'et'.
5 13 MS 'Sa valeur et sa vie'; Södergård corrects what is evidently an eyeskip to next line. In the text below, MS readings and variants are signalled wherever interesting differences occur (for very minor differences, see the edition). Passages in square brackets indicate extra lines from another MS (a footnote explains each); single words in square brackets are clarifying interpolations. Notably different readings from MSS online are likewise signalled. For 'valur' in vv. 12 & 13, see Glossary.
6 14 'De translater ci ceste vie': for 'translater', see *La Vie Seint Edmund le Rei*, Denis Piramus, Introduction, p. cxiv: meaning more 'to transfer' than to translate in our modern sense (the work is dated *c.* 1170). This author is another who used English sources (pp. cxxix–x).
7 19 'En terre est primes coruné': MS W frequently has 'est' for 'ert' (Södergård's note); further occurences silently corrected.
8 Laurent marks this mystical passage (*Plaire et édifier*, pp. 260–62). See my Introduction for the poem's Themes, and p. 29, above.

So much does this gazing delight them that they cannot be sated.[9] What they do,[10] they do longingly, and they long for what they already have. The more they see him, the more they are drawn to him; the more they have, the more they long for. From their strength is their desire born to them,[11] and their strength feeds their desire: they have power to gaze at him, and their will is born from their gaze. To the abundance of this sight of God, King Edward is now come. He delights in this plenty, for his joy is perfected in it. Oh, wonder! What great nobility, and what two-fold felicity! He has abundance here below, and abundance there – but he despises the former, and he loves the latter. He knows the former to be fleeting and vain, the latter to be lasting and full of all good things. Here he made God rule his body, so that he would always find[12] his heart poor in sin, in crime, in vainglory, in wicked pleasures.[13] So he, who can be as rich as he was and yet hold himself poor; and who thus follows poverty, he may indeed be rich in deserving; therefore he was rich and poor, as he wanted to have both together: humility in riches, and the virtue of poverty. Now let us pray God, who is so good and who accepts his own people everywhere, who despises not the poor, nor is satisfied merely by riches – that by his great bounty, without which no good thing is given, he may give us a share in his joy, that he has now given to Saint Edward.

---

[9] 30 'ne se poënt saüler': first of several examples of holy craving and its fulfilment. 'se soûler' means to get drunk, in modern French. This is interesting in view of what comes later, about Edward *drinking* the news of St John with lover-like ecstasy (see ch. 25). But generally in the poem it means sated, not drunk (see Glossary).
[10] 31 'ceo qu'il funt': MS 'unt'; Södergård corrects, for clarity.
[11] 35 Södergård thinks two lines are missing here (his note); MacBain emends 'prist' to 'paist' ('Apprenticeship', p. 18), which I follow.
[12] 50 'truver': MS 'turner'. Södergård corrects, for the sense (his note).
[13] 51-2 'Povrë en pechié, en delit, En veine glorie, en fol delit': Bloch claims 'delit' is first found in 1392 (Södergård's note to v. 51). Here as elsewhere it is not always easy to judge where pleasure ends and wickedness begins (see Glossary).

Chapter 1
Of his Lineage (69–142)[1]

Introduction

MS P begins here (v. 69). The Nun's sections, except for these first two, correspond with those of her model; each is introduced by a chapter (§) number from *Life*. The very personal *occupatio* ('I should have to hold up my story ... I could tell much more about them ...') is added by the Nun. Aelred passes over the matter in fewer words. However, Aelred begins his first chapter with a short sermon on God's chosen. He cites examples from Scripture, finally quoting the Parable of the Vineyard (Matt. 20:1–16) to illustrate Edward's worthy end. The Nun makes no such parallels here. The end of Aelred's chapter (a glance forward to Edward's story) contrasts with the Nun's statement of opinion ('Ethelred did wisely ...') and her address to the audience. She does not take the opportunity of mentioning Edward the Martyr here, but jumps from Edgar to Ethelred. Ethelred was Edgar's son by his third wife; the son by his first wife was Edward the Martyr, said to have been murdered by his step-mother. Södergård (note to v. 74) gives the succession of kings; see chapter 37 (the Sewing-Girl), and Introduction (p. 34 above), for possible connections between the family and Barking Abbey. Ethelred's surname, 'the Redeless', means 'lacking good counsel' (in modern English, the 'Unready'). During his troubled reign the Danes and Norse began their invasions, and his attempt to buy them off with 'Danegeld' was held to be shameful. Compared with Aelred, the Nun makes more of Emma and her family.

❧ ❧ ❧ ❧ ❧ ❧ ❧ ❧ ❧

¶In the days of good Englishmen, formerly, Alfred reigned in this land.[2] After him, it was held by his heirs, who wielded great power. The fathers handed so much to the sons, and brother reigned after brother, so that after they were dead the lot then fell upon Edgar. This Edgar was a potent king, wise in God and courteous in the world.[3] He overtopped them all in goodness, glory, and surpassing holiness. His goodness pleased God very greatly, as he showed at his birth. For at the very hour Edgar was born, angels sang on earth 'Joy be to the Angles,[4] peace be to earth! May his days

---

[1] *Vita*, 740D–41C; *Life*, §1. Cf. *Estoire*, vv. 102–54; *History*, pp. 54–5.
[2] Södergård's note to v. 70, describing Alfred, is wrongly labelled v. 72. See Legge, *Background*, p. 63, for interest in Alfred during Henry II's reign.
[3] 78 'en siecle curtais': the Nun recognizes the importance of this quality, whether God or human behaving 'courteously' (see Glossary).
[4] 84–5 'Unt li angles en terre chanté: «Joie aient angle ...» ': the identical 'angel' and 'English' deliberately juxtaposed. Cf. the famous phrase *non angli sed angeli*, in the Legend of St Gregory (*GL*, I, p. 172. The story is not necessarily fictitious; see Bede, *History*, note to p. 98 on p. 365). See Södergård's note to v. 77, for Edgar. The passage, expanded from Aelred's *Vita*, resembles rather a corresponding one in his *Genealogy* (which the Nun probably knew); see p. 96, and cf. *Life* p. 131.

be free from war!' This song came true in time, for as long as he held the kingdom the English had joy and England had peace – free from all war. His son was King Ethelred, in whose time the Danish came to England; they took it and subjected it to their power. Then King Ethelred took a wife, most noble and beautiful, her name was Emma.[5] She is daughter to the Duke of Normandy, that noble man of saintly life. Her high birth, her reputation and courage, the saintliness of her good father [Richard Sans Peur], her nephew [Robert the Magnificent], and her brother [Richard II, the Good], together with their valour and virtue, are now known to everybody.[6] England knows this still, for through her own is her war ended:[7] by the glorious King Henry [Henry II], who sprang from this godly lineage and who has freed England and enriched her Church. I should have to hold up my story for a long time, were I to list all his goodness. But may God, from whom he has good will,[8] grant him long life and health, and to govern his people so well that he may reign with God in Heaven. On earth let him have peace, prosperity, and health; God give strength to his heirs so that they may hold land in such a way as to please God. Grant them such wisdom and power as their good ancestors had: Count Robert, the good Richard, and William the noble Bastard.[9] I could tell much more about them, for the subject is both noble and fine; but I shall say just that their good life was completed by holy death. Their holy death adds to their glory, and their life and their rest is in God.

¶King Ethelred did wisely when he took a wife of such lineage: his heirs were able to take after her, in loving God and doing good. For it often happens, that whoever is born from the good may easily achieve good.[10] From these noble lords came the good Edward, the friend of God, as you shall hear by and by, when you know more of the story. It will be of benefit to all who hear, and it will be a delight to lovers of God.

---

[5]   The Nun expands, making more of Emma than Aelred does (*Life*, pp. 131–2).
[6]   96–104 Emma is (not 'was') the Duke's daughter; the passage leads into a statement about the present (see my notes on Translation).
[7]   This refers to years of strife during the time of Stephen and Matilda.
[8]   113 MS 'Mes Deu, par ki ad bone volunté' (retained here): Södergård corrects to 'par ki ad la bunté' because the line is hypermetric.
[9]   Aelred mentions their 'praiseworthy' life and 'priceless' death (cf. the Nun's 'holy', below); William of Malmesbury stresses their virtues but mentions no holiness (*Kings* tr. Stephenson, Epistle, p. 3). The Conqueror's nickname, common in c12 (examples: Sinclair, 'CCC 405', p. 225; Barlow, *William I*, pp. 1 & 11–12; Mason, *House of Godwine*, p. 107 & note 1 on p. 229), suggests the Nun knew a source in which he was called 'the Bastard'; not a term of abuse, but noteworthy because Aelred does not call him that. However, 'the *noble* Bastard' seems to be her own (the phrase is used by Aurell without comment (*Plantagenet Empire*, p. 136), in discussing the Nun's work).
[10] 136 'Ke ki de biens vient süef eolt': Morawski, 1886, 'Qui de bons est soef fleire'; cf. *Estoire* vv. 97–101, 'Quant racine est de bone ente, Droiz est ke li fruz s'en sente …'.

Chapter 2

Edward is chosen King (143–266)[1]

Introduction

Aelred, like the Nun, steps straight into the story at the beginning of this chapter. Its ending is also similar, expressing the people's hope, although the Nun expands. In particular, she recasts the prayer to Jesus. She dwells at greater length upon the marvellous choice, made by the greatest in the realm, of an unborn child to be king. They wanted to ensure a safe succession, but in the days of high infant mortality and failed pregnancies it would have been a remarkable occurrence. Doubt whether the child will be born is addressed in the narrative, but people choose him in spite of that doubt. The picture of the unborn child (vv. 232–4), knowing the secrets of the womb and feeling its restrictions, is an addition to Aelred's account. The Nun may have known about childbirth at first hand, before joining the Abbey. Women not infrequently entered nunneries later in life, and there is no evidence the Nun was young. Women who have never had (or wanted) children are less likely to feel such empathy, so it cannot be argued that this is merely a typical woman's comment. Alternatively, the Nun may be exploiting a legend, so far unidentified, that the unborn Christ felt oppressed inside his mother – perhaps a notion explored in womens' prayers which emphasize the holy infant's humanity.[2] If so, it fits with the way the Nun aligns Edward with Christ elsewhere in the poem.[3] The idea that follows, of ruling upon earth without having felt or seen earth, is taken from Aelred but expressed in a more concrete manner (cf. *Life*, p. 133: 'someone whom the land had not yet received is designated lord of the land').

☙ ☙ ☙ ☙ ☙ ☙ ☙ ☙ ☙

¶Ethelred had a first son, a good soldier, strong and brave. His name was Edmund Ironside, and he was a well-loved knight. His mother was of high lineage, for Count Theodred was her father. But by Emma, whom he married next, he had a son he named Alfred.[4] A long time after his birth, the greatest in the realm assembled: the bishops and abbots, the counts and powerful lords, all were moved to anger, for they had heard news that the Danish had arrived in the land and all wished to destroy them. And they saw several signs,[5] of the great evils they would soon endure. For sure, it

---

[1] *Vita*, 741C–2B; *Life*, §2. *Estoire*, vv. 155–74; *History*, p. 55.
[2] But see Tasioulas, 'Heaven and Earth', for medieval thinking about the status, and feelings, of an unborn child.
[3] See p. 5, above.
[4] Södergård believes Alfred was the elder (note to v. 150, and IPN), but see *Life* (note on p. 132), and introduction to ch. 3, below.
[5] 159 'plusurs enseignes dunc virent'; MS P reads 'enseignes lor vindrent' [signs came to them]: see note to v. 240. Aelred has 'indications of the coming conflict' (*Life*, pp. 132–3 and notes).

often happens that promised evil is fulfilled. What bodes ill often comes to pass, and good fails when one trusts in it most.[6] Evil comes more quickly than good, for the smallest reason, in all matters. Therefore the English were suspicious of these Danes' intentions. They took counsel together, and all agreed as one man: they wanted to ask their king to take charge of the land and to choose one of his sons, who would have the kingdom after him, who would be able to rule the land and overcome its enemies. As soon as the king was asked, he wanted to know their opinion: whatever each of them thought best they should tell him and he would do it. Some wanted to have Edmund, for they knew him to be hardy and bold. Others demanded Alfred, by virtue of his kinship with the noble lords of Normandy, whence they hoped for much aid. But God, from whom nothing is hidden, neither strength nor goodness, knew who would have the land and who would rule it best. He saw that those the English elected would soon die. The King Edward, who is their brother, who is then still in his mother's womb, is the one God then made to be chosen; those chosen first, he made to be disdained. The two grown ones are refused in favour of him who is not yet born.

¶Dear Lord Jesus! Who can understand thine intentions or comprehend thy reasons,[7] thou, who canst work thy will everywhere and who hast power to do whatever thou wishest; compared to thy wisdom, human wit is foolish and simple and void of all reason! Who could ever be thy counsellor? When didst thou ever have need of another's wisdom? Who could better thy judgement, and whose judgement could work without thee? When human counsel works without thee, it is but folly and lawlessness.[8]

The English thought they were doing well, and using their judgement beneficially, when they chose Edmund first for his great prowess, and then Alfred for his high lineage and the power of his family. According to human reasoning the English had good reason:[9] they saw them well-grown and suitable in their strength, and wanted them to have the land and defend it from war. But God, who knows the higher law, sees what is to come: the early death of the two chosen ones,[10] and the long and fruitful life of Edward. He overturned their choice and curbed their collective will; all their will is given over to his will alone: they elected as king the child who knew nothing but the secrets of his mother's womb where he lay, and whose oppression he still felt.[11] Now he is elected king upon earth, who has never yet felt or seen

---

[6] 164 'Le bon faut quant l'em plus espeire': MS P reads 'Que maus fait, mal espeire' [Who does evil, expects evil]. See Morawski, 1979–83 for sentences similar to the latter; the former is not listed, and nor are many of the Nun's proverbial and monitory sentences. For 'evil comes more quickly than good', see ibid. 1093: 'Les maulx sont tost venuz'. P omits the next two lines; as will be seen, this scribe has a tendency to cut to the chase, even if not always very elegantly.

[7] 201–11 The bulk of this prayer, and first line of the following narrative, omitted in MS P.

[8] This prayer contrasts with Aelred's; he says 'These are your deeds, Christ Jesus ...' (three Bible passages noted, *Life* pp. 133–4), but he does not burst into *apostrophe*.

[9] 217–18 'raisun ... achaison': different kinds of 'reason'.

[10] 225 MS P reads 'Des autres vit la mort hastive' [sees the others' early death].

[11] 232–4 See above for this addition.

2 Edward is chosen King (143–266) 63

earth. Nor was any of them certain that the child would be born; if he was born, they granted him the land, and swore their allegiance and trust to him.[12] There was none among them who did not feel happy, with joy at this new eventuality. For it was a great comfort to them all, that God had chosen him as king. They had been in despair, and now they were consoled. Although it was hidden from them, why God had acted thus,[13] they took good hope from having God's chosen one for their lord. Whomever God made to reign would be able to govern the kingdom well.[14] They all feel comforted in their faith, and hoping exhorts hope. As their hope mitigates the present evil that afflicts them, so they are the more hopeful about the good king they await. Often good faith can alleviate present evil, and often great joy can come directly out of grave fear. Therefore the English did well, who were so troubled by events.[15] With good faith they suffered them bravely, because of the good results they expected.

---

[12]   240 'Lijance et fei lui unt juree': 'they' are the lords in council (previous paragraph). We are not told how God made his choice known, unless the 'signs' mentioned earlier (v. 159 and note) included this remedy for evils to come. The pre-natal choice of Edward is in Aelred, where God turns the wishes of all to the unborn child (*Life*, p. 133), but not in *Estoire* (see p. xxv, note 29); for the earliest Life see *Anon*, pp. lxix & 7–8.
[13]   245–8 'They had been in despair ... had acted thus'; MS P omits these lines.
[14]   253–66 MS P omits this homiletic passage (no obvious parallels in Morawski), from here to the end of the chapter.
[15]   264 'cil furent grevé de rien': 'rien' without 'ne' has a positive meaning (something, things, even 'a person' – from Latin *res*).

Chapter 3
The young Edward (267–354)[1]

Introduction

Both Aelred and the Nun plunge straight into this next part of the story, although the Nun amplifies in (for example) the passage about Ethelred's feelings, and in the hint about Edward and homosexuality. In the light of Phillips' enjoyable article,[2] one may conclude that the Nun is exploiting current rumours about Edward's childlessness: hinting so as to excite an audience's curiosity without appearing to satisfy it. Aelred mentions only the shortcomings of youth, without making explicit suggestions. It is possible, given his reference to Gen. 39:23, that a different kind of temptation may have been in his mind: the attentions of some older woman, forbidden not only because of the boy's chastity but also because of the woman's married state. The Nun could have heard something like this about Edward. It is also possible that some story was circulating about princes in her time, and the bad habits of young men, especially since MS P says the vice is common at court. P reads, for v. 319, 'Dunt cil de la cort sunt blasmé'. Accusation is thereby shifted from 'there' [over there, abroad] to 'at court'; the latter could mean royal courts of France or of England. The modern suggestion that Richard I may have been homosexual is refuted by Gillingham (this goes also for Philip Augustus, with whom Richard is reported to have shared a bed). Richard was born in 1157, aged six at the date of Aelred's *Vita*. However, the mention of court "practices" does not appear until the later P-text. It is conceivable that something was in the air regarding the French, if not Philip himself (b. 1165). The families of Henry II and of Eleanor's first husband Louis VII had close ties.[3]

The rumour persists into our own time.[4] It has never been substantiated, nor its source traced, as far as I can discover. There is a suggestive passage in the Prologue to Aelred's *De Spiritali Amicitia*, cited in Squire, *Aelred of Rievaulx*, chapter 5 (at p. 99); also in Gray's anthology, where Aelred speaks of his own youth: '... among the habits and vices which that age is wont to be troubled by ...'.[5] It is not unlikely the nuns knew Aelred's treatise on virginity, written for his sister. Given the Nun's emphasis on friendship in *Edouard* it seems reasonable to assume she knew his treatise on friendship, together with his reference to youthful vice.

In both *Vita* and *Vie*, this chapter ends with a mention of Edward's two special friends, who will reappear at the end of his life. The Nun characteristically phrases

---

[1] *Vita*, 742B–D; *Life* §3. Cf. *Estoire*, vv. 231–66; *History*, pp. 56–7.
[2] 'Gossip'.
[3] See Gillingham's *ODNB* article on Richard (www.oxforddnb.com/view/article/23498), accessed 11.5.2010; also Ailes, 'Male Couple', pp. 232–4.
[4] See, for example, Clarke, *1000 Years*, p. 30 (and see above, p. 8). Clarke tells me his notes for the book were lost when his computer gave up the ghost, so cannot enlighten me as to the source of the rumour.
[5] Gray, ed., *Norman Conquest*, p. 27; Squire translates 'habits and faults'.

3 The young Edward (267–354)   65

this as a promise to an attentive audience. By contrast, MP makes little of Edward's *enfances*: he mentions the family being sent to Normandy, then goes on to talk about Edmund Ironside.

At v. 307, the Nun says Edward was the younger son. In fact Alfred was the younger (see also *Osbert*, p. 71 and note 1). William of Malmesbury,[6] and several *Lives*, even some modern history books, declare Edward to have been the younger, but see Barlow (*Edward the Confessor*, esp. pp. 28–30). In Gaimar's account of Edward,[7] Alfred is given as the younger. Gaimar's editor remarks 'most authorities make Alfred the elder' (note to v. 4780).

¶It was not very long before the child was born. He was baptized, and named Edward; thus he took God into his dwelling. As soon as he was anointed in baptism, he was joined fully to God[8] so that God resided completely in him and he was completely in God.[9] God resided completely in his thought, and he in God's will. In his heart he placed the Holy Spirit, so that his body and heart were made perfect.[10] He was well nourished in his care, this good little boy who grew up well. Certainly, he ought to grow well, whose nurse was God.[11]

¶After the child was born, it was not long before the Danes prepared themselves,[12] increasing their numbers of men and arms. They came into port with a great navy, fiercely proud and fearfully violent. They burned castles and sacked towns, laying waste the land and all the [safe] places;[13] they completely overran the greater part of the country. King Ethelred saw his land burned, destroyed by the war. He was very much afraid of being taken, and that he and his sons would be beggared. Without wasting time in deliberation, he took his children, with his wife [Alfred, Edward, and Emma], and sent them into Normandy where they would be safely received. As soon as he had placed them somewhere peaceful, he felt relieved of a heavy burden. He thought he could better defeat his wicked enemies, or suffer being defeated by them, now that he had sent his sons to safety.[14]

---

[6] *Gesta Regum*, vol. I, p. 337.
[7] *L'Estoire des Engleis* ed. Bell, vv. 4528ff.
[8] 271–2 Omitted in MS P (the sense would be 'he took God into his dwelling, so that God resided completely ...'). The Nun amplifies Aelred's citation of I Cor. 10:16.
[9] 273–4 John 14:10–11, a Gospel reference not in Aelred.
[10] 277–8 This sentence, about the Holy Spirit, omitted in MS P.
[11] 282 For the MS P reading of this line, and of v. 325, see the online version (Södergård's readings are incorrect). The Nun expands Aelred's description of the boy, notably with this homely little picture of God playing nurse.
[12] See Södergård's note to v. 285ff.
[13] 290 'Gastent la terre et ses asiles': *AND* glosses 'asile' (citing this line) as 'refuge' with a question mark. However, Södergård corrects the MS reading 'asises', perhaps because it does not rhyme with 'viles': the original reading may mean 'places' or settlements (cf. MS P, which reads 'manandies', that is, dwellings etc).
[14] This passage expands Aelred's, giving Ethelred's personal point of view (cf. Cnut's, in ch. 5).

Edward, who was the very youngest,[15] and who was sworn to the kingdom, grew in bravery and bounty,[16] mighty in God's might. For God was with him everywhere, and supported all his deeds.[17] In the house of his senior kinsman[18] he gave joy, never sorrow, to everybody. He wanted to obey the poor, and he made himself their equal everywhere. He was a youth among the young men; nevertheless, he was clean of the vice for which those from over there are notorious – but you'll not hear a word about that from me![19] With the old people he was mature and wise – because of his great good sense and in spite of his age.[20] Chastity was his treasure: he was chaste in heart and body. Rarely did he speak, but wisely and with marvellous forethought.[21] He was too simple to do evil, but he was clever at attracting all that was best. His desire was so much in God, that God always fulfilled him. He was beloved of everybody, and he wished well to everybody.[22] He was so deserving of love that nobody could hate him for any reason. As well as being full of goodness, God had given him the great good fortune that almost everything he did was pleasing to both God and men. Before age gave him the knowledge, and before reason could show him, why one visited churches where services to God were held, he often used to go there to hear mass and to pray.[23] [He learned his letters with the children, and paid attention to all good things. He learned something of reading, and then he learned of chivalry.][24] Because of his true love for the good monks he knew to be there, he would go to see them.[25] For God's love he loved them all dearly, and nevertheless he found two of them, whom he loved more tenderly and with especially true affection.[26] In his last illness, when it overtook

---

[15] 307 'tut li puisnez'; the Nun counts all three sons, with Edmund Ironside. MS P has 'ki estoit li puisnez' [the younger]; the online version reads 'Hedewars qui estoit li mainsnés' (which means the same).

[16] 309 'valur ... bunté': 'valur' means (modern) valour, or bravery, but also worthiness (see Glossary).

[17] See Genesis 39 for the story of Joseph and Potiphar's wife.

[18] 313 'En la maisun a sun aol' (Södergård's glossary gives 'ancestor'). The household where the exiles went to live was not his grandfather's; MP also thinks Emma's father took them in (note to v. 237 in *Estoire*).

[19] 319–20 The Nun refers to the (Norman) French; she may mean just plain vicious, or she is hinting about homosexuality. The coyness of her comment, which is in neither *Vita* nor *Estoire*, suggests the latter. 'les vallez', in v. 317, might mean his servants (although there is no possessive pronoun), or, more generally, that young Frenchmen are said to be guilty of this vice. MS P reads 'Dunt cil de la cort sunt blamés', that is, the vice is restricted to those at court, rather than to Frenchmen (see introduction to this chapter).

[20] 321–2 'Par sun grant sens, nïent par age'; for *puer senex* as hagiographic cliché, see Curtius, *European Literature*, pp. 98–101 (also in *Life*, p. 135).

[21] 325 See note to v. 282.

[22] 331–2 This sentence omitted in MS P.

[23] This resembles young Jesus in the Temple (Luke 2:42–7).

[24] 344 After this line, MS P adds 'Letres aprist o les enfans A toz biens fais ert entendans Auques ot apris de clergie E puis aprist chevalerie'. To learn 'clergie' is to learn clerical skills such as reading, or general literacy; the idea of 'chevalerie' is infrequent in the Nun (she often stresses the courtly, but rarely the chivalric, nature of Edward's virtues). Clemence uses such words more frequently; see introduction to ch. 8, below, and General Introduction for the Nun's identity.

[25] 346 In MS P he goes to them to learn, not for love: 'Por bien aprendre a els aloit'.

[26] 350 'fin desir': an example of the Nun's rich love-language; earlier in this passage she speaks of 'bien amur' and 'bon' amur', implicitly contrasting it with worldly, imperfect, or unchaste love. MS P has 'Et mult forment les honora' for v. 348, then omits vv. 349–50; the sense would be '... all dearly, and he valued them very highly. In his last illness ... these friends (sc. all the friends) ...'.

him, these friends appeared to him; you shall hear about this in due course, if you wish to know about it.

Chapter 4

Brihtwald's Vision (355–510)[1]

Introduction

The Nun expresses her intention, in typical first-person style, of telling the next part of the story; Aelred plunges straight into it. She expands slightly, while omitting some Bible references. Her chapter ends with a homily; Aelred's with the bishop preaching to the people. Brihtwald is the first example of somebody who, like Edward, can see visions. Such people are usually very pious or virtuous (for example, the hermit in chapter 12). After Edward's death, there are many who see Edward himself in a dream or vision, often in the context of a healing miracle, although few see prophetic visions (cf. chapter 33).

≈ ≈ ≈ ≈ ≈ ≈ ≈ ≈ ≈

¶I want to turn now to England, which was still at war. The country is bereft of friends, and filled with strong enemies.[2] Everything had been cruelly torn away; everywhere there was sorrow and lamenting. There was slaughter everywhere, with no respite for any reason. Sighs and tears were widespread, with groaning and great torment. Despair was all abroad, and terror was seen on every side. They laid waste the monasteries and burned the churches, destroying them in every way they could.[3] They drove out all the priests, who left their posts with great anguish. These could find no peace anywhere, for the war was unrelenting. And so they hid themselves, most sorrowfully, and bewailed the common woe. [They took refuge in deep woods; the Danish did them terrible damage.][4]

Among those who thus wept was a holy man, a friend of God. This man's name was Brihtwald, and he was bishop at Winchester.[5] He entered Glastonbury Abbey weeping, pensive, and troubled. He would often pray to God, to put an end to all war – and would say to him these words:

'And thou, sweet Lord, how long wilt thou turn away thy face from us? And how long wilt thou forget our miseries and our pains? There is nobody who helps us. Thy people have chosen death, and thine others have suffered.[6] Lord, there is nobody who makes us safe, nor who redeems us, except for thy grace. Lord, I know and I understand that thou hast done to us whatever thou hast done in right judgement.

---

[1] *Vita*, 742D–3D; *Life* §4. See also *Estoire*, vv. 597–713; *History*, pp. 61–3.
[2] 357–8 MS P omits this sentence.
[3] The Nun deletes Aelred's reference to Ps. 79:3 (78 in *LV*), without even paraphrasing the idea.
[4] 374 After this line, MS P adds 'Fuient en grans boscajes Li Danois lour funt grans damages'.
[5] See IPN, and note to v. 597, in *Estoire*: Brihtwald was Bishop of Ramsbury, not of Winchester (error copied from Aelred, *Life* p. 136).
[6] 390–91 MS P omits two lines. The sense would be 'Thy people have chosen death, and nothing can redeem us ...'.

Lord, can it ever be, that this scourge so long-enduring will have an end?[7] Lord, when wilt thou take care of us?'

¶Then, with these pious prayers, and in these holy tears,[8] the saint felt somewhat weary, and gave himself to sweet sleep. And in this vision[9] he saw Saint Peter, the noble lord. He saw him sitting in a high place, in brilliant light, in worthy garments. Before Saint Peter, it seemed to him, was a man: he had a bright face, his form was fine and well-grown, he was clothed in noble royal robes. Then Saint Peter consecrated him and made him king with his own hands. He taught him the way of salvation and especially commended him to guard his chastity, and then told him how long he was to reign.

¶The bishop, when he heard this spoken, was marvellously awed by the miracle he had seen, of the king whom Saint Peter consecrated. He begged the saint to tell him what this thing means: what it is and what it will be, and who this is that he has made king; above all, of the great danger that had put the kingdom into exile. He humbly begged the apostle to tell him what would befall.[10]

¶Then, when Peter had looked at him[11] with an expression of sweet humility, he said to him very gently:

'This realm is Our Lord's, for he made all kings and all kingdoms, and is Lord of all people. He gives realms, and takes them away,[12] and thus he makes to reign whom he wills. His people have done evil towards him; for their sins, they are so tormented and so cruelly maltreated by those who hate them most. But God has not so forgotten that he does not still have mercy on them. Anger does not exclude his bounty,[13] for he hears all those who beseech him. But in these days it will not happen, that God will grant this grace. The bountiful God will choose a man, who shall be after his own heart.[14] To him he will give power to fulfil his will. This man will have my help and thus shall conquer England. Through him the suffering, by the fury of the Dane, is ended. He will be acceptable to God, and pious and helpful to his people.

---

[7] 396–7 'Sire, sera ja que fin ait Ceste merveillie …': 'merveillie' can have negative meanings; it may further be used adverbially [greatly, extraordinarily]. Cf. the words of Dan. 12:6, one of Aelred's references: the Latin is *mirabilium* (*wonders* in AV). Brihtwald's prayer in the Nun, as in Aelred, is filled with echoes from the Bible. Many are psalms, and the Nun retains about half of them. Aelred says, as the Nun does not, that the bishop gave himself up to prayers *and psalms* (*Life*, p. 136, my emphasis).

[8] 400 'holy tears'; MS P has 'lermes si pleneres' [so plentiful]. 'suveraines' [sovereign] means supreme, perhaps high-minded; 'sovereign' also has a meaning 'remedy', so the tears could have been comforting to him.

[9] 403 'avisïun' (P 'vision'). According to medieval dream-thory there are various kinds, and sources, of dreams; 'vision' is the Nun's preferred term unless rhyme or metre demands something else. Her handling of dream and vision differs from Aelred's (see Introduction, above).

[10] The Nun expands this passage, in which the bishop spells out what he wants to know (see *Life*, p. 137).

[11] 429 MS P has 'Saint' for 'Quant'.

[12] Dan. 2:21 (as in Aelred).

[13] 442–4 MS P omits these lines; the sense would be 'But God has not forgotten, but in these days it will not happen …' (see Södergård's note to 'esclot' in v. 443).

[14] Cf. I Sam. 13:14. The Nun reduces and paraphrases three more of Aelred's Bible references here.

He is terrible to his enemies, gentle to all those of his land.[15] He is profitable to Holy Church, for in his time it shall have liberty. Then, when he has reigned so long as God has decided the term, the great peace he has made on earth and the justice he has established there, and the praiseworthy life he has led, is fulfilled by holy death.'[16]

¶When Saint Peter had shown him the whole matter, he went away; later, it was all fulfilled in King Edward, his dear friend. Then the bishop awoke, very much heartened by the great comfort he had seen, and praised the name of Jesus for it. Again he wept sweet tears; humbly he begged God to make the vision come true, and to have mercy on his people. Nevertheless, he was aware that peace would not come in his time. But so perfect was his desire, that the good to come in the future comforted him in the present evil and awakened his desire.[17] And it does often happen, when somebody has yearning hope for what awakens desire to accomplish his good hope. Often hope gives greater joy than even its achievement. But that is only the hope which is born and comes from evil desire, for wrong desire when it wants evil thinks it is drawing towards joy, but as soon as it achieves the evil it loses the joy of hoping. But they who here on earth desire God alone, and who draw towards him by good hope, the more they have their desire so much the greater joy they hope for – for their desire feeds (on) their hope[18] and hope feeds (on) their will – thus the bishop did, who placed his desire in the bountiful God, and from God received hope and the perfection of joy. Even though he never saw what his hope promised him, even so it was joy and comfort to him that it would come to pass after his death.

---

[15] 458 MS P reads 'Et tous enemis toz ses amis', corrected online to 'E dous envers toz ses amis' [and gentle to all his friends].
[16] The foregoing contains a number of tense-changes. These may be partly the Nun's attempt to show the vision with more immediacy, or merely adjustments to regularize the syllable-count.
[17] This passage makes more sense if we assume a stop omitted from the end of v. 484 in the edition. Laurent describes it as 'mystical' (*Plaire et édifier*, p. 262 and note 59). MS P omits vv. 479–510, the whole section from 'Nevertheless ...' to the end of the chapter; this corresponds approximately to the expanded passage in the base MS, which adds several sentences to Aelred's short closing passage.
[18] 501 'lur desir paist lur espeir': the verb can mean both feed *and* devour. The Nun plays on the two: 'their desire feeds their hope and is fed by it; their hope feeds their will (desire) and is fed by it.'

Chapter 5
Exile and Return (511–850)[1]

Introduction

This chapter, opening with the bishop's sermon (which ended Aelred's previous chapter), contains notable additions: vv. 601–6 and 727–90. Generally, the Nun's narrative of historical events is more detailed than Aelred's, suggesting one or more supplementary sources. Aelred begins with a quotation from a psalm, and description of England's woes similar to the Nun's, before going on with the story. His chapter ends with a link to the next (third-person: 'what follows will tell'). The Nun does likewise, though characteristically in the first person: 'as we shall recount presently ...'. *Estoire* follows Aelred more loosely, so that precise collation is difficult.

᛫᛫᛫᛫᛫᛫᛫᛫᛫

¶After this vision, he exhorted the people with a sermon; he promised them God's mercy, if they kept to themselves, if they repented of their evil and valued penitence henceforth. But although some did not take much notice of him, it did so happen to them later. Deceit and fraud are everywhere, and covetousness and treachery; the abundance of outer evils sets inner evils at discord.[2]

The one hardly had faith in another, and no one had faith in himself. They kept no faith with themselves, while they found it neither in themselves nor in others. All the land was filled and invaded with traitors. To cheat was all their care; nowhere was there sure trust.[3] No one had true love for any other,[4] for they were all full of anxiety. They were so tormented by guile that each held every other guileful. And worse: some had this habit, that when they had evil intentions they would condemn others and believe their own madness to be in them. And the English believed these others to be thus, because of the great evil they found in themselves. No one can trust in another, nor can one find true love among them. So much do discord and envy grow, and so much is hate fostered, that they are betrayed by their own selves to the foreigners who hate them.

¶Once the King [Ethelred] was dead,[5] then treason came into its own; and those who had no power to do treason fulfilled themselves by theft. It was by the treason of

---
[1] *Vita*, 743D–5C; *Life* §5; *Estoire* vv. 714–883; *History* pp. 63–5.
[2] 521–2 'De la plenté del mal forain Se (MS 'Si') descordent lui dedenzain': a tricky passage, unless 'lui' is read as 'les'. It could perhaps read 'the inner evils quarrel over the abundant supply of outer [foreign] evils' (MS P omits vv. 521–4). Aelred's chapter begins here, citing Ps. 107:25 (106 in *LV*); he says 'Civil discord was added to outside evils'.
[3] 530 MS P reads 'En nului ne metent fei ...' [they put trust in nobody].
[4] 531 'Nul n'out vers autre fin amur': for MacBain, unsuspicious or disinterested love ('Vocabulary'). The rhyme with 'errur' in the next line is telling ('fin amur' occurs again in v. 542). MS P omits vv. 531–40 ('No one had true love ... they found in themselves'), and the last clause (vv. 545–6).
[5] Aelred, too, omits to name the dead king (*Life*, p. 138).

the English and the craftiness of the Danish that the greater part of the land was given over to King Cnut, who waged war against them. They granted the kingdom to him, and forgot the rightful heirs. They soon broke the promise they had faithfully made to Edward. They killed Edmund Ironside, the king's eldest son, who was a strong and proud king, most wise in counselling the great; as long as the king his father was alive he governed the realm. He undertook great tasks and achieved great honour. They killed him by treachery, and with cruel intent. His sons, whom they found in the cradle, they sent to the Danish to be put to death – they sent them into exile, into suffering and dire peril.[6]

¶King Cnut was a man of great cunning, for he had the land in his power, and everything was now as he wished, just as he had formerly desired. He wanted to act wisely, to provide for himself at others' expense. He feared that war would spring up against him, from those he had once warred against, and he did not care to suffer the evils that he had once inflicted on others. He thought he would lay claim to Emma,[7] who had formerly been the queen. It made him feel hopeful, that if he were able to take Emma, then through this alliance he would have the Normans where he wanted them: he would be better liked by them, and his men less feared. He was very anxious about the rightful heirs, to whom the whole land belonged. He was afraid they would strengthen themselves and challenge him for the land, by their own force and with the help of their kinsmen of Normandy.[8] He feared their strength and their right, and the wrong he had done to them. Because of the sons he feared, he took the mother and married her.[9]

¶This time passed, and another came by, as is the nature of things. Whoever expects bad luck may stumble upon it suddenly. Rarely can he avoid it, if it has chosen him.[10] It could be said that Alfred was courting bad luck: he wanted to see his mother, so he obtained leave to go, and a retinue. So he arrived in England, where he met a harsh welcome. The Danish, who were his enemies, and the English who should have been his friends, put him cruelly to death with extraordinary cruelty.[11] It has been fully

---

[6] 559–72 The king of Sweden, reluctant to act as the Danes' butcher, sent them to King Stephen of Hungary, where they remained in exile. Edmund died young, and Edward returned to England years later (see Södergård's note; *Estoire*, note to v. 1426; and Ronay, *Lost King*). Details are more elaborate than in Aelred, who mentions neither treachery in context of Edmund's death, nor the young princes' destination (*Life*, p. 138; but see *Genealogy*, pp. 111–13).
[7] 583 'requereit', MS P 'queroit'.
[8] 596 MS P reads 'lur genz' [their people of Normandy].
[9] Details are expanded from Aelred, especially in the description of how Cnut was thinking (cf. Ethelred's thoughts in ch. 3).
[10] 605 'Relment la pot cil eschiver'; MS P reads 'Forment lui doit ci escever' [he must try hard to avoid it]. These commonplaces sound proverbial, although no analogues are listed in Morawski.
[11] 615–16 'Par merveillieuse crüelté L'unt a crüele mort livré': cruelty is deliberately doubled in the Nun's words.

told elsewhere, why and how it happened; I have told you of his death briefly because I do not know the story.[12]

¶Now Edward was alone, without a brother, and bereft of his good father. All human aid had abandoned him, but God's aid was near. He was exiled from his realm: by force, by pain, and by sin. But his thought and his care dwell on goodness and justice. Exiled from human honour, he is yet rich in the love of God; nevertheless he greatly feared the cunning wickedness he had heard about. From all sides grief assaults him – anguish, heaviness, and anxiety. He was suspicious of his friends, lest they do him treason – that they would sell him to his enemies or give him up to be killed. Now he knows not what he can do; on all sides anguish rises up against him. He fears treason from his own, and death from others. He can see no counsel but one, that could be of any use to him. To this Counsel he has recourse immediately, and weeping says humbly to him:

'Lord, I know very well that I can expect no help from my own strength nor from my own life. Those I have greatest need of are separated from me and far away. My friends are against me – against me are my nearest ones.[13] Lord, I understand that my father is dead; my brothers are dead by treason and my nephews are exiled – cruelly chased out of the land. And my mother has married him who drove us out.[14] She has made the enemy my step-father; they have all abandoned me to thee.[15] Thou art my help and my refuge; I am thy poor one, thine orphan.[16] Thou who once gave to Edwin succour from his pains – a noble baron of our line, who was close neighbour to death – Lord, thou didst preserve him from death, and restored life and kingdom to him. And Saint Oswald, Lord, thou didst save – and raise from exile to king. He overcame all his enemies by the Cross, with which he signed himself.[17] Now I make a promise to thee – with firm purpose, if thou preserve me from death, and if thou wilt that thy power be with me so that I may have my kingdom. Verily I shall believe in thee as God and honour thee as lord. Saint Peter is my protector,[18] and as an honoured father to me. Lord, if I have thine aid, and thy grace for company, I promise this: I shall go to visit his holy body as soon as ever I can.'

---

[12] Cf. *Estoire*, vv. 714–815; *History*, pp. 63–4 (MP blames Godwin for Alfred's murder, see also *Estoire*, vv. 414–43; *History*, p. 59). It is not 'fully told' in Aelred's version, but told even more briefly than here (*Life*, p. 139). Although the Nun says she does not know the story, she seems to have knowledge of a fuller version, so far unidentified. *ASC* shapes the story differently, mentioning Godwin's opposition and the people's favour of Harold. Neither the C version, which contains further details in the lament or 'ballad', nor the D version says Alfred was courting bad luck, which seems to be the Nun's own idea (*ASC*, pp. 158–60). Her remark about the harsh welcome is likewise her own, unless culled from another source.

[13] 652 Supplied from MS P (Södergård's note).

[14] 658 MS P reads 'Celui qui nous a fait damage' [him who has caused us harm].

[15] 660 MS P reads 'Par qui sunt mort tot mi ami' [by whom all my friends are dead].

[16] Aelred cites Ps. 10:14 (9 in *LV*); the Nun's phrase is closer to Ps. 46:1 *God is our refuge and strength, a very present help in trouble* (45:2 in *LV*).

[17] For Edwin and Oswald, see Södergård's note to v. 664; and *Estoire*, note to vv. 801–3. The Nun here matches Aelred more closely than earlier in the chapter (*Life*, pp. 139–40 and footnotes).

[18] 679 'Saint Pere est a mun avoé', see note: Södergård thinks this construction unusual (MS P reads 'ert mes avoes', that is, without preposition).

¶When Saint Edward had done this, and made the vow that he afterwards fulfilled, he received true comfort from God and his joy and hope revived. He surrendered himself completely to God's will, and awaited his joy patiently. 'Who trusts in God's help has it indeed' – he did not want to forget this.[19]

And then Cnut died, the king who had conquered the English. After him his sons died, taken away by sudden death. And so the English were freed from servitude to the cruel Danes. They remembered the rightful heir, who had been driven out of the country; the kingdom had been sworn to him since before he was born of his mother. They all fastened their hopes on him and wished for his power to fulfil those hopes; they sent to him, to come quickly. He should be king and take his kingdom.

¶When Edward heard the news that his enemies were dead [he gave thanks for it, to Our Lord Jesus Christ his Maker],[20] he came back to England with the intention of doing everything for the best. With gladness and celebration they acclaimed him as their lord, and with all honours the two honourable archbishops crowned him.[21] Bishops and abbots, noble and esteemed princes, made him their king and sovereign with great pomp and splendour. Could one but see such joyful people, he would be overjoyed with the joyful!

Anger is fled away and peace returns.[22] Joy shows itself, sadness withdraws,[23] for the former blessedness that was once in the kingdom is returned in abundance. The joy of the people is greatly increased; and it often happens that one can rejoice more, after severe trouble, in a small happiness than one could before that trouble.[24] For when the trouble withdraws and the lost happiness comes back, it returns with a greater sweetness than it had before the great trouble – for no happiness brings such joy as the joy that consoles trouble, nor does any joy please so greatly as the joy that is lost and then recovered. Because the English lost the blessedness they once knew, so much more did they desire it to be restored by Edward, and so they rejoiced more than they would have done without the loss. And we too must do likewise: draw towards that great blessedness for which we were created, and from which the Devil has separated us. By him, and by our sin, we were long in exile. Then when King Jesus was born and crowned on earth, he reigned in the Holy Cross and called us back from harsh exile. Therefore we do very wisely to flee that first wrong, and hold to the joy that we have thanks to the King Jesus – that neither by foolishness nor by

---

[19] The saying seems proverbial; Morawski, 1840, 'Qui bien desire bien luy vient', is the closest. Aelred cites psalms, to similar effect, here; the Nun may be paraphrasing the idea.
[20] 708 After this line, MS P adds 'Grasces en rent nostre seignour A Jhesu Christ, son creatour'.
[21] 713 'l'unt coroné Les deuz arcevesque honuré': the first coronation, in Winchester, was 3rd April 1043 (*Life*, p. 140). Later coronations are either anniversaries, or simply occasions where the crown is worn (see ch. 9, for example).
[22] Cf. *Estoire*, vv. 872–933 (*History*, p. 65), as below.
[23] 721–2 'Ire s'en vait et pais revient. Hait se mustre, tristur s'aprient'. This example of chiasmus is rare; the Nun tends usually towards antithesis. MS P reads 'Ire s'en vait tristors remaint' [remains], which spoils the sense.
[24] 727–30 These sentences may be proverbial; cf. Morawski, 109 *et seq*. There is a fine line between what is proverbial and what is homiletic.

excess may the Devil have power over us. Destroyed is his power, and his Danes have gone back to hell,[25] to their own land, whence they still move war against us. But between us there is a sea, that often makes them return – that is the Holy Cross of Jesus Christ, where God placed his holy Body for us, where he suffered the tempest of death, that is now a safe harbour for us. But when this sea draws back, then the Devil and his own are glad. With great noise and harsh violence they then enter upon our shores. Therefore it behoves us to be watchful for the moment this sea withdraws; with great virtue, with fierce effort, fight those Danes at the ports – as the English did who guarded their shores well, so that the Danish could neither come back nor make trouble within. Once Edward was crowned, then the Danish are driven away.[26] Now let us pray God, in whose likeness Edward achieved the deliverance of his people,[27] to take us out of the hands of the cruel Danish and set us into our heritage. May Jesus Christ give us our own, as Edward did for his people.

¶As King Jesus freed Holy Church when he suffered death, so also did Edward free it, with all his might, all his life.[28] In his day religion flourished, as did knowledge and faith, prosperity and reason; he so ordained the ordained priests that he kept them all to the service of God. He dispensed peace and justice to the people, happiness and prosperity to the land: both heaven and earth gained richly from his plentiful bounty. The country became more stable,[29] the air more healthful, the sea more patient. It was right that it happened thus, because God made him reign so well that heaven and earth had peace and relief from pestilence. The good justice that he wrought, and the goodness that was in him, became known in every land and his good reputation grew. All the neighbour kings who heard of his good fame marvelled at his deeds and desired his friendship. They made alliance with him for love; they settled peace treaties, and they cast out fear. Not only were his neighbours devoted to him for his fine reputation, but also the emperor now ruling in Rome was inspired to send to King Edward, so as to establish a firm friendship between them. They had good reason to love each other, for the king's nephew, Edmund's son, whom King Cnut sent into exile, was now married in Rome. The emperor thought highly of him, and had given him his cousin.[30] So he was especially delighted at the good he heard about his uncle. The King of France is his neighbour; they were closely related, and the

---

[25] 762–3 'Et ses Daneis s'en sunt ralé En enfern': the Nun calls the devils Danes, not the reverse (the passage is an addition to Aelred's).
[26] 784 Si sunt les Danois delivrez': MS P reads 'des Danois' [they are delivered *from* the Danish]. The verb can have either meaning.
[27] 785–6 '... Deu, en qui semblance Edward fist as suens delivrance'. This passage, continuing below, is one of several where Edward is aligned with Jesus the Saviour.
[28] 791–4 Edward is again aligned with the Deity (see p. 5, above). Aelred adduces a different parallel: Joshua 10:13.
[29] 803 'fermable'; MS P has 'fuisonable' [fertile, plentiful].
[30] Edward the Exile married Agatha, daughter of Emperor Henry II (see Södergård's notes to vv. 569–72 & 826; and *Life*, p. 141).

power of friendship renders their relationship even closer.[31] God bestowed on him the same gift that King Solomon used to have: what caused all the kings on earth to seek him out and listen to him for his wisdom,[32] and thus these kings made peace with Edward.[33] Only Denmark remained, that still threatened him with war, for it was not yet sated[34] with killing and battle; as we shall recount presently, when we come to the right time and place,[35] how God put a stop to their cruelty and tamed their greed.

---

[31] 833–4 Henry I, King of France, married Adèle, daughter of Richard III of Normandy. His father, Richard II, was the Confessor's uncle (see Södergård's note). Aelred stresses the importance of friendship (*Life*, pp. 141–2), but the Nun makes even more of it. In these two lines, the verb 'to be' is first present (est) and next imperfect past (esteient).

[32] See II Chr. 9:23 (as in Aelred).

[33] 837–42 Solomon = peace *and* wisdom here. Solomon was not associated with wisdom so much as with peace in c11 (Barlow, *Edward the Confessor*, p. 192).

[34] 845 'saülee'; this more like Clemence's use of the word (see Glossary).

[35] 848 Södergård notes this hypometric line.

Chapter 6

Description of Edward (851–978)[1]

Introduction

Both Aelred and the Nun begin this chapter with a description and end with a link to the next. Aelred offers a story which became famous ('let us give one example ...'). The Nun ends with a personal address: 'We will now tell you an example ... and show you the deed.' Aelred's chapter has four Bible references; the Nun rewords or expands each idea, keeping the sense. MP's description of Edward, between the coronation and the story of the treasure, tends more to the political than to the moral, mentioning neighbouring countries, the cessation of Danegeld, and comparison with King Arthur. Then, before introducing this story, *Estoire* adds another about how Edward lost interest in his treasure after having driven off a black devil from sitting upon the money-bags (vv. 934–79; *History* pp. 65–6). Some, but not all, of Marzella's ω group contain this Danegeld episode, so MP must have used one of those.[2] It is hard to believe the Nun would not have exploited such a good story, so we may guess she did not see a copy that contained it. This narrows down the number of manuscripts whose archetype she had access to.[3]

❧ ❧ ❧ ❧ ❧ ❧ ❧ ❧ ❧

¶The king was most greatly blessed, and he was loved by all far and near. He also wielded great power, of riches and of wisdom.[4] Never, for any honour done to him, nor for any goodness he felt to be in himself, did any foolish pride enter his heart, nor was there any shadow of wrongdoing in his conduct. He knew and understood perfectly well that all his goodness came from God, and so he humbly made the most of it and was grateful to God alone for everything. He loved his close friends very dearly, and honoured them as his equals.[5] He is benevolent towards the priesthood, merciful and charitable towards the people; he comforted the sorrowful, the sick, and the needy. But his devotion was wholly to true religion; there, he applied all his care to build and restore monasteries. He established the holy life, with good rule, in great churches everywhere. He supported poor people everywhere, and made sure they all received their rights. He never wronged a poor man for the sake of any rich or

---

1   *Vita*, 745C–6B; *Life* §6. Cf. *Estoire*, vv. 872–933; *History*, p. 65.
2   'La tradizione'.
3   In addition to MP's version, see Richard of Cirencester (ed. Major, vol. ii, pp. 214–17) for this episode.
4   In Aelred (*Life*, p. 142), the king ponders a verse from 'Wisdom': Ecclus. 32:1 (in *AV* Apocrypha). The idea of a king's equality with all, paraphrased by the Nun, is contained in this verse although she does not refer to it.
5   863 'Ses privez': Aelred does not mention friends specifically; the Nun thinks the idea important enough to add.

well-connected one.[6] Anybody he knew to have good qualities, he treated as if they were gentlemen. [He gave poor people their rights, speaking gently to them.][7] Even though he was so powerful, an earthly king with earthly riches, he did not therefore despise those in misery when he saw them. He was a gentle father to orphans, and is devoted to all the needy.[8] His wealth is a commonwealth, so that everybody thought of it as theirs; therefore they held it as their own and they all had ample. He did not think of the treasure he possessed as his own, and he spent it on everybody as though he owed it to them. Nobody ever asked for some of it without receiving as much of it as he needed. When he saw any being taken, he kept quiet as though he had not noticed. He was ashamed to take anything belonging to another, and overjoyed to give of his own belongings.[9] He never forgot a gift from anybody, but always forgot his gifts to others. The holy goodness that dwelt in his heart could clearly be seen in his beautiful face.[10] His heart was perfect and wise, his body was fair and his face was sweet; his look was gentle, mature, and handsome, and he never lacked wisdom and assurance. His behaviour was always decorous, as though he had been brought up in the cloisters. His speech was at once happy and gentle, truthful and glorious, for before it ever came forth from him God's grace had sweetened it; so that all those who heard him had their hearts sweetened towards God. The greater part of what he said was about God and his Mother. His words were wise, and well suited to the occasion: he was strong and severe with fools, gentle and confident with the wise. He scolded the foolish roundly, and with wise blandishments.[11] Nobody ever saw him swollen with pride, nor his body tormented with anger. He is moderate in all things, and his moderation was steadfast: he was never seen to over-indulge either in eating or in drinking. He never acted wrongly in any matter, unless he was deceived by somebody else. But because of his simplicity[12] and his righteous thinking he believed that nobody would tell him anything that he would perceive to be evil, and so if ever his intention erred it was because of some such happening.

¶Who is worthy to remember his goodness, or to praise his deeds? He was so gifted with chastity that he was filled with it to perfection. He never let go of it, neither in

---

[6] The Nun replaces Aelred's reference, to James 2:1, with an explanation of favouritism (cf. *Life*, p. 142).
[7] 880 MS P adds 'A droit tenoit la povre gent Sis apella mult doucement'.
[8] In *Life*, p. 142, Ps. 68:5 (67:6 in *LV*) is quoted; the Nun's more inclusive phrase omits mention of widows. Here again the verb 'to be' changes tense within the sentence.
[9] 900 'de suen doner est joius'. Aelred quotes II Cor. 9:7, that he was a cheerful giver (*dator hilaris*, see Rewriting Aelred, above).
[10] 903-4 Laurent notes that 'bunté' (v. 903) translates Aelred's *spiritus sanctitatis*; the saint is instrument or 'conductor' of God's work (*Plaire et édifier*, pp. 419-20).
[11] 924 'blandisement': Södergård's glossary gives 'flattery', but it is unlikely that the Edward of hagiography would flatter the foolish, or even the wise (see note to v. 4243). Aelred has *blandiens* [coaxing]; the Nun amplifies the idea (cf. Clemence's use of the word in its usual bad sense; see Introduction, p. 42, above).
[12] 933 'sa grant simplicité': MS P reads 'humilité', although at v. 950 'simpleté' replaces 'good thoughts'. Aelred gives his inborn simplicity (equated with sincerity) as a reason for his sometimes being deceived in people (*Life*, p. 143); candour or openness, not stupidity, is meant. Simplicity as a medieval virtue is expounded in (for example) *Les Paroles Salomun* ed. Hunt, lines 168-99 & 298-321.

6 Description of Edward (851–978)

deed nor in desire. In exile, it was his health,[13] and his comfort in poverty. As the king exerted himself for the country he had recovered, so he reinforced his chastity by good deeds and good thoughts.[14] But it rarely[15] happens nowadays, that anybody improves through becoming rich: very often great power creates an evil desire to do evil, because one never felt that desire until one experienced the power. Riches cause much evil to be done, where poverty dares no attempt. But when Edward became rich,[16] he did not adopt the habits of the rich. Never did he abuse his great power by any desire to do evil. He despised avarice so much that he could never take pleasure in it. No regret entered his mind when he lost his riches; no more did he feel joyful when his loss was restored to him.[17] Such was the good king Edward, in whom was no avarice, no foolish pride or malevolence, although he held supreme power. We will now tell you an example of his inexpressible goodness[18] and profound humility, and show you the deed – how pious and charitable he was, and how tolerant about loss to himself.

---

[13] 945 'seinteé' (health; note the similarity to the word for sanctity – see Glossary); MS P reads 'seurté' [security, safety].
[14] 949–50 'enforça sa chasteé Par bons faiz': the Nun adds another virtue to Aelred's list (*Life*, p. 143, but see Preface to Laurence, p. 128). Treatises on virginity stress that one cannot achieve grace without proper virtue. By analogy with the Parable of the Sower, good wives score thirty, virtuous widows sixty, and true virgins one hundred (Matt. 13:8 & Mark 4:8); and see 'Beatitudes', in *Cher Alme* ed. Hunt.
[15] 951 'reument': MS P reads 'souvent'. This would make sense only if 'nul' in the next line were read as a negative: 'often ... nobody improves'. But it is probably a mistake, being not the only instance of P reading 'often' for 'rarely' (see note to v. 1112, where context renders the meaning unquestionable).
[16] 959 'riche' can mean powerful, as well as rich; the Nun regularly contrasts it with 'poor' (see Glossary).
[17] 968 'sa perte restora'; MS P reads 'sa tere recouvra', but Edward was happy to recover his land. Of P's interesting variations, some make less sense than the base MS.
[18] 973 'sa nun disable bunté'; Södergård notes examples of 'nun' before adjective in Old French (and cf. *Catherine*, v. 1190: 'nun disable sa bunté', although it is no evidence of common authorship). MS P has 'merveilleuse bunté'; it also omits the last clause below.

Chapter 7

Edward's Treasure (979–1080)[1]

Introduction

This story, not in earlier Lives, appears to be original to Aelred: he heard (or read) it 'in the celebrated language of the English' (*Life*, pp. 143–5). He allows himself a rare outburst of praise for Edward, in his own voice (1st p. sing.) and personal in tone, although he does not call it a favourite as the Nun does. For her, the deed is worth more than all his other good deeds, including his miraculous cures, because it shows his humility and his reluctance to play the judge, even of wrongful actions. Poverty is shown to be a reason, even an excuse, for theft; furthermore, the Nun adds no authorial censure of the crime. She gives the episode as an *exemplum* against the sin of avarice. It shows exceptional generosity in the Nun too: the fellow is not despised for his sin, because of his poverty.[2] She makes more of the thief's plight and his reprieve than MP does. Her words resemble a saying, well known to English ears: 'thy need is greater than mine'. Aelred has 'Perhaps the person ... needed it more than we do' (*Life*, p. 145). There are many stories on this theme, ranging from David's sacrifice of water at the Well of Bethlehem (II Sam. 23:15–17), through Alexander of Macedon's refusal to drink while his men thirsted, to words credited to Sir Philip Sidney as he gave his own drink to a dying man (Battle of Zutphen, 1586).[3] The Nun is unlikely to be referring to David, who does not give the water to a needy companion; this expression of unselfish charity seems to be her own. For MP, the action is an example of Edward's simple humility, and is compared with Jesus' pardon for the repentant thief at the Crucifixion. This comparison is in *Estoire* only (vv. 1050–57); not in Aelred. But in *Estoire*, Edward's ability to predict Hugelin's arrival is not, as here, ascribed to the power of the Holy Spirit (Aelred says simply *in spiritu* = spiritually, *Life* p. 144), nor is this miracle a favourite. Although the Nun follows Aelred closely, her account spells out that the servant's punishment would have been death.

The last paragraph of the preceding chapter, a discussion of Edward's virtue and his hatred of avarice in particular, also serves as introduction to this story. The account is thus framed by two passages praising Edward: 'Who is worthy to remember his goodness' (above), 'Who can tell his great sweetness' (below) – these give it special rhetorical weight.

---

[1] *Vita*, 746B–D; *Life*, §7. Cf. *Estoire*, vv. 980–1057; *History*, pp. 66–7.
[2] Johnson and Cazelles, '*Le Vain Siecle*', p. 145; the authors offer comparison with Brendan (The Stolen Goblet, vv. 307–54, in *The Anglo-Norman* Brendan ed. Waters).
[3] See Yonge, 'The Cup of Water', digital.library.upenn.edu/women/yonge/deeds/deeds.html (accessed 5.9.2013).

7 Edward's Treasure (979–1080)

¶One day the king had lain down and prepared his mind for sleep. But thoughts came, that deprived him of this rest; it often happens that sleep flees because of thought. So as the king lay there – he who had no evil thoughts – he saw his treasurer, and saw him come to the treasure. Then the man opened the chest and took from it what he wanted: as much as he needed for what he had to do. But he forgot to shut it, because he was in a hurry to go somewhere else. A poor servant realised, seeing how the other had opened it, and knew that it was not shut – he went over to the place. This fellow used to serve the cooks[4] and collect their dishes. Because he was poor, and saw such great riches, he made poverty a reason to be a thief of those riches. So he helped himself lavishly to some treasure, and put it in his breast to hide it. He went straight out of the room and into a secret place, then he emptied his breast of the gold and hid it away cunningly. Yet again he went to the treasure, and again he did as he had done before. All the time the king was watching what he did with the treasure. The young man went to work a third time, to take more. But the king could see, and I believe it was by the power of the Holy Spirit, that the treasurer was near – he whose responsibility the treasure was. To the thief he said gently:

'Boy, you have erred most wickedly. If you believe me, you'll run away now! And take with you what you've got! I swear by God and his Mother – you can be quite sure of this – if Hugelin manages to catch you, he won't let you take a penny away.'

He who had this name was the king's chamberlain.[5] The servant, when he heard this, immediately ran away. Presently the keeper of the treasure arrived; he very soon saw that some of the treasure the king had put him in charge of had been stolen. Fear assaulted him, anguish overcame him – immediately he gave himself up to grief: he turned pale, turned livid, strength failed him; he sighed and moaned and wailed aloud. By the sighs and by the cry the king heard his anguish. He asked what this grief was about, as if he didn't know the reason. He told him what he already knew, about the treasure that had been stolen. The king said:

'Hush now! Don't be so upset about it! Perhaps the one who took the stuff did so out of great need; he has greater need of it than you have.[6] Now he has it, let him be glad of it. Surely the rest, that he left, will be quite enough for us.'

Thus the king concealed the deed, and redeemed the young man from death. Who can tell his great sweetness,[7] his charity, his great virtue; or his generous benevolence, or his gentle simplicity? That he, so noble and so honoured in heaven and earth, saw a wicked boy steal from his great treasure and carry it off – he didn't want to give him away, and so he told him to flee. He pardoned his crime and, what is more, saved him from death. Everybody may judge their king as they see fit, on this matter, but I judge

---

4 999 'kius': *pace* Södergård, whose note glosses it as 'the blind'; cf. *Estoire*, v. 992.
5 1027 & 1030 For Hugelin, a historical figure, see Barlow, *Edward the Confessor*, pp. 165–6. He reappears in the story of Gille Michel (ch. 13).
6 1051 'Greignur mestier en ot de vus': here as elsewhere 'de' used instead of 'que' (Södergård's note).
7 1057 MS P has 'dolour' instead of 'duçur', which makes less good sense; it also reverses vv. 1059–60 (without altering the sense).

that this worthy act ought to be treated as a great miracle.[8] For he who cured the sick, and he who gave sight back to the blind and made the crippled to walk – more than I can now remember – all this should be put in the shade beside the deed he did for the thief. He ought to be praised more for this than for the other works he performed.

---

[8] 1072 Aelred does not call it a miracle; but inserts Gospel references, about the eye being the light of the body, which the Nun does not include.

Chapter 8
Edward and Edith (1081–462)[1]

Introduction

The opening of this chapter amplifies the source, for example, in its reference to Original Sin. This doctrine teaches that everybody is born sinful because of Adam and Eve's sin in the Garden of Eden (variously considered to be disobedience, gluttony, and/or lechery). An apparently innocent child, dying unbaptized, will thus be condemned to Hell. The chapter is more personal than Aelred's: reference to Edward's worthiness or valour, additional direct speech (notably Edith's), ideas about friendship further developed. There is a cluster of courtly terms and love-vocabulary: 'amie', below, can be translated only as 'lover',[2] one of the Nun's references to 'fin' amur' occurs here. Aelred says Judith's chastity saved the city, but the Nun says God saved Judith (adding 'curteisement'). MacBain notes Clemence's 'language of chivalry' (*Catherine*, p. xxiv), but his examples are words meaning knightly, noble etc., rather than the vocabulary of love and courtesy (see also Glossary). The extended address to the Virgin Mary is fitting prologue to a description of the virgin Edith, idealized to the extent that a parallel with the most virtuous of all women must be intended. After this, Edith does not appear again until the scene of Edward's last illness, where evocation of Mary grieving at the death of her Son is also apparent. Notable differences between these Lives and MP's account are that, in the latter, Edward's prayer is to Saints John and Peter (instead of invoking Joseph, Susanna, Judith, and the Three in the Furnace). The Nun's choice of stories is significant: historically Susanna and others are linked with appeals for deliverance of the soul (in Middle English romance, ultimately from prayers of priests officiating at a death-bed).[3] Further, MP's refutation of those who misunderstood the couple's childlessness is shorter and less polemical. Aelred allows himself a rare personal opinion on this matter (*Life*, pp. 148–9), but the Nun's argument comes across as more personal still. Södergård's note to v. 1253 (see also Analyse) sketches contrasting opinions of Godwin in the source-texts. Edith, the rose born from the thorn, is his daughter and thus a controversial choice. Godwin, as will be seen, hopes to be forgiven for crimes against Edward's family by marrying his daughter into it. Furthermore, people think the couple are barren because Edward wants no child from that accursed family (discussed at the end of this chapter), though there was nothing but his purity and integrity to prevent him getting one 'en concubinage' with another woman. The latter observation ('could he not find another ...?') is not in Aelred. It suggests the Nun was familiar with more than one rumour about

---

[1] *Vita*, 747A–8C; *Life* §8. Cf. *Estoire*, vv. 1058–278; *History*, pp. 67–70.
[2] Edward says 'Pur amur a ta chaste amie' (v. 1205).
[3] Dalrymple, *Language and Piety*, pp. 131–7.

Edward's childlessness.[4] Södergård thinks the king's sterility would be construed as saintly virginity (note to v. 1090). So, of course, would the queen's.

¶Saint Edward was a very worthy king,[5] and he was powerful in every good quality. He had grace, wisdom, and virtue from God; from his neighbours he had peace and love. He had established things so well in his land that nothing could be bettered. Wise people who observed this, and who were sensible of the common good, were very anxious about his death, and worried that he had no heir. They called a council together on this matter; then they begged their king that he would be pleased to take a wife, from whom he might have at least one heir to hold the land after him and maintain his people with right. When the king heard their request he was both sad and shocked. He did not know what to say or do, nor whose advice he might follow. He feared that if he took a wife he would offend his Creator. And the treasure of chastity, that he had preserved so honourably:[6] he was afraid that if he married a woman this treasure would be reft from him; it was in a frail vessel, that could soon and too easily fall to pieces. This vessel is the human body, and no virtue is safe in it; above all, chastity rarely finds safety there.[7] No human body is so strong – such is this life – nor its strength so well prepared, that it will really not fail when one has most need of it. None should trust in it, nor have faith in bodily virtue. The body of a man is so weak in itself that it cannot even trust itself: what it desires today it will come to hate tomorrow. It fell into this weakness when it lost its true nature, for which God created it, from whom sin separated it. Never, since then, has the body been worthy to recover its strength; as long as it is here on earth it must fear evil and sin.

Saint Edward understood this very well, that a man's body is so weak. Although he had strengthened his saintly body against all the sins, he was afraid that natural weakness would alter his resolve. On the other hand, he reflected that if he were to gainsay the counsellors' will he would then have to confess the sweet secret of his heart. And so notwithstanding he agreed to them, that he would gladly take a wife. But to God, who knew his heart, he prayed fervently for strength:

'O good Jesus, listen to me, for without thee I see no comfort. Lord, thou canst save me – who once did save the young men from the burning fire into which they were thrown, that was so cruelly stoked up. By the praises they sang to thee, they escaped the flames alive.[8] By thee, Joseph escaped from the lady who loved him so; nor did he lose his chastity, either by deed or wanton thought. The lady obtained

---

[4] See p. 8, above.
[5] 1081 'reis mult vaillanz': 'valiant,' or ' having the properties proper to one's position' (see Glossary). Reminder of Edward as God's soldier is added to Aelred's account. MS P's next line reads 'En boines oevres' [in good works], instead of 'tutes buntez'.
[6] 1104 MS P reads 'Qui si longement ot gardé' [preserved for so long].
[7] 1112 'Relment i trove seurté': MS P reads 'souvent' (see note to v. 951).
[8] The story of the Three in the Furnace is in Daniel, ch. 3.

nothing more than the coat he left with her.⁹ Susanna was saved by thee, who was coveted¹⁰ by the mad priests – thou didst guard her from their madness and deliver her from blame.¹¹ Thou didst save Judith courteously¹² – who, in order to save thy people, dressed her beautiful body most beautifully and presented herself to the pagan. She deceived him by holy dissimulation, and he was greatly delighted with her. She took much trouble to please him, with honour and drink and food. But neither for food nor for honour, nor for pleasure or love, did the lady waver, nor did she come near to his madness; nevertheless she tricked him so well that she killed him with his sword. What is more, Lord, it was thy doing.¹³

'This is what everybody in the world receives happiness from – human sense cannot understand it,¹⁴ and must render thanks for it – that thou who art Creator by thy nature didst later take human form. And that flesh that thou didst take, before man was, thou madest her. Thy daughter thou madest thy Mother, thou wert the Son of her whose Father thou wert. She was both mother and maiden: handmaiden on earth and queen in heaven. She was chaste, and chaste thou didst find her; chastely didst thou love her body. Her chastity pleased thee so, that from her body was thine born. Thou didst undergo marriage with her, but maintained thy chastity. She was not degraded by wedlock, nor was she touched by her husband.¹⁵ O sweet and pious, glorious King! This is what I desire, for my part, that I may wed thus, that my body need not be degraded. Lord, hear my plea. I am thy servant, and son of thy handmaid.¹⁶ Thou madest me when I was nothing. Whatever I am, I am surely thine. For love of thy chaste lover, keep me in my chaste life. I cannot compare myself with her, nor dare I wish to, but truly – as much as I can – I want to emulate her chastity.¹⁷

'Again I pray thee, dearest Father, for the love of my lady thy Mother, that you¹⁸ have mercy on me, for I have no faith in myself for anything. And you – my Lady, sweet flower, mother¹⁹ and wife to my Lord – with your Son, help me as you are well

---

9   Genesis, ch. 39.
10 1160 MS P reads 'saisie' [seized].
11 In *AV*, the story of Susanna is in the Apocrypha, where the Book of Judith also appears.
12 1163 'Judith salvas curteisement': comparatively early use of one of the widest and loosest terms in medieval vocabulary. Here, it means 'in courtly fashion, as a truly noble king (sc. God) should ... '. MS P has 'bonement' [benignly], as though the copyist disliked the word 'curteisement' (see my Introduction, and Glossary for the Nun's uses of it).
13 This thirty-line passage diverges from and amplifies Aelred's two lines (see Wogan-Browne, 'Clerc u lai', pp. 72–3 and note 61).
14 1180 Instead of the following, MS P has 'Ne cele grant hautece estendre' [nor can it reach out to such great highness] – although 'entendre' [understand] would make better sense.
15 1196 'Ne de sun barun atuchee': 'baron' means 'lord' or 'husband'. Here, both God and Joseph are meant (Aelred does not include this comment; *Life*, p. 146); see note to v. 1216.
16 1202 Ps. 116:16 (115 in *LV*); also in Aelred.
17 The next few lines resemble the 'credo épique' of *chansons de geste* (Laurent, *Plaire et édifier*, p. 369).
18 1211–15 'te pri jeo ... Ke vus': the address is 'vous' from here (see my note on Translation, above).
19 1216 MS P reads 'Fille et espouse' (daughter and wife); medieval thinking makes much of the paradox by which Mary is wife, daughter, and mother to God. In ch. 29, Edward talks of Edith as of a daughter or sister (see v. 5082).

able to do: let me undergo marriage in such a way that the lady[20] may not cause my undoing, nor my chastity be led astray by our coming together.' [Thus Saint Edward made this prayer to the Lord God.][21]

¶Once he had begged leave from God, because he was so reluctant to take a wife without the desire for one, then he let his barons know that he would do as they wanted as soon as he could hear of a suitable woman. So they sent out to enquire, asking whether anybody could find a woman both beautiful and wise.[22] She must be high-born enough to be the king's friend,[23] and must be of blameless life. They sought and made enquiries until they found one suitable.

¶There was a Count in this land, a powerful man and strong in war,[24] but he was known to be a traitor for killing his overlords. He had often betrayed the country, for he was filled with wickedness. He was so extremely cunning that he deceived all his neighbours. His dissimulation was so clever that he was never blamed, because his deeds were never apparent; he never failed to conceal what he did, about any thing he wanted. While he was so capable in his deeds, he was well capable of pretence. He knew just how to attract everybody to the evil that he himself wished to do. His name was Godwin, in that language,[25] and he was of very high lineage. He had a most beautiful daughter: the maiden's name was Edith. But like a rose from thorns this girl was born to him.[26] She took her flesh from his, but she gave herself to the will of God. And God, to whom she had given herself, had endowed her generously with wisdom, virtue, goodness, and perfect chastity. For the benefit of Edward, his dear friend, God had nourished her saintly body so that it would be chaste for the chaste king. What she found in him, she had in herself: it was true chastity that she would find in her lover. God adorned her body with good manners, good virtues, and beauty. In her youth she was as wise as though she were of mature age;[27] she never had any love for impropriety or worldliness. She stayed in her room industriously,

---

[20] 1220 MS P has 'ma femme' [my wife], as though he has already married her.
[21] 1222 After this line, MS P adds: 'Sains Edward fist en tel maniere A Damedieu ceste priere.'
[22] 1230 MS P has 'S'en la terrre peust trover Femme …' [whether a woman … could be found in the land].
[23] 1233 'd'estre amie …'; the Nun stresses the importance of friendship for Edward. Aelred says 'fit for the embraces of such a king' (*Life*, p. 146).
[24] 1238 'riches … puissant': see Glossary.
[25] 1253 'en cel language' (MS P has '… nun icel language', online 'itel' now corrected to 'en cel' as here). The phrase may be a line-filler, or a clue about whether the Nun was a native English-speaker. The comment is her own; Aelred says 'the most powerful of all was Earl Godwin' (*Life*, pp. 146–7), without remarking on his name. The Nun rarely remarks on names or language; perhaps this indicates awareness that the language of England was different in those days, more than a century before the date she was writing.
[26] 1257 The rose born from thorns is a common description of Mary (cf. Song 2:1–2); see also *History*, note 114 to vv. 1175–6. In *Gilte Legende* (ed. Hamer and Russell, II:165, p. 879) St Catherine is also described thus, because born of pagan parents (though not in *GL*, or Clemence).
[27] 1273–4 'En sa juvente esteit si sage Cume s'ele fust de grant eage'; for the old-young woman, variation of the *puer senex* theme, see Curtius, *European Literature*, pp. 101–5. The young Virgin Mary is conventionally described as wise beyond her years (see 'Young Mary', in *Cher Alme* ed. Hunt).

where she did her beautiful handiwork. She was wonderfully clever at crafts:[28] sewing with silk, embroidering with gold; she could draw anything, and paint a marvellous likeness. When she wearied of her work, she enjoyed herself with fine books. She was never found in idleness, or not absorbed in some worthy thing. She was full of all goodness: good deeds, and good life. The lady was very unlike the wicked scoundrel who begot her; so much more should she be praised, for changing herself from this evil nature. Whoever comes from the bad, and yet is good, does honour to herself and to her own.[29]

¶The count, my lords, is a powerful man; he is well versed in all sorts of cunning.[30] So he is fully aware of the great evils he has wrought against the king: of Alfred, his brother, whom he killed with treason and much wrong[31] – and of many other crimes that he took on[32] and achieved. And for this, fear haunted him, that the king hated him bitterly. He planned to arrange things so that the king would take his daughter, so by this connection the old anger would be pardoned. He begged the king's familiars – by these gifts, by these friends – to help him in this need and to praise him to their lord the king, that he would deign to take his daughter and thenceforward love her as his consort.[33] These men are pleased with his request, and they counselled the king very fully about it – the more because they loved him more – they advised him to take the woman, for they knew the count to be wicked and had often had the proof of it. Therefore they would benefit substantially if the count were to ally himself to the king. He asked them for a short respite, then assigned a fixed day. Then preparations for the nuptials began: both friends and strangers were invited. Bishops and abbots came, and others in abundance. The day had not elapsed before they had all arrived from all sides. The king wedded the lady and crowned her queen. They had great pleasure in the marriage, and then they moved on to the wedding feast. It had been prepared satisfactorily, for which they were extremely glad.[34] I cannot name the rich dishes, for I was not there and so I tasted nothing. But you will know that they were such as ought to be for that occasion.[35] The king, on whose account all the joy was, had the least joy of it. He went away to a private place and then sent for his queen.

---

[28] 1279 'A merveilles sout bien ovrer': Södergård notes that this form 'A merveilles' predates previously recorded occurences. The list of Edith's accomplishments is expanded from Aelred's (*Life*, p. 147).
[29] The latter part of this description goes beyond that of Aelred, who does not expand on the difference between Godwin and his daughter (*Life*, p. 147). The last sentence here looks like a proverb, although I cannot find it recorded. It is typical of the Nun to add such sentiments.
[30] 1295–6 MS P reads, instead, 'Li quens ses peres est riches home, Cil Godwine que jo vous nom' [her father ... this Godwin, whose name I'm telling you]. Note the address to audience, that the description shifts into the present tense, and also that the word 'riche' here means 'powerful' (see Glossary).
[31] For Alfred's death, see ch. 5; for Godwin's punishment see ch. 23 (and note in *Life*, p. 147).
[32] 1302 'K'il out aprise': 'aprendre' usually means 'learn', but MS P reads 'emprise' [undertake, enterprise], which makes good sense.
[33] 1314 'cume sa per': see Glossary.
[34] 1335–8 In MS P these lines (They had great pleasure ... extremely glad) omitted.
[35] 1342 'Cum a cel'ovraigne': MS P reads 'noeces' ('ovraigne' = work or business). The Nun's remarks about not having been there are her own.

He begged and urged her to keep true chastity; not – for wanton worldly love – to be taken away from serving God, nor to lose the dignity in which God himself rejoices.

'This is the perfect chastity by which man is brought close to God. Chastity is so glorious that she becomes God's bride, for God is supreme chastity. He leads her into his presence, and there he bestows on her all the sweet enjoyment of his divine love.[36] Wherever he is, there shall she be, and wherever he goes she will follow him.[37] Nor can anybody ever have this sweet closeness without chastity. Therefore I tell you, my lovely friend,[38] that you should maintain a chaste life. In Heaven you will surely be honoured for it, and be the more beloved of me.'

The lady heard; she was very glad, and joyfully said to the king:[39]

'Dear sweet lord, dearest friend, with all my heart I give you thanks for your welcome request. You find me ready to grant it, for I have always wanted to offer my chastity to God; so also I beg you to heed my prayer – that you keep yourself just as you have begged me to. Now you want what I want, so I will do your pleasure. I shall honour you as lord, and love you chastely. Now let God give you the strength as he has given you the will.'[40]

¶When the king had what he desired, he sighed sweetly with joy, he laughed sweetly with the sigh. And he gave thanks to Jesus Christ for having given him a lover in whom chastity was so manifest. They made a solemn covenant between themselves, and they kept it for ever after; they took God as witness to the covenant they had set between them. They took great delight together, as the chaste lover and his chaste lady. She was wife, but without the deed that makes a woman to be called wife. She was wife in name only, for there was no question of the deed with her. The king was called husband, without the deed or any desire for it. So they lived their friendship without wicked pleasure and without sin. Their love was great joy to them – true pleasure and refined sweetness. She honoured and served him as a wife should a husband, ready to do anything for him; and he loved her as his queen. So their love was sustained with no lust either committed or desired. If any of you disagrees, that their sweet delight could be like this, may you be willing to acknowledge your error. There was nobody in the whole kingdom from whom their chastity was concealed – everybody was quite certain that no wrongful pleasure took place between them, and these people often debated among themselves, and guessed at wrong reasons, for their wit could not comprehend their holy love, nor understand it. They said he was a simple man . . .

---

[36] 1360 'sa fin amur': MacBain points the contrast between this and 'fole amur mundaine', v. 1349 ('Vocabulary'). MS P has 'douce' instead of 'fin'.

[37] See Ruth 1:16; this reference, and passage of direct speech, not in Aelred: unusually, the Nun adds a Bible reference. The story perhaps had special significance for nuns.

[38] 1365 Södergård places quotation marks at the beginning of this sentence, but there is much to be said for repositioning them a few lines further up (because of the word 'therefore').

[39] The Nun's is the only Life to give Edith a point of view, or even a voice (see, for example, Wogan-Browne, 'Clerc u lai', pp. 68–70).

[40] 1385–6 Edith's prayer is not unlike the short passage added to the description of Edward at the end of his life. He strives to love God more (that is, he wills) as his strength diminishes (see vv. 4167–8, and introduction to ch. 25). This sentiment, like the other, is homiletic but not recorded as proverbial.

'And he cannot love the lady because of the treason Godwin, her father, committed against his brother. This must force the king to be dishonest with his wife, that he does not wish to father children on her[41] who would certainly resemble their grandfather, who was a murderer.'[42]

But this reason is wrong. I would like them to prove their saying and put it to the test of truth: if he could not love the lady because of her wicked father, could he not find another with whom to slake his lust? He was capable of finding another, had he wished to do such folly.[43] God, who was his only reason, showed by living proof that any who believed those things were wrong in their judgement. For had he been chaste because of hate he ought not to have had grace and favour.[44] But God, who knew the reason – and even was himself the reason – why he kept his chastity, richly rewarded him, so that in his frail chaste life he had the spirit of prophecy: he knew what was to come as well as what had been. And by this it is clearly proved that he kept true chastity not for worldly hate but for heavenly love.[45]

---

[41] 1432–3 MS P's version suggests the lady did not want a child that would resemble its grandfather.
[42] The foregoing is marked as speech in the edition; I have moved the opening quotation marks by half a line (closing quotation marks are missing). If it is direct speech, then they ought to go where I have placed them: at the end of v. 1435. It would be possible to cast it as reported speech, but I prefer (as Södergård evidently did) the immediacy of popular gossip which the Nun promptly contradicts.
[43] 1442 & 1444 MS P has 'deduit' [pleasure, delight] and 'solas' [comfort, delight] instead of 'folur' and 'folie', as though the scribe took a milder view of Edward's possible aberration.
[44] 1450 MS P has 'Gré ... ne amor fine', adding the idea of courtly or perfect love.
[45] Aelred closes with '... as the following chapter shows' (*Life*, p. 149). Edward's first vision naturally follows the account of his chastity.

Chapter 9

The Vision of the Ships (1463–640)[1]

Introduction

It will be noticed that Edward appears to have several coronations; in fact those occurring after chapter 5 are special occasions when the crown was worn.[2] He is shown with it one Easter Day (v. 3945), and at Christmas (v. 4546). It may also have been his practice to wear it on the anniversary of his coronation (see note to v. 713). Södergård's p. 4 mistakenly says this crown-wearing is Easter, not Pentecost.

An example of the way the Nun rewrites Aelred is, in this chapter, where she replaces a psalm-reference with a sentence about pride. Even if Aelred was more learned in Bible-knowledge than the Nun, it is unthinkable that she would not know the Psalms, for example; every religious would be familiar with them. We must assume she re-words such passages deliberately. Perhaps she prefers, instead of citing the psalm, to cut straight to what she considers the moral. Here the sinner falls into the pit because of pride (see General Introduction, Audience, and Rewriting Aelred). Another version of this story appears in Aelred's *Genealogy* (pp. 89–90); yet another in Aelred's Sermon.[3] The Nun describes the Danish king coming in a small boat to embark on the great one; he slips while jumping from one to the other. Aelred seems to envisage the king capering excitedly at the prow of the ship he is already standing on (*Life*, p. 151). But, with regard to the latter, manuscripts of the family ω contain a passage much closer to that of the Nun: ... *et pedes et crura sinuose divaricans, dum de scapha in navem conscendere pararet, pede lapso inter utrumque in mare corruit.* ... *Sicque morte sua utrumque populum, Danorum scilicet et Anglorum, a peccato pariter et periculo liberavit* (*scapha* is the smaller boat from which the king jumps). Marzella also points out that Aelred's text contains a reference to Jonah 2:6 (2:5 in *AV*), which the Nun here omits.[4] Nevertheless, she retains a later one, from Genesis.

☙ ☙ ☙ ☙ ☙ ☙ ☙ ☙ ☙

¶The year had run its course, and time had duly brought round once again the day that was recorded as being the holy day when God sent the Holy Spirit he had promised to his beloved apostles.[5] When he ascended from earth into heaven, he sent

---

[1] *Vita*, 748C–9D; *Life*, §9; *Estoire* omits the introduction about Pentecost. MS V begins here, becoming Södergård's base MS; as with MS P, variants from MS W are signalled in notes.
[2] See William of Malmesbury, *Kings* tr. Stephenson, p. 214, note 5.
[3] ed. Jackson, pp. 55–7, pp. 72–5, and notes 33 & 36.
[4] 'La tradizione', pp. 360–61 (the 'famiglia ω' prefacing the first cited passage should of course read 'famiglia ϱ', as will be obvious when examining the second passage).
[5] 1470–71 Two lines (When he ascended ... down to earth) missing from MS W (the sense would be 'to his beloved apostles, to visit his faithful ...'). For Pentecost, see Acts 2:1–4.

his Holy Spirit down to earth, to visit his faithful and help them.[6] It comforted his followers in their sorrow, and filled them with its sweetness. It increased their desire to do good, and strengthened them in suffering evil.[7] The day, which brought solace to all the world, is called Pentecost.[8] On this day King Edward wore his crown with the greatest honour. He prepared his royal person as the occasion demanded; he had to attend the festival, for this was his coronation day. As his outer person was adorned with human splendour, his inner heart was likewise adorned with divine virtue. Little did he prize outward honours; he took them for no more than they were worth. All the best of the realm were gathered there that day. For the festival and for the king each one of them busied himself: to make his heart clean for the festival, and to deck his body finely for the king.

The king entered the church, and with him his powerful barons. The place is called Westminster, and Saint Peter is its patron.[9] The holy priests spoke the mass loud and clear. The king was overjoyed, and quickly commended himself to God. He gave himself up entirely to God's pleasure: his body and heart, and his whole desire.[10] The whole world was wearisome to him, and he made sweet Jesus his refuge. His heart was so rapt in God that he put the whole world out of his mind. Then when he came to the sacrament, that was offered for all humankind, he felt the glory so intensely that he gave it all his thought. He begged God for his sweet grace, and to have mercy on his people; and this he prayed humbly, that he would give them peace, strength, and help. When all had taken communion – those who had the opportunity to do so – Edward the King suddenly smiled a sweet wise smile. With happy face, with gentle look, he raised his eyes smiling. He smiled with a fitting restraint, although he saw great joy. All those who saw his smile[11] marvelled very much at it. But some were sure that he had very good reason. When the service of this solemn day was completed with all honour, those who had seen the king and noticed his expression begged the king politely to explain the reason for his smile. The king, who was a simple man, told simply what he had seen:[12]

---

[6] 1472 'quere' [to seek], the Nun's usual verb for visiting a holy place (see Glossary).
[7] 1476 MS P has 'de Dieu servir' (in serving God).
[8] *Estoire* begins the chapter here: vv. 1279–372; *History*, pp. 70–71.
[9] Laurent remarks that for the Nun Westminster Abbey is only one of many [churches], while for MP it is thematically central (*Plaire et édifier*, pp. 145–6).
[10] 1507–8 The next two lines (The whole world ... his refuge) missing from MS P.
[11] 1527 'ceus ki sun ris veü unt': in modern French, 'ris' would mean 'laugh', cf. 'surris' [smile], but here they *saw* his 'ris.' At v. 1533, MS W has 'ris' for 'rei' (those who had seen the smile, not 'seen the king'). See also note to v. 3989. In Aelred, he 'broke out in moderate laughter'. Where Edward refers to his own smile, at the end of his speech in the Nun, in Aelred he says he had laughed (*Life* pp. 150–51).
[12] 1537 MS P has 'qui sages hom esteit' (who was a wise, not a 'simple', man). Edward's simplicity was innocence, not stupidity (see Carpenter, 'Origins', pp. 890–91, for the simplicity of Edward, and of Henry III). For the enemy king, see Södergård's note to v. 1539; also notes to vv. 1319–21 in *Estoire*, to vv. 1318–44 in *History*, and footnote in *Life* pp. 151–2. Swein, or Svend, king of Denmark throughout Edward's reign, actually outlived him by some years. Magnus [of Norway] died suddenly in 1047, on board ship according to some accounts.

'The Danes', he said, 'were all gathering; they were getting good and ready to make war. They had all drawn towards the sea, so as to do what they had done before: destroy us, take our land, as they previously did in other war. They wanted to trouble our country, but God would no longer suffer them, that the peace we had from him we should ever again lose to them. Because of the old sin, God had now chastised us. Our ancestors did him grave wrong – rarely and little did they repent – and for this he delivered us into the hands of the Danish. But the Danes did not realise that God had put us into their power. They did not understand the judgement of God,[13] that he wrought upon us for them: they thought it was by their strength that he had so confounded us. Therefore they now thought to afflict us again in the same way. They do not know how God is good, how quickly he gives succour to his own. Those whom he loves most, he chastises most;[14] he makes to die and then brings to life. He heals the wounds that he made; he leads them into affliction and brings them out of affliction. And as much as he causes bitterness, by so much is joy increased. But the Danes understood nothing of that. They trust too much in their own folly.[15] Their king, in his insane pride, today – this very day – had gathered them. They had all come towards the sea; he commanded them to prepare the ships. They had the wind they wanted, so they hastened all the more. They had their stores brought; the ships provisioned and prepared. The mariners brought everything the ships needed. The soldiers went aboard the ships, and took the best quarters for their own use. Then they were ready to haul on the sails, so as to make the voyage more speedily. The king was in a boat that was coming towards the big ship. So arrogant was his thought, that his body could not endure the delay; thus a very foolish desire seized him: he wanted to leap into the ship. He stretched out his body and his legs, to do his leap in noble fashion. Because he forced himself too much, his feet slipped from the deck. Between the boat and the ship he slipped, easily, into the sea. Without pride, the sea received and held fast the prideful king;[16] and by his death alone did we and the Danes all benefit.[17] No longer shall they harm us, nor shall we sin against them. Thus has God delivered us, by his death, from their cruelty. To him, himself, fell the harm he wished to us. The Danes, when they saw him dead, made for the nearest harbour. For this I hope, in God our Father and in his sweet Mother, that in my lifetime they never come again nor ever do their evil will. By the grace of God I saw this, and I smiled

---

[13] 1558–9 The next two lines (that he wrought ... by their strength) missing from MS W (the sense would be 'the judgement of God, that he had so confounded us').
[14] 1565–7 'Ceus qu'il plus aime, plus chastie ...'; for these Bible quotations, expanded from Aelred (*Life* p. 150), see first Prov. 13:24, Heb. 12:6, Rev. 3:19. For the next phrase, see I Sam. 2:6. Job 5:18 is how God wounds and then heals; the leading into and out of affliction is not readily identifiable (cf. the wanderings of the troubled Jewish people, OT, *passim*).
[15] 1573–4 The next two lines (Their king ... gathered them) reversed in MS W.
[16] 1600 See *Life*, p. 151: Aelred refers to Ps. 7:15 (7:16 in *LV*), *he ... is fallen into the ditch that he made*. The Nun replaces this with a sentence about pride.
[17] 1602 MS P has 'Orent Daneis grant desconfort' [were the Danes thoroughly defeated].

and rejoiced very much; and so will those who smile with me, and all those who will hear it after me.'[18]

His barons, when they heard this, noted the hour when they saw the smile of their king, and his looks; and they sent immediately to Denmark to find out. They learned that it was all true, what the king had said to them, and the time, and the thing he saw – that their king was thus drowned for pride and for his sin. All the neighbouring people who heard this made concord with King Edward. Each one could see for himself that God was fighting for and through him. The Danes, since they heard this, sought peace and made concord. Thus was the king honoured – feared by all, loved by all. But among this fragile human love he did not forget his Creator. In his richness he did not forget him who had comforted him in his poverty.[19]

---

[18] See Gen. 21:6.
[19] 1635–40 The last lines, after peace was made, added by the Nun: typically to end with some pious comment. The word 'forget' links into the next part of the story ('he did not forget ... he remembered'), another of her methods for marking off sections of narrative.

Chapter 10

Edward's Pilgrimage (1641–2018)[1]

Introduction

The Nun amplifies, adding personal touches. In the opening passage, and in Edward's speech, she renders the sense in a way very similar to Aelred's, although without following the words of many of his Bible references (those retained are noted). Her citation from Numbers is an example of her changing, rather than deleting, a Bible reference. She is clearly not making any assumption that her audience would be unfamiliar with such citations. Preachers were only too ready to add them to their texts; there is no reason to suppose the Nun's practice should be so very different. One of her characteristically personal comments, that there is something she does not know, appears in this chapter. Another example of Edward as a type of Christ occurs here. Her remark that the letter had to be translated is not in the source (an example of her deictic style). MP says 'E tel est de l'escrit la summe Ki est en latin apert Noté, ke en seit chescuns cert' (*Estoire*, vv. 1652–4; *History*, p. 74). However, the text in front of us is in French and not Latin. 'Here is the whole of what was written clearly in Latin, so that everybody may be sure of it' is preferable to *History*'s 'Here is the entire text, set down clearly in Latin, so that ...'. Her final paragraph is expanded.

¶One day the king remembered that he had promised in his poverty to visit Saint Peter as soon as he was able to do so.[2] Now he saw that he could, and he began to wish to do it. Often he thinks and tells over to himself the great mercies that God has done him: he comforted him in exile, he brought him safely through many perils. From a slave, he had made him a sovereign, and he had given him back his proper estate.[3] He had raised him from poverty to royalty, and by his grace Edward was universally loved; he had fulfilled his desire in every way, for honour, goodness, and wisdom. And so he wanted to fulfil the vow he had made as a poor man. He gathered his provision together, and prepared the rich gifts that he would make. Judiciously he purchased and purveyed everything necessary for the journey. Next he summoned his barons, and then, when they were gathered, in these words he opened his mind to them: that he wished to make his promise the deed and do the pilgrimage he had promised to God faithfully:

---

[1] *Vita*, 749D–52A; *Life*, §10. Cf. *Estoire*, vv. 1391–654; *History*, pp. 71–4.

[2] 1643 'requerreit' (see Glossary). Aelred has *ad limina*, for visiting the tombs of Peter and Paul and by extension the Pope (*Life*, p. 153).

[3] 1652 'Si li ot rendue s'onur': 'onur' is frequent in this text, and 'honour' (virtue) is not always what is meant: many great medieval estates were called 'The Honour of ...' (Henry of Huntingdon, *Chronicle*, p. 309).

'My lords,' he said, 'you know very well how God has delivered us from the cruel scourge with which he chastised us. In his mercy he punished us for our sins as his children, and comforted us as his chosen. His justice was perfect love, and his scourging was true gentleness.[4] He has turned our tears to laughter, and our sorrows to gladness. He has humbled the mighty who were exalted over us. He has raised up the meek, and satisfied the hungry. I know you have not forgotten how the Danes harmed us, how they invaded our land, and then the damage they did to us. They took our people with violence, then savagely killed them.[5] They put the prisoners to slavery and humiliating ill-treatment. Many of them were exiled in great suffering and sorrow, so that all our lineage lamented the cruel outrage.[6] There was nobody in our land who was not deeply dishonoured. The more powerful they were, the greater were their depredations. All were in despair, and almost completely disinherited. Then, when my father died – as we all shall do – my two brothers were murdered by evil men of this land. As you know, I was driven out and exiled from my country. The enemies who hated us wreaked their hate upon us. The fine exploits they performed everywhere were bitter and hard for us. Everything that suffering took away from us was given joyfully to them. They were full of confidence, and we were in complete despair. Although there was nothing in all the world to give me hope, nevertheless I clung to the sweet hope that never fails good faith. I surrendered myself completely to the King of Kings, and in my heart I prayed for his mercy: that his strength would maintain me, that he would render me my land and my estate. So that he would grant my prayer, I eagerly made him a vow: as soon as I could, I would visit the tomb of Saint Peter. I commended myself into his keeping, and I received his mercy in answer to my prayer. He did not despise my prayer, and he sent me to my land and to gladness. More than this: he gave me great glory and victory over my enemies. His generous liberality has made me rich and powerful in worldly good. Without bloodshed or atrocity he has restored my great loss. He has confounded and overcome all our enemies with gentle peace. Our ills have ended in joy, and we shall accomplish what we have long desired. It is right he should be rewarded, because he saved us from death and gave us back our own. We must praise his holy Name, by which we receive joy and honour. With firm faith and perfect heart let us do what the Prophet says:

---

[4] See MacBain, 'Vocabulary', for 'fin amur' at vv. 1675–6. The first passage is inspired by Ps. 89:32–3 (88:33–4 in *LV*.); the next by the *Magnificat* (Luke 1:46–55; likewise in Aelred, *Life* p. 152). The tone of the speech differs in Aelred, where Edward's language is less personal (*Life*, pp. 152–4: for example, he uses second-person address less than in the Nun).

[5] 1688 MS P, instead of 'crüelment', repeats a phrase from the previous line: 'par lor esfors' [then with violence killed them]; not necessarily a mistake, for such poetic repetition is not untypical of the Nun's style.

[6] 1691–4 MS W omits these lines (Many of them ... the cruel outrage).

"Make a vow to the Lord our God, and render the deed you have vowed."[7] Therefore I wish to render to him the vow I made when I was poor.

'Each of you now look around, and I shall myself look around,[8] to see whom the land should be given to, by whom it may be rightly ruled, who shall hold it in his possession, to make peace and keep justice. Take care, if foreigners assail you, lest your own closest counsellors then fail you. Place a protector over you who shall be respected for his wisdom, who shall know how to love good people and quell the wicked, who understands the common need and can give and receive right judgement. If he keeps his friends around him, let him not fear his enemies. To him alone do I commend you, who is powerful to guard you. May he alone guard you by his mercy from death and war and sin. The peace that he alone gave us, only he, I trust, shall maintain it. You will remain in safe keeping if you are kept by him. He will stay here with you, and, if he pleases, he will be with us. He will keep you in joy and peace, and, if he pleases, he will bring us home.'

¶As soon as the king had explained to them his vow, and then his intentions, there was not one of them but burst into tears or trembled with fear. With deep sighs and painful tears they showed their great distress. They were afraid already, of being overrun by their enemies, the cruel Danes. They dreaded to lose, through his going away, the peace they had regained through him. A cry went up from the people, who groaned and wept bitterly, as though the whole country had been set on fire and aflame. Then you could see the poor weeping and raising their hands to God in heaven. They all think they are going to die of hunger, if the king has to leave them thus. They no longer care for their lives, but all are thinking of their graves. Rich and poor cry out with a loud voice, and all with one voice beg him not to leave them to die in such misery, nor leave his realm so to perish; not to give his people, his land, and his friends to his enemies. For if they were abandoned by him, alone, then they would soon be invaded by those enemies. The peace that God had given them and that he had established for them would, they feared, turn to war if the king departed from the land. God who restored their loss gave them their king as a hostage: while he was their king the land would have peace and happiness. Therefore they are all complaining together, that he could go and leave them to such a fate. They urge him to take pity on them, that it would be a sin to abandon them. He ought not to bring so many terrible things on his people for the sake of doing one good thing. One good deed could not make up for so many ills, that so many people would have to complain of. The priests conjured him, and commanded him on God's behalf, to stay with

---

[7] Num. 30:2: *If a man vow a vow unto the Lord, or swear an oath to bind his soul with a bond; he shall not break his word, he shall do according to all that proceedeth out of his mouth* (the prophet is Moses). Aelred refers to a similar law, but from Ps. 76:11 (75:12 in *LV*; *Life*, p. 153). In the following, the Nun deftly pushes at the notion of the Protector: at first Edward seems to mean a human Regent, then it becomes clear that the Regent is to be God (also in Aelred, but less dramatically done).

[8] 1753–4 'Chascuns enguard ore endreit sei E j'esguarderai endreit mei': this is more personal (and endearing) than Aelred, whose Edward says merely *Decernite ergo mecum* [Consider with me, then], *Life* p. 153.

10 Edward's Pilgrimage (1641–2018)   97

them as was fitting and look after his land and his people. The lay folk beg for his mercy and entreat him strongly to stay with them; if he still would not give up his plan could he at least postpone it.

When the king saw such misery, he felt a marvellous tenderness. Everywhere he saw his people lamenting, and he saw himself moved by their tears. He knows not what best to do: whether to proceed or to desist. He knows not which to follow: his pity or his desire. His desire to go spurs him forward, but Pity tells him to hold back.[9] His desire made it clear to him that he must fulfil his vow to God and, if he did not do it now, he did not know whether he would ever do it. On the other hand, Pity told him that it would be too cruel a sin if he would not have mercy on their sorrow and their tears.

Now he did not know how to decide, but he asked God to give him to do whatever would be most acceptable to him and most profitable to the people. Then the king took what he believed to be the best counsel: he would not give up the enterprise altogether, but he would delay his journey until he could find out what the Pope thought. He wanted to act by his advice, either to stay or go, and whatever he recommended the king would willingly do.[10] He told this to his men and granted them the respite. When they heard of their respite, they all fell to rejoicing as much as they had done the day they made him their lord, when he was recalled from exile and crowned with such gladness.

¶Then they all came away,[11] happy and joyful at their reprieve. Each one prayed to God earnestly, as best he could, that the king would not regret this delay, and that he would not go back on it. They all gave generous alms in thanks for it, according to their means, and they repeatedly promised the king that they would go to Rome for him on this matter. The most important thing was that they should send to Rome, that the Pope would release the king and that he would stay here. And so they chose messengers, intelligent, polite,[12] and honest ones, who could understand and answer reasoned discourse in any court on earth: a holy archbishop of York,[13] and Herman the bishop of Winchester. Then they chose two saintly abbots who were known to be very wise, and a good number of clerics and lay-folk – as many as the business required. Then, when they were all ready, they assembled all together. The king told them all his intentions, about the vow and the delay he had granted. As soon as they had heard his words, they took their leave and set off. [He told them the whole business and they put it into their letter, and they sealed it up well; then they

---

[9] 1841–2 MS W omits 'His desire … hold back', about Edward's internal conflict in which his feelings resemble personifications.
[10] 1863 MS W omits 'and whatever he recommended'.
[11] 1873 MSS W and P both have 'the barons came away'.
[12] 1888 'curteis' (see Glossary).
[13] 1891 'Verwich': Södergård's IPN gives Warwick, but *Vita* reads *Eboracensis* (751B; *Life*, p. 155; and see Legge, *Background*, p. 60, note 2).

all went off together.]¹⁴ I don't know which route they took, nor how long they were on the journey,¹⁵ but when they arrived in Rome they were given a joyful welcome. They found the full council in progress, just as God had planned: the holy Pope Leo had called this meeting. He was making decrees and sitting in judgement on cases pertaining to Holy Church. God had arranged for the Great Senate to be assembled.¹⁶ It was as if they were there to decide about releasing Saint Edward from his vow. This is why God brought them together: he wanted to assure their king that it was by general agreement he should restrain his eagerness a little.

¶The messengers greeted the Pope and the others who were there. The whole reverend company was delighted at their coming; they were as joyfully received as if they had arrived from Heaven. All together they praise God, who fulfils to each his need and gives to each his desire, that such good people had found a gathering of such holy people. The Pope ordered room to be made for the messengers.¹⁷ Everybody is to be quiet and pay close attention, and all listen to the messengers. Then the messengers explained the vow that the king had sworn and the reason he made it: that God might give him back his kingdom. Now he had his land in joy and peace, he did not want to leave undone any longer the fulfilment of the vow he swore to God in his poverty. Then they tell of the people's grief, of their tears and groans, and of the crying and weeping of the poor folk whose only succour he was. They tell of the orphans' cries, how they weep and wail for their king so that none had ever seen or known such grief for a mortal man.¹⁸ There was not a soul in all the land who had not been overcome with grief or terror. The grief was for his departure, and the fear was that he would not return. Everybody wanted to die rather than let the king be separated from them, for they were certain of this: that the Danes would come again and destroy the land as they had done before. When the messengers had told all their errand, and asked for what they wanted, then all those who heard them were very glad of their request. They gave thanks to the King of Heaven for granting the king such good fortune, that he was so loved by his own and so feared by outsiders. When the Pope had heard of the vow and of the outcry that resulted from it, that the kingdom would perish if the king fulfilled his vow, [he ordered a plan of action, about what King Edward was to do;]¹⁹ then, with the assent of the reverend company and by their

---

14   1902 After this line, MS P adds 'Tot son afaire lor a dit Et il l'ont mis en lor escrit Et si l'ont bien enseelé Puis se sunt tot ensamble alé'.
15   1903–4 'Ço ne sai jo quel veie il pristrent Ne cumbien il all'eire mistrent': not in Aelred. It is typical of the Nun's confidence that she does not hesitate to say when she does not know something (for example, v. 1342 and note).
16   1913 'Le grant sené': this occurs again at v. 2009, and has a different origin from Aelred's 'synod' = 'meeting' (*Life* p. 155). I retain the Nun's suggestion of wise heads gathered together (see Glossary); in v. 1907 she calls it 'Un grant concilie'.
17   1934–6 In MS W three lines 'room to be made ... had to say' are only two: 'Que as messagiers tuz entendent Tant cum lur raisun et lur voler rendent' [that everybody should listen to the messengers, as well as their reason and will could do so].
18   1952 'Pur un seul hume': 'only a man', or 'just one man.' Here, as elsewhere, the Nun implicitly characterizes Edward as a type or imitation of Christ (see p. 5, above).
19   1974 MS P adds 'esgart a faire commanda Que li roys Edwar en fera'.

common judgement, he absolved the king of the vow and commanded him to stay at home. He was to look after his land for peace and common good; he was delivered of his bond by the holy authority of Saint Peter, his patron. He was to make a church in his name and furnish it with royal honour; he was to restore other churches and repair destroyed ones. The treasure he had gathered together, that he wanted to bring to Rome, he was to spend on the poor – in this manner he would make good his vow to God.

When the Pope had said this and confirmed it by his writ, the messengers asked for his blessing and then asked leave to depart from all who were there. Next, they went to see the relics of Saint Peter, and presented him with the gifts the king had entrusted to them when they left their country. They took leave of Saint Peter and went away well contented; they made all the haste they could until they arrived in England. They found their lord the king, who had assembled his council against their arrival – for it was known of in advance.[20] First they greeted the king, then they told and showed him from beginning to end all about the judgement of the Senate of Rome. Then they handed over the letters, and the greetings from the Pope. You can imagine how the people were burning with curiosity to hear the letters.[21] The king had the letters put into the common tongue and read to them.[22] This is how the letter began, that the Pope sent:

---

[20] See ch. 12.
[21] 2014 MS P has 'Et de la joie molt joiouse' [and beside themselves with joy], instead of 'E de briefs oïr curïuse'. In the previous line I translate 'veïsiez' (lit. 'you would see', a characteristic and very personal tag used by the Nun) as 'You can imagine ...'. Marzella makes much of the one place where Aelred (or whoever made the ω version) addresses a plural audience, remarking it as unique ('La tradizione', p. 363). Therefore we do not expect, even in the full critical edition when it appears, to find addresses to the audience scattered through the ω text; the Nun must certainly have added them.
[22] 2016 'en commun language': the Pope writes in Latin. Södergård notes that 'en commun language' means French, as spoken at court in c12 (when the Nun was writing); but it ought to mean 'English', because English was the common tongue in c11 (the date of the event). All three MSS have this passage; Aelred does not say the letter had to be translated (*Life*, p. 157).

Chapter 11
Pope Leo's Letter (2019–108)[1]

Introduction

Leo IX (1048–54) was Bruno, bishop of Toul, before his election. This letter is found in Edward's first charter (dated 5th January 1066).[2] There is no mention of the charter in notes to *Life*, *Estoire*, or *History*. Barlow says Aelred got the letters, including Edward's to Pope Nicholas in chapter 15, from Osbert (*Anon*, p. xxxvi); also that 'according to Westminster tradition' Edward was seeking papal privileges for the Abbey.[3] The Pope's instructions for the establishment of a 'congregation of monks' may be compared with instructions given by Nicholas in chapter 15, where the Rule of Benedict is cited (see my note to v. 2883). The Nun follows Aelred rather closely in this chapter, but the comment at the end is her own.

❧ ❧ ❧ ❧ ❧ ❧ ❧ ❧ ❧

¶'I, Leo, servant of God's servants: greetings and holy blessings to my dear son Edward the King, and for his good will towards me.

'We deem that your desire is praiseworthy, and acceptable to the King of Heaven whose goodness we admire in you, for we find that you are filled abundantly with it. For God is in every place and is close to all his supplicants;[4] the Apostles are members of him, and whatever their Head does, they also do. All those who ask their help, either in life or in death, they help them with God's help. Therefore know that they have not forgotten you. And so we say this to you, regarding your vow that we have heard about, that you want to depart from England to visit their relics in Rome.[5] We shall not permit you to do this because of the grave danger we perceive to your land, which will perish as soon as it is out of your sight. You preserve its noble freedom; rule it with justice, because of the good that we now see and the bad that we fear. Be absolved of your vow to God, and of all your other sins, by the authority of Jesus Christ as he said to his apostles: "Whatsoever thou shalt loose on earth shall be loosed

---

[1] *Vita*, 752A–C; *Life*, §11. Further, cf. *Estoire*, vv. 1655–722; *History*, pp. 74–5.
[2] Södergård, note to vv. 2019–102, refers to Dugdale, *Monasticon*, p. 293 (the 1970 reprint has the same page-numbers). The charter is pp. 293–5, and the letter prefaced *hanc epistolam mihi scripsit*.
[3] This likewise refers to Edward's letter to Nicholas; see *Anon*, p. 34 note 5. Södergård's note to vv. 2801–932 refers to Edward's third charter (same date); see *Monasticon*, pp. 295–7: this contains both letters including the Pope's reply (see introduction to ch. 15).
[4] Ps. 145:18 (144 in *LV*). Aelred cites Prov. 8:15 in the preceding sentence.
[5] 2037–8 MS P reads, instead of the above: 'De saint Piere mon avoé Que a requere aves voé' [of Saint Peter my protector, whom you have promised to visit].

in heaven."[6] By this authority we receive power from God to absolve you of your vow.

'And we command you further, by holy obedience instead of true penance:[7] you must spend on the poor the goods you gathered together over many days, that you would have spent on the long journey to fulfil your vow. And we lovingly advise you yet further: you must make a new church in the name of Saint Peter and in his honour, where there shall be placed a congregation of very holy monks to glorify the place. If you do not wish to do this, restore an old one, then make a church rich in rents and good possessions. Endow it from your own estates with so much that the good men[8] will have enough to drink, to eat, and to clothe themselves, that they may be ready to serve God. As they do service to God and honour to the holy Apostle, so shall your holy memory be celebrated with glory in Heaven. Whatsoever you endow the church with shall be established and vouchsafed by God and his saints, and by us; then let it be confirmed by you. Whatsoever you shall find in the church, and whatsoever you shall place there of your own, let it remain there for ever so that none shall suffer want. Let it be inhabited by holy monks, and revered, for ever. In no wise do we allow it to be placed in the care of laymen, but only a sovereign of the land, to whom it must appeal for its rights.[9] You shall establish such privileges there that God shall be worshipped in that place; to this end we grant and confirm in God's name that all who gainsay these things or wrongly falsify them shall be eternally cursed and have damnation without end.'[10]

This was the whole text of the letter, and as soon as it had been spoken then everybody who had been in despair regained their peace of mind. The king rejoiced at it, and all the others rejoiced for their king.

---

[6] Matt. 16:19 (Christ's words to Peter authorize the giving of absolution for sins); this Gospel quotation reappears in the next chapter. Two Bible references are retained in this paragraph, neither deleted nor paraphrased.
[7] 2058 'En liu de veire penitence': 'penitence' can mean *either* 'penitence' *or* 'penance': the context shows which (see Glossary). The Pope refers to penance enjoined by a priest as reparation for sin, in this case, Edward's failure to keep his vow. Repentance is the regret or compunction felt by a sinner, not the reparation to be performed. Aelred's 'obedience *and* repentance' is subtly different (*Life*, p. 157).
[8] 2074 'les seignurs': it is not always Latin *seniores* that the Nun is rendering. Aelred says *fratribus* [for its brothers], *Life* 158. Elsewhere she translates *monachorum* as 'seignurs' (I write 'good men' in the next chapter, for example).
[9] 2094 Södergård notes the use of 'estuet' in this line.
[10] 2103–8 The following, to end the chapter, is added by the Nun.

Chapter 12

Saint Peter and the Hermit (2109–284)[1]

Introduction

This story is another that shows Edward is not alone in having visions (see chapter 4), even in his lifetime. There will be many beneficent and healing dreams later, after Edward's death. MP, like Aelred, ends the Pope's letter without comment (see above), but begins the section corresponding to this one with an introductory passage. By comparison with Aelred, the Nun above all stresses feelings of love, between Saint Peter and Edward, as well as between Peter and the hermit. Osbert names the latter Wlsino (*Osbert*, p. 80).

❧ ❧ ❧ ❧ ❧ ❧ ❧ ❧ ❧

¶Saint Peter, the noble lord, who was the reason for their anxiety, wanted to increase their joy and reassure Saint Edward. For before the messengers returned – they were not yet far departed from Rome – Saint Peter appeared to a man who was his intimate friend.[2] For some years this man had been enclosed beneath the earth in shadowy seclusion. Beneath the earth, he wanted to avoid what he saw reigning on the earth: pride, folly, and covetousness; hate and wicked cunning. He wanted to abandon it all, that he saw so much on earth; this is why he hid himself under earth. But God in Heaven was his friend: Saint Peter appeared to him, with sweet voice and pious looks. He told him of the messengers, and of the letter, in these words:

'King Edward, my friend,[3] has just lately sent to Rome because of a vow he made before, when he was in exile, in distress: that he would come to visit my relics as soon as he had established his land in peace. Then he wanted to carry out his vow, by good works and good will. He saw in his people their great trouble, and their desperate anxiety. Because of this great trouble he saw, and he being the only cause of it, the king sent to Rome: he wanted to be advised about the matter, and what he should do about it, whether he should stay or go. But by my authority he is absolved from the vow that he swore.[4] The Pope in a letter tells him – and commands him as penance – to make a church in my name, but the command comes from me. I want him to follow his counsel, if he acts as my faithful servant. He has always loved me

---

[1] *Vita*, 752D–4A; *Life*, §12. Cf. *Estoire*, vv. 1723–876; *History*, pp. 75–7.
[2] 2116 'un umme ki ert sun dru': Aelred says he was *dilectus Deo et hominibus* [beloved of God and human beings], *Life* p. 158. The word 'dru(e)' is often used of lovers, and 'drüerie' of romantic love (see Glossary). Such affective language, and emphasis on God's love, is typical of the Nun. Aelred points out that the man knew nothing of what had happened; the Nun omits the comment here, only to make more of the fact later.
[3] 2131 'li miens amis': Aelred's Peter does not call Edward his friend.
[4] 2148 The line 'he is absolved ... he swore' is missing from MS W (the sense would be 'by my authority the Pope tells him ...'). It thus lacks the reference to Matt. 16:19, which is also in Aelred.

very dearly, therefore he chose me as patron. In his land I have a church that once had many goods and possessions,[5] but because of the sin of the people the place is now hideously destroyed. From rich it has become poor; from high it has become low. Once it was noble and honoured; now it is poor and dishonoured. This place is near to London, it was in the western part;[6] it was chosen and loved for me, but now it is changed from its former renown. I revisited it from Heaven, and dedicated it with my own hands.[7] God has worked many miracles there, for the sake of me who so loved the place. I commend this place to my Edward, that he may soon give it some attention, and enrich my house with religious monks; make fine buildings there for me, and I shall put my blessing in the place. He is to establish lands with endowments, and establish the good men lavishly. This place shall be the door of Heaven, for God shall make it his house.[8] Those who wish to ascend to Heaven will be able to find a ladder there by which they may come to it – by doing good, with perfect desire.[9] By this ladder the angels will descend, to carry back to God the pious prayers of the people he holds dear. I shall open the door to Heaven to my friends whom I know to be there. And as far as my task is concerned – to bind and to unbind – with which Jesus our Saviour anointed me by his great sweetness, there I shall unbind the bound, and receive the unbound. Because they shall be justified and amended of their sins, the door of Heaven shall be open that before was closed because of their undeserving.[10] And to you I command, and I pray, that what you have heard from me you will please put in writing and send quickly to King Edward, so he may be assured that his vow has been pardoned him – he will do more devoutly whatever is according to my command. In my love he will be the more complete, and in my service the more submissive.'

¶When Saint Peter had said this, he went away wherever it pleased him [he vanished suddenly, and went up into Paradise].[11] The good man made no delay, but soon called

---

[5] 2153–8 The lines 'I want him to follow ... and possessions' omitted in MS P; readers would have to guess which church was meant.

[6] 2166 'En la partie estait del west': 'west' spelt as in English. This tells us nothing about the Nun's native language: the pronunciation of French 'ouest' is similar, so it suggests no more than that the word was used thus in French as written by the scribe (see Södergård's note to v. 2506). MS W has 'est' [east], a mistake: Aelred writes *in occidentali parte* (*Life*, p. 159).

[7] See ch. 14, Mellit and the Fisherman.

[8] See Gen. 28:17 (& 12, for the ladder).

[9] 2186 'parfit desir'; 'parfit' can for once be translated as 'perfect' (see Glossary). MS P reads 'avec bon desir', meaning with good will, or virtuous as opposed to wicked desire.

[10] This passage follows Aelred quite closely, with biblical references: Matt. 16:19, Heb. 11:13–16, Ps. 118:19 (117 in *LV*).

[11] 2214 'Si s'en ala, si cum li plout'; MS P adds, less mysteriously, 'Il s'en est tost esvanis Si s'en monta en paradis' (after v. 2213). The Nun stresses the visitor's supernatural character. Cf. Aelred: *lux con loquente disparuit* [The light disappeared with the one speaking] (*Life*, p. 160). *Estoire* also mentions light, in the saint's bright face, which disappears when he does: 'of la luür Desparuit devant le jour' (vv. 1748, 1813–14). 'He disappeared with the light [that had appeared with him], before day broke' is my translation, slightly more exact; cf. *History*, p. 76: 'he disappeared before the first light of approaching day'. See also Introduction, From Latin to Medieval French.

a scribe who put everything into writing that he had just heard and seen.[12] Then he delivered it to the messenger, who carried it to King Edward. He came to the king that day, as God had planned, the same day that the messengers came back to announce the decision from Rome. As soon as their letter was read through and they had spoken the whole of their message, here comes this man running![13] He came close up towards the king, rendered greetings to the king and his entourage, and straightaway held out his letter to him. With great joy the letter was read, for they had great joy to hear it. Everybody holds up their hands to Heaven and gives thanks to God for the letter. They give thanks to Saint Peter, who has done so much for his friend, who has so greatly honoured him and comforted his people. They join their hearts the more to God, and move away the more from doing evil. Certainly nobody can be in any doubt about this sign: for how would the good man know what they had done in Rome, he who was near Worcester and who stayed underground all the time, nor know which day the messengers were to come back to King Edward – unless he knew it by God? He could not know it by man.[14] King Edward believed it fully, and all his people did too. All the wealth he had gathered, with which he had intended to go to Rome, he spent upon God's poor, as he was commanded to in the letter. To restore the church of Saint Peter – to this he bent all his thoughts.

He paid for the work from his own treasury: wherever he saw need he paid in full. Then he remitted the tribute, to be held quit for ever, that the people had paid in the days of his father when the Danes first arrived.[15] When that taxation by the crown was set up, everybody was bound by it; he generously freed them from this unbearable burden.[16] Thus he liberated his country and gladdened all his people. Day by day his bounty increased, from better to best. The King of Heaven, who created him to be like this and who placed such great good in his person, that he was able to rule the land so well and that he had no equal in the land, wanted his virtues to blossom so that they would bear celestial fruit. He enjoyed abundance of the world's good, and of Heaven's good, as God demonstrated by the cripple he healed through him. We shall tell you of this next, according to what we know of the story.

---

[12] 2218 MS P reads 'que sains Pieres lui ot dit' [what Saint Peter had told him].
[13] 2227 'Este vus cestui vint errant': Aelred does not include this tiny word-picture (*Life*, p. 160), an example of the Nun's livelier style.
[14] Cf. *Life*, p. 161: Aelred writes this passage in the indicative; the Nun recasts it more dramatically as a rhetorical question.
[15] 2261 'le treü': the notorious Danegeld. See, for example, *History*: notes to vv. 923–7, 955 & 957, 1884–9.
[16] In Aelred, the following resembles *apostrophe* rather than description (*Life*, p. 161); the Nun deletes several Bible references, to stress the results of Edward's virtue.

Chapter 13
Gille Michel the Cripple (2285–480)[1]

Introduction

The cripple's name is of some interest: Gille Michel, or Gillemichel, is one of the common devotional names of Gaelic origin.[2] Originally such a name (meaning Servant of [Saint] Michael), and others like it, was given to dedicate a child to a chosen saint. However, by the twelfth century, such names could well have lost their etymological meaning when used outside a Gaelic-speaking society and had become ordinary forenames like any other (many are now family names or surnames).[3]

The *PL* text gives it as all one word (*Life*, p. 162). *Estoire* gives it in two parts (v. 1927), as the Nun does: Guil Michel. It is not clear why both Anglo-Norman writers, independently of each other, separate the name into two parts, nor why the later text introduces the spelling Gu-. *Estoire*'s editor makes no note on the name; the IPN entry reads 'Guil Michel (Gilla Michael)' without further explanation. Although no variant spellings are printed in Södergård's edition, the online texts give the following: MS V 'Gille Michel'; MS W 'Gille Michiel; and MS P 'Ghile Micel'; the prose version spells it 'Gile Michiel'. None matches the Gu- spelling found in *Estoire*, but all are two words instead of Aelred's one. The Nun's spelling resembles the French Gilles [Giles]; MP's spelling appears to be a confusion with William [Guillaume]. These, together with any idea that the man had been nicknamed 'Boy' ('gille' can mean 'lad', *inter al.*; see below), are all very wide of the mark.

Loss of the original and correct semantic content may explain a misunderstanding found in two other medieval Latin texts. A margin note in one manuscript of *Vita*, described by Marzella, reads *Gyllmychel, id est, filius Michaelis, Hybernice* [that is, son of Michael].[4] There is another person of this name in Simeon's History: he is *Gillomichael ... id est, puer Michaelis*; though, it goes on to say, he were better called the devil's boy.[5] Here, the Latin word for 'boy' could mean 'son', or indeed 'servant'. These two passages show that names in Gil or Gille were susceptible of being misunderstood even in contemporary writing.[6] The word (or rather, the half-name) must have been rendered into Latin as *puer*, which can mean lad, servant, and also son – hence the misreading *filius*. It is curious that confusion with modern 'gillie',

---

[1] *Vita*, 754A–5D; *Life* §13. Cf. *Estoire*, vv. 1919–2022; *History*, pp. 78–9.
[2] I thank Dauvit Broun, Linda Gowans, and Frances White for their help here.
[3] For modern Anglicized forms such as Gilchrist, Gilmory, and so on, see Yonge, *History of Christian Names*, pp. lxv & 259–63.
[4] 'La tradizione', p. 352.
[5] *Historia Ecclesiæ Dunhelmensis* ed. Arnold, Lib. III, Cap. XVI (*c.* 1071); this is obviously not the same person as the cripple in our story.
[6] I thank Graham Edwards for his useful comments.

which ought to be irrelevant in a twelfth-century text, has some parallel in other Latin writing of the period.

Given the currency of names such as Gillemichel, any suggestion that the name means he was a gillie, or servant, because of the modern definition (OED *s.v.* ghillie) is misleading (*History*, note to vv. 1927–8). Baswell, cited in *History*'s note, makes no comment on the name except to call the fellow 'Michel' for short, which is incorrect.[7] The man's name does not mean Michael who happened to be a servant in his twelfth-century story.

Aelred remarks that the man's name is *secundum proprietatem linguae illius* (that is, the Irish language). The translation renders Aelred's remark as 'according to the peculiarities' of the language; but in the context I would judge that 'after the manner' of their language would be a better rendering, because there is nothing 'peculiar' about it. The Nun makes no comment on the language; in any case she is generally less interested in names than he is.

The Nun follows Aelred fairly closely. Södergård remarks that many changes are 'pour les besoins de la versification' (p. 29). However, her style often differs more markedly than the needs of the verse might call for. Aelred expresses the scene, where the cripple rides on the king, in a sort of hymn of praise [O necklace splendid with every gem! O precious torque ...] which is more dramatic but somehow less descriptive than the Nun's homely and even comic picture, where the king's own feeling rather than that of the writer is stressed: 'Never was precious golden necklace so delightful to the king as this poor fellow's hands ...'. We may contrast Aelred's evocation of David and Michal, and of Saint Martin (*Life* pp. 163–4), with the Nun's burlesque evocation of a horse-race or tournament, and people cheering both steed and rider. In addition, the Nun replaces the cripple's support, a small stool [*scamnum*], with crutches [*eschameus*]. This picture of the man dragging himself about is easier to envisage than Aelred's, and, hanging in the church afterwards, the crutches provide a more descriptive symbol of a cripple's cure.

¶ King Edward was staying in London, his royal city. Close by is Westminster, which is wholly dedicated to Saint Peter. The king loved the place, for love of his patron Saint Peter. Wherever he was, far or near, his thought was always close to it. One day, when the king was there, a cripple arrived. This unfortunate man was Irish, and his name was Gille Michel. He had no use of his legs, and indeed they were nothing but an encumbrance to him: the tendons at the backs of his knees were seized up so that his legs were cramped in behind his thighs. And his thighs were twisted back towards his loins, so his heels were impacted and growing into the flesh of his behind. His whole body, below the belt, was a mass of almost one single limb; his limbs were so welded together that the whole body was deformed. He crawled

---

[7] 'King Edward and the Cripple'.

painfully into the king's court as best he could, with the help of two little crutches that he wielded with his hands. His body was so burdensome to him that he went about dragging it behind him; everybody who saw him like this was moved with horror and pity for him. He was not merely crippled, for he had many other ailments. One was the torment of his poverty, that had rendered him close to death; another was a dreadful weakness that mounted in him day by day. In this suffering and agony, he crawled feebly across the court. Luckily he met Hugelin and accosted him;[8] this man was the king's chamberlain and privy to all his secrets. He wanted to walk on past, but the other began to call him, saying,

'Hugelin, my friend, have you no more pity for me than this? Can't you be sorry for a wretch so horribly afflicted?'

The chamberlain responded, 'What do you want me to do for you, friend?'

The other said, 'Have you ever seen such a human carcass! I've been to Rome six times like this, and I've prayed to the body of Saint Peter for the health I'm longing for, but to this day I'm without it. I'll get it when God wants me to. It wasn't refused to me there, but Saint Peter has deferred it. He's delayed healing my body so as to demonstrate Edward's saintliness. He'll be his collaborator in the deed, because of his great devotion. I've been to Rome six times, and I now feel the need to go for a seventh time in case I can get some good there. I heard a command from the Apostle, that I must come straight to the king and tell this message without embarrassment: the king must make himself humble enough to carry my body on his back, from the chamber as far as the church that's been established in Saint Peter's name. If the king is willing to carry me there, I can get my health back; my limbs will be completely healed as soon as they touch his.'

¶Hugelin went off immediately. He told the king everything he had heard. King Edward was delighted, and thanked the King of Heaven. [You must believe it as true: he was overjoyed, and he raised his hands to God on high];[9] he said he would willingly do what Saint Peter had commanded. The poor man was soon called, and then he came to the chamber. The king awaited him humbly, and was very glad as soon as he saw him.[10] He had no peace in his heart until the moment he had him on his back. This man was neither stupid nor boorish, he linked his hands around the king's neck and hugged him close, and the king was overjoyed. The dirty hands settle on his chest, and the deformed arms clasp him.[11] The filthy torn clothes are pressed close to the royal robes. Never was precious golden necklace so delightful to the king as this poor fellow's hands, to which he bent his neck. He embraced the royal bosom and had

---

8   2326 For Hugelin, see note to v. 1027.
9   2368 After this line, MS P adds: 'Sacies de voir molt s'esjoi A deus ses mains al ciel tendi'.
10 2374 Instead of this line, MS P reads: 'Et li contrais les bras tendi' [and the cripple held out his arms].
11 2381–2 Rhyme-words 'sient' [settled] and 'apriment' [clasped]. Södergård finds this the only example of assonance in the poem. He judges it unlikely to be authorial, because MS P reads 'Ses ordes mains al piz li furent Ses bras sor les espaules jurent'; 'furent' [were] and 'jurent' [lay] are true rhyme. Neither is markedly closer than the other to Aelred's 'he has his filthy hands and scaly arms clasped around the royal breast and neck' (*Life* p. 163), and so not much can be concluded from the different reading.

a right noble ride. Then you could see people gathering to watch the tourney. The king went forth at a good speed, and the cripple held on well. Then you could see the king roundly mocked, and laughter caused a riot. [The people took him for a madman, because he had the cripple on his shoulders.][12] They said he was too simple to realise his shame at the hands of a peasant, who had tricked him into carrying him on his back. Such goodness and kindness they judged in him to be folly.[13] But however they mocked and however they laughed, King Edward finished the course. But before getting into the church, and even before getting very far from the palace, the sufferer's tendons relaxed to give free circulation to his blood. Now it took its natural course, and ran through the veins everywhere. His bones were washed with it, and were adorned with new flesh. His bones hid themselves under the flesh, and the flesh over them revived. His flesh quickly warmed up, as soon as it was given the drink of blood. His heels came away from where they had been stuck. When the cripple felt this, he stretched his legs downwards. The blood streams from the wretched body, and poison pours out of his wounds. This filthy matter of his weakness soaked into the royal vestments. Then everybody called out to the king that he had carried him far enough: the cripple was straightened, and his royal clothes were filthy.[14] They urged him to put him down, to throw the filth into the road. But the king had not forgotten what he had first been ordered to do. He carried him right up to the high altar and presented him to the King of Heaven; with gentle mien he presented him to Saint Peter, his own lord. The sacristans who were there received him from his shoulders, and they washed his wounds; God healed them very quickly after that. When he could walk without pain, and sit down and get up again easily, then they gave him back to the king and everybody praised the name of God. The king fits him out handsomely; then gives him as much of his own money, that he will have enough to spend on the journey to Rome, on his pilgrimage.

¶He took his leave of the king, and then he set off on his journey. He thanked Saint Peter warmly for having healed him, through the king, so well. The crutches, that he used to crawl with when he could not walk, were hung up in Westminster as witness to the deed. The king was overjoyed because of it, and so were all his people. If he loved the apostle so much before, [to serve him, and to do good to the poor so as to please God better,][15] now he laboured even more in his love; he was devoted to the saint's place, and he devoted himself and his goods to honouring it. To this end he bent all his efforts: to refurbish Westminster for his patron Saint Peter, who had loved it above all the places anywhere on earth. Therefore he made this request to the king, that for his love he should love the place and glorify it above all others. He loved it most dearly, especially for the wonders that he saw there and that he had

---

[12] 2396 Instead of 'E meint ris fait desordené', MS P reads 'Meint ris et maint gabois jeter' [they hurled laughter and jeers]. It then adds 'La gent le tenoient pour fol Qar le contrait out sor son col'.
[13] 2401 MS P reads 'His shame and his great dishonour they judged ...'.
[14] 2428 MS W reads 'vermeilliez' [reddened, crimsoned].
[15] 2459 MS P adds 'De lui servire et de bien faire As povres pour a Dieu meius plaire' after this line.

heard about; Saint Peter had performed them there once upon a time, in the good old days that were now passed away.[16] I should like to tell you about one among them all[17] – though it does not belong to my subject: nobody could hear it without delight, provided they had a longing for God.

---

[16] Cf. the passage in ch. 17 (The King's Evil), contrasting 'good old days' and now.
[17] 2477 'Un de tuz en vuldrai dire': Södergård notes 'vuldrai' as an anglicism; he refers to several other instances.

Chapter 14

Mellit and the Fisherman (2481–696)[1]

Introduction

The Nun follows the Latin source fairly closely, although vv. 2584–90 are amplification. See below: 'but with differing powers: one fished to cure souls; the other, fish to feed bodies. One, sustenance for the souls of the people, the other for their bodies. Very different were their intentions, and their powers were not the same'. Also notable is her variation on the celebrated pun of the Gospels (vv. 2623–4, and see Glossary): 'Jo sui numé Pieres, ami, Od mes piers ...'. This is interesting not only for her added Bible reference but also because she does not usually make much of names.

Edelbert [Ethelbert] was king of Kent, 560–616; Sexbert [Sebert] king of Essex, d. 616 (*Life*, p. 165). Among Westminster foundation stories, Aelred's is the first to make Sebert founder of both St Paul's and St Peter's (*History*, note to vv. 2049–52). Södergård's Analyse says Edelbert planned the churches (p. 6), but it seems clear that Sexbert was responsible for them: one inside, and another outside, London. The story of a new church being dedicated, before the ceremony can be held, by supernatural hands may be a common hagiographic theme.[2] Traditionally this dedication took place in the days of Mellit (*Osbert*, p. 7), a Life of whom was written by Goscelin. Mellit (Mellitus) was a Roman abbot sent by Gregory in 601. He was the first bishop of London, and Augustine made him bishop of the East Saxons in 604.[3]

❧ ❧ ❧ ❧ ❧ ❧ ❧ ❧ ❧

¶In the time of good King Edelbert and of his nephew Sexbert, these kings were converted by Augustine, the friend of God.[4] The uncle king was in Kent; the nephew stayed in London. It was the principal seat of his realm. There the king was inspired to make a church within the walls, to be established in the name of Saint Paul. He wanted to make it a bishop's seat, so as to bring great honour to the church. He made Saint Mellit bishop, with great honour and great joy. Saint Mellit was a very good man: he came from Rome with Saint Augustine, who turned England to God, the same that Saint Gregory sent. King Sexbert was worthy and wise, and also he was of great virtue. Then the king had an idea, that as he had honoured Saint Paul he wanted to honour Saint Peter – he would make a church in his name. Outside the walls of the city, to the west,[5] the king founded a church in honour of Saint Peter – which he

---

[1] *Vita*, 755D-7C; *Life*, §14. Cf. *Estoire*, vv. 2042–265; *History*, pp. 79–83.
[2] See William of Malmesbury, *Kings* tr. Stephenson, §25 (p. 23).
[3] See also *ODS*; and Mirk, *Festial*: SS Peter and Paul, vol. I:45, notes on dedication of churches in vol. II.
[4] 2484 MS P reads 'Par saint Augustin lor ami' [by their friend Saint Augustine].
[5] 2506–8 The abbey was originally built on Thorney Island (Södergård notes 'west' here). MS W omits v. 2507.

ever after held most dear. The king granted it great lands and established many rich rents. Then came the time when it pleased God it should be dedicated. People came from near and far; they prepared whatever was necessary for the proceedings of such a high day, for the place and for the love of God. Saint Mellit was very thoughtful, and all night was attentive to the ordering and preparation of what he would need next day. The people were happy about it all, though they were far from true faith. They attended the dedication, even though they did not believe in God – more to see the marvels than out of devotion – and because they had never before seen anything like it they were the more joyful.[6]

That night a fisherman had put his boat into the Thames, that ran right there beneath the church. He got into it, to go fishing. The boat went towards the other bank and arrived quickly. There Saint Peter appeared to him, dressed like a pilgrim, and told him he would have a good reward if he would take him across the water. He willingly agreed, and Saint Peter got in with him. When they came to the other side, the apostle got out of the boat, then he went into the church – the fisherman saw it all. When the apostle had entered, he soon showed the power of God. From Heaven came a brightness that lit up the place. Its splendour was so abundant that night was turned to day. To join the apostle came that noble company of citizens of Heaven above, over whom reigns King Jesus. The angels and the saints go ahead, with bright radiance and with sweet song. In earth there is no mouth that can tell how sweet was the melody, how complete was the joy, how beautiful was this light. Who can tell the sweetness of the heavenly fragrance, when the celestial nobles accompanied the terrestrial?[7] All the earth rejoiced at it, and gloried in the glorious. There the angels go up and down,[8] and give back the song from heaven to earth. [The place was sanctified from top to bottom, and dedicated by the holy angels.][9] When Saint Peter with his company had dedicated the Abbey, and done what he had to do that pertained to the dedication, then he turned back to the boat of the fisherman who had transported him. This man had been so frightened he was nearly out of his wits. His frail body cannot endure to see nor hear such things. So Saint Peter gently comforts him and brings him back to his senses. He brought his boat to land, and one fisherman went with the other.[10] The two fishermen went into the boat – but with differing powers: one fished to cure souls; the other, fish to feed bodies. One, sustenance for the souls of the people, the other for their bodies. Very different were their intentions, and their powers were not

---

[6] *Life*, p. 166: the Nun makes more than Aelred does of Mellit's sleepless night and of the people's ignorant wonder.
[7] 2561–4 Aelred does not cast this as a question; cf. the Nun's more dramatic style (the word-play on 'glorious', below, is intentional).
[8] 2567 Aelred has 'as if on Jacob's ladder' (*Life*, p. 167); the Nun prefers, instead, the idea of giving back the song. See Gen. 28:12.
[9] 2568 After this line, MS P adds: 'Li lieus fu toz saintefiés Et des sains angeles dediés'.
[10] 2582 'l'un peschur od l'altre vait': cf. the fishermen of the Gospels. Laurent considers this 'allegory' remarkable (*Plaire et édifier*, pp. 215–18). In fact, the Nun is following Aelred, who refers to Peter as 'the great fisher of men' (*Life*, p. 167; see Matt. 4:19); although she elaborates, contrasting sustenance for the soul with sustenance for the body, below.

the same. Then Saint Peter remembered the dear sayings of his master Jesus. How could he forget his sayings, whom he knew how to love so sweetly? How could he lose the memory of that wherein his whole desire lay?[11] So sweet was the sweet Jesus, his heart was so sweetened that the bitterness of sin nevermore took the place of the sweetness. Therefore he cannot but remember the sweet sayings of his sweet friend. He addressed his companion, and said to him:

'Haven't you anything to eat?'[12]

'No, indeed,' he replied. 'I caught nothing, because I was here, waiting for you. I was certain of my promised reward, and so I didn't want to go to work.'

Immediately Saint Peter said to him, with gentle look and kindly manner:

'Let out your nets, put them in position.'

And he did so, in his usual way. Quickly the net was so laden that he could scarcely draw it towards him. He pulls the fish to the bank, and puts them in the boat with great satisfaction. Saint Peter said to the fisherman:

'Take the very biggest of the fish – you shall carry it to Saint Mellit. You are to present it to him, from me. The others shall be your reward, that I promised you for your crossing. I am named Pierre, friend; with my peers[13] I came down from Heaven to dedicate this, my church, which is established here in my name – and by my own authority I have sanctified this place. I hastened more than the bishop did, for I dedicated it before him! You will tell him tomorrow, friend, all you have seen and heard. He will see such a sign in the church, by which he will believe your words. It will no longer be necessary for him to set his hand to it, nor undertake to dedicate it, but as soon as he performs the service that day – tomorrow – in the church, and then says the sermon to the people, so he gives them my blessing. Let him reassure them and tell them that in this place they shall have my help. I shall often hear the prayers of God's faithful, whom I know to be here; so I shall open the great door of Paradise to my friends.[14] Those who live here chastely shall never find it closed.' With this, Saint Peter went away; soon afterwards, the dawn broke.[15]

¶Saint Mellit rose in the morning; he had thought much during the night about performing the dedication so as to please God and the people. The fisherman met him and presented him with the fish. Then, from beginning to end, he told him what he had seen and heard of Saint Peter. The bishop was overjoyed, and marvelled greatly at it. He had the doors of the church opened, and saw that what he had told him was true. They found the two alphabets, which had been properly set out. They found the

---

[11] 2595–6 The second of the two questions is omitted in MS P as if deemed unnecessary.
[12] This conflates episodes in Luke 5:1–7 and John 21:5–11 (see also *Life*, p. 167).
[13] 2623–4 'Jo sui numé Pieres, ami, Od mes piers ...': Aelred's Peter mentions 'fellow-citizens' [*cum meis concivibus*] (*Life*, p. 168) without punning. See also v. 2916.
[14] Aelred cites Titus 2:12, about the sober, the upright, and the godly; the Nun's saint says he will open Heaven to his friends (her mention of friends is typical; cf. *Life*, p. 168).
[15] 2650 MS P reads, instead, 'Après molt tost l'abei trova' [Soon he came to, or found, the abbey] – perhaps to recheck his night's work. This chapter uses the words abbey *and* church, so 'abei' is a not unlikely reading (this spelling not listed in *AND*, but see 'abeie'). At v. 2885, P has 'aves' for MS V 'habez'; the latter corrected to 'abés' [abbots].

twelve crosses, that were anointed with holy oil. Of the twelve candles, they found the remainder fixed to the crosses. The church was still wet with the scattered holy water.[16] As soon as they had seen this, they believed all the rest completely. None could have any doubt, now God had assured them of it. Saint Mellit went to the people and recounted this miracle. As soon as he went, he told them, then he showed them what he had already seen. Straightaway they praised the King of Heaven, and for joy and piety they wept – that by this holy dedication he had given faith to his people.[17] The fisherman and all his lineage, father and son, thenceforth used to reckon the tithe of their fish and take it to Westminster. But nevertheless one of them held this back, for his own gain, and it so happened that he was never able to catch fish again until he had begged for Saint Peter's pardon.[18] When Saint Edward heard of the miracle I have told here[19] – by writing and by re-telling – he took much trouble to cherish the place. He made the church, and he had houses built, to draw rich rents for the establishment.

---

[16] 2663–70 'Les deos abeces ... Les. XII. cruiz ... Des dudce cirges ... encore arusee': this conforms to the ritual of consecrating a church (*Life*, p. 168 and note). The alphabets may in some cases have been painted or drawn (MS P has, for v. 2664, 'Les letres mult bien painturé'). The crosses are incised, not free-standing, and candles stuck onto them. 'La remasille' [the remainder]: this means they had been lit, by no mortal hand, and had been burning all night (*History*, notes to vv. 2194–203 & 2204–5). Södergård's glossary gives 'chandelier' for 'cirges'; but candlesticks would not have been used.
[17] 2679–82 MS P replaces the foregoing with 'Les remansilles des candoilles Moustra les gens dont ont merveilles' [He showed them the remains of the candles, at which they marvelled].
[18] Aelred's chapter ends here, citing Acts 5:1–5; he begins the next chapter with a rather longer account, including several Bible references, of Edward's response to the miracle. The Nun ends with the following, adding personal comment.
[19] 2692 'Le miracle qu'a' (corr. 'ai' or 'ay') cunté ci': see Campsey website. Two of three online versions have first-person form, which makes better sense than third-person: who but the Nun has told it?

Chapter 15

A Visit to Pope Nicholas (2697-960)[1]

Introduction

Södergård says this chapter is a free reproduction of Aelred's text. The Nun makes more of Edward's thoughts before preparing his letter, and omits some Bible references. Personal touches include her linking sentence between the two letters. Södergård makes one section of Aelred's three; there is much to be said for either arrangement, although putting it all together makes good sense. This papal letter, like the earlier one, seems to be historical. Södergård says, correctly, that the Pope's letter appears in Edward's third charter dated 5th January 1066; he refers to Dugdale, vol. I, pp. 296-7 (his note to vv. 2801-932). In fact both letters appear in that third charter: Edward's to Pope Nicholas, and the Pope's reply (the former, vv. 2753-98, receives no mention in Södergård's notes). The text of the letters corresponds closely to Aelred's Latin.[2] Nicholas II (1059-61) succeeded Benedict X, who had been appointed 'in an irregular manner' (Södergård's same note), and who gave the pallium to Stigand when the latter took over the archbishopric of Canterbury.

☙ ☙ ☙ ☙ ☙ ☙ ☙ ☙ ☙

¶Then it came to his mind that he would like to have it confirmed, what he had given to the church and what he had found there, by the Roman authority of the Pope and the Senate:[3] that the church would keep its rights, as God permitted to the world. The king was still in doubt about the vow that he had once made. He often thought about the Judgement, where all the world would be gathered, and he often felt great fear of the stern and merciful Judge: stern to those who have abandoned him, and merciful to those who do his will. The king often thought about this, and in himself he trusted for nothing, for he was never in that place but God was before his eyes. He knew and understood that God sees into all hearts;[4] he did his works and his will as best he could to please God. Even though he had been released from the vow he formerly made, he still felt doubt, and felt puzzled in his mind. And he had another good reason for wishing to send to Rome: he wanted to petition the Pope for his churches of England, for the king to take care of them all, and to have rights in everything – church and lay people – that each one should hold to the rules. He sent an archbishop, who chose two to go with him. One was to serve at Hereford,

---

[1] *Vita*, 757C-60B; *Life*, §15-17. Cf. *Estoire*, vv. 2324-513; *History*, pp. 83-5.
[2] See Dugdale, *Monasticon*, pp. 295-7, for the whole charter; cf. introduction to ch. 11.
[3] 2702 See Glossary for 'sené'.
[4] 2717-18 omitted in MS P; MS W has 'tuz les suens veit' [sees all his own].

15 A Visit to Pope Nicholas (2697–960) 115

the other at Wells, as I remember;[5] they were leaving England for this purpose, they were to be consecrated at Rome. One was named Gise, and the other Walter. The archbishop was named Aldret, and he was of York. [He carried with him documents and letters from the king, and showed them to the Pope, in order to find out about what the king wanted.][6] They found the Pope, who was at the Lateran Council that he had convened,[7] just as God arranged it. They were welcomed warmly and received with great joy. Next, they presented their letters, and told their wishes for the other things.[8] The letter that the king sent began like this:

¶'To our lord and father,[9] vicar of God, to govern and take care of Holy Church and feed us as his children. Edward, who takes care of the English, titled king by the grace of God, sends greetings, and does homage in good will tempered with good sense. Let us praise God who takes care of the world,[10] who is so mindful of us to have placed our holy mother Church in the guardianship of such a father; you who have been given the holy seat that Saint Leo had before you. By your great holiness, and in our weakness, [we beseech your high wisdom to reinforce our powerlessness, so that we may serve God fitly, in deed, in desire, and in thought. Your works and your knowledge, Your advice and your might][11] – we beg you to grant us what he [Leo] who was before you granted us, and then to confirm what you have granted us. Please do as we beg you. By his command I built a Minster, because of a vow I once swore that I would go to Rome as soon as I could. For the absolution of all my sins, by which I was released from my vow, I honoured that church and glorified it in the name of Saint Peter. We beg for your confirmation of everything we have placed there. Improve and enhance our privileges, and renew them, that the church may have its dignity as long as humankind shall endure. And I, as long as I live, shall surely take care of it with the accustomed wealth it has been used to enjoy in England. I have placed my royal gifts at the disposal of Saint Peter our patron. I send to you, to urge you to consent to pray for us, for my people and for my land, that God will protect us from war. With great honours, perform a commemoration of his feast, in presence of the saint's relics.'

---

5   2736 'cum jo record'. It is typical of the Nun, who presumably has Aelred's text before her, to say 'as I remember'. 'record' provides a rhyme for 'Hereford', but such fillers often have a special use: providing a sense of immediacy and personal involvement. She confuses the bishops: Giso was bishop of Wells (1061–88), and Walter of Hereford (1061–79), not the reverse (*Life*, p. 170). See also Mason, *House of Godwine*, p. 95.
6   2742 After this line, MS P adds: 'Chartres et bries o lui porta De par le roi si li moztra A l'Apostoile pour savoir Çou que li rois voloit avoir.'
7   2744 MS W has 'A la trone' [on his throne].
8   2750 'De l'el dient lur volentez': these would include consecration of Aldret's companions.
9   2753 MS P has 'A l'apostre nostre pere' [to the Pope our father].
10 2762 Instead of the following, MS W has 'Ciel et terre et tutes choses fist de nient' [Heaven and earth and all things made from nothing]; the sense would continue 'and who has placed ...'.
11 2768 After this line, MSS W and P add 'Requerum vostre grant saveir D'esforcier nostre nunpoeir Ke a Deu puissum servir a gré En faiz, en voleir, en pensé. Voz faiz et vostre conissance Vostre conseil et vostre puissance ...'. The omission, in MS V, is due to eyeskip from one line beginning 'Requerum' to another (Södergård's note).

Now we have told you the king's letter, we shall tell you the reply:

¶'Nicholas, elected servant of God, to King Edward his beloved son. Glorious and worthy of affection, ruler of England, I send you warmest greetings and give you my blessing. Let us give thanks to the Almighty King for the great things we hear of you. Your benevolence and great nobility are so illumined with his grace that you are pleasing to God and to all. You are found to be so praiseworthy, that you love Saint Peter so much, and to honour the apostle you wish to do as his servants do, and you seek the friendship of us who hold the seat in his name. We send you letters wherein we gladly grant you fellowship in the holy body, together with our goodwill. Let us request his mercy as well as we are able,[12] that he will give you a share of our good things, if you are seen to be worthy before him.[13] As soon as this is made known to us, I wish you to be able to share it. May the King of Heaven in his grace make us brothers and companions. From henceforth we shall pray for you:[14] may God keep you in his peace and place your enemies in subjection to you, may he send you wisdom and strength to deal justly with all those who think to make war on you, may your patron Saint Peter uphold you and your kingdom. May he be comfort and aid to you, and joy in all your troubles. The kings who reigned before you often had, because of Saint Peter whom they so loved, great victories, and they are remembered with reverence. They were redoubtable, thanks to Saint Peter and his great virtues. May God in his power grant you remission of your sins, and by his almighty grace accomplish all your desire. And when you come to the end of this life, may he receive you into his company, in the joy that never comes to an end, where his commandment endures. We confirm your privileges;[15] we renew and increase them. This is to say, you shall be absolved of the vow you have been so anxious about. In addition, we fully absolve you of all your sins, by the highest Authority that has been granted me, unworthy as I am, to be governor of his Church in peace and stern piety.[16] The church you have restored and honoured in the name of the apostle, that he dedicated long ago and consecrated for his own, in those days it was a royal seat, we have been informed. By the authority of Jesus Christ and his chosen apostles, we henceforth grant and command, and we confirm in perpetuity, that it shall from now on be a royal seat and that it shall be honoured accordingly. First, let there be crowned and anointed there all those who are made to be kings; let the royal treasure be deposited there, that all the kings of the land shall possess. Let the place be perpetually filled with holy and well-regulated monks. Let the rule of Saint Benedict be enforced rightfully

---

[12] 2824 MSS P and W replace the foregoing with 'Senz ki rien faire ne poüm'; the sense would be 'Let us request his mercy, without whom we can do nothing ...'.
[13] 2826 'Se devant lui *puet* valeir rien'; MS W has 'poez'.
[14] 2831 Södergård's text reads 'Pur vus serrum' [we shall be for you]: MS P reads 'prierons', which I follow because it makes better sense.
[15] 2855 MS P omits this line (evidently a mistake).
[16] 2864 MS P replaces the last phrase with 'Qui de par lui sui gouvernere' (possibly a mistake, because of the identical rhyme).

15 A Visit to Pope Nicholas (2697–960) 117

among them;[17] let them elect abbots from among their number,[18] and let them receive suitable benefices. Let nobody from any abbey of strangers ever have the rule of it, unless it be by common consent or by the will of God. We grant freedom to the place and to the church, that no bishop shall ever say mass there; he may not enter it to give orders, nor may he command anything there, unless he is invited by the abbot and the good men who are established there. Whatever pertains to the glory of God, with whatever lies within our power, we grant most cordially, and we shall maintain the foundation for ever.[19] The lands given by the kings who reigned before you, and the other possessions you and your barons have given, let the charters in which they are written down be enacted and enforced. From henceforth all those who sell these lands, and who diminish these possessions, let them be damned evermore without redemption. We condemn them with the wicked Judas,[20] and we cut them off from merciful God. Let them beware, they shall be judged on that day when God shall come to judge the world. Saint Peter will wreak vengeance on them, and with his peers he will judge them.[21] We now command you, and humbly beg you, and all those who shall come as kings on earth after you, to uphold this church in prosperity, that it may lose none of its franchises. All the other churches established in our land [of England] we commend to you to protect and rule according to God's will, with the guidance of the priests, the bishops, and the abbots. Whatsoever needs mending, mend it; whatsoever is good, take care of it. You shall be rewarded by him who is one God in Trinity.'

¶When the Pope had spoken this, and all had then been put into writing, those who had come there for this purpose returned again with the letter.[22] They delivered it to the king; he was very happy when he saw it. It lifted from him all the fear he had felt about the vow he swore before. He put away all worldliness from his thoughts. He commended his kingdom into the protection of great princes of the land, and the best men he could think of, to carry out his justice. Thus he was freed from cares, and God would have all his thoughts; as much as he attended to the world, so much he lost of God's sweetness. He surrendered himself to this sweetness, that delighted him body and soul. This Sweetness was his delight, by whom he was sweet and perfect. He had

---

[17] 2883 'Sulunc la riule saint Beneit': Barking was a Benedictine foundation. The Nun follows Aelred's mention of Benedict's rule, as does MP (*History*, note to v. 1764). For Benedict (*c.* 480–*c.* 550) and his rule, see *ODS*: an important prescription was that religious must read and study as a matter of routine. This passage refers to Rule 64:1–6 (*Life*, p. 174).
[18] 2885 'eslire habez' (MS P 'aves'); corrected online to 'abés' [abbots].
[19] 2874–900 Westminster Abbey as a 'royal seat': although it has not been a monastery since dissolution in 1540, it is still a 'royal peculiar,' subject only to the crown and not to the bishop of London (*Life*, p. 174).
[20] 2909–11 In MS P these lines are differently written (the sense is much the same).
[21] 2916 'od ses pers les jugerat': the Nun omits Aelred's reference to Matt. 19:28, to make another play on 'Piere' and 'pers'.
[22] 2935–7 MS P differs: 'O larmes en sunt returnez Ki pur ço furent la alez. Tant ont erré et cevaucié Al rei, lur reignur, l'unt baillé. Isnelement fu desploiés ...' [those who had come there for this purpose returned, with tears. They travelled, riding, for so long that they came to the king and gave it to him. It was quickly unfolded; he was very happy ...], one of P's somewhat rambling interpolations.

such sweet desire for God that he was often able to see the heavenly glories on which his desire was fed, as you shall hear presently, if God gives you the desire to do so.[23]

---

[23] Aelred ends this section similarly, by introducing the subject of the next, but the address to audience is the Nun's (*Life*, p. 175).

Chapter 16

Edward and Lievrich (2961–3074)[1]

Introduction

This chapter demonstrates Edward's sanctity in a special way. It comes just after the Pope has re-confirmed Edward's release from his vow, and has given his churches – in particular his favourite Westminster Abbey – dispensations to protect them in perpetuity. His mood is of relief from the old burden, and exaltation that he may henceforth give all his attention to God. Profoundly mystical, this incident is fittingly placed here. The Nun follows Aelred in the main, but adjusts and sometimes amplifies in a manner personal to herself. She deletes or paraphrases several Bible references, perhaps in order to focus more fully on the very affective scene of devotion.[2]

Lievrich was Count of Mercia (d. 1057), and after Godwin the most powerful man of the realm. His wife was said to have ridden naked, but for her long hair and her chastity, through the town of Coventry in protest against taxation of the people. The story, well known from Tennyson's poem *Godiva*, was recorded by the thirteenth-century chronicler Roger of Wendover (and see *History*, note to vv. 2522–9). The Nun omits Aelred's explanation of the name Godgiva: that she wonderfully fulfilled its meaning by being or by continually offering 'a good gift' (*Life*, p. 176 and footnote). Aelred's understanding of English words is apparent here; the Nun's narrative is almost entirely free of name-play in any language.[3] This is no proof the Nun did not understand English (her repetition of 'God' and 'good' shows awareness of the name's meaning), but suggests that etymology did not greatly interest her. The problematic variant identified by Marzella in the ω family of manuscripts of Aelred's *Vita* has not been followed by the Nun any more than she follows the *PL* version (family ϱ) at this point.[4]

The miracle is given authority by its unusual provenance: what Edward saw must be kept secret, so as to prevent improper feelings of pride or envy in anybody, but his companion manages to publish the account in such a way that it will come to light long afterwards. Documents such as this share with prophecies mentioned by Strohm a kind of magical authority. They appear opportunely to authenticate a significant happening, and as magically they disappear, having served their purpose.[5] The context of Strohm's argument is political rather than hagiological, but in either case a document is 'recruited to bear fitful witness to a current inevitablity' (p. 14).

---

[1] *Vita*, 760B–61C; *Life*, §18. Also cf. *Estoire*, vv. 2514–97; *History*, p. 86.
[2] See Dinzelbacher, 'Beginnings of Mysticism', for this kind of vision.
[3] For etymology as a habit of medieval thought, see Curtius, *European Literature*, pp. 495–500.
[4] 'La tradizione', p. 365: *quod talem feminam ecclesie sancte profectibus pietas divina contulerat* [either because Divine Piety had conferred such a fine woman for the profiting of Holy Church] is more effusive than the version in family ϱ (I am grateful to Graham Edwards for help with this translation).
[5] *England's Empty Throne*, The Uses of Prophecy.

We are to understand that it is lucky the historian was able to copy the account before it vanished, so that we may be reliably enlightened. The story comes, ultimately, from an Old English source (the *Vision of Leofric*), whence Osbert learned it either directly or orally.[6]

❧ ❧ ❧ ❧ ❧ ❧ ❧ ❧ ❧

¶One day the king was at Westminster, as God ordained; he had come into the church to hear God's service. Before the altar, sacred to the name of the Holy Trinity, he stopped – joyful, and certain of salvation.[7] Count Lievrich was with him, in whom was the grace of God: he was full of true goodness and perfect charity. His wife was named Gudeve, who had given her love to God; she never ceased from serving God, either by good intention or by good deed. Her lord was both worthy and wise; he loved God with his whole being. He made many monasteries and churches, and added to them great benefices. He had made the Almighty King heir to his lands and his goods.[8] This man was with the king in the church, worthy to bear witness to the beautiful miracle he saw there – it has never been recounted without delight. The mass had already begun, and the holy moment approached when the priest who said the mass held the true salvation of the people gently between his hands: it was the true Body of Jesus Christ. Then the good, the merciful, the sweet Jesus appeared at his altar.[9] He showed himself, clearly and corporeally, to his friends; he raised his holy right hand and blessed the king gently. The king bowed his head and bowed his whole body to that divine presence – to the joy that never ceases, to the beauty that never grows old, to the goodness that performs all good things; to that supreme sweetness he bowed with supreme love. Count Lievrich marvelled why the king thus bowed himself; he did not know he had seen the lovely, the benign Jesus. He wanted to make him share the glory that he saw. He took a great step towards the king, but the king saw his purpose, and said to Lievrich:

'Stay, stay! I can see what you are seeing.'

Then they began their prayers again, and began most tenderly to weep. With sweet sighs they were sustained, and with sweet tears fed. So abundant was the delight that they were entirely fulfilled with it. They were intoxicated[10] with holy sighs, refreshed with holy tears. When the service was finished, the count drew near to the king.

---

[6] Leyser, 'Texts', p. 49 & note 2; *Osbert*, p. 92 and note 1 for the monk Maurice. See also Stokes, 'Vision of Leofric'.

[7] 2967–8 A small dramatic detail not in Aelred, who says simply that the king attended the mysteries (*Life*, p. 176).

[8] 2981–4 MS P reads 'He made the Almighty God heir to his lands and his goods. This man was with the king in the church; he was worthy to come close to all good things.' Aelred cites Titus 2:12; the Nun's words about his worth and wisdom paraphrase the sentiment.

[9] Aelred cites Ps. 45:2 (44:3 in *LV*).

[10] 3023 'saülez': not quite the modern 'drunk' (see Glossary). But the author is pushing on the meaning: the companions were replete, almost delirious, with sweetness (cf. v. 3036, where it means 'sated'). In the next line 'abevrez' [refreshed] means their thirst was quenched. See Ps. 36:8 (35:9 in *LV*). Aelred's translator gives 'intoxicated'; the Latin is *inebriabuntur/bantur* in Aelred and *LV* (in *AV, abundantly satisfied*).

Between themselves they told what they had seen – what it was, how it had been. As soon as one finished his speech, the other began his right away – and when the other had to stop then the first began to tell again. With the words were mingled sighs, and tears with sweet desire – neither of hearing nor of telling could they be sated.[11] The king said to his companion:

'What we have seen, by the majesty of Jesus Christ, I conjure you to promise me that nobody shall know of this as long as we live:[12] so that vain pride may not assail us because of the praises of the common people, nor that the envious should believe and because of it become disloyal to God.[13] I do not want them to sin, nor us to be exalted in pride.' [He understood, and was very glad. When this had been agreed ...][14]

¶The count left the court; he was joyful with great joy. He went to Worcester, and there he sought out a holy man. In confession he told what he, with the king his lord, had seen. He asked him to put it in writing and never tell it in their lifetime; it should be put in such a place where it could be found again. This man did the writing and shut it up with the relics. It was in safe guard, for[15] except himself no mortal knew of it. Then, when it pleased the will of God, and the king had passed out of this world, the reliquary was found to be open,[16] without anybody having been near. And they found the writing inside there, with the relics. They read the letter, so they saw how the king had seen the King Jesus. Thus did the merciful Jesus show what King Edward had concealed; thus was the miracle believed and the king held to be a humble man.[17]

---

11 3036 'saülez': see note above. The Nun omits Aelred's citation from Ps. 19:2 (18:3 in *LV*; *Life*, p. 177).
12 3042 MS P omits this line (the sense would be 'promise me that nobody shall know, so that vain ...').
13 3045-6 'U que les envïus nel creient E par ço vers Deu se desleient': it is suggested that these might lose faith, because not so favoured (MS W reads 'les enemis' [enemies] instead of 'envïus').
14 3048 MS P adds, after this line, 'Cil l'entendi si fu molt liés E cis com s'en fu otroiés ...' (it continues: 'the count was greatly delighted. Then he left the church ...'). The Nun, although usually eager to portray Edward as a Christ-figure, omits Aelred's comment that Edward was following the example of Jesus in Matt. 17:9 (*Life*, p. 177); see p. 5, above.
15 3062: 'ke' [that, which] means 'car' [for], here. Södergård's note says the suggestion of Provençal influence is undermined by the fact that it appears, much earlier, in *Brendan* (see *The Anglo-Norman* Brendan ed. Waters, v. 904; there is no note for this word 'que'). MS P reads 'Car nus hom fors il n'i aloit' [for no man but himself had gone there].
16 3065 'vaissel' [container, vessel] can also mean coffin; we are not told whose relics were kept at Worcester at the time of the story.
17 The Nun shortens Aelred's account of the disclosure, but reiterates what the disclosure was about and what it signified.

Chapter 17

The King's Evil (3075–256)[1]

Introduction

Edward, together with his successors, was reputedly able to cure scrofula by prayer and the laying on of hands, hence the name 'The King's Evil'. Elizabeth I is said to have cured nine people in this way, while staying at Kenilworth.[2] Shakespeare (*Macbeth*, IV:3) names the disease, mentioning Edward's virtue. William of Malmesbury tells of the King's Evil cured by a woman: a royal virgin, but no king.[3] Another cure, by Frideswide, is in *Acta Sanctorum*. This cure of a woman begins the first series of Edward's miracles. His doubts about dreams have not yet appeared: he is delighted to hear of the woman's vision, and not until the next chapter does he begin to wonder about the reliability of such things.

The Nun adds, to the description of the sick woman's suffering, a passage lamenting the ills of 'nowadays',[4] which resembles an outburst in Malory's *Morte Darthur*. Her regretful tone recalls a well-known passage, at the opening of 'The Knight of the Cart' episode, with which it may be compared. The words 'dangier' (v. 3152) and 'pru' (v. 3154) have extra meaning in the 'courtly love' game, and their use here prepares the reader for a further set of courtly notions: 'franchise', 'valur', 'fin' amur', 'honur' (3155–9). Malory calls to mind 'olde jantylnes and olde servyse', contrasting it with 'the love nowadayes'.[5]

The Nun's distinctive style is much in evidence in this chapter: frequent deictic comments, calling the 'here and now' to mind. Her introduction is longer and more personal than Aelred's, and her description of the woman's excited arrival at the court is more vivid.

꙳ ꙳ ꙳ ꙳ ꙳ ꙳ ꙳ ꙳ ꙳

¶After the king had seen him he loved so much – our Jesus, our Lord, our comfort and strength – his power and goodness increased by divine power, so that God healed many people of their infirmities through him, and we shall now tell you as well as we understand it.

Near where the king was staying lived a wretched woman, who passed her days, her youth, in pain and agony. She was doubly afflicted, and her double complaint

---

[1] *Vita*, 761C–2B; *Life*, §19. Cf. *Estoire*, vv. 2598–683; *History*, pp. 87–8.
[2] Södergård, note to vv. 3221–2; for studies, see notes to v. 2613 in *Estoire* and *History*. See also Barlow, *Edward the Confessor*, pp. 270–71; and his 'The King's Evil' (*EHR* 95, 1980, 3–27), cited in Dunbabin, *France in the Making* (p. 135 and note 5; pp. 259–60 and note 11).
[3] *Kings* tr. Stephenson, §216, p. 206.
[4] See Harden, 'Ubi Sunt', for changes rung on this theme.
[5] *Works* ed. Vinaver, p. 649. For love without ulterior motive, see MacBain, 'Vocabulary', p. 271.

tormented her terribly. One was that she could have no child, and had lost all hope of being a mother. The other was such a horrible disease that she had no hope of being cured. An ugly tumorous lump had grown on her face,[6] which was black and swollen; all the blood was putrefied. Her body-fluids had turned to poison, but continued to flow under her skin. The poison could not flow out, because of the skin; it was close to the swelling, and disgusting maggots came from it. The worms have eaten away her flesh, and such a stench comes forth that nobody will come near to give comfort or help. Her husband avoids her, night and day, because of the stink; he loved her even less because she could have no child. Indeed, her dreadful disease made him conceive a hatred for her, so that instead of dutiful love he gave her spite and loathing. He wished her no comfort but a speedy death. The poor thing was well aware that her husband despised her; his contempt doubled her suffering and increased her anguish. Pain overwhelmed her from all sides, for all comfort failed her. All her relatives loathe her, and nobody gives her help or relief. The more her suffering increased, the less she could find any good friend. This often happens still, when anybody falls into severe affliction of poverty or disease or other great misery. If it goes so badly with them that nobody believes they will get better, then people quickly come to hate those nearest to them, and regret that they go on living. Where they ought to be finding help, they find nothing but a wish for their death. While they can talk and be pleasant to them, and give them things,[7] then they will find plenty to help them – when they need to ask nothing. But when great need comes upon them, then all help quickly fails them. No wretch suffers more than the poor, when they become weak. They are despised for their poverty and spurned for their weakness. No pauper, once fallen sick, can find any friend to trust in. As soon as he cannot help himself, he will look in vain for others' help.[8] Nowadays, nobody is capable of loving anybody else unless they can see some advantage in it; nowhere in the world can selfless love,[9] in generosity and moral worth, be found. All their love is based on pleasure and greed; love's honour is not enough for them, unless they can get some profit or some lustful enjoyment. Because Lust is their master and Greed their keeper, they have no pity for their friends when they see them in trouble.[10] If it were really love they felt, they would suffer for their friend's trouble as for their own. But nowadays it rarely happens, that anybody loves purely for love. So it seems to me that a poor man has no friends, especially if he has

---

[6] 3096 'sur la face': MS 'suz les faces'; Södergård corrects to 'on', but 'under' is more accurate. Aelred writes *sub faucibus* [under her jaw] (*Life*, p. 179): she has lumps *quasi glandes* [like acorns]; the disease causes neck-glands to swell, so the lumps subside on healing ('acorns' are not expelled). Latin *glans* means 'gland', as well as 'acorn' (and 'bullet'), presumably because of the shape.
[7] 3139–40 MS P rephrases, omitting the idea of talking and being pleasant; and omits v. 3142 ('when they need to ask for nothing'), which does not alter the sense much, given what follows. Sentiments expressed here are analogous to 'L'un bien actraict l'autre, et l'une povreté l'autre' (Morawski, 1124).
[8] 3152 *AND* cites this passage for an unusual meaning of 'avoir dangier' = 'to look in vain' (cf. perhaps our modern and ironic 'no danger!'). Södergård's glossary gives 'besoin' (= he will have need of their help).
[9] 3156 'fin amur', in all three MSS. See Glossary, and MacBain, 'Vocabulary'.
[10] 3165–70 The following, 'If it were really … has no friends', omitted in MS P.

no health – he is soon loathed by his own people, just as this poor woman was.[11] All her family, and her husband, had developed such a hatred for her that they would not willingly see her, even, nor hear her talked about. The poor woman had nothing with which to win strangers to her side, nor to pay doctors; nor did she know who could get one for her. Now she was in pain and misery, and groaning day and night; she could see that all human help was utterly and completely lost to her.

So she betook herself to the help that is the relief for all burdens: this is the lovely merciful Jesus, who is the salvation for all who suffer. To him she prays for all succour, and again and again she begs for his mercy: that he will put an end to her great suffering, or else put an end to her life.[12] When she had finished her prayer, a vision then came to her, that she must go to the king's palace, where she might hope for true healing. If the king would vouchsafe to touch her, to wash and bless her with his own hands,[13] through the virtue of the king she would recover her own health. The woman awoke then, and was very happy at what she had heard. She set off for the palace, going quickly and leaping for joy; she did not recollect that she was a woman, and decorum did not hold her back. She entered the palace and threw herself at the king's feet in front of everybody, and she told him what she had dreamed. The king was filled with joy and compassion, and he called for water to be brought; then he begins to wash her face. Tenderly he strokes the swelling; the stench never made him hesitate. The king humbly touched all that part of her face where the poison had set in, and he signed her with his saintly hand. Suddenly, after this saintly handling, the skin cracked open! Then you could see those worms coming forth,[14] and the poison seething out with them. Quickly all the swelling went down, and the pain came to an end. Thus God cured that body, by his friend King Edward. Those who witnessed this wonder were overjoyed at the miracle, and they praise the name of Jesus who gives the king such virtue. All marvel at his goodness, his virtue, and his sanctity: that he, who was an earthly man, could do heavenly deeds. The woman stayed there until the ulcer was healed; soon the holes close up and hide all trace of the wounds. The servants and the palace people fed her as much as she needed;[15] then she went joyfully back to her house, completely whole. Her husband was full of gladness, as were her friends and relations. [Those who heard of this miracle gave thanks to the

---

[11] 3175–84 The following, 'All her family ... day and night', omitted in MS P, as if to shorten and simplify the Nun's account (see previous note).
[12] See *Life*, p. 179, for Tob. 3:13 (3:15 in *LV*): *Take me out of the earth, that I may hear no more the reproach.* Sara, daughter of Raguel, is eventually saved by the angel Raphael.
[13] 3200 'De sa main laver e seignier': 'seignier' means to make the sign of the Cross; 'seignier' sounds and looks like words meaning 'to bleed' (when transitive, a healing process), and also 'to make whole or sound'. A similar example of homonymy, that our author delights in, occurs twice in this passage: 'sancté' as health or healing, and also sanctity (see Glossary).
[14] 3223 'Dunc veïssez ...': the Nun makes her story more vivid (Clemence never uses this expression). Aelred introduces the passage with 'What more shall I say?' but uses no phrase about his audience seeing (*Life*, p. 180).
[15] 3242 MS P adds that they dressed her.

Lord God.]¹⁶ Nor did this gladness fade, for soon she had conceived a baby. This is how God honoured the king, and filled him with virtue: through him he healed the woman and gave the barren one a child. She had despaired of both, and now she was fulfilled in both: her husband loved her ever after and, as is proper, honoured her.

---

16   3246 MS P adds, after this line, 'Chil qui ceste miracle oirent A Damedieu graces rendirent'.

Chapter 18

A Blind Man sees Edward's Beard (3257–438)[1]

Introduction

The Nun expands Aelred's pious opening. The citation from Job is not in her source (his first is from Corinthians); unusually, she adds a Bible quotation. For the action of the story, she extends description of Edward's inner struggle, and adds the detail of the towel (not mentioned by Aelred). Direct speech, in the passage where people (including Edward) ask questions, is added by the Nun; so too is the paradoxical observation that the man's sight troubled people's perceptions (cf. *Life*, p. 182). For the important discussion about the reliability of dreams in this chapter, see General Introduction (Rewriting Aelred) and Appendix.

❧ ❧ ❧ ❧ ❧ ❧ ❧ ❧ ❧

¶The gifts of grace are diverse, nor do all possess them all. God bestows them as he wishes, and as he pleases he takes them away.[2] To some he gives the wisdom to speak so as to teach others. Some possess simple good sense that benefits themselves alone; they cannot demonstrate it except by good works. These are models of good conduct, but they cannot impart their wisdom. So the gifts are shared out according to the will of the Holy Spirit; gifts of grace are bestowed by him, exclusively to God's faithful.[3] Although King Edward had a generous share of such gifts, that he was wise and powerful, valiant for God and for the world,[4] and that he could heal the sick and make the lame and the crippled to walk, yet he had one gift above all, especially greater than others. By the grace of the Holy Spirit, he had the perfect gift of being able to render sight to the blind, however it might be that they had lost it. It was right he should have this gift, of bringing light to the blind, he who by the most pure chastity was so entranced within his heart that he could see nothing in the world to delight him.[5]

Near to the king's court there lived a wretched man who was blind; it was common knowledge to everybody that he had lost his sight, and because of this real misery he prayed to his merciful Creator to take a little pity on him and give him back his sight. In his sleep God showed him that he would have healing from the king, he was of such great virtue. If he could get the towel he had dried his hands on, and the water he had washed them in, then as soon as he had washed his face and wiped his eyes with the towel, he would have his sight back immediately if he believed perfectly in God.

---

[1] *Vita*, 762B–3C; *Life*, §20. Cf. *Estoire*, vv. 2684–823; *History*, pp. 88–90.
[2] 3259–60 'Deu les dune si cum il volt E si cum li plaist les recolt': Job 1:21.
[3] I Cor. 12:4–11 (cf. *Life*, p. 180).
[4] 3276 'vaillainz', see Glossary, *s.v.* 'valur'.
[5] 3289 MS P says he loved none of it in his heart.

The man wakes up and feels full of joy, and then he comes to the court. He tells the king's chamberlains about his dream and his own need. These repeated to the king what he had said to them. The king was filled with pity, and yet greatly angered that men believe so much of him when he feels himself to be nothing but a mortal sinner; he says it is no business of his, but of God's. He ought not to take upon himself what concerns the Almighty King. He says the man is deceived and bewitched by the dream, for not all dreams are to be believed.[6]

They answer: 'Not all dreams are false, for often they have spoken truth. Daniel the wise knew by dreams what the weather would be, and to Saint Joseph an angel appeared secretly by night, telling him to go into Egypt and take the Child and his Mother.'[7] They tell him not to stay his hand from fulfilling God's commands, for God by his grace gives power to his faithful, to help the needy and comfort those in pain. They tell him that none must oppose the divine succour, and if God wishes to act through him he must act as best he can.

¶The king listens humbly to them, torn by pity and by doubt. But Pity constrained him so that he was pulled away from the doubt that insisted on his powerlessness; Doubt did not take away his belief that God could perform cures without the help of any man if he wished to. But if God wished to work this thing through him, then he would fulfil all his wishes. In spite of his misgivings, he was encouraged to do it all. He prepared to go to the church, for it was the Vigil of All Saints.[8] He washed his hands and then dried them, and at once went to the church. As soon as the king was in the church and hearing the service, the servants sent for the man and washed his face and eyes. Privately, they prayed that God in his divine power would restore health to the sufferer through the king's virtue. As soon as the water touched him, he raised his eyes and saw the light of day and the brightness of the sun. He was astounded at everything he saw, for it was all new to him.[9] The sweet delight he felt made him weep for happiness. Those who witnessed what had happened praised God and his power. The healed man ran into the church to offer up praises to God; those inside the church beheld him with wonder. Because they had seen him blind, they now did not know him; his sight troubled theirs, and his certainty made their error.

---

[6] Edward had no hesitation, in ch. 17, about believing the woman's dream (as in Aelred).
[7] Dreams and prophecies of Joseph (Genesis chs 37, 40, & 41) conflated with Daniel's prophecies about things and times to come (*Life*, p. 181). The Nun adds the idea of weather (3330 'quel tens avendreit', perhaps with Joseph's prediction of famine in mind); she names 'Christ's foster-father' Joseph, and the Holy Family's destination (Aelred does not: Matt. 2:19–22).
[8] 3360 'la serveille': two days before All Saints (see *AND* 'veille'), properly 30th October.
[9] 3376 'Kar nule rien ne cuneseit'; lit. 'he recognized nothing at all'. In Aelred, he sees *quasi denuo* [as if restored to him anew]; the Nun told us earlier that he had lost his sight and hoped to regain it, but now it seems he never had it (cf. *Life*, p. 182). She omits reference to the Pool of Siloam (John 9:1–11), part of Aelred's account of the healing: the Gospel miracle resembles the present miracle, even to there being no towel in Aelred's version. Further, neighbours in the Gospel story feel uncertain about the cured man's identity, as here.

One says to another, 'Is that him?' and the other replies, 'No, of course not!' [This is what some people say, that this is how he made him see.][10] So then they ask him, 'Is that you?' and he says, 'Of course I am!' They went on arguing until the service was over.

The king came out of the church, and his men ran up to him; they told him of the miracle and how the sufferer was cured. As soon as he hears this, he goes straight back to the church and calls the man to him.

'Can you see?' he says, 'Tell me the truth.'

'Lord,' says he, 'really, I can see! I thank you, and I thank God.'

The king puts out his right hand, then says to the poor wretch, 'What am I doing now, tell me?'

And the poor man answers the king, 'I can see your blessed hand, stretched out towards me – God was pleased to give me healing by it.'

He wants to try him further, so he says, 'What am I doing now?'

He says, 'I can see you raising your finger – you're going to stab it into my eye!'

A third time the king says, 'Tell me what I'm doing now, if you can see it.'

'Faith,' says the poor fellow, 'you've taken hold of your beard with your hand!'[11]

When the king hears him say this, he begins to weep for joy. He lays himself before the altar, to worship the power of God. He transmits all the credit to God, who made him and who made the miracle.[12] He is not deceived into vain pride, for he counts his virtue as nothing. The less he reckoned his own worth, the more he was worthy of the deed – thus his virtue was demonstrated, but he wanted it all kept secret. The more beloved he was, the more the deed was reported. Not to believe it was impossible, for all the people had seen it, and he who was the proof of it stayed thenceforward in the king's court and received his livelihood every day and year there, this is why it cannot be kept a secret.

---

[10] 3390 MS P adds, after this line, 'Si est çou dient li auquant Qu'il a donc fait issi voyant' (one of P's rather unclear explanations).

[11] 3418 MS P: 'you've taken hold of your beard with your two hands'.

[12] Aelred's chapter ends here, citing Ps. 115:1 (113:9 in *LV*). The Nun's words paraphrase the idea, as do the words of the Gospel cited above (John 9:24, *Give God the praise*...). Characteristically, the Nun continues about Edward's virtue (impossibility of keeping the secret is part of Aelred's introduction to the next chapter). See Glossary 'valur', for 'vertu'.

Chapter 19
The Blind Man of Lincoln (3439–500)[1]

Introduction

Aelred opens with a passage broadly corresponding to the end of the Nun's previous chapter: that the cured man remained at Edward's court. He goes on to cite Ps. 67:4 (66:5 in *LV*), which the Nun does not. He tells as part of this introduction that Edward is a prophet. The Nun delays the remark until the blind man's speech. Her account of the dream is slightly expanded. Her last sentence of this chapter is added as extra explanation of how Edward's special fame was spread abroad.

It is curious that the Nun, or whoever copied the *Vie*, spells Lincoln 'Nichole' (v. 3447, no variants noted). This is common in Anglo-Norman and a peculiarity of French scribes, even in Latin, according to the editor of Jocelin of Brakelond's *Chronicle*.[2] *Estoire* spells it Nicole; the *PL* text of *Vita* spells it conventionally (763C), as does Osbert (*Osbert*, p. 95).

❧ ❧ ❧ ❧ ❧ ❧ ❧ ❧ ❧

¶Fame celebrated this deed, and would not allow it to be concealed. There was nowhere in the land where it was not talked of, and everybody delighted in hearing of it. It flew from one place to the next, until in the city of Lincoln and in all the country round this marvel was recounted. At that time there was living in Lincoln a citizen who was blind. He heard the story gladly, and was cheered by good hope. In spite of his affliction, his heart lifted in hopefulness – it was now the third year since he had fallen into this misfortune. I don't know the circumstances,[3] by which this evil happened to him, but great suffering befell him who was bereft of his sight. But now he took comfort, and his hope revived. He often said to himself:

'What am I doing? Alas, what should I do? Why do I delay going to seek a cure, when there is a prophet in our land who can heal the sick and tell what is to come? And I stay here, wretched, in darkness,[4] and pass my life in pain. Our king has such virtue as the holy Apostles had, that he can render their sight to the blind, however they might have lost it.'

While saying these words, he nodded and fell asleep.[5] Somebody said to him that he would soon be cured, if he could get the water the king had washed his hands in,

---

1 *Vita*, 763C–4A; *Life*, §21. Cf. *Estoire*, vv. 2824–93; *History*, pp. 90–91.
2 ed. and tr. Butler, note 2 on p. 69; *Prose Brut* ed. Pagan, spells it Nichole (IPN, p. 272).
3 Another personal comment; Aelred says 'an accident or an illness' (*Life*, p. 183).
4 Luke 1:79 and Is. 9:2; Aelred echoes the verses more closely (*Life*, p. 184).
5 3474 MS P adds two lines: 'Vint vers [illegible], ce li fu vis E com il fu bien endormis'. The online version supplies 'heui'; Russell (pers. comm.) supplies 'Vint veiz huem ...'. Thanks to this clarification, the passage reads: '... fell asleep. A man's voice came, it seemed to him, and as he was deep in slumber it told him that ...'.

and the cloth he had dried them with. This way he could regain his health, just as the other blind ones had done. As soon as he had dreamed this, you can imagine he did not hesitate another minute. He comes to the king's court, and privately he begs the chamberlains[6] to speed his cure for the love of God, and get him some of the water. They agree, and reassure him, then they bring him the holy water. As soon as he washed his face, the sight came back to his eyes; by that water he quickly regained the health he had so long desired. He gives thanks and praise to God, who has thus cured him through the king.[7] Then he goes back to his home, bringing great joy to his folk; he tells everybody how it was, the royal and holy power. In this way his goodness and his saintliness were made known.

---

[6] 3484 'les chamberiens': the online version prefers MS W's 'des' (he begs *of* the chamberlains that …).
[7] 3494 MS P says 'by the water' instead of 'through the king', weakening the sense of Edward as God's instrument.

Chapter 20

The Blinded Woodcutter (3501–628)[1]

Introduction

The Nun follows Aelred closely, but not word for word. Södergård remarks, 'as usual, the narrative is somewhat developed' (Introduction, p. 30). An example is an added sentence describing the villagers' zeal, and a comment about the woodmen's appetite for dinner. The female advisor differs from the same figure in *Estoire* (*History*, p. 92), who is scantily described. It seems clear not only from these, but also from Aelred's picture of her, that this bringer of Heaven's message is not supernatural. The words 'decent' and 'respectable' conjure up the image of a good-natured neighbour (*Life*, p. 185). Although she has unusual knowledge about how the woodcutter can be healed, note the matter-of-fact way the Nun describes her: 'She had an exceedingly good reputation, having proved herself good by good deeds ...'. The woman's goodness is expanded from Aelred, and that she is sent by God spelt out. Edward has learned his lesson, that he must do God's will and cure people when required to do so (he no longer grumbles that dreams cannot be trusted, as in chapter 18). He takes it for granted that the woman's promise was a message from God. William of Malmesbury's version of this story specifies eighty-seven churches (note to v. 3569); Osbert, eighty.[2]

¶After that man had been cured, it was not long before it happened that in one of the king's towns – it was called Brukeham,[3] I think – a house was ordered to be built for the king. Timber was to be hauled from the forest; all the woodcutters of the region were summoned to assemble there. Every villager was envious of every other who knew anything at all of woodcraft. Once they had all gathered, most of them set off into the woods. They felled a good number of big oak-trees, and then they chopped planks out of them.[4] When dinner-time comes, they sit down to eat, and drink merrily, as is the custom with such folk.[5] Then they went back to work. The hot sun, and the long day, make their labours very harsh. They go to rest in the shade, and when they have slept a little they go to work happily, for their rest has

---

[1] *Vita*, 764A–5A; *Life*, §22. Cf. *Estoire*, vv. 2898–3018; *History*, pp. 91–2.
[2] *Kings* tr. Stephenson, §224, p. 210; *Osbert*, p. 96.
[3] 3504 'Brukeham': Brill, in Buckinghamshire. Aelred has Bruheham (*Life*, p. 184). See *Estoire*, note to v. 2898: 'Brehull' was the site of a royal hunting lodge. The Nun's pretended uncertainty adds to the personal flavour of her narrative.
[4] 3514 'borz': Södergård's glossary says the cut wood is 'de sapin [fir] probablement', although we have just been told the trees are oak (fir was not native; see Mortimer, *Guide*, p. 25 & note 9). The 'granz cheines' detail is not in Aelred (*Life*, p. 184).
[5] 3518 The Nun frequently adds comment of this kind (for example, vv. 3847–50 and note).

cheered them up. One of them who had rested, whose name was Ulwine,[6] woke up with the others, but not so cheerfully. He opens his eyes, and he can see ... not a thing![7] He could not understand it, and turned his head from side to side, repeatedly rubbing his forehead.[8] He scrubs hard at his eyes with his hand, but he realises it is of no use. Once he knows there is nothing for it, then he weeps and moans, crying out loud. He calls his mates to him, and tells them his distress and misfortune. They comforted him as best they could, and led him home to his house. There he remained, in pain and suffering, and in darkness both night and day. Nineteen years he lived like that, miserably, without help.

One day, as the poor fellow wept, as he so often bemoaned his plight, a woman came to talk to him and comfort his distress. She had an exceedingly good reputation, having proved herself good by good deeds. She had spent the days of her age in the good habits of a good life.[9] She asks, enquiring about his state, and he speaks as is proper to reply to her:

'I suffer, and I'm miserable!'

She tells him to hush, 'Don't cry any more, my friend,' says she, 'for God has sent me here. If you will believe what I tell you, then understand that you will soon be cured.'

When he heard this, he was so happy that he trembled all over for joy, and he promised he would do whatever she commanded right away. When the lady heard him promise, she said:

'Now, my friend, you must visit eighteen churches,[10] and make sure you do them all. In your woollen shirt, with bare feet,[11] you shall go, and beseech the saint of each one that they will pray to the merciful Creator to put an end to your pain. Then you must go to the king's court, full of hope and good faith. Understand this: if you believe truly then you will be cured by the king.'

He delayed not a moment longer, and hired a guide immediately. [He went to do his pilgrimage like a wise and worthy man.][12] Then he goes to the king's court, full of hope and good will. He begs the servants to tell the king he is here, and to intercede for him. But they don't want to listen, and order him to be quiet. But the more they threatened him the louder grew his cries; he harrasses them and beseeches them so,

---

[6] Aelred's name for him is similar; *Osbert* nicknames him *Vastans annonam*, meaning Spillecorn (p. 96 and note 2).

[7] 3531 'gute ne veit': as in modern French, the Nun says 'to see not a drop' for being able to see nothing at all. *Estoire* is more vivid: 'blind as a stump' [zuche], poetically appropriate for a woodcutter (v. 2919, and note to v. 3322).

[8] 3534 MS P says he rubbed his head and his face.

[9] 3551-4 'good' repeated five times, doubtless intentionally.

[10] 3569 'dis e oit': an error. Aelred specifies *octoginta* [eighty]; *Life*, p. 185, and *Estoire*, v. 2940).

[11] 3571 'En langes e nuz pez': standard for pilgrimage or penance (see *AND*, s.v. lange). Aelred says *absque lineis* [without your cloak], *Life* p. 185. *Estoire*'s glossary (for v. 2942) gives 'confession' for 'lange', but see *AND*; and *Prose Brut* ed. Pagan, glossary (p. 247).

[12] 3580 'duitre': MS P reads 'garçon' [boy], and adds: 'Si a fait son pelerinage, Come preudom et come sage'.

they hear his plea.[13] To their lord the king they tell of the poor man and his suffering. The king heard what he wanted to hear, for he was quite used to hearing and doing such things, and so he said:

'Send him to me. Who am I, that I should not grant what God has chosen to work through me? I should not be worthy to do it; nor must I go back on his promise. For if he promised a cure through me, it will be through his sovereign might. I shall not be afflicted by it, and so I should be overjoyed!'

Then he made them bring the blind man, and ordered water to be brought. Humbly, he washes his face for him, and prays for divine grace. He holds the holy Cross to his eyes, and the grace of God comes to pass. Immediately, the blood bursts forth, and his eyes see the light. The swelling goes away from the lids, and the pupils quickly clear.[14] So his sight is restored, as the king and all his court can see. As soon as he was free of that affliction he said to the king:

'I can see you quite well, and I see such glory in your face, as if an angel were standing in front of you!'[15]

When the king sees that he is cured, he gives thanks to God for it. He made them give him everything he needed, and he put him in his service at the palace of Westminster. He stayed there for the rest of his days, until England was conquered and made subject to King William. [For King Edward had taken no care about who was to have the kingdom. And so there were bitter wars in England, in the time of William whom God greatly favoured.][16]

---

[13] Cf. Mark 10:46–52; Luke 18:35–43. The woman's insistence on true faith echoes the Gospel story.
[14] 3614 MS P says 'and soon the corruption goes out of them'.
[15] 3620 'Cum s'un angele fust devant tei': Aelred (*Life*, p. 186) compares Edward's face with that of an angel (like Stephen's: Acts 6:15). In *Estoire*, a line is missing after v. 3002.
[16] After v. 3628, MS P adds 'Car le rois Edward n'ot vuleir Qui son regne soloit avoir Pour çou avoit molt puis grant gerre Al tens Guillaume en Engleterre En qui Dieus avoit molt grant part'. This remark, not in Aelred, does not find its way into *Estoire* (see *History*, p. 92); perhaps the P-scribe favoured William.

Chapter 21

Seven Blind Eyes (3629–92)[1]

Introduction

The Paris manuscript omits v. 3631 to v. 3932. It therefore reads: 'We have heard a great marvel, but next we shall hear a much greater one. God is full of glory in himself, and in his faithful he is marvellous …'. The latter sentence is the opening of chapter 24, The Seven Sleepers. The present miracle, and two chapters about Godwin, are thus missing from the P-version. In a previous chapter Edward learned a lesson about dreams; now Edward's servants are learning how to perform, with suitable humility, miracles on his behalf. The number seven allows the writer to mention the gifts of the Holy Spirit (Isaiah 11:2): six expanded to seven by taking the last one twice (*Estoire*, note to v. 3095; *History*, note 206). In Aelred, see *Life* (p. 188), where Is. 11:2–3, and I Cor. 12:4–11 are cited. The Nun declines to list the gifts, confident that her audience will know about them.

☙ ☙ ☙ ☙ ☙ ☙ ☙ ☙ ☙

¶We have heard a great marvel, but next we shall hear a much greater one – for as soon as this man [Ulwine] was healed there were found four sufferers at the king's palace, before the door, who had one eye between them and no more. And this one's sight was a common comfort to three: for the fourth in his kindness, who had one eye, was their leader. In him was all their help, for the three could not see a thing. This one always went ahead, and then each of the others following. A servant of the royal palace sees that they are all afflicted. His heart kindles with great sadness, and he is filled with pity. This man had kept some water,[2] and hidden it, in pious theft: it was what the others were cured with, as you have heard earlier. Because the water had healed one, he kept it so as to heal others. For he knew and believed that if it cured one man then by that same virtue many would regain their health. He goes for the blessed water immediately, and takes the poor fellows aside; he commands them[3] to have faith in God and to pray for his mercy, that for the merit of their king he will take care of their affliction; he tells them that if they believe the king able by God's power to make their disease better, then they could recover their health. Then he took the water that he had brought, and humbly washed their faces with it. He made the sign of the cross with his thumb upon their eyes, and began to pray to God, that he would show his power that day for the sake of his lord's merit. Behold, here comes the divine help that brings health to the afflicted. They raise their eyes to Heaven, and

---

[1] *Vita*, 765A–D; *Life*, §23. Cf. *Estoire*, vv. 3013–128; *History*, pp. 92–4.
[2] 3647 'de l'eve': Edward's washing-water, now known to have curative powers.
[3] 3659 MS W 'he asks them …'.

all the darkness goes out of them. Light is reborn to their eyes, and gives them back perfect sight. The four recovered seven eyes, for they were enlightened by seven.[4] The fourth of just one, the three of six – they were all given one holiness.[5] By these seven lights, restored to the sufferers who had lost them, is a thing truly proved and assured to God's faithful: that King Edward was perfect in the seven gifts of the Holy Spirit – as we can prove to you, but it is a long matter to tell. And we have already said so much that it should suffice the believers.

---

[4] 3680 Aelred cites Rev. 4:5 (the light is like 'seven lanterns'); the Nun omits this.
[5] 3682 'sancté': the author enjoys playing on 'santé' [health] and 'sancté [holiness]; cf. 'salu', which means health *and* salvation (see Glossary).

Chapter 22
The Fate of Godwin's Sons (3693–766)[1]

Introduction

The Nun's account is slightly expanded from Aelred's, making more of the characters' feelings. Her account of Harold, however, is mild compared to MP's. For this, and for legends of Harold's survival after Hastings, see especially *History* (Introduction), pp. 24–5. At v. 3757, she says 'Harald e Tosti ad occis' [Harold Godwinson 'killed Harald, and Tostig' too]. Here she differs from Aelred, who says the Norwegian king fled (*Life*, pp. 189–90; the note says they were both killed).[2] *Estoire*, too, does not say he fled, but that he was killed (*History*, p. 95). At first reading, it would seem that perhaps both writers corrected Aelred's apparent error, from the later account (*Life* §34, p. 218) of the real battle predicted here, in which 'both leaders were thrown down' (this alternative story is not to be found in *Genealogy*).[3] However, it has recently been pointed out that manuscripts of his *Vita* vary in just this chapter, which fact explains the discrepancy: both the Nun and MP used manuscripts containing a corrected narrative (Marzella's pp. 361–2). Of five significant variants which distinguish the two families of manuscripts, three are important for the present study. This is because they match places where the Nun's difference from Aelred really does suggest she was using a copy of the *Vita* which differs from the *PL* version that everybody has used up until now. Of those five mentioned by Marzella, a fourth is not relevant here because it occurs in Aelred's Prologue. The fifth, about Godiva (chapter 16), is not relevant because the Nun omits the passage in question. There remain many other differences, which are less likely to have arisen in this way, but until we have Marzella's new edition of the *Vita* containing all the variants we cannot identify any more such passages. The fact that she does not always follow readings in Marzella's family ω suggests that our argument, that her work is not a straight translation, remains valid.

ta ta ta ta ta ta ta ta ta

¶King Edward was a perfect man, and he was filled with such wisdom that he knew what was to come as well as what was past. He often recounted events, from beginning to end, and it always fell out just as he said – as it did about the two sons of Godwin.

One day he was seated at dinner, together with many worthy barons. Count Godwin was sitting with him, he who was the queen's father. The count's two sons were in the hall; they were small and young then. The elder's name was Harold, and the younger was called Tostig. These little boys were playing around the hall, but their

---

[1] *Vita* 765D–6B; *Life*, §24. Cf. *Estoire*, vv. 3133–252; *History*, pp. 94–5.
[2] For Aelred's 'mistake' at this point, see Marzella, 'La tradizione', p. 367 (and note 82).
[3] See ch. 34 for the real battle.

22 The Fate of Godwin's Sons (3693–766)

game turned to anger. They beat each other with their fists, and knocked each other to the ground. It was Harold who turned the play to fighting, attacking the other with his strength.[4] He got his two hands entangled in his hair, and would have given him death without respite had he not been hauled off him, for he wanted to strangle him. When the king had seen them separated, he said to their father the count:

'My lord count, tell me your opinion of that battle you've just seen. Do you think it was only play?'

The count replies, 'I don't believe it was anything different.'

The king says, 'I understood something different, in just that game I saw. I see clearly what will happen to those boys,[5] as soon as they are out of their boyhood and have sense and strength of their own: anger and hate will come between them, and one will rise up against the other. Conspiracy and treachery will take the place of the games they have done with. The stronger one will exile the other, and will finish by killing him – though he will quickly atone for his death, because he will be crushed by it.'

Everything came about as the king said, for this was where their story began. England witnessed it, and so England connived at their war. We know that after Edward died, Harold reigned next. He exiled Tostig, his brother, wanting to do even worse to him; he drove him as far away as Norway, where Harald [Hardrada] reigned.[6] He [Harald] welcomed the exile, and kept him at his court. He served the king much to his satisfaction, and he threw himself on his mercy, so that the Norwegian gathered his host and went with him against his brother. But Harold [Godwinson], with his English host, fought fiercely and killed both [King] Harald, and Tostig too, and took most of his men prisoner. In the same year that he committed this sin, England was reft from him. Some say that he was killed, and others that he remained alive.[7] Whatever the truth of the matter, he shamefully lost the kingdom. Thus ended those two brothers, and proved that the words of the king were true.

---

[4] 3714 'requere', attack (cf. *Life*, p. 189).
[5] 3727 'Bien vei qu'as vallez avendra': Södergård notes that lack of antecedent 'ço' is not uncommon; read 'vei ço qu'as vallez …'.
[6] 3748 'Harald Harfager': confusion between Harald 'Fairhair' (d. 930) and Hardrada was common among chroniclers (*Osbert*, p. 115 note 1). See Södergård's note; *Estoire*, and *History* (notes to vv. 3210 & 3222). Aelred says *cognomento Harfager* (*Vita*, 766B); *Life* translates as Hardrada without comment (pp. 189–90). See also v. 5524.
[7] Marzella refers to a story that Harald Hardrada escaped and became a hermit, as Harold Godwinson is said to have done ('La tradizione', p. 362, note 67).

Chapter 23

The Fate of Godwin (3767–932)[1]

Introduction

The murder of Alfred was mentioned in chapter 5, where the Nun says she does not know the story; and in chapter 8, among reasons for Edward not to marry into Godwin's family (see *Life*, note on p. 147). This chapter amplifies Aelred's account, especially in its anti-Godwin sentiments.[2] Certain details, such as the servant hurrying in the hall, seem to be further additions by the Nun. The blessing is a distinctly Eucharistic touch, bold in that the resulting transubstantiation is death-dealing rather than life-giving. It adds to the notion of Edward as a Christ-figure (see p. 5, above). The servant's hurry explains his stumble. In fact the detail of the fateful comment, that brother should assist brother, also appears in William of Malmesbury's account of a different pair of brothers: The Birth of Ethelstan, and the Murder of Edwin his Brother.[3] A variant in family ω, described by Marzella, adds *Cumque vir sanctus bucellam manu benedicens signasset, miser ille ori inferens* etc. [With that, the holy man signed the morsel with his hand, and the wretch ... (the passage continues as in the *PL* copy)].[4] The king blessing the bread alters the death-scene. Instead of divine vengeance acting directly upon the culprit, our story makes Edward its instrument; it thus becomes another of his miracles.[5] The variant in family ω continues, a few lines down, with the following: *Hinc, fratres karissimi, hinc liquido apparet quantum vim et efficaciam illa sancta manus habuerit, ad cuius motum bucella modica in tantam virtutis molem excrevit et neque eici posset, nec per solitos meatus traduci, sed mox eum vita privavit, qui nec in verbis veritatem, nec in divini nomininis adiuratione reverentiam observavit.* [Hence, dearest brothers, it is limpidly clear what great power that holy hand holds, at whose motion a small morsel grew into so great a heap of virtue, and could neither be swallowed, nor led through the usual channels, but all at once it deprived him of life, who observed neither truth in his words, nor reverence in his oath by the divine name.][6] This, and other variants in the manuscript family in question, indicates that the Nun used one of these manuscripts and not one of those

---

[1] *Vita*, 766B–7B; *Life*, §25. Cf. *Estoire*, vv. 3253–340; *History*, pp. 95–7.
[2] See Le Saux, *Companion*, pp. 215–16 for demonization of Godwin in Wace's *Rou*; p. 219 for his account of Godwin's death, from English sources.
[3] *Kings* tr. Stephenson, §139, pp. 122–4.
[4] My translation, and see below.
[5] See Talbot, 'Duped', p. 208: during the Inquisition a 'test of the morsel' was used as a form of lie-detector. See also *History* (note to vv. 3312–34); but 'Modern legal historians have reached no consensus' about how such an ordeal might have worked.
[6] 'La tradizione', p. 363 (I thank Jane Burkowski for help with the translation); see p. 364, note 71, for possible sources.

on which *PL* is based; a few of the passages apparently added by herself turn out to have been taken from Aelred after all.

In fact, Godwin did suffer a sudden illness at the king's table; he died on 15th April 1053 (*Life*, p. 192). Aelred for once begins on a personal note 'I think I should ...' (*Life*, p. 190), and there are no biblical references in his chapter. The Nun often replaces Bible passages with proverbial or homiletic sayings; here she begins with one.

ta ta ta ta ta ta ta ta ta

¶We have often heard it told, that whoever does or intends evil, it often falls back on himself and he suffers the worst of it. Sooner or later the evil he does, or wishes to do, returns upon him.[7] This is what happened to Count Godwin, who did so many bad deeds. He did much wrong to King Edward, and he delivered his brother to death. Then, by vengeance of divine anger, the evil turned on him so that afterwards he died shamefully, in the presence of the king and all his noble court. He was extremely wicked and treacherous, and accomplished in all craftiness: there was never felony undertaken by him that did not achieve its end. He did wrong as though it were just and right. He committed great outrage in the land, and anybody who did not submit to his will, however clever and wise they were he chased them right out of the kingdom.[8] He was so sure of himself that he often tried it out on the king, as to how he could trick him into doing what he wanted. In the end he had managed so well, manoeuvring and bribing, by lies and treachery and flattery, that he had turned almost all, but a few, of the king's closest associates against him. Cousins and relations and friends, he drove them all out of the land; clerks and laymen and ordained priests, even bishops and abbots whom the king had brought with him when he arrived in England. And so he separated the king from those who best knew his secrets: when these failed the king, then he must needs turn to himself. This is how he thought to tempt the king to do everything he wanted. But the king, even though he was aware of all this, made no sign. Because he saw him to be so powerful, and so set in all his ruses, he pretended not to see any of the wickedness: he could see that this was neither the time nor the place to do anything about it. Therefore he wished to endure the more patiently lest worse should come of it. For if the count knew for sure that the king was wise to him, he would hate him the more and punish him the sooner; once a villain realises that his villainy is known, then his strength will kindle to unbridled wrath. His desire will never be ended, until he has achieved his desire. Therefore the king acted wisely, guarding himself against disaster. Nevertheless, he often said publicly, even in his hearing, that God would take vengeance on him for the great wrongs he had done. His words certainly came true, and it was now not long to wait.

¶The king was holding a banquet, to which the noblest of the English came. The king seated himself to dine, and Godwin took his seat near him, little knowing what

---

[7] 3768–72 Similar sayings are listed in Morawski: 1939, 1979, & 1983.
[8] 3790 MS W says 'he quickly [tost] chased them ...'.

was to happen to him so soon and so dreadfully. The servants bring dishes to them, and invite them warmly to eat; this they do gladly, after the manner of English people.[9] But there was one of those who dined, who would never partake of another dish. As the king sat there, beside his secret enemy,[10] here comes one of his servants hurrying across the hall at top speed. His foot somehow tripped on something, so that he nearly fell over. But thanks to the other foot, which was firm, the stubbed foot recovered its strength quickly, and resumed its proper place. One of the feet had helped the other so well that no harm was done. Many laughed loudly, saying how courteously one foot had helped the other,[11] so that no harm had come to it. Count Godwin laughed with them, and said:

'It is customary, and quite proper, for one brother to help the other and come to his aid when he needs it.'

As soon as the king heard this, he said sharply, 'My brother would do the same for me, had Godwin allowed him to do so.'

When the count heard this he looked stunned and unhappy. His face falls and his looks grow doleful, and he says to the king in front of everybody:

'My lord king, I can see and understand that you still suspect me, that your brother was killed through my doing, and that I have despised you since. You are still in the confidence of those who say that about me. But God, who knows the secrets of all hearts, judges according to the right. Let him allow me to swallow the mouthful I'm about to eat, without difficulty. If it will go down my throat and I stay in good health, then I never did treason against you, and I had nothing to do with his death.'

With that, the king raised his hand and blessed the fatal food.[12] Then the wretch, miserable soul, put the morsel in his mouth. He swallowed it into his throat, but it stopped halfway down. He gulped hard at it, but it stuck fast and would not go down. When he sees that he cannot swallow, he tries frantically to cough it out. But the harder he struggles, the more he feels afflicted. The passage of his throat is stopped, and soon his breathing stops; as he lost his breath his eyes began to turn in his head. Death's agony seized him, he flung out his arms, and fell headlong. When the king sees the wretch endure the hideous pangs of death, he understands that it is the wrath of Heaven. He says to them, 'Drag that cur outside!'

Here, everybody who is prepared to heed this example can understand clearly how the king's holy hand had supreme virtue in itself: the morsel that it signed with the

---

[9] 3847–50 This characteristic comment is added by the Nun. It is not clear whether she is distancing herself from, or identifying herself with, the English (whose customs Aelred does not mention); cf. the woodcutters (v. 3518 and note).

[10] 3854 'sun privé enemi': this could mean 'private', or even 'personal'.

[11] 3866–7 'Ad l'un pié l'autre sucuru': MS W lacks 'pié', reading 'one had helped the other'. Coincidentally, a corresponding line in *Estoire* also omits the 'foot' (v. 3288; the translators nevertheless supply it: '... his other foot held', *History* p. 96). The idea 'courteously' is an addition to Aelred's narrative (*Life*, p. 191). It underlines the bitter irony of a situation where Godwin's less than courteous behaviour to Edward's brother is in everybody's mind.

[12] 3896 'le mortel mossel seigna': both alliteration and double entendre are present in this phrase, a play on 'mor' meaning both food and death (Aelred provides no adjective).

cross was so quickly transformed that it cruelly killed the body that it ought naturally to have nourished. For at the moment the king blessed it, it took on such hugeness that the man could neither swallow it down into his body nor drag it back up into his mouth. So it caused the death of a traitor, who neither showed loyalty in his words nor bore any reverence towards the name of God, by whom he swore falsely.[13]

---

[13] 3917–32 'Ici poet chascun … a tort jura': for this 'personal reflection' (Södergård, p. 31) see my introduction to this chapter. Not only does Aelred here address a wider audience, the passage also reinforces Edward as instrument of divine vengeance. For the scene as imitation of the Last Supper, see Marzella's p. 364 and reference to I Cor. 11:29.

Chapter 24

The Seven Sleepers (3933–4164)[1]

Introduction

This is a well-known legend, exploited as evidence for Edward's prophetic power.[2] MS P, after missing three chapters, resumes here. It contains added description and action, and the answer to how long the Sleepers will sleep (see notes below). In Anglo-Saxon England, the feast was 27th July (*Life*, p. 194). See Södergård's note to v. 4043, and the Anglo-Norman version (Chardri, *La Vie des Set Dormanz*). For the earliest appearance of Edward's vision, see 'In translacione' ed. Jackson, p. 72, note 29. MP says Edward told the legend in Latin (*History*, p. 97; see note 223 to v. 3390).

❧ ❧ ❧ ❧ ❧ ❧ ❧ ❧ ❧

¶God is full of glory in himself, and in his faithful he is marvellous; he reveals his secrets to them, and he shows them the "why".[3] He does his will, as one who has the power. There is no need to marvel at this, if he, the marvellous, performs marvels and draws his own people to marvels; so he did to Edward the King, who did so many marvels himself,[4] as you have heard before and shall presently hear.

One Easter Day he was crowned,[5] rather by custom than by his will. King Edward, with high honour as is proper to this high day, was adorned nobly – as is proper for a coronation – crown on head, sceptre in hand, and heart full of good thoughts. As his body was adorned with gold and purple from head to foot,[6] so was his heart enriched and filled with the love of God. When the king had taken communion, he approached his palace. All the barons of the realm, and the bishops and the abbots, were at the feast that day for love of the king, their lord. The king sat down at the table to eat, then each one sat down according to his rank. Many a gentleman served that day, and many a worthy of high renown. [Many fine silken clothes embroidered with gold, and many rich clothes beautifully worked,][7] much good cloth, and many fine ornaments could be seen there that day. The plate was of gold and silver, finely worked, rich and beautiful. The king saw the noble life led by his great barons, the

---

[1] *Vita*, 767B–9A; *Life*, §26. Cf. *Estoire*, vv. 3341–452; *History*, pp. 97–8.
[2] See Magennis, 'Seven Sleepers', on the legend, sources, and references; in Otter, 'Prolixitas', the anonymous Edward is one of three texts examined (Merlin's prophetic laughter also discussed). See also *Osbert*, note on p. 100, for the legend's antiquity; and ibid. p. 103, note 2, for possible sources and an analogue for the vision.
[3] 3936 'met en eus le purquei': Södergård's note refers to a similar phrase at v. 5959, and adduces other examples of this curious usage. MS P omits vv. 3935–6.
[4] 3938–42 The Nun uses 'marvel ...' five times in five lines (six in nine lines).
[5] 3945 'ert curuné': the Nun refers to 'curunement' at v. 3950. This was an occasion when a king's crown was worn, cf. Aelred's *caput ornaret corona* (*Life*, p. 193), not a re-coronation. See introduction to ch. 9.
[6] 3954 MS P has 'e de pierres coronés' [his body was adorned with gold, and crowned with gems].
[7] 3966 MSS P and W add, after this line, 'Maint bon samit a or brusdé Et maint bon pailie bien uvré'.

jewels and the arrogance,[8] the golden cups and the great feast; he saw himself crowned and knew his great power – he feared that he might take vain delight in the vain glory that he saw. Then he controlled his thoughts so that vain delight could not enter there. He shut himself away from the whole world, and sent his whole heart to God. As the king sat there, wholly ravished in God, suddenly he was illuminated and his face was greatly beautified. The joy inside his heart appeared outside, in his face; soon after, he laughed,[9] and then resumed his former expression. His face then darkened as it returned to its usual look. The servants marvelled greatly, and the feasters took counsel with one another; each was sure that he had seen marvels. But there was not one of them there so daring, that he would ask what it was he had seen – as best they could, they kept still.[10] When they had drunk and eaten enough, and they were happy with the different things, they drew the cloths and removed the tables, then went on to the songs and the stories. The king left them to amuse themselves; he withdrew his body, and his attention. Then he went into a chamber and took off his royal adornments. Count Harold went after him, and he took a bishop with him, and an abbot who had seen this; then they all three came to the king, and gently asked him to explain his laugh to them. The king, when he hears the request, grants it very amiably:

'Exceedingly blessed', he says, 'is he who places all his thoughts in God and who trusts in him for everything, and who forgets these great vanities.[11] As much as he is far from them, so is he closer to that very great certainty that despises all vanity. Now just then, when I was sitting at dinner, I saw these big goblets of pure gold, and fine foods arriving thick and fast in big silver dishes; I saw good wines brought wherever they were wanted, and saw all my nobles dressed so richly – I shut my thoughts up tightly in myself and put all this into oblivion; in all things I rendered myself to God. By his mercy he received me, and he empowered my heart with his grace.[12] He illumined the eyes of my heart, and the beams darted a very long way – as far as the city of Ephesus and then to the great Mount Celiun. There I saw the Seven Sleepers lying, whose sleep has no end.[13] I saw the size of their cave and the colour of their silken clothes, and I saw their faces and their looks, and how big their bodies were. All this I saw clearly – of course I laughed at it. But suddenly I saw something else: a troubling and deathly sign. For I saw all these seven Sleepers, who had reposed and slept for so many years on the right side, that they turned onto the

---

[8] 3973 MS P has 'Les estrumans et les banoi' [the musical instruments and the entertainments, or games]. The scribe seems to be enjoying this scene, already expanded by comparison with Aelred.
[9] 3989 'fait un ris': most likely a laugh. Nobody here mentions 'seeing' a smile (cf. v. 1527 and note): the word is always 'ris' not 'surris'.
[10] 4000 MS P has 'A grant force s'en sunt tenu' [with great effort, they kept still].
[11] 4017-20 Aelred cites Ps. 40:4 (39:5 in *LV*); the Nun expands the idea slightly (she rephrases another psalm reference a few lines down; see *Life* pp. 193-4).
[12] 4038 'E mun quoer de sa grace pout': Södergård notes (to v. 6548) that the verb may be used in absolute, not merely auxiliary, sense.
[13] 4044 In the legend, the Sleepers wake many years later; for this endless sleep see note to v. 4086.

left.[14] I know that this movement is a bad omen to humankind.[15] Henceforth the saying shall be fulfilled, that we have heard in the Gospels:[16] one people will rise up against another and one reign will persecute another. Pestilence and famine will come, there will be earthquakes here and there. The enemies of God, the pagans, will rise up against the Christians,[17] and God will take cruel revenge on his people who have done him so much wrong. The servants will hate their masters, and will take away their honours from them. Kings will make war with one another,[18] and princes will play one another false. Seventy years will the wars last, all over the world in all lands – and so long will they lie on that side to which they have now turned.'

¶These men were very much dismayed when they heard this from the king, for never before had they known anything of the Seven Sleepers who slept so. They ask the king who they are, why and how long they will sleep. [There is none present who does not beg him to explain the prophecy.][19] The king told them their story as though he had it written before him – and their names and their martyrdom,[20] and the reason for their sleeping. [He told them that they will sleep from now until they come to Judgement Day, when those who caused them such torment shall receive judgement.][21] The three took counsel together about it, they wanted to send to that country because they wanted to advise all those who would come after them. The count found a messenger – a well-spoken and good knight; the bishop found an ordained cleric; the abbot found a monk. Then they gave them a letter where it was written, from beginning to end, what the king had seen and how and in what way [that the seven brothers lay like this, who had been sleeping so long].[22] They sent them to the Emperor, whom they knew to be in Constantinople, to ask him for an escort to go on as far as the mountain where the Sleepers were, and that by his great power he could make the messengers see them. The messengers travelled until they

---

[14] MP says 'they had turned'. Here Edward saw them moving; in William of Malmesbury's account (*Gesta Regum*, vol. I, bk. ii, 225.2; p. 411) he sees them turn over. Aelred says 'As I was looking on ... they turned' (*Life*, p. 194).
[15] 4058 MS W has 'Mut merveilliaint cele umaine gent' [Mankind marvels greatly ...], a weaker idea.
[16] Matt. 24:7 (and Mark 13:8): *For nation shall rise up against nation, and kingdom against kingdom: and there shall be famines, and pestilences, and earthquakes, in divers places.* For 'parsivra' in v. 4062: the first meaning is 'follow'; here it probably means pursue or persecute. The Nun keeps the Bible quotation, telling us where it is to be found, although another psalm reference, a few lines down, is more characteristically paraphrased (*Life*, p. 194).
[17] 4066 After this line, MS P adds four lines of to-ing and fro-ing between the pagans and the Christians (the pagans are finally conquered). For the seventy-year age of wars, predicted below, see Otter, 'Prolixitas'; and note to v. 3402 in *History*.
[18] 4072 MS W has, instead of the following, 'Et mult granment se forceront' [and will greatly expend their forces].
[19] 4082 MS P has '... dormi unt' [how long they have slept], then adds 'N'i a celui qui ne li prie Qu'il descuevre la prophesie.'
[20] 4085 Södergård's glossary gives 'suffering' for 'passion', but the meaning includes 'martyrdom'. They are called 'martirs' twice, below. Chardri, *La Vie des Set Dormanz*, calls their walling-up a 'seint martirement' (v. 773).
[21] 4086 MS P adds, after this line, 'Si lor dist que il dormiront De ci c'al jugement venront A donc aront le jugement De ceus qui lor font tel torment' (other MSS do not give this explanation).
[22] 4098 MS P adds 'Que li set frere ensi gisoient Qui longe dormi avoient'.

found the Emperor. At Constantinople, where he then was, they were received with great honour. He read King Edward's letter with great joy and delight – that God had showed to the English the rich treasure of the Greeks. He sent them to Ephesus, and commanded the bishop to honour them and show them the Seven Sleepers. And he did it willingly; he went to meet them with clerks and laymen.[23] He leads them in great procession, thus making their satisfaction sure. Then he lets them go into the cave, and has the martyrs shown to them. So they saw it was all truth, that the king had told them – of their looks, of their clothes, of their names and their form. And they found them all lying on their left side. They are very happy at what they see,[24] but they are very much amazed that the king had seen them from so far, by the power of the Holy Spirit. They make their prayer to the holy martyrs, make their offerings, and take their leave. They go back to their land, and gladden everybody they find there. To the king, they tell what they have seen, and that what he saw was the truth; in the hearing of all they have proved that he spoke the truth about it all. The king was not deceived in what he said and what he saw. For when God called him to him,[25] his words very soon came true – for all Syria was conquered by the pagans and their dominion. They burned cathedrals and churches, and brought them all to the ground. There was then no land in the world that did not experience very cruel war. For several of the kings who held them had already gone to their deaths: of Greece, of Rome, and of France.[26] And England had great misfortune after the death of its good lord, as appears still to this day.[27] It is clear that in his life he had the spirit of prophecy, and that he was very intimate with God – when he showed him such secrets, that he in one moment saw both what had been and what was – nor could what was to come hide itself from his senses.

---

[23] 4118 'Od clers e lais ...': this probably means 'with a sizeable group of [all manner of] people'.
[24] 4129 Aelred says great fear seized them (*Life*, p. 195). A typical switch of tense occurs in this line and the next: 'mult sunt liez, Mais mult se sunt esmerveillez': the reader's eye sees two apparently matching forms with 'sunt', but one is followed by an adjective (are happy) and the other by a participle.
[25] 4143 MS P reads '... quant devant eus en parla' [when he spoke of it, before them]; this (or 'what he said of it ...') makes better sense than MS V's 'quant Deus a lui l'apela'.
[26] 4153 MS P omits mention of Greece.
[27] This reference to post-Conquest troubles is not in Aelred.

Chapter 25

King Edward and the Ring (4165–476)[1]

Introduction

This story is remarkable for one of the poem's mystical passages. It also demonstrates the Nun's use of 'fin' amur'. The miracle of the ring is among the most celebrated of the wonders attributed to Edward; although *GL* attaches it to King Edmund (in the legend of Saint John).[2] It first appears with Aelred, as if he sought to characterize Edward as a true Anglo-Saxon hero and 'ring-giver' (*Life*, p. 196, and editor's note p. 23).[3] Its appearance in one manuscript of *Osbert* was probably an interpolation, therefore unknown to Osbert.[4] However, Marzella examines this version:[5] written before Edward's canonization in 1161, it could be Aelred's source for the story. Dutton argues that Aelred probably was the first to put it about, wherever he got it: the abbot Laurence took a ring from Edward's body when the tomb was opened in 1163 – a ring that had been present when the tomb was opened earlier in the century. Had the story been current at this earlier date, the ring would probably have been taken then, for safe-keeping.[6] In the *Early South English Legendary* it is likewise found in John's legend, but is told of 'Seint Edward þat was nouþe late'. One manuscript says the ring is still at Westminster, for pilgrims to wonder at: an example of the widespread 'still-there' topos of medieval narrative.[7] The two collections were made at around the same time, neither being derived from the other.[8] Lipscomb is mainly concerned with the pilgrims' return to England and does not mention the Nun's version. He does not remark on the fact that *GL* attaches the story to Edmund, but does lay stress on whether the saint 'vanishes' or simply 'departs'.[9] There is a comparable story in *Gesta Romanorum*: a king receives gifts from the Magi in a vision, and is vouchsafed information about his own death, in return for his gifts to them. The extant *Gesta* post-dates Aelred's work, but such stories probably circulated freely in medieval culture.[10]

John the Apostle (see *ODS*) was thought to be one of the Evangelists, and also author of the Book of Revelation (Apocalypse). This belief was widespread, although

---

[1] *Vita*, 769A–70D; *Life*, §27. Cf. *Estoire*, vv. 3453–600; *History*, pp. 98–100.
[2] *GL*, I, p. 55; neither Edmund nor Edward has his own entry.
[3] See also 'King Edward's Ring', for versions of the story.
[4] *Anon*, pp. xxxvi (note 1) & 116; and 'King Edward's Ring'.
[5] 'L'anello del re' (abstract in English, p. 255).
[6] 'Ælred, Two Portraits'.
[7] ed. Horstmann, p. 417; Owst, *Literature and Pulpit*, p. 147; for something 'still there', see note to v. 5948.
[8] *The Early South-English Legendary* ed. Horstmann, pp. vii–viii. See further Laurent, *Plaire et édifier*, pp. 303–7.
[9] 'Legend of the Ring'.
[10] See *Gesta Romanorum* ed. Herrtage, p. 518, and Introduction for sources and dates.

25 King Edward and the Ring (4165–476)   147

Eusebius cites Dionysius' doubts on the subject.[11] The editor of a thirteenth-century *Revelacion* cites 'renewed interest in St John as a pilgrim', in context of Henry III's promotion of Edward's cult. But, though Aelred describes the saint as *in habitu peregrino* [in the garb of a pilgrim] (*Life* pp. 197 and 199), the Nun 'a pilgrim' (vv. 4266 and 4415), *Estoire* uses neither figure: he calls him 'un povre' throughout, thus deleting the pilgrim persona.[12] At v. 4296 the pilgrim vanishes mysteriously; this disappearance is a sign that he is supernatural (see my note).

Södergård marks the episode as one which amplifies the source (p. 31). MacBain gives details as follows: Aelred says only that Edward burst into tears [*prorupit in lacrymas*] and enquired most diligently about everything the pilgrims had seen. The Nun expands considerably, with a good deal of direct speech as well as the added prophecy of Edward's death. She stresses his insatiable love for the saint, and his burning desire to hear more and more. 'Like Chrétien and Marie ... the Nun of Barking appears to be well acquainted with the new love ideology'.[13] Dates for Marie are uncertain, but she is thought to have been writing a little later than the Nun.[14] MacBain guesses the Nun was a lady of the court before taking the veil; her knowledge of Latin shows she was a highly educated one. Her richly sensual expression of the love between John and Jesus, and of Edward's gluttonous delight in hearing of John's appearance to the pilgrims, is matched by Aelred's powerful language in his account. She uses the verb 'enivrer' [intoxicated, delirious]; in Aelred, John drinks wisdom and love from Jesus' breasts (*Life*, p. 197).

The episode is coloured with a sense of mortality. The prediction of Edward's death is adumbrated near the beginning (vv. 4167–8) by a phrase that invokes the words of Byrhtwold as he rallies his doomed men before the defeat of Maldon: 'Cum sun cors plus s'afiebliseit, Sun quoer de tant plus s'esforceit ...'.[15] In the Nun's poem, Edward is characterized as a soldier of God, even though she does not always care to stress his qualities as an earthly warrior. Her words here recall an earlier scene, where Edith prayed that God would give her husband strength to fulfil the desires of his will (see note to vv. 1385–6, in chapter 8).

❧ ❧ ❧ ❧ ❧ ❧ ❧ ❧ ❧

¶King Edward was already afflicted by the weakness of mortal age. As his body grew weaker, so his heart strengthened itself the more, to love God and his Mother and to honour his saints everywhere.[16] He loved and served them all, but he had

---

[11] *History* ed. Louth, 7:25, pp. 240–43.
[12] Note to v. 36 of *Revelacion* ed. Pitts, p. 102. In Mirk, *Festial*, the saint is a 'pylgrym' (vol. I:35); note (vol. II p. 366) for the ring still at Westminster in 1388.
[13] 'Vocabulary', p. 274.
[14] See for example Crane, 'Anglo-Norman cultures', p. 46.
[15] 'Our resolve must be so much the firmer, our hearts so much the bolder, our courage so much the greater, by so much as our strength diminishes' (*A Guide to Old English*, Mitchell and Robinson, p. 252, lines 312–13 and note). See my Introduction (English Literature) for discussion: this sentence does not appear in proverb-collections or other repositories of traditional wisdom.
[16] Aelred lacks the Nun's poetic antithesis (*Life*, p. 196).

chosen two of the best. One was Saint Peter, whom he cherished as his patron, for he had given him much comfort and held him back from many perils. He chose Saint John next – he who is Jesus Christ's beloved – he loved him above all for his unique chastity.[17] In these two he had set his heart, and so received from them the good hope that they would help him in all things as soon as they knew of his need. The king often used to wonder which he should love most, but his Thought told him they were both God's companions: for although he had given riches and power to one, he had filled the other with delight and sweetness by his love. To the less-beloved one he gave the greater dignity – lordship and judgement over the whole Holy Church – and though he gave less to the other he made it up to him by his love, for he loved him more tenderly and with special intimacy. At the Supper this was clearly seen, when he lay upon the breast of his Master. Then, when God wanted to announce how his time drew near, that he must buy us by death and go from the world to his Father, he said to his disciples that one of them would betray him. As soon as they heard that they made signs to Saint John, to ask him which one it was, for each one doubted himself. But John asked him only which was the beloved, the familiar friend. He took it upon himself, as one who has the right to do so.[18] Saint Edward loved him dearly for that, and honoured him as much as he could. He dearly loved Saint Peter, who is the shepherd of all humankind. He did not know which to praise more, nor which he should love the more: either him who was gate-keeper of Heaven and who could grant the right of entry,[19] who was prince of the apostles and governed Holy Church – or him who was beloved of the Lord of Heaven, Creator of earth, whom God laid on his breast and made all drunk with his love.[20] From the sweetness he drank there, he received such worthy knowledge that he understood more of the deity than any mortal man born in this world. King Edward, who knew this, pledged himself with great tendernessness; he tenderly granted his love to his pious Creator's beloved.[21] And nevertheless he loved Saint Peter more – his good patron – it was necessary to cajole[22] him, because he had the power of entry[23] to the royal Court where no evil may ever come in. Next to this revered gate-keeper, the king loved Saint

---

[17] 4180 MS P has 'for his most holy chastity'. For Christ's beloved, see John 13:23, 19:26, 20:2, 21:7 & 20 (and *Life*, p. 196). In the following, the Nun makes more of Edward's thought, about both saints, and Aelred gives more detail of the Gospel stories. John introduces himself in person, as the beloved friend of Jesus, later in this chapter.
[18] 4181-218 In Aelred (*Life*, p. 197), as here, are references to Gospel accounts of the Last Supper.
[19] 4226 'le dangier': see note to v. 4244. MS P reads, instead, '... entree fu ses mestiers' [it was his task to guard the entry].
[20] 4232 'E de s'amur tot l'enivra': cf. 'saoul' = 'sated' or 'drunk' (see Glossary).
[21] 4240 MS W ends here, for reasons unknown, in the middle of introducing an important story. The break was probably not intended to remove the mention of Barking Abbey several chapters later.
[22] 4243 'losengier' usually has a negative meaning (flatter, slander), but see v. 924, where Edward apparently 'flatters' fools in order to reprove them; and p. 42, above.
[23] 4244 'le dangier De l'entree': 'dangier' (from Latin *dominiarium*) has several meanings; see vv. 3152, 4226, 4380 (and Glossary).

25 King Edward and the Ring (4165–476)   149

John. He often used to speak of him and deplore his own high estate, and talk with great humility of his chastity and his virtue.

¶Then it happened that a church was established in the name of the Apostle, sacred to the honour of God and erected in the name of his beloved.[24] King Edward was at the dedication-day for love of him.[25] The business gladdened him very much, for the sake of his dear friend Saint John. There were many great knights in this royal company; the king and all the barons followed the procession. As the king was duly making his way, a pilgrim appeared to him. He asked him very politely, in Saint John's name and for his sake, to give him something that day. The king was happy when he heard, and put his hand into his alms-purse. But it was wasted effort, for in such deeds it had already given out as much as had earlier been put into it.[26] When the pilgrim saw that there was nothing in the purse, he pressed the king eagerly and begged him most insistently.[27] But he had nothing to give him, nor knew which way to turn so as not to find him crying out in front of him. The king was very upset, and upset about the pilgrim.[28] Then he called his treasurer, who could not get near him for the crowds around him. The king felt shame and annoyance, that he could not get free of him and that he had nothing to give him.[29] Then he thought of his ring, rich and beautiful on his hand. Quickly he took it off and gave it to the pilgrim, who thanked him politely and then went away or vanished [so that he never knew what had become of him. The king often remembered him, and marvelled greatly how he had lost him so quickly].[30]

¶Soon after this dedication, there were two men of England travelling to visit the Holy Sepulchre. As they went on their way with their companions, suddenly they went astray – they left their right road – they didn't know the reason, but it was only

---

[24] See *History*, p. 98 & note 228, for what church this might have been. The story originates with Aelred, so it cannot have been a c11 church refurbished in c13, as suggested there (Aelred seems to be talking of a new church). MP may have been thinking of a contemporary dedication service, but he is more probably following the source, as the Nun is.

[25] 4257 'pur sue amur': Södergård would normally expect 'pur la sue ...' here, but cites several examples of an article omitted.

[26] 4274 MS P reads, instead, '... U il plot molt au roi Jhesu' [it had already given out what was most pleasing to King Jesus].

[27] 4279-84 The next lines, 'But he had nothing ... about the pilgrim', are omitted in MS P. Aelred gives the idea more briefly: 'The pilgrim pressed him, increasing his entreaties' (*Life*, p. 198). But see note to v. 4290.

[28] 4283-4 Södergård thinks 'anguissus' is repeated by mistake, because the sense is the same ('rime équivoque' calls for a different sense), and is unable to correct from another MS.

[29] 4290-91 Södergård notes the construction 'rien ne li out que doner', and about the Ring story. MS P adds, after v. 4290, 'Li pelerins molt l'angoissa Et plus et plus li demanda'; the line-order here is somewhat different.

[30] 4296 'Si s'en ala u esvani': this vagueness suggests he is supernatural; see Aelred: *vel recessit, vel disparuit* [either withdrew or disappeared] (*Life*, p. 198). *Estoire* has 'Partiz s'en est e envaniz' (v. 3480, 'went away *and* vanished'); the translators conflate: 'he vanished' (*History*, p. 98). See my Introduction, From Latin to Medieval French. MS P says 'Et puis s'en est esvanis', simplifying the departure; it then adds 'Que onques ne sot qu'il devint Souvent de lui au roi souvint Et grant merveille en a eu Qu'il si tost l'avoit perdu'. This amplifies Edward's feelings, and incidentally makes a pun familiar to all members of Lady Margaret Hall, Oxford: 'Souvent me souviens' (the College motto). See also my note to vv. 2213-14.

those two who turned aside from the way.[31] They are troubled at this adventure, and presently night has overtaken them. Then they didn't know which way to turn, nor whether to stay still or go forward. One said to the other:

'How did we get here? What sin has beset us miserable fellows, that has brought us here?'[32]

While they were lamenting like this, they saw a great company, who seemed to be young men dressed in white garments. They were very beautiful people, and nobly attired. The two who went right at the head of the group carried two candles in their hands, so that this great light robbed the night of darkness; they passed along the road where the pilgrims were standing. After the great procession, there came a lord of kingly manner. Two barons escorted him handsomely, and led him with great honour. He was white-headed, but very fine-looking, for he had the colouring of a youth. His body was beautiful, his face bright and worthy of grace; his countenance was noble and wise, his looks were sweet and his expression pious;[33] he was of royal stature and priestly deportment. When the pilgrims saw him, they felt greatly comforted. As soon as he came near them, he stayed his pace a little. He looked at them kindly, and then spoke to them:

'Where are you from, friends?' he said. 'From what land do you come here? What law do you submit to? What king have you, and what country?'

They replied very readily:

'We're from England, King Edward is our king, and we hold the Christian faith. We were born in England, and we had resolved to visit the Holy Land where God lived and died for us.[34] But today, as we travelled, we went astray by chance and lost our companions. But we don't know any reason for it. To tell the truth, we don't know this place. This land is strange to us; we don't know whom to ask for shelter nor who will be kind to us. There's no doubt about it, we're completely lost!'

'Now follow me,'[35] he replied, 'and God will provides adequately for us; he alone takes care of all beings, and gives good measure to all.'

The pilgrims thank him heartily, and obey his instruction. So he led them with him into a most noble city. There he entertained them for the night with great plenty,

---

[31] 4302–482 MS P reduces the following to forty-seven lines. See note to v. 4482, for the ending of the P-version.

[32] 4311–14 Direct speech is added by the Nun; Aelred just says they were discussing what had happened (*Life*, p. 198).

[33] 4333–6 'face', 'semblant', 'reguard', 'visage': repetition is an important feature of the poem's style, but this passage contains a sudden variety of words for 'face'. It is more detailed than in Aelred (*Life*, p. 198).

[34] 4355 'requere', 'visit': for the Nun, 'to seek' a saint or a holy place means to visit them, in prayerful pilgrimage. She stresses the act of seeking as beseeching; corresponding passages in *Estoire* and *Vita* stress the making of the vow, even the making of a pilgrimage, over this sense of pious travel (*Estoire* 'quere' 3484, 3514; *History* 'to find, to seek'). Aelred uses 'visit' in just one of these instances: *sacratissima ... loca visitare disponimus* [to visit the most sacred places] (*Vita* 770A; *Life* p. 198).

[35] 4367 See Södergård's note on word order.

25 King Edward and the Ring (4165–476) 151

with great delight. Then, when they are well satisfied and rested from their travels,[36] they go to lie down on fine beds – they don't stay awake for long.[37]

¶When the bright day had appeared, their host came to them. He led them out of the city, then told them what he had to say:

'Dear brothers,' he said, 'don't be afraid, for you will return safe and sound to the land where you were born, with joy, with great prosperity – and God who is our salvation will lead you by his power. He will make your way prosperous, and will keep you for my sake; you will have my help for the sake of your good king. As long as you are on this road my eyes will be upon you every day. I shall make your journey light;[38] you will accomplish it without hindrance. Perhaps you want to know who I am that is talking to you. John Evangelist is my name, and I am called Apostle. I am a disciple of Jesus – the one he made his beloved friend. I and the king, your lord, are bound by one love. I love him for his great chastity, and he loves me, in turn, for that. Give him greetings from me, and, so he will not hesitate to believe you, take this his ring with you and give it him as a sign – he amiably gave it to me, on the day of my dedication. I was the pilgrim who begged from him and took the ring from his hand. Then tell him that I send to say his day is fast approaching. Within six months it will come to him[39] – he will see it as a friend, and he will follow the Lamb with me.[40] Where he goes, he will go with him, for his chastity is very fine and remains ever perfect. He has gathered in himself all goodness, of manners, of deeds, of good thoughts.'

¶When Saint John had told them this, and other things he wanted to say, the pilgrims found themselves in the place they wished to be – they came there suddenly, just by wishing and with no pain.[41] Then they joyfully went and related everything to the king – how they lost their companions and how then Saint John came and that he, for his sake, lodged them so honourably. Then they presented him with the ring and with the greeting that he had bidden them. Then they drew him aside from the

---

[36] 4378 'travail' (and v. 4397, see Glossary): Södergård gives only 'labour, work' in his glossary (as modern French). But in Anglo-Norman it has the added meaning 'travel'; see also v 6501.
[37] 4380 'Del dormir ne funt nul dangier': Södergård's glossary has 'delay' for this line (*AND*: willingly, or not refusing to). See note to v. 4244, and Glossary. The Nun's comment suggests they were tired out from their troubles.
[38] 4397 'travail' (see Glossary).
[39] 4419 'El siste mais' (Aelred: *infra sex menses*). Södergård's glossary gives 'May' for 'mais', but he must be mistaken and the unusual spelling be scribal for 'meis' [month]. Furthermore, 'el' is a contraction of 'en le' [in the]; unlikely if a single day were meant. He died on 5th January (see note to v. 5220), and the 'May' date is never mentioned again. See also *Catherine*, note to v. 2641, where a reading 'cel mais de novembre' is cited.
[40] 4421 'l'aignel': Södergård's glossary gives 'ring' (his entry for 'anel'), but 'Lamb' matches Aelred and conforms to the citation. Rev. 14:4: ... *they are virgins. These are they which follow the Lamb whithersoever he goeth* (*AND* gives spelling 'aignel' for both 'ring' and 'lamb'). Edward cannot follow the ring, even metaphorically on John's hand, because John has just given it back (see *Life*, p. 199).
[41] 4432 'turment' has another meaning, 'storm' (*AND*, sense 5). This implies the travellers did not have to endure a Channel crossing. In Aelred, they seem to have got to Jerusalem, 'the place they desired', and *then* returned home (*Life*, p. 200). Here, the place they wished to be was England, to see the king as soon as possible.

crowd and told him privately what he had said about his death, and the promise of comfort.[42] As soon as the king heard his friend named, Saint John, he wept for joy and pity – moved by their sweet friendship. He could not get enough of listening to them, nor of asking what he was like, how he spoke, and about the place where he lodged them. These men told and told again;[43] it was delightful for them, to recount the great sweetness of the Creator's noble friend – his deeds, his words, his lovely looks. The king drinks it all in, like a true lover.[44] As he drinks more, so he desires more. All that they could say was but little to him. As much as they said to him, so much the less had they fulfilled their duty – because, by all that they said to him, his desire and delight increased, hearing talk of dearest John, whom God names as his beloved. Although the king can never tire of this listening, he tries to control his desire a little, so as not to sin against moderation.[45] Presently he let them rest, then began to thank them warmly. Next, he gave them so much of his own riches that they departed joyful. Then they went away elsewhere, with great gladness and with great honour.

---

[42] 4445ff. Laurent marks the following as extravagantly affective, bordering on erotic (drinking of words compared with drinking of the love-philtre in Tristan romances); she refers to late-medieval mystics and their metaphors of ingestion and sexuality. Because of this 'total abandon of souls lost in the contemplation of God', she argues that the target audience was more likely convent than court (*Plaire et édifier*, pp. 460–64). But Aelred likewise stresses the love-relationship between Jesus and St John, and nobody argues that Aelred's version is solely for enclosed contemplatives (see esp. *Life*, p. 197, where John drinks love and wisdom from Jesus' breasts).
[43] 4453 'Cil li unt cunté e dit' (MS 'Cil i unt' ...): it is often possible, and desirable, to match doubled words in intense poetry such as this. Södergård concedes that 'i' may stand for the indirect pronoun; he prefers to see it as a copying error and corrects accordingly.
[44] 4458 'cum finz amanz': bold use of courtly love language. See MacBain, 'Vocabulary' (pp. 273–4): holy desire is like a lover's thirst for his lady (note 'dru' for 'friend' in v. 4456). The following sentence is proverbial (Morawski, 1755; folk-wisdom meets the mystical).
[45] 4470 'Qu'il n'ofendist a sa mesure'; moderation was among Edward's principal virtues (see *Life*, p. 200, for Aelred's shorter ending).

Chapter 26

Edward's Last Illness (4477–638)[1]

Introduction

The Nun follows Aelred, but as usual she amplifies, with thoughtful alterations or additions. She extends Aelred's idea of the messengers that Edward sends ahead of him, developing them into personifications. There are several other places in the poem where the Nun's style asks for capitalization of certain qualities. She expands his explanation of Edward wanting to dedicate the church; and also expands the role of the queen (who now reappears, unnamed), stressing the honour that accrues to her by her actions. She uses fewer biblical references than Aelred: five in his Latin but only two in her French. For example, she does not translate Aelred's suggestion that the king lowers his head as if saying 'it is finished' (as Jesus did on the Cross).[2] Nor does she make reference to the *patria* that the dying man will go home to: she talks of 'inheritance' instead.

¶As soon as the king had heard the message from his friend, he knew that his time was near; he must leave this world, and enter into the inheritance for which he had been born.[3] He saw that time was short, and the journey he had to undertake would be hard and painful until he came where it pleased God to bring him. By this road that he feared so much he sent two messengers, to broaden the way, that he might travel it without hindrance. One of the messengers was Sweet Tears, who lingered, to soften the hard road, so that he should not feel its rigours. The other was Good Alms, the neighbour of all good things; he wanted his help to quench whatever still burned in him of worldliness. As water quenches fire, and by its nature cancels it out, so Alms cancels out the sin entrenched in the heart of man. The king understood all this, and divided his treasure among the orphans and the needy, the sick and the suffering. He prepared the way so well that whatever day he was called,[4] he could depart safely, without fear of any torment.

The king often wondered to himself, being always anxious to know how he could please God and estrange himself totally from the world. He had already completed the

---

[1] *Vita*, 770D–71D; *Life*, §28. For Edward's death and the Vision of the Tree (below); see also *Estoire*, vv. 3601–954 (*History*, pp. 100–5).
[2] An opportunity missed; see p. 5, above.
[3] 4482 Södergård's footnote (p. 245) describes the end of MS P: its last lines are 'A itant est li rois fenis Puis est montés en paradis A saint Pierre fu enterrés E fu molt grans Dieus menés' [Then the king died, and went up to Paradise. He was buried in Saint Peter's, and great mourning was made]. The online version removes the capital from 'dieus', which means 'dol, duel'.
[4] 4508–9 Södergård notes the syntax of these lines.

church,[5] which he had established at Westminster in Saint Peter's name – you heard about this earlier, if you were paying attention to the story.[6] So, the king wanted to dedicate it himself before he died.[7] Because of the vow he made long ago, he took on as penance the work of restoring, enlarging, and renewing it. Therefore the king wanted to increase his undertaking to the full; if it could be sanctified in his lifetime he would be fully honoured.

He pondered night and day, about how he could best do it, so that the church would be glorified and the festival celebrated. But he could do nothing now, for the great day was nigh when God vouchsafed to be born in the world – who later humbled himself to die for us – and to clothe his high Godhead in our mortality. He made a virgin to be his mother, who was companion to God in heaven. On this day, he who never had beginning was born on earth.[8] At the feast on this great day all the flower of England was wont to gather, with all nobility, and the king wore his crown.[9]

The king sees that the day is near, but he is constantly settled in his purpose to make his dedication. However, he sets aside the three days of Christmas, so that they would be celebrated with proper honours.[10] Therefore his choice fell on the Feast of the Innocents;[11] he would make the dedication then as best as ever he could. But on the holy night of Christmas his last illness gripped him, and the entire saintly body of the king became acquainted with harsh pains. Now, see how joy is turned to mourning, and the feast is celebrated with tears![12] The king was feeling very ill, but he concealed it as well as he was able, because of the great joy he felt; he saw the great day of the birth of sweet Jesus, the Creator of Salvation. And so he felt a different joy, for the time was approaching that he would see his dear Maker, who was born on earth on this day. He was so glad, for these reasons, that he was able to master his bodily nature, and he controlled his weakness as though he had power over it; he struggled for three days, and endured all the regalia. To honour the feast, and to reassure his companions, he would sit among them at table, more for their sake than for his own

---

5   4515 'Si ot ja parfaite l'iglise': this verb has the sense of finishing or making perfect (see Glossary).
6   See *Life*, p. 200: Aelred says the church was now built. It is typical of the Nun to challenge the audience in such a personal way.
7   4520 Södergård notes the form 'dedié'.
8   4542 'Ki unkes n'out cumencement...': where Aelred echoes Ps. 19:5 (18:6 in *LV*), comparing Christ to a bridegroom, the Nun stresses the paradox that he who has no beginning can be born.
9   4546 This is the last occasion of the king's life when he wears it (see introduction to ch. 9).
10   4551–2 'les treis jurs Fuissent parfaiz...'.
11   4554 28th December. This commemorates the children slaughtered by Herod in his attempt to eliminate the child he feared (Matt. 2:1–18). In *History* (note 236), the translators cite Hayward, 'Innocent Martyrdom', although Edward is not among the saints discussed there. He is indeed a witness to the faith, as the child-martyrs were, but is an old and ailing man when the feast is mentioned. More to the point: the flood of hagiography after the Conquest may have been a response to Norman doubts about the authority of certain cults (Hayward, p. 82, note 6). Emphasis is laid on these saints' chastity, naturally, but chastity is not an issue on the day of Edward's death. See also Fell, 'Hagiographic Tradition', on 'boy-victim' martyrs (which do not include Edward).
12   4561–2 Cf. James 4:9 (*Life*, p. 201). The Nun neither deletes nor interprets, but adds dramatic tone with 'Est vus...'.

26 Edward's Last Illness (4477–638)   155

pleasure. He was joyful beyond his strength, for he knew for certain that his time was come and that he would leave the whole world behind.

Then he had his men called to him, and quickly gave them orders to prepare[13] whatever the church would need, for he wished to put off no longer the morrow that was to be perfect. It was his last wish on earth! He had all his rich gifts got together, with which to glorify the church: gold and silver vessels, and many costly adornments. Then he had all his gifts written down, and all the holdings for the upkeep of the church, by which it would be maintained for ever.

When the day dawned, the bishops arrived, and other folk from far and near so that almost nobody was lacking. All the flower of the land came to be present[14] at the dedication. Then they began the service for the dedication of the church. King Edward managed as much of the business as he could, but the queen took charge of everything, for he could hardly help himself at all. She took good care of everything, and was unhappy only about the king. She took the whole thing upon herself, as though already in the king's place. It fell to her alone, to bring off what the two of them should have done together. But she did it so beautifully that it pleased both God and the congregation. Whatever the king's task, she fulfilled it so well that it will always be remembered. She was in her lord's stead, and she received praise and honour for it.

¶When the service was over, they conducted the king to his bed, and painfully they laid him down, for he was in agony from this terrible sickness that would soon lead him to his death. Now you could see his people weeping and crying, groaning and lamenting! Most of them were well aware of what evils would befall after his death. They could see the country's danger: after his death war would break out, by which its nobility would fall and its freedom perish.[15]

---

[13] 4588 Södergård notes non-elision in this line.
[14] 4606 'Vunt ... requere': the Nun's word for holy visiting (see Glossary).
[15] *Life* (p. 202) cites a comparable passage in *Beowulf*.

Chapter 27

The Vision of the Tree (4639–912)[1]

Introduction

The first sentence, added by the Nun, includes the address 'seignurs' which Aelred never uses; he begins with the bedside scene. The Nun expands the description, and turns a remark about Edward's coma into an expression of personal opinion. Aelred says 'weighed down by his illness, or – what is worthy of belief – rapt in ecstasy' (*Life*, p. 202; and see the Nun's comment, below). We are reminded of Edith's role, and shown how her loving care keeps her constantly beside her husband, tenderly nursing him. For the Prophecy of the Tree, see *Anon* (pp. xxii, xxvi, xxxi, xxxvi, and 75–6, 78–9, 88–90).[2] See also Owst, *Literature and Pulpit*, p. 160, for survival of the story into later texts. The Green Tree image, used by Aelred and the Nun for Henry II, was first applied at the birth of William the Atheling (d. 1120, in the White Ship). Geoffrey of Monmouth probably got it from this tradition.[3] Brown's work discusses the prophecy, but her argument presupposes the Nun writing under Abbess Matilda (she also declares that the Nun dedicates her work to the king, which is not the case).[4]

The passage about Stigand is of interest: the Nun follows Aelred, but expands. She says he climbed into his father's bed (vv. 4853ff.): '... Cum il el lit sun pere entrat'. Aelred says 'who went up to his father's room and defiled his bedclothes ...' (*Life* p. 206). *Estoire* accuses Stigand of simony (vv. 3706–7) but nothing worse. I thank Matthew Kilburn for checking Stigand in *ODNB* for me ... where there is nothing that corresponds to this passage. I am also indebted to Francesco Marzella for a Bible reference not supplied in either *Vita* or *Life*: Gen. 49:4. Reuben is accused of going up to his father's bed and defiling his couch; the concubine, Bilhah, gave Jacob two sons (Rachel was then barren). Without this reference the passage suggests incest. As it is, it means that as Reuben betrayed his father by depriving him of his woman, so Stigand betrayed his father (Archbishop Robert) by depriving him of his bishopric while he was yet alive. Stigand, deposed in 1070, died a prisoner in 1072, having apparently starved himself.[5] The reference in *Life* (p. 206), Acts 1:18, is a version of the death of Judas: having bought a field with the proceeds of his betrayal, he fell and burst his vitals. Stigand's death is similar in Aelred; the Nun adds that the entrails 'formerly had fed his evil body'. More familiar is the account in Matt. 27:3–5, in which Judas gave back the money and then hanged himself; however, the Acts version goes on, in

---

[1] *Vita*, 771D–3D; *Life*, §29. Cf. *Estoire*, vv. 3695–804; *History*, pp. 102–3.
[2] See also Barlow, *Edward the Confessor*, p. 248: the rustic metaphor of the tree is given scriptural 'polish' from Luke 23:31 and Dan. 4:14, 15, & 23.
[3] Legge, 'Influence', p. 684.
[4] 'Cut from its Stump'.
[5] See William of Malmesbury, *Kings*, §199, pp. 189–90, for another version of Stigand's disgrace; and Mason, *House of Godwine*, pp. 133–4, for Edith's care of him, later!

27 The Vision of the Tree (4639–912)

this context: *his bishoprick let another take* (1:20). This indicates that another and more worthy man must take over as Archbishop of Canterbury. For Stigand in Lives of Edward, see *Osbert*, p. 25, note 1; ibid. p. 109 and note 1 for Osbert's version of the prophecy (which does not mention Dunstan).

The reference to Dunstan is noteworthy because, although both Aelred and the Nun mention what he prophesied, the references are different. Aelred says, at the beginning of the chapter following, 'My mind is entirely set against the idea that the holy man Dunstan foretold the calamity and promised no alleviation whatsoever'. Then, more positively: 'It is not to be believed that Saint Edward refused what we know Saint Dunstan promised' (*Life*, pp. 207–9). The Nun says 'Therefore they were without hope; but they did not believe rightly, they had not seen Saint Dunstan's writing, nor had they heard it – he who spoke of this same torment and threatened the land severely. But he promised them comfort afterwards, as King Edward did' (see end of this chapter; and p. 25, above). Aelred is clear about Dunstan's promise, but the Nun emphasizes the people's despair because they had not heard of that promise. The Nun specifically mentions 'the writing'; Aelred does not. It would be interesting to know what writing she means. She may have known *Genealogy*, but she cannot have believed Aelred wrote it *at the time of the story*. Or she is referring to some other record of Dunstan's utterance: oral record, or in his Lives. This extends the range of texts she may have known.[6] For an extended account, king by king, of Dunstan's work and visions, see *Genealogy* (chapters 13–18); his prophecy and his promise, spoken to Ethelred, are in chapter 18 (p. 104).

Dunstan had a long and fruitful life, and is well known for Benedictine reforms carried out by successive kings. It was on his advice that Barking was refounded by Edgar. He also advised the delay of Edgar's marriage – both actions possibly as penance for his sinful pursuit of the lady who became abbess (see General Introduction, above).[7] The Life of Dunstan by Osbern, an Englishman, was rewritten by Anselm's biographer Eadmer and also by William of Malmesbury, because of perceived historical errors. As far as we know, no saint's life supposed to have been connected with Barking is of (or by) Dunstan.[8] The nuns of Barking could have known about Dunstan from Aelred. They could have known William's Life; it has been suggested that William's work – even William himself – was familiar to them. If the Nun knew Osbern's work, as well as knowing Osbert of Clare, this might explain her confusion of the names in chapter 38. Osbert was friends with Anselm's nephew, although there is no mention of Dunstan in *Anon*; *Osbert* does not mention him either. There is nothing to show that Barking held Dunstan in special esteem (it may have revered him as

---

[6] See, for example, William of Malmesbury, *Kings*, §164, pp. 144–5, for Dunstan's prophecy (in which no respite is promised); also *Early Lives* ed. and tr. Winterbottom and Lapidge, pp. cxxvii–ix & 140–43.

[7] See *Early Lives*: Osbern says Edgar raped a nun who subsequently gave birth to Edward the Martyr (p. cliii).

[8] See Lives listed in the Cardiff MS, and those attributed to Goscelin in the MS that later contained *Maldon*. Works attributed to Dunstan are not generally considered genuine; but see *Early Lives*, p. li ff. – although we cannot assume the Nun meant any of this material.

a benefactor). It is not known why Aelred added Dunstan's prophecy – perhaps to remind his audience of the saint's special interest in the royal family of the time. Edward the Martyr was chosen king thanks to Dunstan, but during Ethelred's reign this influential saint went into retirement. His cult was eclipsed under Lanfranc, but revived under Anselm – there could be a link here, given the Barking letters from Osbert previously mentioned.[9]

In Osbern's Life, Dunstan tells Ethelred that because of his aspirations, and the murder of Edward by his mother, cruel troubles will not depart from his house in his lifetime, and his reign will pass to an alien power. This cannot be expiated without extended pain and strife, and there is no promise of ultimate good fortune.[10] William says Dunstan hated Ethelred, prophesying that the sin of all who conspired against the Martyr would not be blotted out except by the blood of Ethelred's subjects. There is no promise of good 'until then'.[11] It would be clear with hindsight, even at the time of the Confessor's death, that those troubles had come to an end with Edward's own kingship. Hagiographers could emphasize his saintliness by reading a promise of good back into Dunstan's prophecy. This hindsight predates the text Aelred wrote for Edward's translation: the promise ('And yet at last the Lord will visit them') appears in *Genealogy*, as already noted. The Lord's visit could refer to the coming of Edward, so it would be interesting to guess at Aelred's motive at this time (see Introduction to *Historical Works*, pp. 15–20). Dunstan's own biographers were not averse to inventing historical circumstances for the miraculous and prophetic stories they added to the Dunstan canon.[12] It is possible the Coronation Order used by the saint at Ethelred's consecration, which contained a three-fold promise of peaceful, just, and good government, may be one of the ideas behind this reported promise of Dunstan's.[13]

❧ ❧ ❧ ❧ ❧ ❧ ❧ ❧ ❧

¶The king, my lords, as I have already told you, was overtaken by his last illness. Around him were assembled his princes and his intimates, and his grieving queen who was both wife and maiden. She sat nearer to him than the others, constantly and without tiring. He who was going away whence he had come;[14] never willingly would she be parted from him. Never was there such sweetness in a woman, nor

---

[9] See also *ODS*, s.v. Dunstan; and Rigg, *Anglo-Latin Literature*, p. 21.
[10] *Memorials* ed. Stubbs, p. 115: '... *non deficiet gladius de domo tua sæviens in te omnibus diebus vitæ tuæ ... regnuum tuum transferatur in regnum alienum ... Nec expiabatur nisi longa vindicta ...*' (*nisi* [unless] is the only hint that things may turn to the good).
[11] William of Malmesbury, *Gesta Regum*, vol. I, p. 269 (*Gesta Pontificum*'s reference to the prophecy is less specific).
[12] Brooks, 'The Career of St Dunstan', p. 3.
[13] See Rosenthal, 'Pontifical', p. 151.
[14] 4647 'Ki ke s'en alast u venist': another passage identifying Edward with Jesus (see p. 5, above). In John's Gospel Jesus talks of his coming death and departure (13:1–3, 14:28, 16:5 & 28); there is no Gospel citation at this point in Aelred. The Anglo-Norman 'Mary's Lament' contains numerous references to John; Jesus says similar words to Mary (*Cher Alme* ed. Hunt, p. 189).

amiability without foolishness, as she now showed him in this sickness – nor did any take as much trouble as she did. Nothing at all could take her away, as long as she sat beside him, from comforting his body and counselling his soul. She supported him on her lap, and settled him in the bed. With her hands she warmed his feet, that had grown completely cold. While they were sitting around him, those who felt his ill as if it were their own, the king became ready to die and estranged from the world. He had lain so for nearly two days, knowing nothing of the world, nor did he say anything, nor hear anything. I would sooner believe his spirit was rapt away, than that the infirmity was causing this; and so it was rightly shown to be, afterwards.[15] By and by the king comes back to the world, as though he has woken up. He opens his eyes and sees his people; with that, he stretches his hands to Heaven. He raises himself to a sitting position in his bed, and says:

'O God, all-powerful King, in whose ward are all things. Before they were, thou knewest them all well. Thou givest and takest away kingdoms, and changest the laws as thou wilt.[16] Dear lord God, now I pray thee – if what I saw was from thee – to give me back my speech, and lend force to my voice, so that all those who hear me speak and recount thy marvels may have fear of thy power and repentance for their sins. Give them such reparation, that thou vouchsafe to withdraw the wrath stretched towards them, and the evil thou wilt do them.'

¶Once he had finished saying his prayer, his strength and his senses came back: he could turn this way and that, and govern his tongue well. The queen and all his people marvelled strangely, that such strength had come back to a body from which it had all departed; and had freed his discourse[17] – sweet speech with clear sound – who before had not strength enough to move his tongue. But when the king feels his strength, he begins to speak again, for he wishes the vision he saw to be known to his people.

¶He began his story thus:

'Lords, when I was exiled, as you know, in Normandy, I dearly loved people of holy life. Although I was a child, I was always wanting to love and be loved by those in whom I knew to be the greater goodness. But nevertheless I found two, whom I loved so tenderly that their word was honey to me and their sweetness fed my heart.[18] Their whole life was sanctified, and they had abundance of all goodness – of speaking well, of good habits, of humility, of high virtues. For this great goodness, I allied myself to them and my heart reposed in them. Now just then, when I was asleep and completely lost to the world, these two friends came to me, for God had sent them. On his behalf they came to announce that after my death he wished to take vengeance for the great evils these people do, for they have come to the end of their

---

[15] 4670 MS 'Kar l'afaire l'ad bien puis mustré'; Södergård corrects the metre by deleting 'bien' (retained here).
[16] 4680–81 'cum tu vols ... ore vus pri'. There is no obvious reason for this switch, so I keep 'thou' throughout.
[17] 4702–8 These lines copied by a different scribe (Södergård's note).
[18] 4719 'lur parole miel m'estait ...': a reference (also in Aelred) to Ps. 19:10 (18:11 in *LV*).

sins.[19] They told me the crimes of my people, clearly by these words: they have so taken their evils upon themselves that they are all filled with iniquity – now there is nothing to say but that they await the wrath of Heaven. They began the disorder, and proclaimed themselves evil from the first. They said they were mad and treacherous; they had broken their covenant with God. They do not keep faith with their subjects and are the first to break the law. The pastors sell their flocks, and are heading with them towards Hell; so long as they have their wool and milk, they will nevermore defend them against the wolves. For this, death will devour both flocks and pastors as one piece of work.[20] The princes are all traitors: they work their own destruction. They do not fear God, their Creator, nor do they honour his law. They hold truth and justice in contempt, and their delight is to practise cruelty. So it is now taken for granted that the prelates do no justice and the subjects no longer care about discipline by law. Therefore God has drawn his bow; he brandishes his sword in righteousness. From now on he will show his anger against your people. His wicked angels will avenge him on his people who have wronged him. One year, in all its days, will God let them work thus: he will send into the earth fire and flame and cruel war.[21]

¶'Lords, when I heard this, from my friends whom I then saw – this cruel menace and the mortal pestilence – know that great grief invaded me. With these words I replied to them:

"O you, who know the secrets of the merciful and sovereign King, I pray you to reveal as much as you know of this people. Can they ever find mercy, if they truly wish to amend? He is always so gentle and so patient, that where he sees the penitent he turns aside his vengeance – he is pacified in repentance – as he did for Nineveh, where he had commanded vengeance.[22] Then, when they undertook penance,[23] God overturned this sentence. I am certain that he has not changed now, neither in goodness nor in pity. Therefore I shall exhort my people to make such amends, that he will have mercy on them as soon as they have returned to him."

'When I had asked that, they replied and asserted that these people would never hear of good, nor willingly repent. They are utterly filled with sin, so their hearts are all hardened; nor do they wish to repent of it, nor do good, nor hear of good – for they have no fear of threats, nor any love for their Creator. They do not wish to do good for love, nor refrain from evil for fear.

¶'Lords, when I heard this I felt very curious to know what comfort would follow this great evil that the people were to undergo. So I said this to them:

---

[19] 4734 'parfait unt': they have perfected, or accomplished, their sins (see Glossary).
[20] 4751–2 Because one sin leads to others (a pastor's neglect allows the Devil to make the flock sin), it becomes one all-encompassing sin.
[21] 4763–72 'God has drawn his bow ... cruel war': see *Life*, p. 204; the Nun retains these Bible references (Ps. 7:12 (7:13 in *LV*), Ps. 78:49 (77 in *LV*), Is. 66:16).
[22] 4789 Jonah 3:5–10. The Nun omits Aelred's second reference, to Ahab (*Life* p. 205).
[23] 4791 or 'when they became penitent' (see Glossary).

27 The Vision of the Tree (4639–912)

"How will it be, that the wrath of God will have no end? If they atone for their sin, why[24] will he not have pity on them? Tell me what comfort they will have for the great evils they suffer? What joy can they hope for? Wherein can they put their trust? If God's anger performs his vengeance, his pity always brings back hope. Therefore, I want you to tell me something of God's will."

¶'When I had put this to them, they told me only so much: that a tree would be riven, and its trunk split so there would be as much space between the two halves as to measure three whole acres.[25] Then, when the tree repairs itself – without help from anybody, by itself and of its own accord, not constrained by any power of others – the trunk will join itself up and the root be re-established. Then quickly it flourishes, and bears flower and fruit again – where before none could hope for any good comfort in the grief that earlier I told you about. When my friends had told me that, straightaway they returned to Heaven and I came back to you to announce what I saw, and what I heard concerning you.'

¶While the king said this, Count Harold sat with him beside his sister, the queen, who bent to hear the words of the king. And the Archbishop Stigand,[26] lover of all evils; who wrongly and openly despoiled the good Archbishop Robert of his archbishopric, and wrongly took over his seat. But when the Pope knew of this and of other things he had done, how he entered his father's bed and doubled his sin in himself, with great shame he suspended him from office, and God soon destroyed him. For it was not long after that his belly burst open and his entrails came out, that formerly had fed his evil body. This Stigand, when he heard how the king warned his people, was never moved by it to fear, nor to pity for the great troubles. He believed nothing of what he said – formerly he had greatly scorned him – he said he was delirious, and that was why he talked thus. He began to laugh, and to mock what he ought to have wept over. But the good people and the wise, who were of a more righteous disposition, wept over it most tenderly, for they were well aware that the people were utterly in the wrong before God, and therefore they readily believed the rest of what he said. In the end they found out that the king had told them the truth. For when Count Harold reigned, the land began its torment: it lost all its freedom, and all were thrown into harsh servitude. When Duke William took it, he made all the richest poor, for none born of the English had any great power in the kingdom.[27] So it was devastating, this torment that most believed would never end – this was why the king had said their torment would end when the tree came back to its trunk. Nobody believed it, for everybody saw the powerlessness of the tree to grow back to its trunk, and so their torment would never end. Therefore they were without

---

[24] 4818 Södergård's note gives 'why' for 'dunt'.
[25] 4832 The size of an English acre [agre] is immaterial: each acre represents a person (Södergård's note, and ch. 29).
[26] 4853 For Stigand, see introduction to this chapter.
[27] Aelred refers to servitude under William, equally blaming Harold; the Nun is more expressive (cf. *Life*, p. 207).

hope; but they did not believe rightly, for they had not seen Saint Dunstan's writing,[28] nor had they heard it – he who spoke of this same torment and threatened the land severely. But he promised them comfort afterwards, as King Edward did.

---

[28] 4907 For the 'escrit', see Södergård's note, and my introduction to this chapter.

Chapter 28

The Tree Explained (4913–5016)[1]

Introduction

Aelred offers a rare personal opinion: 'my mind is entirely set against ...' (*Life* pp. 207–9). The note on p. 207 points out that two previous Lives of Edward, and William of Malmesbury, declare the impossiblity of the prophecy's fulfilment. This prophecy predates its explanation; see note to vv. 3834–8 in *Estoire*. See also *History* note 246 (to vv. 3805–58), on prophecy as historiographical discourse. This 'impossibility' may explain Aelred's defensiveness, and the Nun's likewise. MP also makes much of the prophecy. Aelred's account is briefer than the Nun's, although she omits his biblical references (for example, Henry as 'morning star' and 'cornerstone'), and his mention of prelates and warriors, too, from the new English stock. She expands slightly, stressing damage done by the three 'acres'. She adds a long address to her audience, including the address to 'seignurs' at beginning and end. She comments in detail on her role as reporter and translator, and asks for prayers for the royal family and their heirs for ever. For all her pretended modesty she comes across as quite assertive, especially where she transfers responsibility for the truth to her audience. 'It is remarkable that this nun, who invites us not to disdain the work of a woman, should introduce political propaganda into what appears to be ... a conventional saint's Life'.[2]

≈ ≈ ≈ ≈ ≈ ≈ ≈ ≈ ≈

¶My lords, you who are listening to this book,[3] you may want to know about this: what it signifies, the tree that the king prophesied about. I am happy to explain it to you, as well as I can, having learned about it from other people.[4] If the explanation pleases you, or if you have reason to criticize it, I ought neither to be praised nor blamed, for it does not come from my own knowledge; whatever I have told of the story has been written before by another than myself. But that I have translated it into French is very much against my will,[5] because I feel neither wise nor gifted enough to achieve it properly.

---

1   *Vita*, 773D–4B; *Life*, §30. Cf. *Estoire*, vv. 3805–58; *History*, p. 103.
2   Legge, 'Précocité', p. 343.
3   4913 'ki cest livre oëz': to 'hear' a book is common in medieval parlance, indicating that books were often read aloud in company. It does not necessarily mean that any of the texts in question were invariably recited (it refers rather to a habit of thought; see p. 47, above).
4   4918 The Nun does not name her source(s).
5   4925 MS 'Mais quant romanz...': Södergård corrects to 'Mais en romanz', the online version to 'Mais qu'en romanz'. Elsewhere the Nun says she undertakes the work for love of Edward, and she has just said she will be happy to explain the tree. Perhaps this reluctance is because the explanation is difficult and controversial, as Aelred also seems to find it. See her expression of willingness in ch. 30, for example; and p. 46, above.

This tree the king talked of stood for England, which contained within it a whole wealth of glory and nobility: riches and great worth, power and great honour. The root that nourished all this, and from which all these good things sprang, was the great royal line founded by King Alfred, who was the first of the English to be anointed by the Pope and made a king. His line grew apace, and extended forward so that heir after heir always reigned until King Edward died. But when he departed from the realm, then the tree was hacked apart and separated far away from its stem. For the realm then fell into the hands of a stranger race, who held it in durance vile. This is clearly the meaning of the separation of tree and stem. The three acres between them were the three kings who reigned afterwards, who were of an alien line in no way related to Alfred. For, when Saint Edward died, Harold seized the kingdom. Duke William wrested it from him, and reigned as long as he lived; when he went to his death then his son William reigned. During the time of these three kings I have named, the royal kindred were so scattered that they never came together, nor restored the lineage. But when the good Henry reigned, he restored the ancient lineage. As soon as he had taken possession of the realm, the tree returned to its root, for the daughter of Edward's niece was the one he chose for himself.[6] He was not forced to do it by necessity, nor constrained by envy or lack, nor by fear; only through the force of love did the king make this lady his consort.[7] I have heard her called Matilda the Good.[8] By virtue of this marriage the king was made part of the lineage that had held the land formerly; now it had returned to its rightful heirs. The tree is reunited with its stem, without any force of necessity. When the empress was born to them, then truly the tree came into flower; but it truly bore fruit, to give comfort to the land, when the glorious Henry was born to this empress. With one stroke it made two peoples one, and united two lineages. Now the land had a sovereign and king from the ancient line, through the good Edward, friend of God. And God grant that it will ever be so, that his heirs may reign here as long as the world shall endure. May he grant them wisdom and valour, as all their fathers had. God keep our king their father for us, and their mother our queen. Keep them in true sanctity, in peace and joy and plenty, and grant them the might to overthrow all those who think of war.[9]

¶My lords, we have told of the tree, as we have heard from others. If the explanation pleases you, or if the truth is silent in you, believe it or not as you like. For I leave the decision to you. If you do not agree with it now, then live as long as you may to see the thing differently fulfilled – I have left it in your jurisdiction.[10]

---

[6] 4971 'la fille a la nice Edward...'. Matilda, formerly called Edith, was great-niece of Edward through her mother Margaret, Malcolm of Scotland's wife. Empress Matilda was her daughter by Henry I of England; this Matilda's son (by Geoffrey of Anjou) was Henry II. The 'good Henry' is Henry I; the reigning queen mentioned below is 'the glorious' Henry II's wife, Eleanor of Aquitaine.
[7] 4977 'sa per'.
[8] 4978 Aelred does not mention Matilda as 'the Good' in *Vita* (see Other Sources, in General Introduction).
[9] 4987–5006 This passage suggests an early date for the poem; see my Introduction, above.
[10] Aelred likewise defends this explanation, inviting sceptics to wait for time to fulfil the prophecy differently. He takes issue with Dunstan (*Life*, pp. 207–9), who is mentioned by the Nun at vv. 4907–12.

Chapter 29
Edward's Death (5017-295)[1]

Introduction

Södergård remarks that this account of Edward's death is amplified by comparison with the source. It is greatly expanded from Aelred, and the Nun gives Edward more direct speech. However, she omits a small point in Aelred: Edward asks for his death to be published immediately so that prayers of intercession should not be postponed (*Life*, p. 210). Edith has a central role in the Nun's death-bed scene: Edward's dying wishes are for his wife, and his last words are to her.

❧ ❧ ❧ ❧ ❧ ❧ ❧ ❧ ❧

¶I want to return to King Edward, because I want to relate his death. I know that you have already heard this, if you were paying attention to the story:[2] how the king was suffering agony from his mortal illness. He was racked with the most dreadful pains; the day was now come, that he must leave the world and enter into God's kingdom.[3] Around him could be seen his household, all in tears, and he comforted them very gently.

'My lords,' he said, 'please don't cry, for this death is leading me to life. Put away your grief and dry your tears; your sadness does no good. If you ever loved me at all, you ought to be glad with me, for I'm going to my beloved Father, my Creator and Guide.[4] There I shall enjoy all the delights that God has promised to the blessed.[5] This is not for any good I have done, but in his mercy he brings me there; he is merciful to those he wishes, and is able to give grace to his own.[6] If you really love me, I need you to show it now. The way I must take is hard, and many of my enemies are already on it; they have travelled the whole road, and are lying in wait to harm me. In truth, nobody is so perfect, in this deadly world, that when he has to leave it he doesn't find the meeting with them very hard. Those who are ranged against him are eager to do him harm. If they cannot trouble the kingdom of God, where he is going, they can

---

[1] *Vita*, 774C–6B; *Life*, §31. (A misprint in Södergård's Analyse, p. 12, reads 5275 for the end of the present section, and 5276 for the start of the next.) For *Estoire*, vv. 3859-954; *History* pp. 103-5.
[2] 5020 'Se vus a l'escrit entendistes' [if you were listening to the writing]: ideas of hearing and reading conflated (see notes to vv. 4913 & 5310; and p. 47, above). The Nun's personal tone contrasts with Aelred (*Life*, p. 209, end of previous section), who says merely 'let us now return to the order of the narrative.'
[3] Cf. John 13:1.
[4] Cf. John 14:28.
[5] 5038 'parfis': 'perfect' would sound strange here (see Glossary).
[6] Cf. Ex. 33:19.

often terrify him with their torments and their anguish.[7] So, my dear friends, I'm asking you to help me in my need, by frequent[8] alms-giving, and by your virtuous prayers[9] that God will grant me to accomplish the journey without being molested by the Enemy.'

¶Then he spoke to Count Harold, and to the princes he saw around him:

'My lords,' he cried, 'I beg you as a favour to me, all of you together, that you will all take tender care of the queen for my sake. I pray you earnestly to honour her, and to defend her rights. Do not allow anybody[10] to interfere with her dower after I'm dead; whatever I have given her, I declare it is to be confirmed, and that she must hold it peacefully and rightfully. Let her lose nothing by the hand of any man. Even though she was my queen, I leave her in your hands a chaste virgin. In public she behaved as my wife, in private as a daughter or sister.[11] Whatever I wanted, she wanted too; my desires were hers. In sickness and in health she has cared for me so well that all her wishes are fulfilled. You must show her your gratitude for this.

'If you would please love me even more, I ask another favour for my friends; they are those who came to this country with me when I left Normandy, and are still here with me. Please let them stay here, and be peaceful and loving towards them, and if they don't want to stay with you then please act towards them so that they have nothing to complain of. Send them home with such honour that you shall yourselves be honoured.

'Please, I want to be buried in the church of my dear friend Saint Peter, whom I have so loved, and for whom I founded the holy place. Now, don't leave me, for the hour is near and I must go away. Now it will be seen whether you love me, if in my need you will show it me. For in death it becomes apparent who, in life, had perfect desires. I pray you to help me with your prayers, to lead me home. Now I take my leave of you, and commend you all to God in his mercy.'

¶When the king had asked leave to depart from the queen and his friends, then you could see them all lamenting;[12] their tears and sighs are redoubled. The counts and the

---

[7] At this point Edward's speech breaks off in Aelred. In one MS of the ω group identified by Marzella there is a long interpolation, during which Edward expresses a wish that Duke William should succeed to the throne (I thank Graham Edwards for help with translation). It seems unlikely the Nun used a copy resembling this, Marzella's MS Royal, containing such an interpolation; but there is no further evidence either way (see 'La tradizione'; note that on his p. 356 the chapter number (of *Vita*) should read XXXI, not XXXV).

[8] 5061 'almones suveneres': Södergård's glossary gives 'remembering' (from 'suvenir') for this and v. 5125. But, however attractive the idea that alms (and sighs) are capable of remembering, see *AND* – which cites this line.

[9] 5062 'parfites prieres': see note to v. 5038. The Nun caps her extended development of the adjective 'perfect' with the verb 'parfaire' in the next sentence, for Edward's accomplishing of the terrible journey (see also Glossary).

[10] 5073 See Södergård's note for 'c'om' (c'um) in this line.

[11] 5082 'fille u surur'. See note to v. 1216; the Mother of God was also God's sister (all men and women are God's children, Jesus their brother).

[12] 5115 'Dunc veïssiez cel doel': the Nun often uses expressions like this ('you could see'), to show a scene dramatically; remarked by Södergård (Introduction, p. 34 and note), and rare in Aelred.

barons weep, all that royal house mourns. The servants wail and lament, their cries vying with one another; all that royal company give themselves up to deepest sorrow. But there is nobody who could tell how much the queen mourned, nor her long and frequent sighs,[13] nor her heartfelt groans; for whoever did leave off crying, she could not be sated with crying. Her anguish was so deep it could not have been deeper. Her mourning was so painful that she could not hide her feelings. Her mourning was felt in the chamber, and was taken up eagerly by the many noble and beautiful ladies and young damsels who were there. Many a sorrowful cry, many a loud and pitiful sigh, is heard so that the doleful noise re-echoes all around the hall. Never was any heart so hard, nor any nature so stolid, that if they had but seen this great mourning they would not have felt a part of what these damsels in the royal chamber were feeling. They weep for their lord the king, and they mourn for their lady in her distress.[14]

But all their lamentation availed little, for the hour was now come for the king to pass away. So he asks them to send for his bishops and the holy monks from the church; he doesn't want any of the clerks. So they come in solemn procession, with pious devotion, those who most reverently bear the true Body of Our Lord. When the king sees them arrive, he turns his thoughts to salvation. He calls up the last of his strength, and weeps for sweet piety; bathed in delicious tears he receives the Body of his Creator.[15] Thus he was girded with the arms of certain salvation, thus he was wholly assured in God, in whom is the only assurance. Then he turned his eyes to his companions, hearing their groans and laments. But he saw that the queen was weeping and sighing more than them all. Her painful sighs openly showed how tenderly she had loved him. She was unmatched in her love, as she was now in her grief; nobody there wept as much as she did, and it is certain that nobody there loved him as much as she did. When the king saw her great distress, he spoke to her very gently:[16]

'My darling girl, don't cry. Be comforted by the King of Heaven. Understand this, I shall not die, but I shall go from death to life. I'm leaving this world of death and I'm going to the Kingdom of Life. There I shall see the glory of my Lord, in the land where death has no tears.[17] And so I beg you, my dearest friend, please do not weep for my death.'

¶When he had comforted the queen, he commended her to the King of Heaven. To his Creator he now offers himself – body and soul, heart and will. He renounced

---

[13] 5125 'suspirs suveners': see note to v. 5061.
[14] 5123–48 The description of the queen's sorrow recalls prayers and meditations associated with the Virgin's lament at her Son's death. See for example Gray, *Themes and Images*, pp. 135–9 and notes, for an idea found across the range of medieval devotional literature; and 'Mary's Lament' (in *Cher Alme* ed. Hunt). The Nun may have been inspired by similar texts; in Aelred, the queen is merely 'among the others, sobbing and sighing ...' (*Life*, p. 210).
[15] Aelred does not mention delicious tears and sweet piety: the Nun intensifies this passage.
[16] 5181–90 Aelred has a comparable passage in which Edward addresses Edith as 'daughter' (*Life*, pp. 210–11). In French, 'fille' means daughter *or* girl. Aelred does not use the word 'friend' for her, as the Nun does at the end of this speech.
[17] 5188 Aelred has 'in the land of the living' (Ps. 27:13; 26 in *LV*); the Nun's phrase is, rather, reminiscent of Rev. 21:4.

everything he had on earth; he gave his holy soul to God. As soon as it issued forth from his body, the holy angels received it. Saint Peter, whom he had so greatly loved, came to escort it. He gently comforted this soul, and opened the gate wide for it. Then Jesus Christ's beloved, Saint John, came as he had promised – that at his need he would come to him and would henceforth lead him with him. They carried this soul all joyful, with glory, with delectable song. To their Lord they presented it, and praised it before his face. He received it, in his sweetness, where it will remain for ever without end.

¶A thousand years after God was born, and sixty-six more counted up, the good King Edward died – full of days but more full of goodness.[18] Twenty-three whole years he was king, and twenty-seven days and six months. He reigned so long in joy and in peace; on the fifth day of January he died.[19] No man on earth can tell you how great a fear invaded all the land around, and all those in the country.[20] At the moment of his death, his relatives and his closest familiars were assembled around the king; the queen sat with him, who had always been there constantly. Then they had the holy body laid out, and dressed as a dead man. They gazed long upon this dead body, that they had loved so much in life – for they saw marvels upon him who was most surely dead. For his colour was fresh, and mingled with a most beautiful redness. Then they uncovered his holy body and saw for themselves the truth of God, for they found the entire body in renewed vigour of colour. They marvelled greatly, but nevertheless they are very joyful,[21] for now it is clear to all that his chastity was pleasing to God. As for the colour, they understood that it came by the power of God. The chastity that was maintained in his body wished to show itself outwardly. As it had once adorned the soul and the heart and the thought, thus it now wished to adorn and illuminate the dead body. When they had gazed their fill, and praised God and his power, they had his holy body swathed, and vested it in fine rich silken stuffs. Then they had the alms distributed far abroad, with a generous hand.[22] When the bier was brought, then you could hear grief and clamour. Many sighs were sighed that day, there were many cries and many anguished tears. Bishops and abbots wept, and the monks and priests. Then they carried that holy vessel of chastity towards the church.

---

[18] Several Bible quotations noted in the earlier part of this chapter. Here in the later part, several more noted in Aelred (*Life*, pp. 210–11). But the Nun rewords her text, quite subtly, so that they are lost or altered. For example, here the Latin is *senex et plenus dierum* [old and full of days], Gen. 25:8 (*AV* reads *full of years*). The Nun sacrifices the Bible words, to create poetic apposition between fullness of age and fullness of virtue.

[19] 5220 'El quin jor de genvier fina': see note to v. 4419. Bloch points to confusion in the sources (4th or 5th); see *Osbert*, p. 111 note 1.

[20] This comment, about terror after Edward's death, is shortened slightly by comparison with Aelred (*Life*, p. 211). However, there may be more than one line missing between vv. 5224–5, the copyist having missed one at the top of fol. 25d (Södergård's note).

[21] 5242-3 'Mult par se sunt esmerveillé Mais nepurquant mult en sunt lié': a pair of verbs that match visually ('sunt' plus participle), but may be translated as two different tenses (the first is present perfect, but the second is the verb 'to be' with an adjective). I standardize a few such pairs where they look strange in English, but have preferred not to standardize all.

[22] 5258 'cele almosne' suggests a special ceremony of almsgiving for a king's death.

Next began the psalmody – which was finished with difficulty: they began the chant for the soul, but the tears burst forth[23] so that they could not complete it because of the great grief they felt. His counts and his knights, valets, servants, and squires, and his neighbours and friends and the peasants of the country; weeping they escorted the bier all the way into the church of Saint Peter, that is called Westminster, that he himself had founded. The bishop and those of the church then performed that royal service, with sweet chanting and honour as was proper for such mourning. Then they buried his body in the place he himself had chosen, where God had already worked many miracles for his sake and for his goodness.

Now let us pray God, for his merit, to make us free of all our sins, and to place us in his company at the harsh ending of this our life, and make us sharers in the good things Saint Edward receives by his grace.[24]

---

[23] 5271 'mis avant': there is a gap in this line; Södergård supplies two words, fulfilling the rhyme and following the Latin *prorumpunt*.
[24] Although the final ending of the *Vie* is more abrupt than the *Vita*, the prayer ending this chapter is rather longer than Aelred's (*Life*, p. 212). It is possible the Nun's version of Edward's life initially ended here: the prayer is appropriate, for one thing (there is none in the conclusion we now have). If so, it might explain why two of the three MSS end near here. Perhaps the Nun was asked to add the posthumous miracles, and some information about herself; Legge is of the opinion that it ended here, miracles added as a sort of appendix (*Background*, p. 64).

Chapter 30

Of the Nun Herself (5296–335)[1]

Introduction

This is, naturally enough, not in Aelred, who inserts nothing between his two Books. It comes at a point corresponding to the end of his Book One: a fitting place for the Nun to add personal details. Here, *Estoire*'s author gives a short passage about himself and how he will add pictures to his history for those who cannot read. As has already been remarked, until we have Marzella's critical edition of Aelred's text we cannot know whether his ω version contained any authorial interpolation at this point. Because the Nun chooses to introduce herself here ('if any of you would like to know ...'), it seems unlikely she did so in the lost section of her Prologue. Her reiterated invocation of Saint Edward is further evidence that she is in no sense dedicating her work to King Henry.

¶If any of you, having heard this romance,[2] would like to know where it was made, and who translated it out of Latin, then you shall know – on condition that you will pray to merciful God, to have true mercy on her to whom he gave the grace to do it. This Life was translated at Barking, in the Abbey;[3] a handmaid of sweet Jesus Christ made it, for Saint Edward's sake. But she does not want to say what her name is here, because she knows she is indeed unworthy[4] for it to be heard or read in a book[5] where such a holy name is inscribed.[6] So she begs all those who hear, and all who will ever hear, this romance of hers,[7] that it should not be despised just because a woman has translated it. This is no reason to be contemptuous of it, nor to scorn the good in it. She begs for your indulgence, and asks pardon for presuming to undertake the

---

[1] Cf. *Estoire* vv. 3955–74; *History* p. 105. (As noted above, there is a misprint in the line-numbering on p. 12 of the edition.)
[2] 5297 'cest rumanz': before its modern meaning (a certain kind of story), the word simply meant 'French', or 'text in French'. Early uses may contain shades of both meanings (see Glossary).
[3] 5304 'En Berkinges en l'abeïe': Södergård's note gives a brief account of Barking. Here, and at vv. 6442–4, the Nun identifies herself as belonging to this abbey. Her identification of Barking, together with the withholding of her name (an internal audience would know her), suggests her audience was not exclusively nuns (see Introduction, the Nun's Audience).
[4] 5309 'Kar bien set n'est pas digne unkore'; this could mean 'not yet worthy', but I adopt Wogan-Browne's alternative ('Wreaths of Thyme', p. 50) because it avoids any supposition that this could be a younger woman who will develop into the mature Clemence.
[5] 5310 Södergård cites Chaytor, *From Script to Print*, p. 10ff., for medieval examples of 'hearing' a book; the Nun uses the idea several times.
[6] See Södergård's note to vv. 5306–7.
[7] 5313 'Ki mais orrunt cest soen rumanz': the Nun envisages that her poem will travel and be heard by many. She addresses not only her present but also her absent and future audience.

30 Of the Nun Herself (5296–335)

translation of this Life. If it is not very well done, then blame her powerlessness – she has carried out her wish.[8]

So pray to the Son of Mary for this holy company, including the handmaid of God who made this new Life, to give them his plenteous grace and to perfect their joy in him, and at the ending of this life to place us with the company Saint Edward has joined by his grace, by his goodness – he who reigns and lives and shall reign, who is and shall be, and shall endure for ever. Amən.[9]

---

[8] 5296–323 Legge, *Background*, translates these lines (pp. 61 & 65–6). 'Kar aquité s'ad sun vuleir ...': it is only at one point in ch. 28 that she declares herself unwilling (see note to v. 4925). Here and elsewhere she is happy to be doing the work, and does not sound like somebody writing to order (*pace* Rossi, p. 46 above).

[9] The prayer ending the previous chapter, together with this more extended prayer, would make a suitable ending to the whole text (which as it is ends rather abruptly).

Chapter 31

Ralph the Norman Cured (5336–453)[1]

Introduction

Aelred's second book begins here; the Nun likewise begins again to tell of Edward's miracles, starting with Ralph's cure. See *History*, note to v. 4028, on the importance of posthumous miracles for canonization.[2] The *Vie* predates Pope Innocent's 1199 bull on the subject. Aelred gives two Bible references in this chapter: Ezekiel (see below), and Psalm 116 (115 in *LV*) in the first paragraph. As usual, the Nun's opening remarks are more personal than those of Aelred, who announces Edward's virtue in greater detail but without addressing an audience (*Life*, pp. 212-13). At the moment of healing, Aelred adds that 'some hidden force' acted on the diseased limbs (*Life*, p. 214). For the Nun this would seem to be unnecessary, because the force is obviously Edward himself.

¶Our Lord is so abundantly good, mighty and yet full of mercy, that he wishes to honour his own and show his power through them, as you have already heard about Saint Edward, his dear friend, and what marvels he performed in his lifetime with the help of Almighty God. The virtue manifested in his body while he lived in this world could not perish with his death nor be concealed inside his corpse. Once it had been revived in his death,[3] then God doubled its power. For as he was separated from the world, then he drew nearer to God, and it was right that this closeness should cause an increase in such a thing: as we shall here tell you presently, as well as we are able to speak of it.

¶While the king was alive on earth there was, among the poor people he looked after, a miserable fellow named Ralph, who was born in Normandy. This wretch was a cripple, with the nerves of his legs contracted at the knee so that his feet were twisted towards his loins and met inside between the thighs. This horrible propinquity had deformed all the rest of his body. He could not crawl on his knees because of the pain it caused him. In his need, the poor fellow had bethought himself to buy a vessel, shaped like a basin; it was hollow and quite roomy. So he inserted himself completely, from the waist down, into this receptacle, and he went swimming about in this ship[4]

---

1   *Vita* (*Liber Secundus*), 775C–7A; *Life* (Book II) §32. In *Estoire*, the Norman is unnamed (vv. 3989–4028; *History*, p. 105).
2   References are to Vauchez, *Sainthood*; and Kemp, *Canonization*.
3   5348 'Eins (MS Fins) fud en sa mort avivee': Campsey online corrects 'Fins' (which is printed in the edition but makes little sense) to 'Eins'. I thank Natasha Romanova for help with this.
4   5374 'En cel vaissel alout nagant': 'vaissel' can mean 'ship'; the metaphor strengthened by the word 'nager', in Old French meaning sail or navigate (cf. its meaning 'swim' in modern French). *Estoire* has 'nager', but not 'vessel' (vv. 3997–4001; *History*, p. 105). Aelred has 'as if he were sailing on land' (*Life*, p. 213).

in order to crawl upon the earth. Thus was the poor man, who had used to receive his upkeep, his food and his clothing, without having to work or worry about it all the time that King Edward was alive. But now it failed him, for times had changed and the laws had become harsher all round.[5] When he lost his livelihood, the pain of his disability increased. Now he had lost everything, but nevertheless he remembered the holiness and great virtue of King Edward, who used to feed him. Then good hope dawned in him, and from the hope grew a desire to visit the saintly body and show his suffering to it.[6] With this desire, he so persevered that he managed to reach the saint's tomb within the eight days during which his festival was celebrated.[7] Then he addressed himself to the king, just as though he had found him alive in the flesh. He began speaking, with these words:

'So this is you, my dear lord, who in life used to give your help to all the needy. So have pity on me, I'm now suffering so much from poverty and sickness that I'm comfortless on all sides. Good sir, as long as you were alive you relieved this disease, for then I didn't suffer except from being crippled. I had everything else I could wish for, so that I could very well bear my infirmity. But now I'm in such misery of need and of pain that I've lost all endurance, for now everything makes me suffer. So I'm begging you to help me with it, and give me some sort of relief. I know that you really can do it, and can put an end to my great suffering.'[8]

As soon as the cripple had said this to the good and merciful Edward, then behold! here is the sovereign remedy, and the poor man receives back his health. Suddenly the nerves give way and allow his legs to straighten; his feet go back to their natural position and his bones to their natural joints. The poison drained out of his wounds, and blood quickly replaced it, nourishing the poor bones so that they were soon covered with flesh again.[9] When the patient feels his strength, he stretches his twisted legs out in from of him. Then you could hear people on all sides crying out and praising the name of God, who had made their king as powerful in his death as he had been in his life. When the man felt himself cured, he gave thanks to the King of Heaven and to his dear lord Saint Edward, who had taken pity on his suffering. Everybody who saw him praised the power of God. Thereafter, they often visited the holy body, and paid more attention to how they could honour it and come to his holy place again. For every one of them was convinced that he could cure them all of pain and disease by his sovereign virtue.

---

5   The Nun adds a hint, not present in Aelred, about hard times following Edward's death.
6   'requere' occurs several times in this section (see Glossary).
7   5396 'Dedenz les octaves': major festivals were commemorated throughout the week, culminating in the octave (eighth day). In Aelred, the man arrives within eight days of the burial (*Life*, p. 213); similarly in *Estoire* (vv. 4006–8; *History*, p. 105). The Nun enhances the solemnity of the occasion by making it Edward's festival.
8   5401-21 This speech differs from Aelred's: the man here stresses his suffering, and how being well fed had helped him to be patient. In Aelred he almost bargains with Edward, commenting that he if can't have spiritual pleasures then may he please have at least physical ones (*Life*, p. 214).
9   5432 '... les chaitifs os': Aelred's *arida ... ossa* recalls Ezekiel ch. 37: ... *can these bones live?* (*Life*, p. 214). The Nun stresses the pathos of the man's situation.

Chapter 32

Thirteen Blind Eyes (5454–501)[1]

Introduction

This chapter is slightly condensed from Aelred. However, there are other differences: the Nun sets the scene thirty days after Edward's death instead of three years, doubtless to provide early evidence of such miracles. She gives direct speech to the sufferers as they are cured, making their amazement more lifelike. At the end, instead of simply going home (as in Aelred), the men go about preaching 'par tut'; the short prayer in the last line is the Nun's addition.

❧ ❧ ❧ ❧ ❧ ❧ ❧ ❧ ❧

¶We have already told you, frequently, that the king had the special gift of giving light to the blind;[2] now we can prove it to you. For, thirty days after his death, as we understand, seven sufferers came to visit his body; six of them were stone-blind. The seventh had the sight of but one eye, and he was the only guide those six had. They lined up in front of Edward's tomb, and prayed humbly that he would have pity on them, and that he would work his pity in them. They told him that they knew, and were quite certain of this, that he had not lost the grace he had possessed in his lifetime. If he could restore sight to the blind while he was yet living among the sinners, then he could enlighten them even better now that he was companion to the angels. As they were reciting this to him,[3] the grace of God spread over them, to show forth the holiness and the bounty of King Edward. The seventh man, who could see with one eye and so had to be the others' guide, received a reward for his labours, for he was the first to receive light. Straightaway he raised his head, and he saw that the six were cured. Then they all looked at one another, and they asked among themselves:

'Can it be true? Can we see? It isn't a dream, for we're awake!'

'My faith!' said another, 'It's true, and we are all blessed with light!'

As soon as they realised that they had not been deceived, they praised God's might in loud voices and great cries. Then you could see people running and shouting, to praise God and Saint Edward. The seven soon took their leave and they go their way, preaching far and wide about the holiness of good Edward. May God give us a share in his joy!

---

[1] *Vita*, 777A–C; *Life* §33. Cf. *Estoire*, vv. 4029–66; *History*, p. 106.
[2] 5456 'enluminer', used several times, is more vivid than merely 'giving sight to' or 'healing' the blind.
[3] 5476 'A ço qu'il cest li vunt lisant': being blind, they could hardly be reading. Aelred says 'As they persisted in prayer' (*Life*, p. 215).

Chapter 33

The Prophecy about Harold Fulfilled (5502–601)[1]

Introduction

Estoire's version of the Battle of Stamford Bridge, 25th September 1066, is more elaborate than either Aelred's or the Nun's (see notes in *History*). The Nun begins with a reminder about Edward's perfection, and about his earlier prophecy, whereas Aelred goes almost directly into the story. Although he too cites the prophecy at the end of the section, the Nun does so in more detail. She reminds us of the boys' play turning to anger and hate, and reminds us (in characteristic first-person) that she has told of the matter before. In this chapter both Harald Hardrada and Tostig are killed, as predicted in chapter 22. Aelred contradicts himself (*Life*, p. 218), saying both were killed, whereas in §24 he said the Norwegian escaped (see note below).

ea ea ea ea ea ea ea ea ea

¶Here above we have often said how King Edward was perfect, that he had the spirit of prophecy even while he was in this life. What he said of the sons of Godwin, and the war he promised them, came true after his death, as now will be shown you. As soon as Edward died, know that Harold reigned. Against nature, against right, he made his own what belonged to another; wrongly he seized the kingdom he had promised to Duke William. He exiled Tostig,[2] his brother, and drove him as far as Flanders; it was within the king's lifetime that the brother had done this outrage. Tostig took great offence, that his brother had so disgraced him. He next went straight to Norway, for the help he wanted to seek. Harald [Hardrada],[3] who was king there, welcomed him. He granted his request, and then gathered all his host. They set off to Northumberland, which they took in a great battle. They completely overthrew the people, then turned towards York. Harold, who was king of England, heard tell of this war and how his brother had invaded, and felt himself deeply scorned. He had all his men summoned, then set off swiftly towards York – where was the one whom he hated and who hated him. While he was on the march, Saint Edward appeared to an abbot of holy life, of the Abbey of Ramsey.[4] The abbot was very much afraid of the king and of his splendour, but Saint Edward comforted him and spoke to him thus:

'Go at once, and tell Harold to be resolute in this assault. He will most certainly vanquish his enemies: my people will have my help. I cannot fail my people, for I wish to uphold their right. This time he will have victory, by those people of mine

---

1 *Vita*, 777C–8C; *Life* §34. Cf. *Estoire*, vv. 4095–264; *History*, pp. 106–9.
2 See Södergård's note to vv. 5516–19.
3 5524 'Harfager'; see note to v. 3748.
4 5543 Ramsey in Huntingdonshire. Aelred names him Alxi or Ælfsige, 'the observant abbot', MP Alexe or Ailsius (*Life*, p. 217; *History*, p. 108). He was abbot 1080–87; the story makes him abbot as early as 1066.

he leads with him; and if he doesn't believe what you say, you'll show him proofs by which you will be believed, that this speech is come from me. You'll be able to tell him all his thought: what pain he had yesterday night, and what anguish. In his thigh he had such agony that he was afraid of being crippled;[5] therefore he thought he would hide this pain as best he could, so as not to be despised by his men or less feared by his brother. You will tell him this, what it was he thought; by this I'm sure he will believe you. Now he has relief for his pain, if he does what I have commanded: let him help our countrymen, for in this deed I shall be helping him.'

With that the abbot awoke, then went to King Harold. He related to him the whole matter: how Edward had commanded him and what he thought about his pain. Harold marvelled greatly how this man was able[6] to tell the secret of his own thought. From what he said, he truly believed him, and was much encouraged. Then he had the whole host rallied, and soon went off towards Northumberland.[7] He found his brother Tostig there, with those he had brought thither. The English assailed them; they killed Harald [Hardrada], and the king's brother Tostig, and most of those he led with him. And so the business turned out as King Edward had promised. When these brothers were boys, and struggling together before him one day, their play turned to anger and they wanted to kill each other. The king said truly what would come of it; thus his words came true, as now – and before – I have shown you.[8]

---

[5] *Estoire* tells us the affliction was gout (*History*, note to v. 4152).
[6] 5580 Södergård notes: 'solt' is not a form of 'soleir'. This observation, that the secret was in his own thought, is added by the Nun.
[7] Stamford Bridge; Aelred names it in Latin and English (*Life*, p. 218).
[8] See ch. 22.

Chapter 34

The Bell-ringer (5602–69)[1]

Introduction

MP, though not Aelred, calls the man a sacristan. In *Estoire*, after this miracle there is a paragraph about many miracles (vv. 4413–44), followed by the story of Edward appearing to Harold to chastise him (vv. 4445–510). Next comes an account of William's victory and Harold's death (vv. 4511–638). *Estoire*'s last scene is the finding of Edward's body uncorrupted (vv. 4639–86; cf. chapter 36 below).

The Nun adds detail to the story, making it more vivid. She reminds us that he is a 'poor fellow' when he is having his sleep. She mentions the importance of ringing the bell so that nobody shall miss the services. She says the man 'seemed to see' Edward (in Aelred, he simply sees), further, that Edward actually comes towards him. She makes a little play on words as the unhappy man is happy to watch the king. She expands his delight and astonishment at his cure, and he actually runs to tell the monks, where Aelred just says 'he disclosed the vision' (*Life*, p. 219).

¶In those days there lived at Westminster a young man who was blind. He was born of a noble family,[2] and was blessed with great beauty. But, because he could see nothing, his good looks were of little use to him. However, the holy monks of the church generously took pity on him, and kept him in the Minster; they gave him a job to do, to ring for all the hours so that nobody should miss them.[3] They taught him which bells to ring for the high festivals, when he knew them; for double offices, and for weekday services[4] – they taught him everything there was to know about it. He learned their doctrine well, and carried out his duties with a glad heart. He was to be found in the church more often than not, always busy in God's service. He was often in devout prayer, and he often begged Saint Edward to heal his disease and restore his health to him.[5]

---

1   *Vita*, 778C–9A; *Life* §35. (Note misprint in Södergård's Analyse: 5502 for 5602.) See also *Estoire*, vv. 4365–412; *History*, p. 110.
2   5604 'Si esteit de bones genz nez': detail of his birth not in Aelred. The Nun stresses the disparity between the youth's advantages and his disadvantages.
3   5612 'tutes les ures': Södergård's glossary gives 'heur' [good fortune] for this line, but clearly 'hours' are meant. While it is possible a bell was rung for every hour of the day, here the reference is to canonical Hours (daily services or Offices). See note to v. 5641, and Glossary.
4   5616 'as dubles e a sursemaine': Södergård's glossary suggests 'two-part singing' for 'dubles', but *AND*'s interpretation seems more probable, since if a saint's feast coincides with a Sunday (for example) then both are celebrated (see Slocum, 'Goscelin and the Translation', p. 79 note 23, for the 'ranking' of feasts: *duplex* or double indicated a major feast).
5   Marzella prints a variant found in some MSS of *Vita* at this point, but it does not correspond to any apparent addition by the Nun here ('La tradizione', p. 351).

It was not long after this that it happened, one summer day, that all the holy monks were asleep having their siesta. The poor fellow I've been talking about was taking a much-needed rest.[6] It seemed to him as he slept that he saw Saint Edward coming out of the tomb where his body lay. He came swiftly towards him, ordering him to get up and ring for Nones immediately. He said he had overslept: the hour was come, and almost gone, that the good men should have got up to sing the Office of Nones.[7] Then it seemed that he saw in his sleep the king going away again.[8] He saw him going towards the altar, wearing his crown on his head. The unhappy man felt great happiness watching the king in his beauty; then, as he watched, King Edward vanished.

The young man woke up, full of gladness at his vision, and he hurried to the bells to ring them. The bell-ropes – that he used to have to feel for – he could see them! He looked at the bells, and the walls; he could hardly believe that he had regained his sight! He turned his head this way and that; his joy rendered him certain, and he gave thanks to God for it. Then he ran to the monks, and told them of the vision he had seen. Those good men believed him entirely, for it was proved in his own person that everything he said was true: then he was blind, now he could see. So they all praised the name of God, who had so glorified their king that he could give light to the poor blind man just by the fact of seeing him in his sleep.[9]

---

[6] 5631 'Se fud al mestier reposé': Södergård's glossary gives 'dining-room', for 'mestier' in this line. But the man is more likely to be somewhere in the church, where he can see the tomb (as in *Life*, p. 219), so the usual sense 'mestier' = 'need' is preferred. A siesta is prescribed in the monastic rule (*The Life of Aelred*, Walter Daniel, p. lxxv).
[7] 5641 'E l'ure de nune chanter': about three o'clock in the afternoon (see note to v. 5612).
[8] 5643 'li reis s'en parti': Södergård notes that verbs of movement were frequently reflexive (cf. modern French 's'en aller').
[9] 5662–9 This short exposition, how the miracle was effected and why the monks were so eager to believe, is the Nun's. Aelred simply reiterates Edward's ability to work miracles after his death (*Life*, p. 219).

Chapter 35

Saint Ulstan (5670–949)[1]

Introduction

This episode is not in *Estoire* (see introduction to chapter 34),[2] nor in William of Malmesbury's life of Wulfstan. Saint Wulfstan, here called Ulstan, is not to be confused with the earlier archbishop Wulfstan, c. 1008–95 (see *ODS*). See *Anon*, p. 118, for Osbert's handling of the Edward miracles. The Nun expands, as follows. First, she develops the reference to Psalm 33 (32 in *LV*) with which Aelred begins, rounding off her little homily with an introductory mention of Saint Ulstan. The explanation of Lanfranc's involvement is developed, with more of his reasons being given.[3] The Nun omits Aelred's extra description of Stigand's sins, having expanded the passage about Stigand in chapter 27 (*Life*, p. 220; the Nun's earlier description is stronger than Aelred's). Then, Aelred says Ulstan approached Edward's tomb 'with his men' (*Life*, p. 221). The Nun shows him going forward alone 'to the sepulchre of his lord', which is more affecting. After Ulstan deposits the staff, there is a scene where everybody crawls about, looking to see how it has stuck. The Nun makes the onlookers a good deal more vocal: shouting instead of murmuring, direct speech expressing amazement, and so much talking that the news reached the senate.[4] The scene where Gundulf tries to take the staff is expanded and dramatized; the portrayal of King William is subtly enhanced. Finally, whereas in Aelred only one of the company asks for the saint's blessing, in the Nun they all crowd around him, for blessings and kisses (*Life*, p. 225).[5]

The incident may have inspired the Sword in the Stone episode, of Arthurian romance; the sword first appears in the *Merlin* attributed to Robert de Boron.[6] There seems no reason why the writer should not have adapted this attractive story to the new Arthurian legends appearing thick and fast by the thirteenth century. Mason suggests, quite plausibly, that the story may have been inspired by yet another incident that occurs, in *Liber Eliensis*, to the other Wulfstan. That the sword story should have

---

[1] *Vita*, 779A–81D; *Life*, §36.
[2] See Södergård's note to vv. 5670–949, for what Matthew Paris says elsewhere of Ulstan (*Quasi homo idiota* ...).
[3] Lanfranc, archbishop of Canterbury 1070–89; see Macdonald, *Lanfranc*, pp. 114–15, for more on this story.
[4] Aelred's 'synod'; cf. *Life*, p. 223. The Nun also has 'sené' for the synod in ch. 10 (see note to v. 1913, and Glossary).
[5] At Edward's translation (1163) Becket took the gravestone, in which Ulstan's staff had stuck, as a trophy (Barlow, *Thomas Becket*, p. 95).
[6] See Dutton, 'The Staff in the Stone'. The Ulstan story first recorded in *Osbert*; the Arthurian episode in *Merlin* ed. Micha. However, Mason thinks Osbert got the idea from *Liber Eliensis* ('St Wulfstan's Staff'); both could be right. For Archbishop Wulfstan's staff, see *Liber Eliensis*, II:87; and III:43 for Osbert's connections with Ely. See *Anon*, pp. xxxiv (note 1), 118, & 132–3: Osbert adds miracles unknown to *Anon*, and to William of Malmesbury, including Lanfranc's attempt to depose Ulstan (*Osbert*, ch. xxix). The anecdote, unhistorical, is presumably associated with the events of 1070–71 (Mason, p. 161).

developed in one step, from an accident involving a staff jammed between flag-stones to a full-blown marvel that identifies a king, seems less probable than that this Wulfstan story, in the miracles of Edward, in fact occurred *in between* Ely and Arthur. The story develops, as it were, in two steps (at least). It is also possible that Osbert's narrative, followed by Aelred's, and then by the Nun's in French, had become generally well known, and that the *Merlin* author got it from somewhere else. Mason discusses this wider context, but leaves exploration of Arthurian development to another time or another scholar.[7]

※ ※ ※ ※ ※ ※ ※ ※ ※

¶It greatly pleases Our Lord that his people abide in fear of doing evil, and do good; and that they love those who hate evil. For he makes him perfectly good, who utterly eschews evil. God himself gives the good to his own; and nevertheless he rewards them for it. He makes them to be honoured for his good, and wants to reward them for his gifts: just as he did King Edward, who had his gifts in good measure, and also Saint Ulstan as you shall now hear presently.[8]

When King William had seized all England into his hand, everything was soon disposed to his liking: the land and the people and the wealth. Once all the rebellious English in the land had submitted to him, then the king wished to see that Holy Church was receiving its due rights.[9] He summoned bishops and abbots, and all the wisest of the realm.[10] When all the senate was gathered, then the cardinals arrived. They had already deposed Stigand, whom I told you of before, and in the see had already placed the wise and noble Lanfranc,[11] who was full of all goodness and educated in every faculty. He was master of all the arts, as one who knows them all. He was perfect both in God and the world, as one who had been chosen for such a position – who nourished, augmented, and upheld Holy Church. Since he had occupied the seat, he had briskly undertaken to redress what was wrong and to establish right everywhere.[12] Because he was so assiduous and eager to do right, much

---

[7] Thompson, *Motif-Index* (accessed 28.9.2010, pm.nlx.com/xtf/view?docId = motif/motif.00.xml), has four entries for a motif of this kind (vol. 3, H31.1): the well-known Arthurian version, a sword drawn from a tree-trunk in *Volsunga Saga* (and related legends), a parallel in Irish myth, and finally one in Indian myth. There may be others.

[8] 5683 'Cum vus orrez or en present'; this nudge, typical of the Nun, is not in Aelred.

[9] Here Aelred says 'he began to deal with his own people concerning ecclesiastical affairs' (*Life*, p. 220). The Nun's rather warmer mention of 'due rights' could be, like her earlier praise of William, because he confirmed Barking's rights in 1066–67. She also tones down what Aelred says about harsh subjugation of the rebels.

[10] 5693–4 See Glossary, for 'senez' and 'sene' in these lines.

[11] 5699 'Le sage Lanfranc...': MS 'franc'. Södergård corrects, apparently thinking the word an eyeskip from 'franc' in the following name. However, the Nun may have intended a deliberate pun (see v. 5718). At v. 5726, Lanfranc is said to be 'courteous': a word the Nun does not use lightly (examples noted, as characteristic of her style). See my discussion of 'courtly' language in both the Nun and Clemence (Introduction, p. 41, above).

[12] Aelred refers to Jer. 1:10; the Nun omits the passage (about plucking up, overthrowing, and destroying; *Life*, p. 220), so as to focus on Lanfranc's more constructive talents.

blame of Ulstan's simplicity had been reported to him: that he was an illiterate idiot who had no right to bear the staff.[13] The noble Lanfranc[14] heard so much from the accusers that he consented to their will – for he believed them to be right and that the king himself wished him to be deposed, lawfully,[15] because he was accused to him. After this there came a day when Lanfranc, the wise and courteous,[16] held his senate at Westminster, and the king was there then: he wanted to help the archbishop to enforce the law of God more strongly. When the archbishop had arranged and set right all the business, he said to the good Ulstan, in the presence of all, that he must give up the staff and the ring. But Saint Ulstan is nothing daunted, for he has placed himself under God's protection. He could feel no grief at giving up, nor any joy at keeping. He took his staff and arose, and thus he gave his reply:

'Lord Archbishop, it is the truth – for my deeds have amply proved it – I am not worthy of this charge. This was true of me when I received it. So I was when I was chosen: those who placed me by force in the see made enough opposition, to the bishops and the clergy. And King Edward, my lord, who sent me to this labour; by the authority of Rome he placed this charge upon me, and by this staff invested me and gave me possession of this bishopric.[17] Now you want it to be given back to you, but it was not given to me by you. You want to take my job away from me, but it is not your business to do so. I fully concur in your judgement, because of the incapacity I feel in myself. But I will not give back the staff, except to him who gave it to me.'

As soon as he had said this to them, he made his way without delay to the sepulchre of his lord; then he said to him very mildly:

'My lord and very dear friend, I know you have not forgotten how unwillingly I received this staff, and from whom, and how I was constrained to it. You know how I fled and how I was caught, how I hid. I was conscious then of my incapacity, but I had to do your will. Truly I received it against my will – to please you. But now we have a new king, new masters, new law; there are already new rules entirely, in place throughout your land. And they claim you were mistaken when you enjoined this task upon me; they blame me for presumption when I received the gift of it from you. Dear lord, who was once a mortal, you could have been deceived. But now you have come to where you are not deceived – so now you know the truth, how I was in need of [your] goodness. Therefore I believe it to be just, that I should render to you the care of your people that you commended to me, and the staff that you gave me; for I

---

[13] 5717 'croce', a bishop's crozier (or abbot's equivalent); not from cross = crucifix, but from the same root as [shepherd's] crook. 'Crozier' sounds rather too modern, so I translate 'staff', since it is also called 'bastun'.

[14] 5718 'Li frans Lanfrancs'; here again, Södergård corrects (this time to 'Li bons'). The word occurs only twice in the chapter; other examples of 'li bons Lanfrancs' are not corrections (see note to v. 5699).

[15] 5722 'par esguard': see note to v. 5989.

[16] 5726 'curteis'.

[17] See *Osbert*, pp. 116–20 for the story, and note 2 on p. 120 for a king investing a bishop.

will not give it to them, whom I know to be mortal and human. I know not whether they are right or wrong – but let the judgement be yours.'[18]

When he had said this to them, he raised his hand a little. He struck the stone where the king lay, and the staff stuck there firmly. Then he said:

'Lord, now take it. Where it pleases you, give it.'

Then he went down from the altar and took off his bishop's robes. He renounced everything to do with the work, then sits himself down among the monks as a simple religious,[19] and sets himself to chanting his psalms. All those who see the marvel are marvellously astounded: the staff stays in the stone, and they cannot imagine how. But they see it standing as firmly as if it has grown there: it does not sway in any direction, and it seems more like nature than art. Several made the attempt, at how one might pull it out from there. But they could not take it out, nor even make it move. Now you can hear the people shouting, telling the marvel forth. Some lie down on the ground to look better, and to see how the stone holds the iron – and that it is not shattered. Now they look in front, now behind, at how the shaft[20] is stuck to the stone. One says to another:

'Look, don't you see? Never before has there been such a marvel!'

They talked so much of this thing to one another that the news reached the senate. But the archbishop does not believe the business happened like that at all. However, in order to find out the truth, he called Saint Gundulf, who was bishop of Rochester – of holy life and of good estate. He ordered him to go there and bring the staff to him. This man went straight to the sepulchre where Saint Edward had been laid, and seized the staff in his hand. He wanted to take it – but it was in vain. He wanted to shake it – but it was for nothing. For the strength of God held it firm in the holy virgin hand of the dead king, who was no longer mortal. When he saw that he could do no more, he went back to the archbishop. In the hearing of the whole senate he told them all: what he found and what he did. When the good Lanfranc heard this he was wonderfully astonished, and soon sent to the king, asking him in friendship to come with all his barons to the senate. The king willingly agreed. Then they went all together to the holy body; and what they had been told, they found. Lanfranc first said his prayer, and then puts his hand to the staff and tries to draw it to him. But the virtue of the holy king held the staff back, so that it would never be moved because of him. When the king sees this, he cries aloud and praises the Son of Mary. The archbishop moans and weeps, and invokes the justice of Heaven, to undo their false judgement and put them out of their error. Then he went to Saint Ulstan and asked for his mercy:

'Truly,' he said, 'God is good, who so shows the rights of his own. Brother,' he said, 'we mocked you and took you for an idiot. But God, who wants to show that you are

---

[18] 5797 'sur tei seit'; 'upon you' would be misleading, though clearly the Nun means 'let the burden of judgement be upon you'.
[19] 5807–8 'Cume cloistrier tot simplement': the point is not whether he was enclosed, but that he had no special rank or office among them. Aelred says *inter monachos ipse monachus* (see *Life*, p. 222), and does not mention him chanting psalms.
[20] 5829 'fust' means wood, but the stone is said to be holding the *iron* (in Aelred it is similarly *ferrum*).

wise in him, showed us to be wrong. And so we request, and command in the power of God, that you take this charge from which you were wrongly deposed. For God has truly shown through you that he loves simplicity more – who is poor in letters, and strong in faith and righteousness – than he does these great subtle minds who have no defence against vain pride. For one sees but rarely great learning without care for vain human praise. Now, dear brother, come away with me to our lord, our king. I know for certain that his hand will release to you the staff that he refused to us.'[21]

When Saint Ulstan heard this, he obeyed him quite simply. Then he went to his lord, and said to him with great mildness:

'O good Edward, see me here, who put myself into your jurisdiction and handed over to you the staff which you formerly gave to me. Now you have proved your dignity and shown your power in me. You have defended my innocence, and I am completely cleared of the false judgement. Now I have put myself in your judgement, so make your resolve known to me. If your will towards me is as it was before when you were alive, when you gave me this staff – and, indeed, often pressed me hard – or if this will has changed, then give it to whom you have chosen.'

With that he ended his discourse, and next his hand took the staff that was locked into the stone, and the staff followed him willingly, as though it were in soft earth, without him applying force to it. When the king sees the marvel, he throws himself down at his feet, and the archbishop as well, and they humbly beg his forgiveness. Now you hear cries mounting up, praising God's power. Bishops and abbots weep, monks and priests weep. Each wants to vie with the others, to ask for his blessing. They all went to his feet, and humbly kissed them. The king takes him in his arms, and kisses his mouth and his face,[22] and the good Lanfranc as well; then they lead him in goodly fashion to the senate where he had formerly been judged. All worship the power of God. The king, after what had befallen, with great care made it his business to honour his holy cousin:[23] he next had a reliquary prepared, embellished with gold and silver and most wonderfully worked, as can still be seen to this day,[24] there where his body lies in great honour.[25]

---

[21] In Aelred's version of this speech, the learned Lanfranc cites the Bible six times; the Nun shortens and simplifies it, keeping the main argument.
[22] This embrace is added by the Nun, perhaps to enhance her picture of the pious king.
[23] 5944 The 'cusin' is Edward (see Södergård's note).
[24] 5948 'Cume encore piert a cest jur': the 'still-there' topos is a common device by which story-tellers claim authenticity for their narrative (see King, *The Faerie Queene*, pp. 48–52, 161–2, & *passim*; Simpson, *British Dragons*, ch. 5. See also introduction to ch. 25, King Edward's Ring). Aelred makes a similar remark, 'as it is seen at the present time', rather less dramatically (*Life*, p. 225).
[25] Aelred's two Bible references, in the last part of this chapter, deleted (not paraphrased) by the Nun. He balances the humility of the great churchmen with that of Ulstan; the Nun stresses the first over the second now that Ulstan is vindicated.

Chapter 36

The Saint's Body Uncorrupted (5950–6071)[1]

Introduction

Södergård says there is 'grande conformité' between this and Aelred. It is indeed close, although the Nun characterizes the incident as one of Edward's miracles (cf. the closing sentences of Aelred's, *Life* p. 228). She deletes a passage of direct speech from the monks' dispute, but expands the idea that 'we' as well as 'they, the people' ought to love the Saint no less (*Life*, p. 226). Other added touches are: that the sweet smell of the uncorrupted body reinforced the beholders' belief, and that the bishop himself (rather than the examiners) kept the original grave-clothes – as if in recompense for the hair he was unable to obtain. Gilbert Crispin was Abbot of Westminster 1085–1117. He was one of Anselm's immediate (English) disciples, and was 'much concerned with the problem of unbelief'.[2] This is interesting in the light of what happens in this chapter, although no evidence that the Nun was familiar with Anselm's work. She adds nothing significant in this regard to what Aelred says about the abbot.

¶After this it came about, as God ordained, that the holy monks there desired eagerly to know whether their lord's holy body was still whole to this day. Because of the great desire they felt, they had an amicable dispute. Some said it was whole, and showed the reason why they were right:[3] that his body was completely whole and lay without corruption – he who was never corrupted while alive, nor had given himself to foolish delights.[4] The others told them to be silent and to calm their presumption. For it could very quickly happen, if the body was not whole, that the people would love him less and, in their simplicity, believe that he was of less merit if his body did not lie whole. They said there was no need to advance this cause, for even if it was dust he ought not to be loved less. And if nature had worked in him as it had in holy apostles, and in martyrs, confessors, and in many holy virgins[5] – it should not then be thought he was loved any the less by God, nor truly ought to be loved less by us, even though he was not whole. The dispute went on so, that it was related to the abbot who was then the incumbent of the place; he was named Gilbert Crespin. As

---

[1] *Vita*, 781D–3A; *Life*, §37. MP sets this story at the end of *Estoire*: vv. 4639–86 (*History*, p. 114), omitting the final miracles of these c12 versions.
[2] Anselm, *Proslogion*, pp. 44–5; p. 57 & note 2.
[3] 5959 'le purquei del dreit': see note to v. 3936
[4] 5963 'fol delit': see Glossary for 'delit'. Aelred does not give this reason for the body's incorruption: merely that his flesh was virginal.
[5] 5979 'E en saintes virgines plusurs': the Nun adds holy virgins to Aelred's list (*Life*, p. 226).

soon as he heard about this pious wrangling he set a day, judicially,[6] to revisit the body and set the squabblers right. Then he summoned his friends: the closest, and those he thought the best. He sent for Saint Gundulf, who held the see at Rochester.[7] Then, when all who had been bidden to this event were gathered, they all went to the sepulchre. Then they took off the lid, and there came forth such a perfect[8] fragrance, such a great abundance of sweetness, that all were comforted by it and reassured in their belief. First they took off the cloth in which the king was swathed. They find it as clean and fair as if it were freshly bleached. Then they take off the next cloths, and find them all white and clean; so their hopes are raised, for what they most want to know about the king. Then they lift up his beautiful arms, and stretch and bend them. They extend and fold his fingers; they touch his breast and body; they found the whole body fair and sound and firm.[9] His flesh was white and fair, coloured with fresh redness. This stimulated their desire to see his beautiful face. But they were not daring enough: they asked Saint Gundulf to do so. So he took it upon himself, in love and in good faith. For love, and the benefit he felt in himself, made him brave – he took courage from both. He puts forth his holy hand to the holy head, and lifts from it the shroud placed over the face. He sees full and beautiful colour, and then he takes the beard in his hand; it was whiter than blossom. He pulled it towards him vigorously, but it was as firm on the chin as it had been when he was alive. When the bishop felt this, he was overjoyed by the miracle. Then a virtuous desire was kindled: he wanted to have a hair. But force could not help him to pluck out a single hair.

When the abbot Gilbert saw what Saint Gundulf wanted to do, 'Dear father!' he said, 'dear friend, leave off this minute, I pray you! And let him remain whole; God will not let you break into him!'

The bishop then replied, 'You have spoken well – I beg your mercy! But I was acting not so much from presumption as from my devotion. For if I could have one hair, I would love it more than all the good things gathered in grace, had I them all in my power.[10] Let him lie whole, and let him rise up whole.[11] I shall do nothing that might hurt him.'

But he kept the cloth that had swathed the body. They attired him in others, very costly, and put him back into the sepulchre. It was in the thirty-sixth year after he had quitted the suffering of the world, that they found his body whole through the power of the Almighty. The abbot was made very joyful, and also the whole devout

---

[6] 5989 Södergård prints 'par esquart' here, corrected online to 'en esguart'. Cf. 'par esguard', v. 5722. 'revisit' (next line) is 'revisder': a rare example of 'visit' in the Nun's vocabulary.
[7] Gundulf was called, in the previous chapter, to help Lanfranc with the business of Ulstan's staff. Edward's tomb was first opened in 1102 by Gilbert Crispin and Gundulf (see the introduction to this chapter; and *Life*, note on p. 227).
[8] 6000 'fait' (past participle of 'faire'); for 'perfect', see Glossary.
[9] 6017 'soldé' = joined (cf. soldered), from *solidare*.
[10] Aelred's bishop says he would value 'a small part' more than the riches of Croesus (*Life*, p. 228). The Nun dwells more specifically on the single hair, and replaces reference to Croesus with mention of all possible good things.
[11] 6058 'e entier lieft': that is, on the Day of Resurrection.

assembly,[12] that God had deigned to work this miracle among them and honour their lord so much.

---

[12] 6069 'cel saint cuvent': these are the pious wranglers.

Chapter 37

The Sewing-Girl (6072–243)[1]

Introduction

This miracle may have originated with Osbert. In Aelred, a prior is mentioned (*Life*, p. 231), perhaps Osbert himself (*Anon*, pp. 124–5). The Nun mentions an abbot, but no prior. Neither Osbert nor Aelred includes the step-mother's involvement in Edward the Martyr's death. The Nun must have known this version of the legend (see General Introduction, above). She alters the figure of the shadowy advisor slightly, playing on the fact that *persona* is gendered feminine in Latin but does not indicate the gender of the person: hence her remark that she doesn't know the person's gender, showing off her understanding of Latin grammar. Aelred's figure ('a certain person', *Life* p. 231) looks venerable, and may be intended as a supernatural messenger: *Dixit, et factum est ita*, translated as 'He spoke, and so it was done'.[2] This suggests a male figure, or so Aelred's translator takes it; such figures are often male. The Nun omits this sentence, concentrating instead on Maud's feelings. A real-life female advisor or messenger is the helpful woman in chapter 20. For the virtuousness of Maud the dress-maker, it is notable that Edith was also skilled in this type of work (chapter 8). Although the Nun may not be drawing any parallel, the Virgin Mary was supposed by legend to be skilful at needlework, so this occupation could be the mark of a virtuous woman (the passage is amplified by comparison with Aelred's). Christina of Markyate was skilled in needlework, which was commonly undertaken by cloistered women; it is possible the nuns of Barking knew her story (see my Introduction, Edith). Aelred calls the craftswoman Matilda; Maud is another form of the name.

¶We have often heard it said that God sends down his wrath upon those who dishonour his saints on earth; their sin is made to devour them, as we can prove by showing you many examples.[3] But of them all I want to write about one, which ought to be enough for the moment: how God avenged Saint Edward because of a wretched woman who insulted him, and then again in his goodness he made her quit of her sin before God.

At this time there lived in London a very clever woman named Maud; she was a craftswoman marvellously skilled at her work of embroidering rich cloth with real gold thread and stitching it finely with costly jewels. When it came to gems and precious stones, she knew all the various secrets of how to apply them so well that

---
[1] *Vita*, 783A–4D; *Life* §38.
[2] cf. Genesis ch. 1, *passim*.
[3] The Nun omits Aelred's examples of Elisha and Paul (*Life*, pp. 228–9), telling instead what the story will be about.

there was nobody to excel her in the art. She had such a reputation for artistry that she was beloved by the highest nobility, who sought her out and honoured her for her work. There was a countess in the land, a very great and worthy lady, who was of hardly less consequence than the queen of the realm. There was no lady in the whole country who could touch her reputation for power and wisdom, and so she had a fancy to put them all in the shade by her dazzling clothes, as she had done so in other respects. She talked to this craftswoman about it, and gave her enough money, so that they came to an agreement for something ornamental – though I don't know what it was, or what it was like.[4] She requests most urgently, and the other agrees, promising most faithfully, that she will hurry on with the work and let nothing delay it.

But a day was approaching that was to be celebrated by the whole of London, and this was the feast of King Edward the Holy Martyr, he who was most shamefully and treacherously murdered by his stepmother, so as to grab the land into her power. She killed him cruelly by her wicked wiles, he who is uncle to our Edward.[5] The craftswoman was desperately anxious: what to do about the feast? She was afraid that if she stopped work the countess would be furious with her, and on the other hand if she did continue her work she would risk the fury of heaven. So she spoke of her fears to one of her workers, to help her decide what was to be done. But she answered, ill-temperedly:

'Is this Edward of Westminster, that the lower classes are so fond of? They think he's a saint and a king, but what's that to you or me? Whoever wants to keep the feast, let them worship him as a saint or wail for his death. To be sure I'll never keep his day, unless you order me to, no more than for any other churl. There'd be no point, I'm convinced of that.'

When her mistress heard her talking like this, she began to quake with fright. Speaking harshly, she reproved her with a torrent of angry words. But the other mocked and laughed at them, for she was a badly-behaved girl. She took her mistress for a foolish simpleton, and spoke foolishly about the saint. Then, the wrath of heaven visited her![6] She was seized with paralysis, and her mouth twisted right up to her ear; then it spread through all her body. She was struck dumb, in great pain, and maddened in her wits. She gnashes her teeth and foams at the mouth; her whole body is in agony, and her limbs all twisted up.

Her mistress watched in anguish, and the women around her burst into tears. Soon the news has flown all over the city, and many people come running to ask what was going on. They tried to console the good woman, for she was beloved by everybody. She asks them what is to be done, and how she is to be helped. At this,

---

4   6109 Typical of the Nun's chatty style; Aelred merely says 'a work of no small value' (*Life* p. 229).
5   6123 Edward the Martyr, half-brother to Ethelred, was the Confessor's uncle. According to his English legend, our Edward was named after him. It is unlikely this story was originally attached to the Martyr (*pace* note in *Life*, p. 229).
6   6152 'L'ire del ciel dunc la requiert': 'requere' meaning 'visit' in a most unusual way.

somebody[7] replied – I don't know whether it was a man or a woman – that they should immediately put her into a boat and take her to the tomb of the saint she had so gravely insulted, to ask his mercy for her sin.[8] The lady listened eagerly to their advice, and then would not rest or relax until she had taken her straight to Saint Edward; then the lady would be relieved. There is the poor wretched girl, in despair of any end to her suffering. Her mistress sobs and weeps and cries, beseeching the saint for mercy and help, that for the love of his dear Lord he would be kind to the unhappy creature.

The good Edward, who had learned well from sweet Jesus Christ's good deeds to render good for evil, and to love where there was hate,[9] heard their prayers. Nevertheless, he suffered her to remain in this suffering, in this pain and torment, overnight.[10] The abbot and all the good monks[11] pray to God with bitter tears, to look upon the sufferer and assuage her pain. They even say the Litany; and each one did everything proper concerned with it.

The lady weeps more than anybody, calling upon the power of heaven. She cried so hard and she prayed so hard that the sweet pity of God, that is never invoked in vain and surpasses all justice, accepted the lady's tears and soon sent alleviation. However, the miserable girl lay all that night and most of next day in the pain and distress that she endured for her sin. During the Vespers they sang, the good monks who were in the church,[12] the sufferer was healed of the terrible pain she had been in, through the goodness of King Edward, towards whom she had done so ill. Her mouth returned to its proper position, and her face that had been twisted backwards now straightened itself. Then she looked around her, wondering what it could mean, that she could see these people weeping. She asked them the reason, and why they had brought her here.[13] When she hears what has happened, she begins to cry bitterly. She gives thanks devoutly to God, and to Saint Edward too, by whose goodness she has been healed. Now you will hear shouting and singing! They all vie with one another, praising God for the poor girl's cure.[14]

---

[7] 6170–71 'A itant li fud respundu – Ne sai se hume u femme fu': the passive 'she was answered' allows the somebody to be either male or female (see introduction to this chapter).

[8] 6172 'en une nef': a boat (rather than a cart, for example) is somewhat unexpected as a conveyance, but this is what Aelred says (*Life*, p. 231); perhaps the most convenient way of getting from London to Westminster in those days.

[9] Matt. 5:43–4; Luke 6:27.

[10] In Aelred (*Life*, p. 232) Jesus, not Edward, makes this decision.

[11] 6194 'toz les seignurs': the Nun often uses 'seignurs' where 'monks' or 'good men' is clearly meant (Aelred has *fratres*, for 'seignurs' at v. 6213; here he refers merely to those singing and praying); see Glossary.

[12] 6212–13 'Entre les vespres qu'il chanterent, Les seignurs ...': Södergård notes this construction, a pronoun subject preceding the noun it is to replace, not hitherto recorded before the fifteenth century. Vespers is an evening prayer (see Hours, in Glossary), so the girl had to wait all day for her cure.

[13] 6225 'il l'unt menee': MS 'il unt'. Södergård notes that although the pronoun may be omitted in Old French, it is unusual with verbs of this type; he corrects, for clarity.

[14] Aelred adds two Bible references expressing praise for God; the Nun omits them, to focus more closely on the cure.

Presently the lady takes leave of Saint Edward and the monastery. She goes home leading her companion, who is now well and happy. The girl, from that day forth, was so frightened of Saint Edward that ever after she could not hear his name without trembling in every limb and changing colour; ever after, she left off her bad behaviour.[15]

---

[15] 6243 This final clause is added by the Nun.

Chapter 38

Osbert's Fever (6244–371)[1]

Introduction

The Nun's account slightly abridges Aelred's, except for her introduction to the audience, and reference to the angels' song at the Nativity. Her addition of a Bible reference is unusual. She calls the man 'Osbern', but this is Osbert of Clare who wrote the 1138 Life (see *Osbert*, pp. 45 note 1, and 56 note 5, although the miracle does not appear in it).[2] Perhaps this cure helped spur the former to do so; he is said to have applied himself thereafter to the service and praise of the Confessor (*Life*, pp. 233 and 236, and indexes B and C); he promoted Edward's cult as a result of his cure (*Anon*, pp. 125–6). Nothing in Aelred's account, which praises Osbert's knowledge, eloquence, and philosophy, betrays the fact that this was the author he himself would be replacing. Two of Osbert's nieces were nuns at Barking. But it is unlikely our Nun was one of them, because if so why would she not translate her own uncle's work? She tells us no more than Aelred does about Osbert's later activities (devotion, and preaching; see end of this chapter, and note introducing the following chapter 39).

❧ ❧ ❧ ❧ ❧ ❧ ❧ ❧ ❧

¶As well as what we have already told, let us tell of another marvel that he performed in his church, where his holy body lies resting. There was a worthy monk in the place, who was well endowed with learning and goodness; this man was named Osbert. He had fallen sick of a very painful disease, a raging quartan fever.[3] It had so tormented him, for six months, that he was completely unrecognizable. His flesh was so wasted he looked more like a phantom than a man. He was pale, faint, and exhausted, for the disease had not been feinting with him.

While he was in this travail, the longed-for day came round that God was born on earth. All the good monks are united in their joy of the festival. But for this man, his pain was doubled: he could not share the joy of the others whom he saw rejoicing, for his sickness attacked him so that he could be conscious of nothing else. But, notwithstanding, his great love for his dear Creator, and the devout faith he had of this holy Birth, so mastered his weakness that he got up in the night for the service. When Matins had been said, and Lauds,[4] for as long as they lasted, then the good monks began the Mass just before daybreak, as was customary on the night in which

---

[1] *Vita*, 784D–6B; *Life* §39.
[2] Osbern of Canterbury, not Clare, is named Osbert in *Acta Sanctorum*; the confusion seems to be common. This man is correctly named Osbert in *Life* (p. 233).
[3] 6253 A type of malaria, so called because it recurs every third day (fourth, by inclusive reckoning; see OED).
[4] See Glossary, for the Hours.

God was given birth. When he hears the Gospel read, he cries for joy, weeping and sighing for the little boy he hears named, who was born to save the world. He hears how those shepherds went to visit the King of Angels born on earth; he hears the voices of angels promising peace on earth to all men of good will.[5] He surrenders himself wholly to glory, and to many tearful thoughts about the surpassing humility of God wishing to be born of a woman. He is ravished by such bliss, both for the Mother and for the Son, that he felt no pain at all and believed himself cured. But God, who performs all things rightfully, and who knows and sees all things, did not send him health. Just now he postponed it, in order to show forth the goodness of Edward, who was to heal him of his disease. Nevertheless, for the whole of two days he was free of pain. He felt no heat or cold, or anything, but on the third day the fever overwhelmed him so cruelly that he had never endured anything like it. For as long as it lasted, it got worse every day. But the longed-for day was near, the feast of his dear lord, when he left this world and passed away to his Father in heaven.[6] That day, at the High Mass being celebrated with supreme reverence, at the moment of the True Sacrament, he stretched his pain-racked body before the sepulchre of his dear lord, moaning and sighing as though he thought his last day had come. His need burst forth in lamentation and agony, for he despaired of ever being cured unless it happened on this day, unless through him whose great feast it was. He began these words:

'O, my good Edward![7] O, my lovely dearest sweet Lord, have you no longer any mercy for me? How long will you forget me? What has become of your pity, that came forth to so many sufferers? Our fathers who saw your deeds and your ways told us how you used to take pity on the strangers who came here. What right have you to disdain poor me, who am so afflicted? Will you let this body die thus, that you deigned to feed for so long?[8] But if it is your design for me to remain in this terrible agony, then I beseech you to let me die and kill my pain in death. But, if ever I may get my health, then I pray you in your goodness to look upon my great suffering, if any suffering is like unto or greater than mine?[9] What burning agony this heat causes me, and what chill then grips my body! I don't know which hurts me more, but it is a burden to me to be still alive. So I beg you to bring on my death, if you want nothing better for me.'

Among these words as he speaks, his eyes pour forth tears, and his heart groans. Then, when the Mass has been sung and the festivities wound up, he lifts himself

---

[5] 6286 'ces pasturs vunt quere ...'; cf. Luke 2:16, *And they came ... and found Mary, and Joseph, and the babe*. The words of the heavenly host, familiar from *AV* Bible (Luke 2:14, *and on earth peace, good will toward men*), differ from *LV*. The Nun's phrase at v. 6289: 'Pais en tere a toz biens vuillanz' [peace on earth to all men of good will] is closer to *et in terra pax hominibus bonae voluntatis*. Aelred refers to the Gospel, but does not cite it directly (*Life*, p. 233). See de Hamel, *The Book*, pp. 320–21, for this variant in the Greek.
[6] 6312-15 According to Aelred's earlier account, Edward died on 4th January (*Life*, p. 211). He may have died on the 5th, the day before Epiphany (as the Nun says, v. 5220); see Mason, *House of Godwine*, p. 136.
[7] 6329-55 Several Psalms are echoed in Osbert's speech (cf. *Life*, p. 235).
[8] 6341 'nurir': he refers to money Edward left for maintenance of the community.
[9] 6348 'esguardez a ma grant dulur ...': see Lam. 1:12, *behold, and see if there be any sorrow like unto my sorrow*. The Latin, in Aelred as in *LV*, is *dolor* (*Life*, p. 235).

from the ground. He feels light, and completely happy, except that he is rather weak. Now he felt an appetite for food, that he had not experienced for a long time. He was completely restored to health! Thus God healed his body, through the goodness of his friend. Ever after being thus healed, he was more devoted than ever to King Edward, his lord, and he preached of his virtue everywhere.

Chapter 39

Gerins Cured Likewise (6372–441)[1]

Introduction

Once again the Nun adds an address to the audience, with the appellation 'seignurs'. Aelred says merely 'This man was a scribe'. Altogether she uses 'seignurs' to the audience four times, and once addresses them as 'sires'. Clemence calls her audience 'segnurs' only once; Aelred, never (see Introduction, p. 48, above). The detail of Osbert being prior, not mentioned at this point in *Vita* (where he is called 'brother ... second to the abbot'), suggests the Nun may have been familiar with Osbert's Life (*Anon*, p. 125). In chapter 38 Osbert is described as a worthy monk. In chapter 37 no prior is mentioned (see introduction to chapter 37, for Aelred's prior who could have been Osbert). This chapter ends with the Nun's homiletic remark about God honouring his own, instead of Aelred's elaboration of the cure.

¶My lords, this man [Osbert] you have heard about, who was healed by Saint Edward, was a learned man and a fine speaker; he was wise in God and worthy in the world. He frequently addressed the people, urging them to do good and love God. He was especially gifted with the ability to talk both beautifully and virtuously. He was overjoyed at his cure, which greatly increased his devotion.

The year passed, and the day of his lord the king's feast came round again. That day he put on his vestments, mindful of the cure he had been given during these festivities. He was to chant the High Mass, and it was his duty and honour to do so, for he was prior of the foundation.[2] The highest nobles of the city came on this blessed day to glorify the great feast and to pray for mercy to the king. When the Gospel had been read, he came forward as usual to face the congregation. He preached the sermon for the day: of the king and his virtue, of his gentleness and goodness, and of his spotless chastity; as for his power, it had been demonstrated on his own body. He told them how this day, one year ago, he had mercifully cured him of a quartan fever so cruel that nobody had ever suffered the like.

There was a soldier among those who heard the sermon, a gentleman named Gerins.[3] He was a guardian of the royal palace, and he had the same fever. It had

---

[1] *Vita*, 786B–7A; *Life* §40.
[2] 6389 'Kar de cel liu priur esteit' (note 'liu' in this context; 'place' would sound awkward in English – see Glossary). The Nun amplifies description of his happiness and eloquence, but omits reference to Matthew's Gospel (*Life* p. 236).
[3] 6406-7 'Uns chevaliers ... Pi udume esteit'; Aelred calls him *miles*; the Nun 'chevalier' but, as is usual with her, not in the romance or 'knightly' sense (cf. *Catherine*, where 'chevalerie' means 'chivalry'); she adds that he was a good or worthy man. See p. 41, above.

so wasted his whole body that he despaired of ever being whole. He had lost all his wealth to the doctors in his search for a cure, and so his suffering was doubled because he had fallen into poverty. When he hears the prior talking like this, and telling his own story, then hope restores him to joy. He thought he would do likewise, and pray to Saint Edward; if he could do it for the prior then he could do it for him. The next night he went to the saint. It was the night of the twelfth day since the Creator was born; on this day he was baptized to purge our sins, on this day he was adored by the Kings who were led by the star. And on this day he turned water into wine:[4] thus it is that this holy feast is celebrated with three-fold honour, and the monks made great rejoicing. Each vied with the others in his singing, but poor Gerins wept. He begged devoutly for the saint's mercy, and the good Edward heard him – he cured him through the power of God, and he never suffered any further pain. So mighty is God to honour his own, and to show their goodness far and wide.

---

[4] Epiphany was also celebrated by the church as the date of Christ's baptism, and of his first miracle. The Nun slightly amplifies this account of the three-fold feast (cf. *Life*, p. 237).

Chapter 40

A Nun of Barking Healed (6442–545)[1]

Introduction

The opening of this section differs from Aelred's because the Nun knows the woman personally.[2] In Aelred, the Bible references are placed at the beginning of the account, and the lady wishes to emulate the centurion's faith (the Nun does not mention the centurion directly). The point of citing this Gospel miracle is that the patient was healed *in absentia*. The lady in the Nun's story echoes the Gospel words later, in her prayer. The story shows the Nun drawing on both oral and written sources. Her acquaintance with the lady of the miracle may be among the reasons for her decision to write the life of Edward.

The Nun follows Aelred pretty closely, although she adds personal touches, including that the lady is still among the Barking sisters. Aelred writes as though she were now dead (see his last sentence, below). It is surprising the Nun's account differs so little from his, if she had the story from the woman herself; we might have expected more detail. Could Aelred have got it from the Nun, instead? Unlikely ... but he must have got it from somewhere. However, she says clearly that he who made the Life wrote about it before. If Aelred had the story from Osbert, in a now-lost appendix to his Life (*Anon*, pp. xxxvi–ii and 124–6), then the Nun could also have known it directly from Osbert. That the woman is still apparently alive when the Nun is writing suggests an earlier rather than a later date for the Nun's work. Furthermore, she speaks of her sister as if to outsiders. It is therefore among several indications that the *Vie* was intended for a mixed or external audience, of visitors, and/or a future audience. Had it been intended for the nuns of Barking only, she might have worded differently this reference ... to a lady presumably present and eager to hear a Life of her saviour (see Introduction, Date of the Nun's Work, and Audience, above). It is also possible that the Nun invented or exaggerated the detail, that she knew the woman at the time of writing, in order to enliven her account. If the woman really existed, the Nun must have known of her. Could Osbert have invented it? Either way a story set in Barking Abbey, where he knew several of the women, is a likely one for him to include in his collection.

¶In time, a lady of our abbey, which is called Barking, came to hear of this marvel. She was a veiled nun there; indeed, she is here to this day, in sanctity and worthiness.

---

[1] *Vita*, 787A–8B; *Life* §41.
[2] Legge translates vv. 6442–51 in *Background*, p. 62.

40 A Nun of Barking Healed (6442-545)

In fact I heard this miracle from her, that I am going to tell you, even though he who made this Latin *Life* wrote about it before.[3]

This lady I am telling you of had already languished for two years with a cruel quartan fever; she had come to believe it would be fatal, because it had lasted so long and had brought her near to death. She no longer dared to hope for health, until she heard tell of the glorious King Edward and how he healed other fever-sufferers. And then her hopes awoke, of receiving her health from him, and she often prayed for his mercy. Then one day it happened to her this way: one morning she was sleeping,[4] and she dreamed she was to travel to her parents in her home country; she had fine folk in her company. When they had gone a little way, one of them called to another and said it would be a good thing if they turned aside to Westminster. They would dine there, for once they were refreshed then their journey would be a pleasure. As soon as the lady heard that, she answered the one who had spoken:

'And I, how am I to go there, when I don't know anybody to talk to? I don't know them, I've never seen them before, and I don't deserve any welcome from them.'

But he answered straight away:

'Don't let that trouble you.[5] Even though we don't know anybody there, we shall find a noble king who will receive us gladly and beg sweet Jesus to give you health, if you pray to him whole-heartedly.'

Then the lady awoke, and had great joy at the vision. She went to the church immediately, and began to chant the Seven Psalms;[6] then she said the Litany, and begged mercy from Saint Edward:

'Lord,' she said, 'I really believe that I should have my health again through you, if I were to visit your relics, as was promised to me in my sleep.[7] But I'm certain you don't need to make my body travel.[8] Nor, on the other hand, lord, do I know how much I would suffer for the trouble of finding companions and horses. Nor am I used to going about in the land, and therefore it's very hard for me, dear lord, to do this journey. And I'm sure that if it's truly your will, you could perfecty well cure me here. Let it not be constrained by my coming, lord, nor weakened by my staying – your great power to give back health to my body. And I do believe you can see how tormented it is; I truly know that in the light which endures for ever you are looking at my pain. Therefore I pray you to have tenderness. By a single word, if you will, heal your handmaiden.'[9]

---

[3] 6451 Here she must be referring to Aelred, although she never names him.
[4] 6466 'se dormeit': Södergård notes that 'dormir' is often reflexive in Old French.
[5] 6483 This reassurance is added by the Nun, as is the remark (below) that the woman had great joy at the vision (cf. *Life*, pp. 238-9).
[6] Penitential Psalms (see Glossary).
[7] 6496-521 The speech begins addressing Edward as 'tu', but switches to 'vus' partway through. I translate 'you' throughout, because she is not speaking to God.
[8] 6501 'travaillier' (see Glossary).
[9] 6520-21 See Matt. 8:8 & Luke 7:7: by the centurion's faith his servant, lying sick at home, was healed. The Nun can recite Psalms and quote from the Gospels; evidence of Barking nuns' knowledge of the Bible.

When she had said this and more, she went straight to her bed, for this was the day the fever was due[10] – the agony she was expecting. But she passed the whole day with little or no pain. With this, hope is reborn in her, and she gives herself up willingly to the good Edward, and prays him to make this cure complete. In great fear, in great anguish, she awaits her fourth day again. When the day came that she so feared, she went weeping to the church. She begged for Saint Edward's mercy, that he would not forget her. Nor did he, in his great kindness, for she felt no pain all day. But nevertheless she was afraid as she awaited the third term; she had recourse again to her remedy, and she received full health. Thus did the friend of God cure, by his virtue, the friend of God.[11]

---

[10] 6524 'a cel jur sun terme esteit': see note to v. 6253.
[11] 6544–5 'Issi ad l'ami Deu guarie Par sa vertu la Deu amie'; this play on 'friend of God' is not in Aelred, who says 'she rendered thanks ... as long as she lived' (*Life*, p. 240).

Chapter 41

A Triple Cure (6546–685)[1]

Introduction

The Nun's account ends rather abruptly once the cure in this final chapter is complete. Aelred extends the monks' rejoicing into a short prayer. Södergård says the account is augmented and developed by comparison with Aelred's (p. 33). This is chiefly in description of the man's feelings, for example, the groans and tears with which he prays for the second cure, and the calm which accompanies that cure. There is no *explicit* in the Nun's version. Aelred's ends: *Explicit Vita sancti Edwardi regis et confessoris, cum miraculis ejusdem* (*Life*, p. 243). It is possible the Nun's text originally ended before the miracle collection, where there is a more substantial *explicit*. She may have added the miracles at a later time; this might explain why two of the three manuscripts end with or before Edward's death. It is also interesting that the French prose version (based on the Nun's poem) has an additional miracle after this one: another Barking story.[2] This raises questions about what, exactly, the original version(s) of the Nun's text may have included.

¶God is very mighty and good, who can so honour his own, and who is powerful,[3] and works at his pleasure. Therefore we must not keep silent about another miracle that he did for his friend where his body lay. A monk in his church,[4] a very worthy man indeed, had a marvellous affection for sweet Edward, his lord; he could barely get his fill of hearing or saying his name.[5] Then it happened by ill luck that he fell into three-fold trouble. For one day there was bleeding in his arm,[6] and the wound swelled up so much, into a raised lump, that it formed an abscess. The blood hardened in the vein and the swelling spread into his body. He was in pain and agony because he could not move his arm. As well as this pain he felt, there was an oppression in his chest so that only with great effort and great pain could the poor man draw his breath. Further, he was much tormented with another thing – with a swelling he had on his

---

[1] *Vita*, 788B–90B; *Life* §42. Södergård's summary (Introduction, p. 15) gives the line number incorrectly (6540 for 6546).
[2] 'Notice' ed. Meyer (and my Introduction, Later Lives).
[3] 6548 'E poet': Södergård notes the verb can be used in absolute as well as auxiliary sense.
[4] 6552 'dedenz sa iglise': as Södergård notes, the pronoun 'sa' (instead of 'son') before a vowel is not unusual.
[5] 6556 'saüler' here means to be sated (not intoxicated, as in other instances – see Glossary). Instead of psalm references at this point in Aelred, the Nun makes the man's piety parallel with Edward's. The latter could never hear enough about God and his friends, this man can never hear enough about Edward.
[6] 6560 'en son braz seigna': it is clear from *Vita* that the circumstance was blood-letting (a routine health precaution); see *Life*, p. 240.

foot, from which he had such agony that he could walk only with great difficulty. While he was in this trouble, the feast came round of the holy day on which King Edward died – on which he lost death and found life. All the good men have great joy of it, except the one who was in this pain. That night, when it is the hour for ringing, the brothers go to assembly. They ring the bells very vigorously for love of their king, their lord. The worthy man was in the church and saw his companions rejoicing. He felt terrible pain in his heart that he could not help them. So strong was his desire, that incapacity could hardly hold him back. In this desire, in this love, he said very tenderly to the king:

'O good Edward, how is it that I can get no other remedy? Do you want to fail me now, and not fulfil my desire? Now help me, for I'm going to get up and go to ring with these others!'

With that he seized a bell-rope, forgetting his arm in his zeal. He pulls and pulls again with great force, and his abscess immediately breaks open. The corrupt blood flows, and the poison loses its hold; the swelling goes down and the pain loses its sway. Now he was healed of one disease, though he was still disabled by two. But he suffered them bravely, for he had great hope that he who had cured this one would heal him of those two. The man often used to keep vigil after Matins in the church, privately before an altar, to say his own prayers. So he watched, on that same night that he received healing in his arm.[7] He went about as best he could, to pray as he was accustomed to do. Weeping, he goes to the saint's tomb. He lays his pain-racked body on the ground[8] and thanks him for the health of the arm he has cured, and begs him to have pity on the breast that so terribly pains him. Tears pour from his eyes, and groans from his heart. Then a sweat broke out, and spread over his whole body; all the heaviness lifts away. The agony departs from his chest, and a great calm enters in its place. He gets up from the ground, for his breast is full of lightness. Now he was cured of two pains, but he was still suffering in his foot. This trouble was a great nuisance to him, because he could not follow the other monks. It so happened that one day he and another reverend monk,[9] who led a very good life, lay together in their sick-room.[10] They talked of several things, and then came to King Edward, and tell again of his great powers to bring healing to many people.

'It's true,' says this man, 'that he has done cures, dear brother; I have experienced myself how the king is of great virtue. I can speak as living proof, for he has done so

---

[7] 6618 'cele meimes nuit': later that same night, or possibly the anniversary of his cure. Matins was sung very early in the morning (see Glossary, for the Hours).
[8] 6623 'Sun dulant cors juint dunc a tere', MS 'Sun dulant juint . . .' [he lays his suffering on the ground]. Södergård corrects the hypometric line by adding the noun which makes most sense in context.
[9] 6641 'un altre seignur': see Glossary for 'seignurs' as monks. Aelred has *seniore* [one of the seniors] (*Life*, p. 242). He rarely uses this word, therefore the Nun is not thoughtlessly translating *seniores* when she writes 'seignur(s)', either of her audience or of monks and other 'good men'.
[10] 6643 'en lur enfermerie': Södergård's glossary gives 'maladie', but Aelred says *in cella infirmorum* [in a cell or room for the sick], which makes better sense (see also *AND*).

much good for me that now I thoroughly know and trust that whatever he asks God for, he will be able to do by his power.'

Then he showed him his foot, which was so ugly and swollen that to look at it was a horrible thing. But the pain was even more horrible.

'Surely,' he said, 'if he loved me enough to vouchsafe to heal this foot – in this matter I don't know how else to pray, except to surrender myself completely to his love.'

Then night came upon them, and each went to sleep in his due place. As soon as day broke, the worthy man who had pain in his foot got up. He puts his hand to it, as he used to do. With his finger he prods up and down, but can feel neither swelling nor pain. The great desire he had for healing makes him hesitate to believe the truth. Then he grasps it in both his hands, and finds it both whole and sound. Immediately he jumps up and shouts; for joy he forgets the rule of silence.[11] Then he told the good monks all about how his lord had cured him of three ills,[12] the very least of which could have been fatal. Now you can hear the happiness and rejoicing that those good men express, for Saint Edward their patron, by whom their brother received healing.[13]

---

[11] 6677 'Pur sun hait sa silence ublie': the Benedictine rule of silence (not in Aelred; see *Life*, p. 243). Barking was a Benedictine abbey, and the Nun reminds the audience that no talking, let alone shouting, was generally allowed.
[12] 6678–9 'ad tut as seignurs cunté Cum sun seignur l'aveit sané': here the Nun plays with two meanings of 'seignur' (Aelred has *sociis*; likewise at 'good men', below). Aelred words this passage differently (*Life*, p. 243).
[13] The last word of the poem is 'sancté'; the Nun enjoys the similarity between this and 'sainteté', which means holiness (see Glossary).

Appendix

Dream and Prophecy

The poem contains many different kinds of supernaturally-transmitted information, occurring in almost every chapter; an account is set out here. They differ from Aelred's in style, but not in content or detail. Barking had quite a history of supernatural visitations,[1] and therefore audience expectations would not be surprised by the relating of visions and prophetic utterances. Henry I is said to have been especially interested in prophecies, which he liked to have interpreted favourably to himself (see *Osbert*, p. 24 and notes). This may have influenced, directly or indirectly, Edward's (and other) hagiographers. Short explains how pervasively the supernatural formed part of the wider literary culture of the age.[2] There is no need for the Nun to emphasize the fact that such things happen: what they say and tell is more important.[3]

The first prophecy, given by angels, happens in chapter 1: it relates to Edgar. In chapter 2, the barons see 'signs' of evil to come. In chapter 3 appears the Nun's proleptic mention of Edward's two friends, who will visit him at the end of his life. The first true vision is Brihtwald's, in chapter 4: he sees Saint Peter crowning an unknown man. Peter then explains who the man is, although it is the Nun who names him Edward before Brihtwald wakes up – the matter of the vision is narrated by the Nun.

In chapter 7 the situation is one of virtuous prescience: Edward is not asleep when he sees the thief, but he knows through the Holy Spirit when Hugelin is about to arrive. In chapter 8, we are explicitly told that Edward's prophetic powers are a reward for his chastity. From now on we are given several examples of full-blown visions experienced by Edward.

In chapter 9 the vision of the ships is narrated not by the Nun but by Edward himself, afterwards, when asked about his mysterious smile. The truth is ascertained by messengers sent to Denmark to make enquiries. In chapter 10 we are advised that Edward and his court knew in advance of the messengers' return from the Pope. It is

---

[1] See references to Bede, in Barking Abbey (Introduction, above).
[2] 'Literary Culture'. See Doherty, 'Merlin and the Angevins', for Henry II's interest.
[3] Petroff, ed., *Visionary Literature*, gives an overview of women's visionary literature, although the Nun's is not among the selections.

not Edward but a hermit, in chapter 12, who is vouchsafed the waking vision of Saint Peter (narrated by the Nun).

In chapter 13 Gille Michel is commanded by Saint Peter, and he himself narrates what he was told to do. The same saint appears to a fisherman in chapter 14; there is no suggestion that the man saw all this in his sleep, and indeed there is much he did not see. He was left waiting while Peter carried out the dedication of the church; the effect of the saint's actions is narrated later when witnessed by Mellit.

Edward's wonderful vision of Christ, in chapter 16, is shared by his friend Lievrich. Coming just after the second letter from the Pope, this gift is a direct consequence of Edward's added holiness now that he is allowed to withdraw his attention from the world. The vision as seen by both men is narrated by the Nun (rather than by either of them), but it is later narrated by Lievrich in confession – the written record of which is duly discovered years later.

The first series of miracles begins with the cure of the scrofulous woman in chapter 17. The woman sees and hears what to do, although no figure is seen. The Nun narrates what she heard, and the woman tells Edward what she has 'dreamed'. In chapter 18 a blind man is shown in his sleep what to do, by God himself. This is narrated by the Nun, and is followed by an important conversation about the truth of dreams, in which Edward tries to resist those of other people. In chapter 19 a sufferer learns by hearsay, and then dreams that 'somebody' tells him, what to do.

The blinded woodcutter in chapter 20 is advised by a messenger from God (a good woman), but the event is not a dream; the conversation is narrated by the Nun in direct speech. In the next chapter (21) it is obvious that the palace servants have learned what to do for blind people, and do it devoutly and successfully.

In chapter 22 Edward makes a prediction about Godwin's sons. There is no vision in this case, but it is clear Edward can see the future that he is narrating. The Nun glances forward proleptically to say that it did indeed come true (it will be told in chapter 33). As for Godwin's own fate in chapter 23, he rashly 'predicts' that he will come to no harm while eating the morsel of food, because he is – he says – innocent. Because Edward blessed the morsel, it is God himself who strikes the villain.

The vision of the Seven Sleepers, in chapter 24, is another that Edward himself narrates. This time the audience is shown him laughing, but the Nun does not tell us why – Edward does so, in direct and indirect speech. This is about the future fate of Syria, and of all lands, we are told. The next 'vision' is another major event in this remarkable sequence: in chapter 25 we hear the story of Saint John's Ring, where there is no dream at all ... the pilgrims meet Saint John, on the road when they are lost. He gives them good lodging for the night, and it is not until next morning that he transports them miraculously, apparently wide awake, to their destination. Additionally, an important message is confided by John to the pilgrims. Edward will meet his death, and his Maker, within six months; it is emphasized that his chastity will be rewarded.

Edward's last vision is the prophecy of the divided tree (chapter 27). He wakes after being rapt away (they had thought him already dead), and he narrates how he saw his two friends – who were introduced in chapter 3 – and what they told him. Everybody believes him except Stigand, who scoffs. The Nun tells us that it did indeed come true, and the explanation continues into chapter 28. The following death scene (chapter 29) contains no vision of any kind, but the Nun manages to make the account of his being taken to heaven more vivid than in Aelred; it is as if she were among the watchers.

There follow two miracles in chapters 31 and 32, where the sufferers (Ralph, and the blind men) pray for healing and receive it. There follows, in chapter 33, the account of Edward's prophecy fulfilled (see chapter 22). It is not narrated by the Nun, but the direct speech of Edward – who appears to the Abbot of Ramsey – is recorded. In chapter 34 the bell-ringer dreams. He seems to see Edward in his sleep, and Edward urges him to ring the bells.

Two miracles at Edward's tomb are narrated without any dream or prophecy, and then comes the story of the sewing-girl in chapter 37. Somebody advises Maud, the girl's mistress, what to do, and the Nun plays on the fact that nobody knows who this somebody was. It is clear she wants us to think the person was a messenger from God.

The occasion of Osbert's cure is rather strange. The sufferer is so enraptured by prayer he believes himself cured, but in fact his cure comes a little later. His preaching in the next chapter, and no vision, is the inspiration for Gerins to come forward and beg for the saint's healing touch.

The last vision (chapter 40) is a strong one, and again involves a woman. This is a nun of Barking who dreamed of a journey, and that somebody told her there was a king who could help her (the dream is narrated by the Nun as it happens); when she wakes she prays to Edward, who does indeed cure her. The final chapter is of three cures in one man. Two are effected by prayer alone; the third is after a conversation with an elder monk who tells the sufferer how much Edward has done for him – although the former is still in the infirmary! However, the final cure is achieved, and the man receives his health through Edward's virtue.

The range of narrative styles and voices, for all these marvellous happenings (more than half the chapters contain some kind of dream or vision), is remarkable. Voices include those of the dreamers, of the apparitions (including apparently ordinary people), of other commentators within the text, and of the Nun herself. This variety enhances the dramatic qualities of the poem. Predictions and fulfilments are followed through: the Nun signals that they are to be found in the story, usually telling us where. Various kinds of vision and intuition are exploited to validate marvellous happenings. The long string of miraculous cures, unremarkable to modern audiences perhaps, are motivated in different ways by advisors earthly and unearthly. Narrating devices are many and ingenious: the hermit's letter, the count's confession, the helpful anonymous neighbour, the royal ring, and the king's mysterious laughter. Messengers are sent as far afield as Denmark and Ephesus to ascertain the truth of visions, and senior saints appear apparently in person to direct the proper course of events.

Glossary[1]

aneme: the word for soul, 'aneme', seems to be reserved more or less for the disembodied entity, so I have usually preferred 'heart' for 'quer'. For example: 'de quer et de cors' is translated as 'heart and body', not 'body and soul'.

beau: one of several words with a number of meanings, 'beau' may be found in (for example) 'beau sire'. This is often rendered as 'fair sir' or even 'fair sire' by archaizing writers, which sounds unlike even formal modern English. The idea of beauty is in the word, but is not strictly necessary; 'dear sir' is a possible alternative, albeit conjuring up a modern world of business letters; 'dear lord' is acceptable if the speaker is addressing somebody above them in rank.

bien: normally meaning 'well', it is often redundant. A translation may silently omit or vary the word for stylistic reasons, *passim*, or exploit it when used for special effect. An example, end of chapter 2: 'With *good* faith they suffered them *bravely*, because of the *good* results (great goods) they expected' [En *bon* espeir *bien* le soffrirent Pur les granz *biens* k'en atendirent].

curteisement: a word used by the Nun several times (see p. 41, above); it adds to the 'courtly' flavour of her poem. Examples are at v. 1163 (how God 'courteously' saved Judith) and v. 3866, where it is part of an ironic comment. At v. 1888, one of the qualities of a good messenger is that he should be 'curteis'. There are several other examples (v. 78 is of Edgar; v. 5726 is of Lanfranc) to set against Clemence's so-called courtly vocabulary, such as 'chevalierment' or similar (cf. the Nun's v. 6406, where 'uns chevaliers' is just a soldier: Gerins).

cuvent: not necessarily 'convent'; it may refer to a house of male religious, or just to a gathering. See v. 6069, 'the whole devout assembly [of monks]'; and v. 6639 (near end of chapter 41), '... follow the other monks'.[2]

dangier: from a Latin word meaning 'power'. In this text the word means variously 'power, right' (vv. 4226, 4244, etc.), 'delay' (or 'object to'; see note to v. 4380), 'need' (or 'in vain'; see note to v. 3152). Our word 'danger' derives from one use meaning 'to be in somebody's mercy', hence to be in their power – which could be perilous.

---

[1] I list words and phrases which may require some explanation or comment. Södergård's glossary is not always accurate; errors are signalled in my text, above.

[2] See for example *The Rule of St Benedict* ed. Dean and Legge, p. 33 and *passim*, and glossary.

The word frequently appears in Old French to express a lady's power of holding a lover at arm's length, so her 'dangier' protects her.

delit/delit: the word may have different meanings: 'delight', and 'delict' [deliction or offence]. Thus they can be used to rhyme with each other (identical rhyme is allowed if the meanings are different). Writers cannot but have been aware of this ambiguity, and doubtless played upon it. Södergård glosses 'delit' to mean 'pleasure' except in just one case, vv. 51–2, where he gives 'crime'. Unfortunately his glossary gives the line wrongly as 55, so one can only guess that line 51 ('poor in sin and crime') and not 52 ('vain glory and foolish delights') is meant.

doux: this word has several meanings (sweet, gentle, kind, even soft) – as with words such as 'grant' and 'bien', some latitude is needed in translation. However, it may be that the poet deliberately uses certain words very frequently, for special effect, and this is rendered where possible.

dru(e), druerie (see **fin' amur** below): this word for friend, friendship, usually has a second meaning of lover, [sexual] love. The Nun uses such words for spiritual love and godly friendship. This is typical of the way she appropriates lyrical language for her own purposes of devotion (Clemence uses this word only once, of the Emperor's intimates; see my Introduction, on the Nun's identity).

fin' amur: fine or perfect love; not 'courtly' love in the romantic sense, which is how it came to be used in secular poetry. There are several examples in the text (it has been well documented by scholars), and each is footnoted because of the Nun's early and very special use of it.[3] Attempts to pinpoint exactly how the notion arrived in Anglo-Norman England, and how the Nun could have come across it, are far from conclusive. Harvey is convinced that Eleanor was not the medium of transmission, although she sets out how troubadour vocabulary and ideas were transmitted to and via Henry's court.[4] See also examples of the term 'fin' amur' in the poems of Marcabru, who contrasts such idealized love not (as one might expect) with non-adulterous married love but with sin and wickedness, as the Nun does.[5] It remains a possibility that the idea originated in a religious context, thence travelling into the wider secular literary world, and not the other way about.

finer: to finish or end; the word is almost exclusively used to mean 'die', and is translated accordingly. It is used once transitively, meaning 'put a stop to' (God ended the Danes' cruelty, in the closing lines of Exile and Return, above).

grant: literally 'great', a very common word. A translator is allowed a certain amount of latitude, because 'great' is less common, by and large, in modern English so a literal rendition would sound stilted or heavy.

Hours: the canonical hours of the day, as observed by religious communities, are conventionally seven in number: Nocturns, Matins or Lauds, Prime, Tierce, Sext,

---

[3] See, for example, MacBain, 'Vocabulary', p. 270.
[4] 'Eleanor and the Troubadours'.
[5] ed. Gaunt *et al.*, esp. poems 15, 31, 32, & 40; see also Eley, 'History and romance', for the term in Benoit's later Chronique.

Nones, Vespers, Compline (the first two often conflated). Services were said or sung at each Hour, beginning in the middle of the night and ending at bed-time. The eight-fold division of each day traditionally opened with contemplation of an Annunciation scene accompanied by appropriate prayers, psalms, and readings, and ended with the Assumption of the Virgin. An accompanying cycle might start with Christ's agony in the Garden and close with his burial.[6]

liu: literally 'place' (Latin *locus*), this word is frequently used for the church at Westminster, or other religious foundations of special importance. English 'place' sounds a little too casual, but the alternatives – sacred space, holy ground, establishment, precincts, foundation – all sound too heavy or not quite accurate.[7] I translate using whatever word seems appropriate (usually 'place', without comment) for the context.

mustier: this word, ultimately from Latin *monasterium*, can mean either monastery or church (cf. OED 'minster', properly the church of a monastery). Södergård's glossary gives only 'église', although it is clear that sometimes 'monastery' is meant. Where the Nun writes of 'mustiers e eglises', she evidently means some of each. Elsewhere, I translate according to context.

parfait: forms of this word are sometimes used where the apparent meaning 'perfect' will not work in modern English. The etymological sense of 'completed', 'as good as it is possible to be', 'very fine', and so on may give a clearer sense of the term. As a verb (in v. 4515, for example), the sense is to finish or make perfect. A broader meaning is demonstrated near the beginning of chapter 26, where Edward waits until the three days of Christmas have been properly celebrated [les treis jurs Fuissent parfaiz …] (vv. 4551–2).

penance/penitence: it is common in Anglo-Norman writing to find apparent confusion between these two terms (see note to v. 2058). They refer to distinct states of the human soul: penitence is sorrow or compunction for sin leading to confession, and penance is the reparation enjoined on the penitent by the confessor. The context makes clear which is meant (in modern French, 'penitence' means both penance and penitence); but cf. Rober le Chapelain's *Corset*, where both words are used and explained.[8]

Penitential Psalms (see chapter 40): there are seven, sometimes matched with the Seven Deadly Sins, as follows: Psalms 6 (6, anger); 32 (31, pride); 38 (37, gluttony); 51 (50, lechery); 102 (101, avarice); 130 (129, envy); 143 (142, sloth); several of the incipits are duplicated.[9]

---

[6] See, for example, *Cher Alme* ed. Hunt, p. 11. In medieval French, the hour of Sext (*sext* = sixth) is usually called 'midi', which would normally be translated as 'midday' into English. Our word 'noon' comes from the name of the ninth hour, Nones, which would properly be mid-afternoon.

[7] In *Liber Eliensis*, *locus* usually means 'monastery', see tr. Fairweather, p. xxxi. Further, see Carpenter, 'Origins', for its use to mean, specifically, [religious] house: p. 877 and note 71.

[8] ed. Sinclair, vv. 1684–5 & 1945–8, and glossary.

[9] The *AV* number of each is given first, *LV* in brackets. Most other references are the same in both Bibles, but most Psalms are numbered differently (see *The Anglo-Norman Lyric* ed. Jeffrey and Levy, pp. 116ff).

per: a mate (help-mate), match, peer, or companion. At v. 1314, Edith is Edward's 'equal', best translated as 'consort' (as at v. 4977). The Nun has her own variation on the Gospel pun (Peter and 'rock'; Latin: *Petrus, petrus*; Matt. 16:18), when she aligns Peter and his 'peers' in chapters 14 and 15 (vv. 2623–4, 2916). Her use of the word is unvaryingly positive.

requere, quere: usually meaning to request, and to look for or seek.[10] The Nun uses them distinctively, some nine occurrences out of ten, to mean 'visit' (see, for example, note to v. 4355). The words occur frequently, in several senses; however, when the context is a holy place or a saint's relics it patently means 'visit'. It occurs in *Estoire* less often (translated 'look for' or 'seek', when somebody visits a saint's relics). Clemence uses it to mean 'find' (not 'visit') only once, at v. 1227. Other uses in *Catherine* are the usual 'beg' or similar (an example of vocabulary that the poems might be expected to share *if* they were by the same writer). In the Nun's miracles, there is much coming and going on the part of sufferers, and it is hard to imagine that in every case they did not know the way to the shrine in question! The blinded woodcutter in chapter 20 has to visit [requere] eighteen churches. Gille Michel the cripple (chapter 13) travelled to Rome six times, to beg Saint Peter for healing. The unhappy Ralph wants to *visit* the king, who used to look after him so well, and show him his misery; he manages to *reach* the place during the octave of the festival.[11] The Barking lady dreams of Edward, and says to him: 'I truly believe I should have my health back again through you, if I were to visit your relics …' ('seek' or 'look for' make less good sense).[12] It is clear that 'requere' (sometimes 'quere') means to visit – usually the shrine of a saint, to beg for healing. The best evidence for '(re)quere' meaning 'visit' and not 'look for' is in two passages not concerned with these miracles. One is about Pentecost, when God sent his Holy Ghost to help and visit his faithful ('aider e quere', v. 1472). The other concerns the dedication of Westminster, just before the king's death. All the flower of the land came to be present [Vunt del dediement requere] (v. 4606).[13] The Nun uses it in other senses too, and there is a fine example where the visiting or seeking goes the other way. A young woman is guilty of insulting Edward, and immediately the wrath of Heaven 'seeks' her out, 'visiting' her with a nasty and painful paralysis – then the verb appears again as the 'seignurs' beseech God to heal the repentant sufferer (see chapter 37). It is frequently used in the context of Edward's vow to visit Saint Peter's tomb in Rome; again, one would not speak of 'looking for' that famous place. Aelred sometimes uses the verb *visitare*; the Nun translates as '(re)quere', not as 'visiter'.

---

[10] Cf. Chaucer: 'The hooly blisful martir for to seke' (*Canterbury Tales*, Prologue, lines 15–17, in ed. Benson).
[11] Ch. 31; 'requere' in vv. 5392 & 5395.
[12] Ch. 40; 'Si j'eüsse tun cors requis', v. 6498.
[13] Sometimes interchangeable: at v. 583 'requereit' is 'queroit' in MS P (Cnut intends to seek the hand of Emma); 'seek out' [go in order to fetch or visit] is more appropriate than 'look for'.

riche: this can mean either rich *or* powerful (cf. the modern German word 'reich'; and 'bishopric' as the area over which a bishop has power). In our poem it is regularly contrasted with 'poor', and Edward's desire not to be a rich man is stressed.[14] Godwin is 'riches' (v. 1295); this must mean powerful, in context (see also v. 1238).

romanz: Romanz = French in the Prologue, but Romanz = 'narrative', 'story', 'life', in the Title – the point being that it is an account in French (it can also mean simply 'book'). See notes to vv. 5297 and 5313; and p. 47, above.

santé/sancté v **sainté/seintée**: health and saintliness do not sound alike in English, but make a resonant pair in French. For example: v. 114 'health': 'santé' echoes 'seintée' [saintliness], at v. 101. This is one of many such pairs, much exploited by our author. The poem ends with the word 'sancté' [healing]; the Nun evidently laying stress on the holiness of this saintly miracle. Cf. *Corset*, in which the writer plays on two meanings of 'sancté'.[15]

saüler (usually refl.): in modern French 'se souler' is to get drunk or inebriated; in medieval French it usually means 'to be sated'. In this poem it may be used for a kind of spiritual intoxication, closer to the modern meaning. In *Jeu Saint Nicolas* it is glossed as 'rassasié' [sated] in a context where 'drunk' might be more appropriate, because the conversation there is about wine.[16] *AND* gives no meaning 'drunk', but the richness of these passages (for example, 'enivra' in v. 4232 and note) justifies such strong terms. For forms of 'saüler' meaning *either* intoxicated *or* satisfied, sated, see vv. 30, 845, 1682, 3023, 3036, 4377, 4449. There is one occurrence in Clemence's *Catherine*, where the word unquestionably means 'sated': the wicked king is not sated with the evil he has undertaken (vv. 2469–72). Clemence does not use it in the sense of 'inebriated, drunk' in the ecstatic mode as Edward, or the angels, contemplate the adored.[17]

seignur(s): a word used by the Nun to address her audience [My Lords], but which also frequently refers to the monks = 'the good men' ('gentlemen', or even 'lords', will not do for the latter). The Latin *seniores* (distinctly less frequent in Aelred than 'seignurs' in the *Vie*) has a range of meanings; it would be simplest to think of it as a term of respect. Her use of 'seignurs' for the audience cannot be taken as evidence that they were all religious. Bloch suggests that *seniores* in Osbert's Prologue may refer not only to senior religious but also to the king (*Osbert*, pp. 12 and 68).

sené: the Nun uses this to translate Aelred's 'synod', but in general 'senate' fits the sense well. It can mean an assembly in general from Latin *senatus*, a gathering of senior and thus usually elderly men. A word with similar spelling but a different derivation is also an adjective for 'wise' (or 'with good sense'), so I usually follow what I judge to be the Nun's choice of a word with more than one meaning: senate.

---

[14] See also Laurent, *Plaire et édifier*, pp. 240–43.
[15] ed. Sinclair, v. 2305 and note.
[16] ed. Henry, vv. 588–90.
[17] See, for example, *The Life of Aelred*, Walter Daniel, p. 21: 'drunk with the wine of unspeakable joy' [*inebriatus*].

travailler: see above in the Ring story; also in the Nun of Barking's cure. The meaning 'travel' is better than the medieval (Continental) and modern meaning 'work'.[18]

valur/virtu: For the word 'valur' (vv. 12 *and* 13), one is reminded of 'virtue' in the sense of Mark 5:30, where Jesus felt that virtue (*LV virtutem*) had gone out of him and into the sick woman as she touched his garment. One may translate as 'power' or 'strength' rather than 'merit' or even 'value'. An associated word is 'vaillant' (variously spelt), with its associated ideas of 'valur': most occurences are in a context where Edward's worthiness goes hand in hand with, but is not obscured by, his valour as a leader of men. There is a nice opposition, between valiant (as a warrior) and worthy (as a Man of God) in v. 3276. 'En Deu e el siecle vaillanz' sums up the dual nature of Edward's virtue. Later, we are told of Edward's 'valur', which could mean worthiness or bravery. On the whole 'worth' is preferred, because it is not generally the Nun's care to emphasize his value as a fighting man. In v. 309, 'valur ... bunté', I have translated 'bravery ... goodness'. But usually she stresses his value as a good warrior less than as a good person.[19]

---

[18] See *AND*; Short, *Manual*, p. 23; and *Catherine*, v. 481, where it unmistakably means 'travel' – perhaps an early anglicism.
[19] See also *Liber Eliensis* tr. Fairweather, pp. xxxi–ii, for Latin *virtus* meaning virtue *or* power.

Bibliography

Primary Texts

Adgar, *Le Gracial*, ed. Pierre Kunstmann (Ottawa, 1982).

Aelred of Rielvaulx, *De Institutione Inclusarum: Two English Versions*, ed. John Ayto and Alexandra Barratt, EETS OS 287 (London, 1984).

Aelred of Rievaulx, *The Historical Works*, ed. Marsha L. Dutton, tr. Jane Patricia Freeland (Kalamazoo, 2005).

The Ancrene Riwle, tr. M. B. Salu (1955; repr. Exeter, 1990), introduction by Dom Gerard Sitwell.

Ancrene Wisse, ed. J. R. R. Tolkien, EETS OS 249 (London, 1962).

The Anglo-Norman Lyric: An Anthology, ed. David L. Jeffrey and Brian J. Levy (Toronto, 1990).

The Anglo-Norman Voyage of St Brendan, Benedeit, ed. E. G. R. Waters (Oxford, 1928).

The Anglo-Saxon Chronicle, tr. G. N. Garmonsway (1953; repr. London, 1986).

Anselm, *Proslogion*, ed. and tr. M. J. Charlesworth (Oxford, 1965).

The Battle of Maldon, ed. D. G. Scragg (Manchester, 1981).

Bede, *A History of the English Church and People*, tr. Leo Shirley-Price, R. E. Latham, and D. H. Farmer, revised edition (1955; repr. London, 1990).

Bodel, Jean, *Le Jeu de Saint Nicolas*, ed. Albert Henry (Brussels, 1962).

Chardri, *La Vie des Set Dormanz*, ed. Brian S. Merrilees, ANTS XXXV (London, 1977).

Chaucer, Geoffrey, *The Riverside Chaucer*, ed. Larry D. Benson, 3rd edition (1987; repr. Oxford, 1988).

"Cher Alme": Texts of Anglo-Norman Piety, ed. Tony Hunt, tr. Jane Bliss, The French of England Translation Series OPS 1 (Tempe, AZ, 2010), introduction by Henrietta Leyser.

Chrétien de Troyes — Arthurian Romances, tr. D. D. R. Owen (1987; repr. London, 1991).

Clemence of Barking, *The Life of St Catherine*, ed. William MacBain, ANTS XVIII (Oxford, 1964).

Corset, Rober le Chapelain, ed. K. V. Sinclair, ANTS LII (London, 1995).

Dugdale, William, *Monasticon Anglicanum* (6 vols, 1817; repr. London, 1970), vol. 1.

Eadmer, *The Life of St Anselm, Archbishop of Canterbury*, ed. and tr. R. W. Southern, Nelson's Medieval Texts (London, 1962).

The Early Lives of St Dunstan, ed. and tr. Michael Winterbottom and Michael Lapidge (Oxford, 2012).

Early Middle English Verse and Prose, ed. J. A. W. Bennett and G. V. Smithers, 2nd edition (1966; repr. Oxford, 1985).

The Early South-English Legendary, ed. Carl Horstmann, EETS OS 87 (London, 1887).

Edward King and Martyr, ed. Christine E. Fell (Leeds, 1971).

La Estoire de Seint Aedward le Rei, Matthew Paris, ed. Kathryn Young Wallace, ANTS XLI (London, 1983).

Eusebius, *The History of the Church from Christ to Constantine*, ed. Andrew Louth, tr. G. A. Williamson, revised edition (1965; repr. London, 1989).

Fouke le Fitz Waryn, ed. E. J. Hathaway, P. T. Ricketts, C. A. Robson, and A. D. Wilshere, ANTS XXVI–XXVIII (Oxford, 1975).

'Fragment of an Anglo-Norman Life of Edward the Confessor', ed. A. T. Baker, *Modern Language Review*, 3 (1908), 374–5.

Gaimar, Geffrei, *L'Estoire des Engleis*, ed. Alexander Bell, ANTS XIV–XVI (Oxford, 1960).

Gesta Romanorum, ed. Sidney J. H. Herrtage, EETS ES 33 (1879; repr. London, 1962).

Gilte Legende, ed. Richard Hamer and Vida Russell, EETS OS 327, 328, 339 (3 vols, Oxford, 2006, 2007, 2012).

The Golden Legend: Readings on the Saints, Jacobus de Voragine, tr. William Granger Ryan (2 vols, 1993; repr. Princeton, 1995).

Goscelin of Saint-Bertin, *The Hagiography of the Female Saints of Ely*, ed. and tr. Rosalind C. Love (Oxford, 2004).

Gray, Douglas, ed., *From the Norman Conquest to the Black Death: An Anthology of Writings from England* (Oxford, 2011).

Grégoire le Grand, *Dialogues*, ed. Adalbert de Vogüé, tr. Paul Antin (3 vols, Paris, 1978–80), f-p into Mn French.

Guidance for Women in Twelfth-Century Convents, tr. Vera Morton (Cambridge, 2003).

A Guide to Old English, Bruce Mitchell and Fred C. Robinson, 5th edition (1964; repr. Oxford, 1992).

Henry of Huntingdon, *The Chronicle*, tr. Thomas Forester (1853; repr. Felinfach, 1991), facsimile.

The Historia regum Britannie of Geoffrey of Monmouth: Bern, Burgerbibliothek, MS 568, ed. Neil Wright (5 vols, Cambridge, 1984), vol. 1.

The History of Saint Edward the King, by Matthew Paris, tr. Thelma S. Fenster and Jocelyn Wogan-Browne, The French of England Translation Series 1 (Tempe, AZ, 2008).

'*In translacione sancti Edwardi confessoris*: The Lost Sermon by Aelred of Rievaulx Found?', ed. Peter Jackson, *Cistercian Studies Quarterly*, 40:1 (2005), 45–83.

Jocelin of Brakelond, *Chronicle*, ed. and tr. H. E. Butler, Nelson's Medieval Texts (1949; repr. London, 1951).

John of Salisbury, *Historia Pontificalis*, ed. and tr. Marjorie Chibnall, Nelson's Medieval Texts (London, 1956).

John of Salisbury, *The Letters of John of Salisbury, vol. I: The Early Letters*, ed. W. J. Millor and H. E. Butler (London, 1955), rev. C. N. L. Brooke.

John of Salisbury, *The Metalogicon*, tr. Daniel D. McGarry (1955; repr. Berkeley & Los Angeles, 1962).

'King Edward's Ring', ed. H. J. Chaytor, in Mary Williams and James A. de Rothschild, eds, *A Miscellany of Studies in Romance Languages and Literatures, Presented to Leon E. Kastner* (Cambridge, 1932), pp. 124–7.

Lanfranc, *Monastic Constitutions*, ed. and tr. David Knowles (London, 1951).

Liber Eliensis: A History of the Isle of Ely, from the Seventh Century to the Twelfth, tr. Janet Fairweather (Woodbridge, 2005).

Liber Festiualis, Alexander of Ashby, ed. Greti Dinkova-Bruun, Corpus Christianorum Continuatio Mediaevalis 118A (Turnhout, 2004).

The Life of Aelred of Rievaulx, Walter Daniel, ed. and tr. F. M. Powicke (London, 1950).

The Life of Christina of Markyate, ed. Samuel Fanous and Henrietta Leyser, tr. C. H. Talbot (1959; repr. Oxford, 2008).

The Life of King Edward who Rests at Westminster, ed. and tr. Frank Barlow (London, 1962).

'The Life of St Alexius', in *Adam Davy's 5 Dreams*, ed. F. J. Furnivall, EETS OS 69 (1878; repr. London, 1998), pp. 17–79.

The Life of St Edmund, Matthew Paris, tr. C. H. Lawrence (1996; repr. London, 1999).

Lives of Edward the Confessor, ed. Henry Richards Luard, Rolls Series 3 (London, 1858).

Malory, *Works*, ed. Eugène Vinaver, 2nd edition (1954; repr. Oxford, 1977).

Marcabru: A Critical Edition, ed. Simon Gaunt, Ruth Harvey, and Linda Paterson (Cambridge, 2000), with John Marshall and Melanie Florence.

Medieval English Lyrics: A Critical Anthology, ed. R. T. Davies (1963; repr. London & Boston, 1978).

Medieval Ghost Stories, ed. Andrew Joynes (2001; repr. Woodbridge, 2006).

Memorials of Saint Dunstan, ed. William Stubbs, Rolls Series 63 (London, 1874).

Memorials of St Anselm, ed. R. W. Southern and F. S. Schmitt (London, 1969), for the British Academy.

Merlin: Roman du XIIIe Siècle, Robert de Boron, ed. Alexandre Micha (Geneva, 1979).

The Middle English Verse Life of Edward the Confessor, ed. Grace Edna Moore (Philadelphia, 1942).

Mirk, John, *Festial*, ed. Susan Powell, EETS OS 334, 335 (2 vols, Oxford, 2009, 2011).

Morawski, Joseph, ed., *Proverbes Français antérieurs au XVe siècle* (Paris, 1925).

'Notice du MS Egerton 745 du Musée Britannique', ed. Paul Meyer, *Romania*, 39, 40 (1910, 1911), 532–69, 41–69.

O'Donovan, A. M., *Charters of Sherborne* (Oxford, 1988).

Of Arthour and of Merlin, ed. O. D. Macrae-Gibson, EETS OS 268, 279 (2 vols, London, Oxford, 1973, 1979).

Orderic Vitalis, *The Ecclesiastical History*, ed. and tr. Marjorie Chibnall (6 vols, Oxford, 1969–80), vol. 4.

Orkneyinga Saga: The History of the Earls of Orkney, tr. Hermann Pálsson and Paul Edwards (1978; repr. London, 1981).

Osbert of Clare, *The Letters*, ed. E. W. Williamson (1929; repr. Oxford, 1998).

The Oxford Dictionary of Saints, David Hugh Farmer, 3rd edition (Oxford, 1992).

Les Paroles Salomun, ed. Tony Hunt, ANTS LXX (Manchester, 2012).

The Prayers and Meditations of Saint Anselm, tr. Bendicta Ward (Harmondsworth, 1973).

Prose Brut to 1332, ed. Heather Pagan, ANTS LXIX (Manchester, 2011).

The Proverbs of Alfred, ed. O. Arngart (2 vols, Lund, 1942, 1955), vol. 2.

Revelacion, ed. Brent A. Pitts, ANTS LXVIII (London, 2010).

Richard of Cirencester, *Speculum Historiale*, ed. John E. B. Major (2 vols, London, 1869), vol. 2, 870–1066.

'*The Romance of Fergus*', Guillaume le Clerc, tr. D. D. R. Owen, *Arthurian Literature*, VIII (1989), 79–183.

Rouleaux des morts du IXe au XVe siècle, ed. Léopold Victor Delisle (Paris, 1866).

The Rule of St Benedict, ed. Ruth J. Dean and M. Dominica Legge, Medium Ævum Monographs VII (Oxford, 1964).

The Saga of the Volsungs, tr. Jesse L. Byock (Berkeley, 1990), the Norse Epic of Sigurd the Dragon Slayer.

Simeon of Durham, *Historia Ecclesiæ Dunhelmensis*, in *Symeonis Monachi Opera Omnia*, ed. Thomas Arnold (London, 1882), vol. 1.

The South English Legendary, ed. Charlotte D'Evelyn and Anna J. Mill, EETS OS 235, 236, 244 (3 vols, London, 1956, 1959).

Thomas à Kempis, *The Imitation of Christ*, tr. Betty I. Knott (1963; repr. London, 1974).

Thomas of Kent, *The Anglo-Norman* Alexander *(Le Roman de toute chevalerie)*, ed. Brian Foster and Ian Short, ANTS XXIX–XXXI, XXXII–XXXIII (2 vols, London, 1976, 1977).
Thompson, Stith, *Motif-Index of Folk Literature* (6 vols, Helsinki, 1932–36).
The Triumph Tree: Scotland's Earliest Poetry AD 550–1350, ed. Thomas Owen Clancy et al. (Edinburgh, 1998).
'La Vie de S. Édouard le Confesseur par Osbert de Clare', ed. Marc Bloch, *Analecta Bollandiana*, 41 (1923), 5–131.
La Vie de Seint Clement, ed. Daron Burrows, ANTS LXIV–LXV, LXVI, LXVII (3 vols, London, 2007, 2008, 2009).
La Vie d'Edouard le Confesseur, ed. Östen Södergård (Uppsala, 1948), by a nun of Barking.
La Vie Seint Edmund le Rei, Denis Piramus, ed. Hilding Kjellman (Göteborg, 1935).
'Vita S. Edwardi Regis et Confessoris', in Aelred of Rielvaulx, *Patrologia Latina*, ed. J-P. Migne (Paris, 1844–64), vol. 195, cols. 737B–790B.
Völsunga Saga: The Story of the Volsungs and Niblungs, with certain Songs from the Elder Edda, ed. H. Halliday Sparling, tr. Eiríkr Magnússon and William Morris (London, [1870]).
Wace, *Le Roman de Brut*, ed. Ivor Arnold, SATF (2 vols, Paris, 1938–40).
Wace's *Roman de Brut — A History of the British*, ed. and tr. Judith Weiss (1999; repr. Exeter, 2002).
William of Malmesbury, *De gestis pontificum Anglorum*, ed. N. E. S. A. Hamilton, Rolls Series 52 (London, 1870).
William of Malmesbury, *Gesta Regum Anglorum*, ed. and tr. R. A. B. Mynors, R. M. Thomson, and M. Winterbottom (2 vols, Oxford, 1998, 1999).
William of Malmesbury, *The Kings before the Norman Conquest*, tr. Joseph Stephenson (1854; repr. Llanerch, 1989), facsimile.
William of Malmesbury, *Saints' Lives*, ed. and tr. M. Winterbottom and R. M. Thomson (Oxford, 2002).
William of Palerne, ed. Walter W. Skeat, EETS ES 1 (London, 1867).
Yonge, Charlotte M., 'The Cup of Water', in *A Book of Golden Deeds* (London, [1846]).

Secondary Texts

Afanasyev, Ilya, ' "Saint lignage": Hagiography and Norman Ducal Genealogy in Twelfth-Century England', *Historical Research* (forthcoming).

Ailes, M. J., 'The Medieval Male Couple and the Language of Homosociality', in D. M. Hadley, ed., *Masculinity in Medieval Europe* (London & New York, 1999), pp. 214–37.

Ashdown, Margaret, *English and Norse Documents relating to the reign of Ethelred the Unready* (Cambridge, 1930).

Ashe, Laura, *Fiction and History in England, 1066–1200* (Cambridge, 2007).

Atherton, Mark, 'Cambridge, Corpus Christi College 201 as A Mirror for Kings? Apollonius of Tyre, Archbishop Wulfstan, and King Cnut' (forthcoming).

Aurell, Martin, *The Plantagenet Empire 1154–1224*, tr. David Crouch (Harlow, 2007).

Auslander, Diane, 'Clemence and Catherine: The *Life of St Catherine* in its Norman and Anglo-Norman Context', in Brown and Bussell, eds, *Barking Culture* (q.v.), pp. 164–82.

Baker, A. T., 'Saints' Lives Written in Anglo-French: Their Historical, Social and Literary Importance', in Edmund Gosse, ed., *Essays by Divers Hands* (London, 1924), pp. 119–56.

Barber, Richard, 'Eleanor of Aquitaine and the Media', in Bull and Léglu, eds, *Eleanor of Aquitaine* (q.v.), pp. 13–27.

Barlow, Frank, *Edward the Confessor* (London, 1970).

Barlow, Frank, *Thomas Becket* (London, 1986).

Barlow, Frank, *William I and The Norman Conquest* (London, 1965).

Barlow, Frank, *William Rufus* (1983; repr. New Haven, 2000).

Barnes, Terri, 'A Nun's Life: Barking Abbey in the Late Medieval and Early Modern Periods' (Ph.D. thesis, Portland State University, Oregon, 2004), deposited in London Borough of Barking and Dagenham archives.

Baswell, Christopher, 'King Edward and the Cripple', in Donka Minkova and Theresa Tinkle, eds, *Chaucer and the Challenges of Medievalism: Studies in Honor of H. A. Kelly* (Frankfurt, 2003), pp. 15–29.

Baswell, Christopher, 'Multilingualism on the Page', in Strohm, ed., *Middle English* (q.v.), pp. 38–50.

Batt, Catherine, 'The French of the English and Early British Women's Literary Culture', in McAvoy and Watt, eds, *The History of British Women's Writing 700–1500* (q.v.), pp. 51–9.

Bell, David N., *What Nuns Read: Books and Libraries in Medieval English Nunneries* (Kalamazoo & Spencer, 1995).

Bell, David N., 'What Nuns Read: The State of the Question', in James G. Clark, ed., *The Culture of Medieval English Monasticism* (Woodbridge, 2007), pp. 113–33.

Bérat, Emma, 'The Authority of Diversity: Communal Patronage in *Le Gracial*', in Brown and Bussell, eds, *Barking Culture* (q.v.), pp. 210–32.

Bestul, Thomas H., 'Antecedents: The Anselmian and Cistercian Contributions', in William F. Pollard and Robert Boenig, eds, *Mysticism and Spirituality in Medieval England* (Cambridge, 1997), pp. 1–20.

Binski, Paul, 'Reflections on *La estoire de seint Aedward le rei*: hagiography and kingship in thirteenth-century England', *Journal of Medieval History*, 16 (1990), 333–50.

Blanton, Virginia, Veronica O'Mara, and Patricia Stoop, eds, *Nuns' Literacies in Medieval Europe: The Hull Dialogue* (Turnhout, 2013).

Bliss, Jane, 'An Anglo-Norman Nun: An Old English *Gnome*', *Notes & Queries*, 254:1 (March 2009), 16–18.

Bliss, Jane, 'Who Wrote the Nun's Life of Edward?', *Reading Medieval Studies*, 38 (2012), 77–98.

Bliss, Jane and Judith Weiss, 'The 'J' Manuscript of Wace's *Brut*', *Medium Ævum*, 81:2 (2012), 222–48.

Brantley, Jessica, 'Vision, Image, Text', in Strohm, ed., *Middle English* (q.v.), pp. 315–34.

Broadhurst, Karen M., 'Henry II of England and Eleanor of Aquitaine: Patrons of Literature in French?', *Viator*, 27 (1996), 53–84.

Brooks, Nicholas, 'The Career of St Dunstan', in Ramsay *et al.*, eds, *St Dunstan* (q.v.), pp. 1–23.

Brown, Jennifer N., 'Body, Gender and Nation in the Lives of Edward the Confessor', in Brown and Bussell, eds, *Barking Culture* (q.v.), pp. 145–63.

Brown, Jennifer N., ' "Cut from its Stump": Translating Edward the Confessor and the Dream of the Green Tree', in Denis Renevey and Christiania Whitehead, eds, *Lost in Translation?*, The Medieval Translator/Traduire au Moyen Age 12 (Turnhout, 2009), pp. 57–69.

Brown, Jennifer N., 'Translating Edward the Confessor: Feminism, Time, and Hagiography', *Medieval Feminist Forum*, 43:1 (Winter 2007), 46–57.

Brown, Jennifer N. and Donna Alfano Bussell, eds, *Barking Abbey and Medieval Literary Culture: Authorship and Authority in a Female Community* (Woodbridge & York, 2012).

Brunot, Ferdinand and Charles Bruneau, *Précis de Grammaire Historique de la Langue Française* (Paris, 1949).

Bull, Marcus and Catherine Léglu, eds, *The World of Eleanor of Aquitaine: Literature and Society in Southern France between the Eleventh and Thirteenth Centuries* (Woodbridge, 2005).

Bussell, Donna Alfano, 'Cicero, Aelred and Guernes: The Politics of Love in Clemence of Barking', in Brown and Bussell, eds, *Barking Culture* (q.v.), pp. 183–209.

Bussell, Donna Alfano and Jennifer N. Brown, 'Introduction: Barking's Lives, the Abbey and its Abbesses', in Brown and Bussell, eds, *Barking Culture* (q.v.), pp. 1–30.

Cameron, Angus F., 'Middle English in Old English Manuscripts', in Beryl Rowland, ed., *Chaucer and Middle English Studies in Honour of Rossell Hope Robbins* (London, 1974), pp. 218–29.

Campbell, Emma, *Medieval Saints' Lives: The Gift, Kinship and Community in Old French Hagiography*, Gallica 12 (Cambridge, 2008).

Carpenter, D. A., 'King Henry III and Saint Edward the Confessor: The Origins of the Cult', *English Historical Review*, CXXII (2007), 865–91.

Chaytor, H. J., *From Script to Print: An Introduction to Medieval Vernacular Literature* (1945; repr. London, 1966).

Cherewatuk, Karen and Ulrike Wiethaus, eds, *Dear Sister: Medieval Women and the Epistolary Genre* (Philadelphia, 1993).

Chibnall, Marjorie, *Anglo-Norman England 1066–1166* (1986; repr. Oxford, 1987).

Clarke, Stephen, *1000 Years of Annoying the French* (London, 2010).

Coleman, Joyce, 'Aurality', in Strohm, ed., *Middle English* (q.v.), pp. 68–85.

Colker, Marvin L., 'Texts of Jocelyn of Canterbury which relate to the History of Barking Abbey', *Studia Monastica*, 7 (1965), 383-460.

Collard, Judith, 'A Lesson in Holy Kingship: The thirteenth-century La estoire de Seint Aedward le Rei (Cambridge University Library MS Ee.iii.59)', *South African Journal of Art History*, 15 (2001), 52–67.

Crane, Susan, 'Anglo-Norman cultures in England, 1066–1460', in Wallace, ed., *Cambridge History* (q.v.), pp. 35–60.

Crick, Julia, 'The Wealth, Patronage, and Connections of Women's Houses in Late Anglo-Saxon England', *Revue Bénédictine*, 109 (1999), 154–85.

Curtius, Ernst Robert, *European Literature and the Latin Middle Ages*, tr. Willard R. Trask (1953; repr. London, 1979).

Dalrymple, Roger, *Language and Piety in Middle English Romance* (Cambridge, 2000).

de Gaiffier, Baudouin, 'Intactam Sponsam Reliquens: A propos de la Vie de S. Alexis', *Analecta Bollandiana*, 65 (1947), 157–95.

de Hamel, Christopher, *The Book. A History of the Bible* (London, 2001).

de Vegvar, Carol Neuman, 'Saints and Companions to Saints: Anglo-Saxon Royal Women Monastics in Context', in Szarmach, ed., *Holy Men and Holy Women* (q.v.), pp. 51–93.

Dean, Ruth and Maureen Boulton, *Anglo-Norman Literature: A Guide to Texts and Manuscripts*, ANTS OPS 3 (London, 1999).

Dinzelbacher, Peter, 'The Beginnings of Mysticism Experienced in Twelfth-Century England', in Marion Glasscoe, ed., *The Medieval Mystical Tradition in England: Exeter Symposium IV, Dartington 1987* (Cambridge, 1987), pp. 111–31.

Doherty, Hugh, 'Merlin and the Angevins: Prophecy in King Henry's England' (presented at the International Arthurian Society, British Branch Conference, Oxford, September 2012).

Dronke, Peter, *Women Writers of the Middle Ages: A Critical Study of Texts from Perpetua († 203) to Marguerite Porete († 1310)* (Cambridge, 1984).

Dunbabin, Jean, *France in the Making 843–1180* (1985; repr. Oxford, 1991).

Dutton, Elisabeth, *Julian of Norwich: The Influence of Late-Medieval Devotional Compilations* (Cambridge, 2008).

Dutton, Marsha L., 'Ælred, Historian: Two Portraits in Plantagenet Myth', *Cistercian Studies Quarterly*, 28:2 (1993), 113–43.

Dutton, Marsha L., 'The Staff in the Stone: Finding Arthur's Sword in the *Vita Sancti Edwardi* of Aelred of Rievaulx', *Arthuriana*, 17:3 (2007), 3–30.

Eley, Penny, 'History and romance in the Chronique des ducs de Normandie', *Medium Ævum*, 68 (1999), 81–95.

Elkins, Sharon K., *Holy Women of Twelfth-Century England* (Chapel Hill & London, 1988).

Elliott, Dyan, *Spiritual Marriage: Sexual Abstinence in Medieval Wedlock* (Princeton, 1993).

Erdman, David V. and Ephim G. Fogel, 'English Literature to 1500', in Erdman and Fogel, eds, *Evidence* (q.v.), pp. 395–420.

Erdman, David V. and Ephim G. Fogel, eds, *Evidence for Authorship: Essays on Problems of Attribution* (Ithaca, 1966).

Evans, G. R., *Anselm* (1989; repr. London & New York, 2001).

Farmer, D. H., 'The Progress of the Monastic Revival', in David Parsons, ed., *Tenth-Century Studies* (London & Chichester, 1975), pp. 10–19; 209.

Faulkner, Mark, 'Gerald of Wales and Standard Old English', *Notes & Queries*, 256:1 (March 2011), 19–24.

Faulkner, M. J., 'The Uses of Anglo-Saxon Manuscripts *c.* 1066–1200' (D.Phil. thesis, University of Oxford, 2008).

Fell, Christine E., 'Edward King and Martyr and the Anglo-Saxon Hagiographic Tradition', in Hill, ed., *Ethelred the Unready* (q.v.), pp. 1–13.

Fenster, Thelma, ' "Ce qu'ens li trovat, eut en sei": On the Equal Chastity of Queen Edith and King Edward in the Nun of Barking's *La Vie d'Edouard le confesseur*', in Brown and Bussell, eds, *Barking Culture* (q.v.), pp. 135–44.

Ferrante, Joan M., *To the Glory of her Sex: Women's Roles in the Composition of Medieval Texts* (Bloomington, 1997).

Fleischman, Suzanne, 'Philology, Linguistics, and the Discourse of the Medieval Text', *Speculum*, 65:1–2 (1990), 19–37.

Fogel, Ephim G., 'Salmons in Both, or Some Caveats for Canonical Scholars', in Erdman and Fogel, eds, *Evidence* (q.v.), pp. 69–101.

Foot, Sarah, *Veiled Women* (2 vols, Aldershot, 2000).

Foulet, Lucien, *Petite Syntaxe de L'Ancien Français* (Paris, 1958).

Fowler, David C., *The Bible in Early English Literature* (1976; repr. London, 1977).

Fry, Donald K., 'Bede Fortunate in His Translator: The Barking Nuns', in Paul E. Szarmach, ed., *Studies in Earlier Old English Prose* (Albany, 1986), pp. 345–62.

Fulton, Rachel, *From Judgment to Passion: Devotion to Christ and the Virgin Mary* (New York, 2002).

Gillespie, Vincent, 'Fatherless Books: Authorship, Attribution and Orthodoxy in Later Medieval England', in Ian Johnson and Allan Westphall, eds, *The Pseudo-Bonaventuran Lives of Christ: Exploring the Middle English Tradition* (Turnhout, 2013), pp. 151–96.

Gillespie, Vincent, 'Vernacular Theology', in Strohm, ed., *Middle English* (q.v.), pp. 401–20.

Gowans, Linda, '*Guillaume d'Angleterre*: Prologue and Authorship', *French Studies Bulletin*, 35 (Summer 1990), 1–5.

Gowans, Linda, 'What Did Robert de Boron Really Write?', in Bonnie Wheeler, ed., *Arthurian Studies in Honour of P. J. C. Field*, Arthurian Studies (Woodbridge, 2004), vol. LVII, pp. 15–28.

Gransden, Antonia, 'Prologues in the Historiography of Twelfth-Century England', in Daniel Williams, ed., *England in the Twelfth Century: Proceedings of the 1988 Harlaxton Symposium* (Woodbridge, 1990), pp. 55–81.

Grassi, J. L., 'The *Vita Ædwardi Regis*: The Hagiographer as Insider', *Anglo-Norman Studies*, 26 (2004), 87–102.

Gray, Douglas, *Themes and Images in the Medieval English Religious Lyric* (London, 1972).

Green, D. H., *Women Readers in the Middle Ages* (Cambridge, 2007).

Greenfield, Stanley B., *The Interpretation of Old English Poems* (London & Boston, 1972).

Harden, Arthur Robert, 'The "Ubi Sunt" Theme in Three Anglo-Norman Saints' Lives', *Romance Notes*, 1:1 (November 1959), 63–4.

Hart, Cyril, 'The Early Charters of Essex 2: The Norman Period', in H. P. R. Finberg, ed., *Occasional Papers, Department of English Local History* (Leicester, 1957), chapter 11.

Harvey, Ruth, 'Eleanor of Aquitaine and the Troubadours', in Bull and Léglu, eds, *Eleanor of Aquitaine* (q.v.), pp. 101–14.

Haskins, Charles H., 'Henry II as a Patron of Literature', in A. G. Little and F. M. Powicke, eds, *Essays in Medieval History presented to Thomas Frederick Tout* (Manchester, 1925), pp. 71–7.

Hayward, Paul A., 'The Idea of Innocent Martyrdom in Late Tenth- and Eleventh-Century English Hagiology', in Diana Wood, ed., *Martyrs and Martyrologies*, Studies in Church History 30 (Oxford, 1993), pp. 81–92.

Hayward, Paul Antony, 'Translation-Narratives in Post-Conquest Hagiography and English Resistance to the Norman Conquest', *Anglo-Norman Studies*, 21 (1999), 67–93.

Heinzer, Felix, 'Holy Text or Object of Display? Functions and Guises of the Psalter in the Middle Ages', *The Bodleian Library Record*, 21:1 (April 2008), 37–47.

Hiatt, Alfred, 'Genre without System', in Strohm, ed., *Middle English* (q.v.), pp. 277–94.

Hill, David, ed., *Ethelred the Unready: Papers from the Millenary Conference* (Oxford, 1978).

Hill, Thomas D., 'The *Liber Eliensis* "Historical Selections" and the Old English *Battle of Maldon*', *Journal of English and Germanic Philology*, 96 (1997), 1–12.

Hill, Thomas D., '*Imago Dei*: Genre, Symbolism, and Anglo-Saxon Hagiography', in Szarmach, ed., *Holy Men and Holy Women* (q.v.), pp. 35–50.

Hollis, Stephanie, 'Barking's Monastic School, Late Seventh to Twelfth Century', in Brown and Bussell, eds, *Barking Culture* (q.v.), pp. 33–55.

Holsinger, Bruce, 'Liturgy', in Strohm, ed., *Middle English* (q.v.), pp. 295–314.

Hoste, Anselm, *Bibliotheca Aelrediana*, Instrumenta Patristica II (The Hague, 1962).

Howlett, D. R., *The English Origins of Old French Literature* (Dublin, 1996).

Hunt, Tony, *Teaching and Learning Latin in Thirteenth-Century England* (3 vols, Cambridge, 1991), vol. 1.

Huntington, Joanna, 'Edward the Celibate, Edward the Saint: Virginity in the Construction of Edward the Confessor', in Anke Bernau, Ruth Evans, and Sarah Salih, eds, *Medieval Virginities* (Cardiff, 2003), pp. 119–39.

Hussey, S. S., 'Introduction', in Hussey, ed., *Piers Plowman, Critical Approaches* (q.v.), pp. 1–26.

Hussey, S. S., ed., *Piers Plowman, Critical Approaches* (London, 1969).

Ingham, Richard, ed., *The Anglo-Norman Language and its Contexts* (Woodbridge, 2010).

James, M. R., 'Manuscripts from Essex Monastic Libraries', *Transactions of the Essex Archaeological Society*, n.s. xxi (1933–4), 34–46.

James, M. R., *Western Manuscripts in the Library of Trinity College, Cambridge* (4 vols, Cambridge, 1902), vol. 3.

Jefferson, Judith A. and Ad Putter, eds, *Multilingualism in Medieval Britain (c. 1066–1520): Sources and Analysis* (Turnhout, 2013), with the assistance of Amanda Hopkins.

John, Eric, 'Edward the Confessor and the Celibate Life', *Analecta Bollandiana*, 97 (1979), 171–8.

Johnson, Phyllis and Brigitte Cazelles, *'Le Vain Siecle Guerpir': A Literary Approach to Sainthood through Old French Hagiography of the Twelfth Century* (Chapel Hill, 1979).

Kemp, Eric Waldron, *Canonization and Authority in the Western Church* (London, 1948).

Ker, N. R., *Catalogue of Manuscripts containing Anglo-Saxon* (1957; repr. Oxford, 1990), reissued with supplement.

Ker, N. R., ed., *Medieval Libraries of Great Britain: A List of Surviving Books*, 2nd edition (London, 1964).

Ker, N. R., *Medieval Manuscripts in British Libraries* (5 vols, Oxford, 1977), vol. II.

Ker, N. R., 'More Manuscripts from Essex Monastic Libraries', *Transactions of the Essex Archaeological Society*, n.s. xxiii (1942–5), 298–310.

Keynes, Simon, 'The declining reputation of King Æthelred the Unready', in Hill, ed., *Ethelred the Unready* (q.v.), pp. 227–53.

King, Andrew, The Faerie Queene *and Middle English Romance: The Matter of Just Memory* (Oxford, 2000).

Knight, S. T., 'Satire in *Piers Plowman*', in Hussey, ed., *Piers Plowman, Critical Approaches* (q.v.), pp. 279–309.

Knowles, Dom David, C. N. L. Brooke, and Vera C. M. London, eds, *The Heads of Religious Houses in England & Wales 940–1216*, 2nd edition (Cambridge, 2001), with new material by C. N. L. Brooke.

Laurent, Françoise, *Plaire et édifier: Les récits hagiographiques composés en Angleterre aux XIIe et XIIIe siècles* (Paris, 1998).

Le Saux, Françoise H. M., *A Companion to Wace* (Woodbridge, 2005).

Lees, Clare A. and Gillian R. Overing, 'Women and the Origins of English Literature', in McAvoy and Watt, eds, *The History of British Women's Writing 700–1500* (q.v.), pp. 31–40.

Legge, M. Dominica, *Anglo-Norman in the Cloisters* (Edinburgh, 1950).

Legge, M. Dominica, *Anglo-Norman Literature and its Background* (Oxford, 1963).

Legge, M. Dominica, 'L'influence littéraire de la cour d'Henri Beauclerc', in *Mélanges offerts à Rita Lejeune* (2 vols, Gembloux, 1969), vol. 1, pp. 679–87.

Legge, Mary Dominica, 'La précocité de la littérature anglo-normande', *Cahiers de Civilisation Médiévale*, VIII (1965), 327–49.

Lerer, Seth, 'Old English and its afterlife', in Wallace, ed., *Cambridge History* (q.v.), pp. 7–34.

Leyser, Henrietta, '*c.* 1080–1215: texts', in Samuel Fanous and Vincent Gillespie, eds, *The Cambridge Companion to Medieval English Mysticism* (Cambridge, 2011), pp. 49–67.

Leyser, Henrietta, *Medieval Women: A Social History of Women in England 450–1500* (1995; repr. London, 1999).

Lindenbaum, Sheila, 'Drama as Textual Practice', in Strohm, ed., *Middle English* (q.v.), pp. 386–400.

Lipscomb, Lan, 'A Distinct Legend of the Ring in the Life of Edward the Confessor', *Medieval Perspectives*, 6 (1991), 45–57.

Lochrie, Karma, 'Between Women', in Carolyn Dinshaw and David Wallace, eds, *The Cambridge Companion to Medieval Women's Writing* (Cambridge, 2003), pp. 70–88.

Loftus, E. A. and H. F. Chettle, *A History of Barking Abbey* (Barking, [1954]).

Love, Harold, *Attributing Authorship: An Introduction* (Cambridge, 2002).

MacBain, William, 'Anglo-Norman Women Hagiographers', in Ian Short, ed., *Anglo-Norman Anniversary Essays*, ANTS OPS 2 (London, 1993), pp. 235–50.

MacBain, William, ' "Courtly Echoes" in Clemence's *Life of St. Catherine*' (presented at Fourteenth International Congress on Medieval Studies, Kalamazoo, 1979).

MacBain, William, 'Five Old French Renderings of the *Passio Sancte Katerine Virginis*', in Jeanette Beer, ed., *Medieval Translators and their Craft* (Kalamazoo, 1989), pp. 41–65.

MacBain, William, 'The Literary Apprenticeship of Clemence of Barking', *Journal of the Australasian Universities Language and Literature Association*, 9 (November 1958), 3–22.

MacBain, William, 'Some Religious and Secular Uses of the Vocabulary of *Fin' Amor* in the Early Decades of the Northern French Narrative Poem', *French Forum*, 13 (1988), 261–76.

Macdonald, A. J., *Lanfranc: A Study of his Life, Work, and Writing* (1926; repr. London, 1944).

Magennis, Hugh, 'Aelfric and the Legend of the Seven Sleepers', in Szarmach, ed., *Holy Men and Holy Women* (q.v.), pp. 317–31.

Marzella, Francesco, 'L'anello del re e il 'Paradiso' dell' Evangelista: Genesi di un episodio della 'Vita Sancti Edwardi Regis et Confessoris' di Ælredi di Rievaulx', *Hagiographica*, 18 (2011), 217–61.

Marzella, Francesco, 'La tradizione manuscritta della *Vita Sancti Ædwardi Regis et Confessoris* di Aelredo di Rievaulx', *Filologia Mediolatino*, 19 (2012), 343–73.

Mason, Emma, *The House of Godwine: The History of a Dynasty* (London & New York, 2004).

Mason, Emma, 'St Wulfstan's Staff: A Legend and its Uses', *Medium Ævum*, 53:2 (1984), 157–79.

McAvoy, Liz Herbert and Diane Watt, eds, *The History of British Women's Writing 700–1500* (Basingstoke, 2012).

McNamer, Sarah, *Affective Meditation and the Invention of Medieval Compassion* (Philadelphia, 2010).

McWilliams, Stuart, ed., *Saints and Scholars: New Perspectives in Anglo-Saxon Literature and Culture in Honour of Hugh Magennis* (Cambridge, 2012).

Meale, Carol M., ed., *Women and Literature in Britain, 1150–1500* (Cambridge, 1993).

Ménard, P., 'Tradition manuscrite et édition de textes: le cas des fabliaux', in Short, ed., *Reid Memorial Volume* (q.v.), pp. 149–66.

Millett, Bella, 'Women in No Man's Land: English recluses and the development of vernacular literature in the twelfth and thirteenth centuries', in Meale, ed., *Women and Literature* (q.v.), pp. 86–103.

Minnis, A. J., *Medieval Theory of Authorship: Scholastic literary attitudes in the later Middle Ages*, 2nd rev. edition (1984; repr. Philadelphia, 1988).

Mitchell, Emily, 'Patrons and Politics at Twelfth-Century Barking Abbey', *Revue Bénédictine*, 113 (2003), 247–64.

Mortimer, Ian, *The Time Traveller's Guide to Medieval England* (2008; repr. London, 2009).

Nelson, Janet, 'Royal Saints and Early Medieval Kingship', in Derek Baker, ed., *Sanctity and Secularity: The Church and the World*, Studies in Church History 10 (Oxford, 1973), pp. 39–44.

Noyer, Ralph, 'Generative Metrics and Old French octosyllabic verse', *Language Variation and Change*, 14 (2002), 119–71.

O'Donnell, Thomas, 'False French and the Monastic Vocation: Twelfth-Century Translations at Barking Abbey' (presented at Leeds International Medieval Congress, July 2009).

O'Donnell, Thomas, ' "The ladies have made me quite fat": Authors and Patrons at Barking Abbey', in Brown and Bussell, eds, *Barking Culture* (q.v.), pp. 94–113.

O'Donoghue, Bernard, 'How European Was the Medieval English Love-Lyric?' (presented at the English Medieval Seminar, Oxford, May 2011).

Otter, Monika, *Inventiones: Fiction and Referentiality in Twelfth-Century English Historical Writing* (Chapel Hill & London, 1996).

Otter, Monika, 'Prolixitas Temporum: Futurity in Medieval Historical Narratives', in Robert M. Stein and Sandra Pierson Prior, eds, *Reading Medieval Culture: Essays in Honor of Robert W. Hanning* (Notre Dame, 2005), pp. 45–67.

Owst, G. R., *Literature and Pulpit in Medieval England*, 2nd rev. edition (1933; repr. Oxford, 1961).

Partner, Nancy F., *Serious Entertainments: The Writing of History in Twelfth-Century England* (Chicago, 1977).

Petroff, Elizabeth Avilda, ed., *Medieval Women's Visionary Literature* (New York & Oxford, 1986).

Pezzini, Domenico, *The Translation of Religious Texts in the Middle Ages: Tracts and Rules, Hymns and Saints' Lives* (Bern, 2008).

Phillips, Susan E., 'Gossip and (Un)official Writing', in Strohm, ed., *Middle English* (q.v.), pp. 476–90.

Pratt, David, 'The voice of the king in "King Edgar's Establishment of Monasteries" ', *Anglo-Saxon England*, 41 (2013), 145–204.

Ramsay, Nigel, Margaret Sparks, and Tim Tatton-Brown, eds, *St Dunstan: His Life, Times and Cult* (Woodbridge, 1992).

Rigg, A. G., *A History of Anglo-Latin Literature 1066–1422* (Cambridge, 1992).

Robertson, Duncan, *The Medieval Saints' Lives: Spiritual Renewal and Old French Literature* (Lexington, 1995).

Robertson, Duncan, 'Writing in the Textual Community: Clemence of Barking's Life of St. Catherine', *French Forum*, 21 (1996), 5–28.

Robinson, Fred C., 'Some Aspects of the *Maldon* Poet's Artistry', *Journal of English and Germanic Philology*, 75 (1976), 25–40.

Ronay, Gabriel, *The Lost King of England: The East European Adventures of Edward the Exile* (1989; repr. Woodbridge, 2000).

Rosenthal, Jane, 'The Pontifical of St Dunstan', in Ramsay *et al.*, eds, *St Dunstan* (q.v.), pp. 143–63.

Rossi, Carla, *Marie de France et les érudits de Cantorbéry* (Paris, 2009).

Rouse, M. A. and R. H., 'Florilegia of Patristic Texts', in [Robert Bultot], ed., *Les genres littéraires dans les sources théologiques et philosophiques médiévales: Actes du Colloque international de Louvain-la-Neuve*, L'Institut D'Études Médiévales (second series) (Louvain, 1982), vol. 5, pp. 165–80.

Ruelle, P., 'Les Synonymes dans le *Dialogue des Creatures*, traduction par Colard Mansion du *Dialogus Creaturarum*', in Short, ed., *Reid Memorial Volume* (q.v.), pp. 180–86.

Russell, Delbert, 'The Campsey Collection of Old French Saints' Lives', *Scriptorium*, 57:1 (2003), 51–83.

Russell, Delbert, 'Notes on the Style of the Nuns of Barking' (presented at the French of England Conference, New York, Spring 2007).

Russell, Delbert, ' "Sun num n'i vult dire a ore": Identity Matters at Barking Abbey', in Brown and Bussell, eds, *Barking Culture* (q.v.), pp. 117–34.

Russell, Delbert W., 'The Cultural Context of the French Prose *remaniement* of the Life of Edward the Confessor by a Nun of Barking Abbey', in Wogan-Browne *et al.*, eds, *French of England* (q.v.), pp. 290–302.

Schendl, Herbert and Laura Wright, eds, *Code-Switching in Early English* (Berlin, 2011).

Schoenbaum, Samuel, 'Internal Evidence and the Attribution of Elizabethan Plays', in Erdman and Fogel, eds, *Evidence* (q.v.), pp. 188–203.

Scholz, Bernard W., 'The Canonization of Edward the Confessor', *Speculum*, 36 (1961), 38–60.

Scragg, D. G., ed., *The Battle of Maldon, AD 991 (essays)* (Oxford, 1991).

Sharpe, Richard, 'Anselm as Author: Publishing in the Late Eleventh Century', *Journal of Medieval Latin*, 19 (2009), 1–87.

Sharpe, Richard, 'Symeon as Pamphleteer', in David Rollason, ed., *Symeon of Durham: Historian of Durham and the North* (Stamford, 1998), pp. 214–29.

Short, Ian, 'Another Look at "Le Faus Franceis"', *Nottingham Medieval Studies*, 54 (2010), 35–55.

Short, Ian, 'Literary Culture at the Court of Henry II', in Christopher Harper-Bill and Nicholas Vincent, eds, *Henry II: New Interpretations* (Woodbridge, 2007), pp. 335–61.

Short, Ian, *Manual of Anglo-Norman*, ANTS OPS 7 (London, 2007).

Short, Ian, ed., *Medieval French Textual Studies in Memory of T. B. W. Reid*, ANTS OPS 1 (London, 1984).

Short, Ian, 'Patrons and Polyglots: French Literature in Twelfth-Century England', *Anglo-Norman Studies*, 14 (1992), 229–49.

Short, Ian, '*Verbatim et Literatim*: oral and written French in 12th-century Britain', *Vox Romanica*, 68 (2009), 156–68.

Simpson, Jacqueline, *British Dragons*, 2nd edition (1980; repr. Ware (Herts), 2001).

Sinclair, K. V., 'Anglo-Norman at Waterford: The mute testimony of MS Cambridge, Corpus Christi College 405', in Short, ed., *Reid Memorial Volume* (q.v.), pp. 219–38.

Slocum, Kay, 'Goscelin of Saint-Bertin and the Translation Ceremony for Saints Ethelburg, Hildelith and Wulfhild', in Brown and Bussell, eds, *Barking Culture* (q.v.), pp. 73–93.

Squire, Aelred, *Aelred of Rievaulx: A Study* (London, 1969).

Stafford, Pauline, 'The Portrayal of Royal Women in England, Mid-Tenth to Mid-Twelfth Centuries', in John Carmi Parsons, ed., *Medieval Queenship* (New York, 1993), pp. 143–67.

Stafford, Pauline, 'Queens, Nunneries and Reforming Churchmen: Gender, Religious Status and Reform in Tenth- and Eleventh-Century England', *Past and Present*, 163 (1999), 3–35.

Stein, Robert M., 'Multilingualism', in Strohm, ed., *Middle English* (q.v.), pp. 23–37.

Stempel, Wolf-Dieter, 'La "modernité" des débuts: la rhétorique de l'oralité chez Chrétien de Troyes', in Maria Selig, Barbara Frank, and Jörg Hartmann, eds, *Le passage à l'écrit des langues romanes* (Tübingen, 1993), pp. 275–98.

Stevenson, Jane, 'Anglo-Latin Women Poets', in Katherine O'Brien O'Keeffe and Andy Orchard, eds, *Latin Learning and English Lore* (2 vols, Toronto, 2005), vol. 2, pp. 86–107.

Stevenson, Jill, 'Rhythmic Liturgy, Embodiment and Female Authority in Barking's Easter Plays', in Brown and Bussell, eds, *Barking Culture* (q.v.), pp. 245–66.

Stokes, Peter A., 'The Vision of Leofric: Manuscript, Text and Context', *Review of English Studies*, NS 63:261 (September 2012), 529–50.

Strohm, Paul, *England's Empty Throne: Usurpation and the Language of Legitimation 1399–1422* (New Haven, 1998).

Strohm, Paul, ed., *Middle English* (Oxford, 2007), Oxford Twenty-First Century Approaches to Literature.

Sturman, Winifred M., *Barking Abbey* (Ph.D. thesis, University of London, London, 1961).

Swan, Mary, 'Imagining a Readership for Post-Conquest Old English Manuscripts', in Stephen Kelly and John J. Thompson, eds, *Imagining the Book* (Turnhout, 2005), pp. 145–57.

Szarmach, Paul E., ed., *Holy Men and Holy Women: Old English Prose Saints' Lives and their Contexts* (Albany, 1996).

Talbot, Margaret, 'Duped', in Sylvia Nasar, ed., *The Best American Science Writing 2008* (New York, 2008), pp. 196–221.

Tasioulas, Jacqueline, 'Heaven and Earth in Little Space: The Foetal Existence of Christ in Medieval Literature and Thought', *Medium Ævum*, LXXVI:1 (2007), 42–66.

Thiry-Stassin, Martine, 'L'hagiographie en Anglo-Normand', in Guy Philippart, ed., *Hagiographies*, Corpus Christianorum (3 vols, Turnhout, 1994), vol. 1, pp. 407–28.

Thomas, Hugh M., *The English and the Normans: Ethnic Hostility, Assimilation, and Identity 1066–c.1220* (Oxford, 2003).

Thomas, Hugh M., 'Lay Piety in England from 1066 to 1215', *Anglo-Norman Studies*, 29 (2007), 179–92.

Treharne, Elaine, 'The Life of English in the Mid-Twelfth Century: Ralph D'Escures's Homily on the Virgin Mary', in Ruth Kennedy and Simon Meecham-Jones, eds, *Writers of the Reign of Henry II* (New York & Basingstoke, 2006), pp. 169–86.

Trotter, David, 'Intra-Textual Multilingualism and Social/Sociolinguistic Variation in Anglo-Norman', in Elizabeth M. Tyler, ed., *Conceptualizing Multilingualism in England, c. 800–c. 1250* (Turnhout, 2011), pp. 357–68.

Tyler, Elizabeth M., 'From Old English to Old French', in Wogan-Browne *et al.*, eds, *French of England* (q.v.), pp. 164–78.

Tyler, Peter, 'Review: The Life of Wulfric of Haselbury, Anchorite by John of Forde, tr. Pauline Matarasso, 2011', *The Brown Book (Lady Margaret Hall, Oxford)* (2013), pp. 102–04.

Uitti, Karl D., 'The Clerkly Narrator Figure in Old French Hagiography and Romance', *Medioevo Romanzo*, 2 (1975), 394–408.

Vanni Rovighi, Sofia, 'Notes sur l'influence de saint Anselme au XIIe siècle', *Cahiers de Civilisation Médiévale*, VIII (1965), 43–58.

Vauchez, André, *Sainthood in the Later Middle Ages*, tr. Jean Birrell (Cambridge, 1997).

Vaughan, Richard, *Matthew Paris* (1958; repr. Cambridge, 1979).

Vincent, Nicholas, 'New Charters of King Stephen with Some Reflections upon the Royal Forests During the Anarchy', *English Historical Review*, 114:458 (September 1999), 899–928.

Wallace, David, ed., *The Cambridge History of Medieval English Literature* (Cambridge, 1999).

Warren, Michelle R., 'Translation', in Strohm, ed., *Middle English* (q.v.), pp. 51–67.

Watt, Diane, 'Lost Books: Abbess Hildelith and the Literary Culture of Barking Abbey', *Philological Quarterly*, 91:1 (Winter 2012), 1–21.

Weston, Lisa M. C., 'The Saint-Maker and the Saint: Hildelith creates Ethelburg', in Brown and Bussell, eds, *Barking Culture* (q.v.), pp. 56–72.

Wogan-Browne, Jocelyn, 'Afterword: Barking and the Historiography of Female Community', in Brown and Bussell, eds, *Barking Culture* (q.v.), pp. 283–96.

Wogan-Browne, Jocelyn, ' "Clerc u lai, muïne u dame": women and Anglo-Norman hagiography in the twelfth and thirteenth centuries', in Meale, ed., *Women and Literature* (q.v.), pp. 61–85.

Wogan-Browne, Jocelyn, 'How to Marry Your Wife with Chastity, Honour, and Fin'Amor', *Thirteenth Century England*, IX (2003), 131–49.

Wogan-Browne, Jocelyn, 'Powers of Record, Powers of Example: Hagiography and Women's History', in Mary C. Erler and Maryanne Kowaleski, eds, *Gendering the Master Narrative: Women and Power in the Middle Ages* (Ithaca & London, 2003), pp. 71–93.

Wogan-Browne, Jocelyn, *Saints' Lives and Women's Literary Culture: Virginity and its Authorizations, c. 1150–1300* (Oxford, 2001).

Wogan-Browne, Jocelyn, 'Wreaths of Thyme: The Female Translator in Anglo-Norman Hagiography', in Roger Ellis and Ruth Evans, eds, *The Medieval Translator IV* (Binghamton, 1994), pp. 46–65.

Wogan-Browne, Jocelyn et al., eds, *Language and Culture in Medieval Britain: The French of England c. 1100–c. 1500* (York, 2009).

Woledge, Brian, *Commentaire sur Yvain (Le Chevalier au Lion) de Chrétien de Troyes* (2 vols, Geneva, 1986, 1988).

Yardley, Anne Bagnall, 'Liturgy as the Site of Creative Engagement: Contributions of the Nuns of Barking', in Brown and Bussell, eds, *Barking Culture* (q.v.), pp. 267–82.

Yonge, Charlotte M., *History of Christian Names*, 2nd rev. edition (1863; repr. London, 1884).

Indexes

Bible References

Numbers in italic type indicate references in the Text, rather than in the Introduction or Notes.

Acts 1:18–20, 156
Acts 2:1–4, 90n
Acts 5:1–5, 113n
Acts 6:15, 133n

II Chr. 9:23, *76*
I Cor. 10:16, *65*
I Cor. 11:29, *141*
I Cor. 12:4–11, *126*, 134
II Cor. 9:7, 14, *78*

Dan. 2:21, 9n, *69*
Dan. 3, 44, *84*
Dan. 4, 156n
Dan. 4:25, 9n
Dan. 12:6, 69n
Daniel, 127n

Ecclus. 32:1, 15n, 77n
Esther 2:7, 25n
Ex. 33:19, *165*
Ezekiel 37, 173n

Gen. 1, 187
Gen. 21:6, *93*
Gen. 25:8, 168n
Gen. 28:12, *103*, *111*
Gen. 28:17, *103*
Gen. 39, 66n, *84*

Gen. 39:23, 64, *66*
Gen. 49:4, 156
Genesis, 127n

Heb. 11:13–16, *103*
Heb. 12:6, *92*

Is. 9:2, *129*
Is. 11:2, 134
Is. 66:16, *160*

James 2:1, 78n
James 4:9, *154*
Jer. 1:10, 180n
Job 1:21, *126*
Job 5:18, *92*
John 9:1–11, 127n
John 9:24, 128n
John 13:1, *165*
John 14:10, *65*
John 14:10–11, 5n
John 14:28, 6, *165*
John 21:5–11, *112*
John's Gospel, 148n, *158*
Jonah 2:5, 90
Jonah 3:5–10, *160*
Joshua 10:13, 75n

Lam. 1:12, *192*

Luke 1:46–55, *95*
Luke 1:79, *129*
Luke 2:14–16, *192*
Luke 2:42–7, 66n
Luke 5:1–7, *112*
Luke 6:27, *189*
Luke 7:7, *197*
Luke 18:35–43, *133*
Luke 23:31, 156n
Luke 24:2–7, 5

Mark 4:8, 79n
Mark 5:30, 212
Mark 10:46–52, *133*
Mark 13:8, *144*
Matt. 20:1–16, 59
Matt. 2:1–18, 154n
Matt. 2:19–22, *127*
Matt. 4:19, *111*
Matt. 5:43–4, *189*
Matt. 8:8, 6, *197*
Matt. 13:8, 79n
Matt. 16:19, *100*, *102*, *103*
Matt. 19:26, 9n
Matt. 19:28, 117n
Matt. 24:7, *144*
Matt. 27:3–5, 156
Matthew's Gospel, 194n

Num. 30:2, *96*

Prov. 8:15, 100n
Prov. 13:24, *92*
Ps. 7:12, *160*
Ps. 7:15, 92n
Ps. 10:14, 73n
Ps. 19:2, 121n
Ps. 19:5, 154n
Ps. 19:10, 159
Ps. 27:13, 167n
Ps. 33, 179
Ps. 36:8, *120*
Ps. 40:4, *143*

Ps. 45:2, 120n
Ps. 46:1, *73*
Ps. 67:4, 129
Ps. 68:5, 17, 78n
Ps. 76:11, 96n
Ps. 78:49, *160*
Ps. 79:3, 68n
Ps. 89:32–3, *95*
Ps. 107:25, 71n
Ps. 115:1, 128n
Ps. 116, 172
Ps. 116:16, 5, *85*
Ps. 118:19, *103*
Ps. 145:18, *100*

Rev. 3:19, *92*
Rev. 4:5, 135n
Rev. 14:4, *151*
Rev. 21:4, *167*
Ruth 1:16, *88*

I Sam. 2:6, *92*
I Sam. 13:14, *69*
II Sam. 23:15–17, 80
Song 2:1–2, 86n

Titus 2:12, 112n, 120n
Tob. 3:13, *124*

Proper Names in Text

Abbot of Ramsey, 175
Aelfthryth, 188
Agatha, 75
Aldret of York, 114
Alfred, Edward's brother, 61, 62, 72, 87, 139
Alfred, King, 59, 164
All Saints, 127
Angles, 59
archbishop of York, 97
Augustine, Saint, 110

Barking Abbey, 170, 196
Benedict, Saint, 116
Brihtwald, 68, 71
Brukeham (Brill), 131

Christmas, 154, 191
Church, 60, 70, 75, 98, 116, 148, 180
Cnut, 72, 73, 74, 75
Count Theodred, 61

Daniel, 127
Danish, 60, 61, 65, 68, 69, 71, 72, 74, 75, 92, 95, 96, 98, 104
Denmark, 76
Devil, 74, 75, 166
Dukes of Normandy, 60, 62
Dunstan, Saint, 162

Easter, 142
Edelbert, 110
Edgar, 59
Edith, 86, 155, 158, 161, 166, 167
Edmund Ironside, 61, 62, 72
Edmund's sons, 72, 73
Edward the Exile, 75
Edward the Martyr, 188
Edwin, 73
Egypt, 127
Eleanor of Aquitaine, 164

Emma, 60, 61, 65, 72, 73
Emperor of Constantinople, 144
Emperor of Rome, 75
Ephesus, 143
Epiphany, 195
Ethelred, 60, 61, 65, 71

Flanders, 175
France, 145
French of England, 56

Gerins, 194
Gilbert Crespin, 184
Gille Michel, 104, 106
Gise, 115
Glastonbury Abbey, 68
Godwin, 86, 89, 136, 139, 175
Gospel, 192
Gospels, 144
Greece, 145
Greeks, 145
Gregory, Saint, 110
Gudeve, 120
Gundulf, Saint, 182, 185

Harald Hardrada, 137, 175
Harold, 136, 143, 161, 164, 166, 175, 176
heirs of Henry II, 60, 164
Henry I, 164
Henry II, 60, 164
Hereford, 114
Herman of Winchester, 97
Holy Cross, 73, 74, 75, 133
Holy Innocents, 154
Holy Land, 150
Holy Name, 95
Holy Sepulchre, 149
Hugelin, 81, 107

Irish, 106

233

John, Saint, 148, 149, 151, 168
Joseph (NT), 85, 127
Joseph (OT), 84
Judas, 117
Judgement, 114, 144
Judith, 85

Kent, 110
King of Denmark, 92
King of France, 75

Lanfranc, 180, 182
Last Supper, 148
Latin, 56, 170, 197
Lauds, 191
Lievrich, 120
Lincoln, 129
Litany, 189, 197
London, 103, 106, 110, 187

Matilda the Empress, 164
Matilda the Good, 164
Matins, 191, 200
Maud, dressmaker, 187
Mellit, Saint, 110
Mother of God, 78, 85, 92, 127, 147, 154, 171, 182, 192
Mount Celiun, 143

Nineveh, 160
Nones, 178
Normandy, 65, 72, 159, 166
Northumberland, 175
Norway, 137, 175

Osbert, 191, 194
Oswald, Saint, 73

Paul, Saint, 110
Pentecost, 91
Peter, Saint, 69, 73, 91, 94, 95, 99, 101, 102, 106, 107, 108, 110, 111, 115, 148, 154, 168

Pope Leo, 97, 99, 100, 102, 115
Pope Nicholas, 114

Ralph of Normandy, 172
Robert, archbishop, 161
Rochester, 182, 185
Rome, 75, 97, 99, 100, 102, 104, 107, 108, 110, 114, 145, 181

Seven Psalms, 197
Seven Sleepers, 143
Sexbert, 110
Solomon, 76
Stigand, 161, 180
Susanna, 85
Syria, 145

Thames, 111
The Prophet, 95
Three Kings, 195
Tostig, 136, 175, 176

Ulstan, Saint, 180, 181, 182
Ulwine, 132, 134

Vespers, 189

Walter, 115
Wells, 115
Westminster, 91, 106, 113, 120, 133, 154, 177, 181, 188, 197
Westminster Abbey, 108, 115, 166, 169, 199
William I, 60, 133, 161, 164, 175, 180, 183
William Rufus, 164
Winchester, 68
Worcester, 104, 121

York, 175

General Index

Abbot of Ramsey, 205
Adelidis, 36, 37, 38, 39
Adgar, 22, 37
Aelfgyth, 26
Aelfgyva, 35
Aelfthryth, 6, 34, 35, 59, 158, 187
Aelfwynn, 35
Aethelgifu, vowess, 27
Agnes, abbess, 36
Ahab (OT), 160n
Aldhelm, 33
Alexander, 80
Alexander of Ashby, 50
Alexis, Saint, 7, 9
Alfred, Edward's brother, 24, 61n, 65, 138
Alfred, King, 19
Ancrene Wisse, 7
Anglo-Norman, 20, 51, 55, 129, 151n
Annalist of St Neot, 22
Annunciation, 209
Anon, viii, 4, 9, 13, 23, 26, 36, 39n, 63n, 100, 142, 146n, 156, 157, 163, 179, 179n, 187, 191, 194, 196
anonymity, 28, 40, 46, 49, 50, 170n
Anselm, 10, 24, 29, 30, 43n, 44, 158, 184
Anselm of Bury, 31, 157
ASC, viii, 19, 21, 23, 73n
Assumption, 209
Athelstan, 3, 138
Audrey, Saint, 4n, 32, 39
Augustine, 110

Barking nun, 6, 26, 32, 39, 49, 196, 205, 210, 212
Battle of Maldon, 4, 19, 20, 34n, 36, 147, 157n
Battle of Stamford Bridge, 2, 175
Bede, 31n, 32, 33, 59n, 203n
Benedictine, 26, 28, 28n, 33, 34, 100, 117n, 157, 201n, 207n

Benoit, 208n
Beowulf, 20, 155n
Bernard of Clairvaux, 56
bishop of London, 117n
Boethius, 26, 32
Boniface, 34
Brendan, 11, 80n, 121n
Brihtwald, 5, 16, 68, 203
Bruno of Toul, 100
Bury, 27

Campsey Ash Priory, 2, 49, 51
Canterbury, 38
Cardiff MS, vii, 23, 27, 28, 40n, 157n
Catherine, viii, 2, 5, 30, 37, 39, 40n, 41, 41n, 43, 49, 56, 79n, 83, 151n, 194n, 211, 212n
Cecilia, Saint, 7, 32
Chadwalader, 3
Chardri's *Vie*, 142, 144n
Chatteris, 39
Chaucer, 210n
Chrétien, 42, 147
Christina of Markyate, 7, 7n, 9, 11, 22, 31, 187
Christmas, 90, 209
Clare (Suffolk), 22
Clemence, viii, 5, 13, 28, 29, 31, 32, 33, 34, 40, 41, 44, 45, 47, 50, 66n, 76n, 78n, 124n, 170n, 194, 207, 208, 210
Cnut, 24, 65n, 72n, 210n
Corset, 209, 211
Coventry, 119
Croesus, 185n
Crucifixion, 6, 7, 80, 83, 153, 167n
Curtius, E. R., 4n, 11n, 31, 55n, 66n, 86n, 119n
Cuthburga, 34

236   Indexes

Danegeld, 59, 77, 104n
Danish, 75n, 208
Danish king, 25, 90, 91n
David (OT), 80, 106
De Spiritali Amicitia, 64
Denis Piramus, 57n
Denmark, 203, 206
Dunstan, 23, 25, 157, 164n

Eadmer, 157
East Saxons, 110
Easter, 90
Edgar, 18, 27, 34, 35, 41, 59, 157, 203, 207
Edith, 4, 5, 6, 7, 8, 9, 12, 25, 32, 43, 50, 83, 153, 156, 156n, 165, 187, 210
Edith, Saint, 34, 35
Edmund Ironside, 24, 65, 66n
Edmund's sons, 24, 72n
Edmund, King, 146
Edmund, Saint, 51, 53
Edward the Elder, 3
Edward the Martyr, 23, 26, 28, 35, 59, 157n, 158, 187
Edwin, 73n, 138
Eleanor of Aquitaine, 6, 38, 164n, 208
Eleanor, Henry III's queen, 57
Elisha, 187n
Elizabeth I, 122
Ely, 179n
Emma, 5, 6, 24, 59, 210n
Emma's family, 17, 66n
Emperor Henry II, 75n
Ephesus, 206
Epiphany, 195n
Erkenwald, 28, 33, 36n
Ermelina, 36
Esther, 25
Ethelbert of Kent, 110
Ethelburga, 28, 29, 33, 39
Ethelred, 4, 17, 23, 25, 34, 59, 64, 71n, 72n, 157, 158
Eusebius, 147

Faith, Saint, 55
fin' amur, 10n, 12, 41, 41n, 43, 45, 66n, 71n, 83, 88, 89n, 95n, 122, 123n, 146, 208
Florence of Worcester, 22
florilegia, 24, 29n, 31
Fouke le Fitz Waryn, 53n
Frideswide, Saint, 122

Gaimar, 21, 23, 65
Genealogy, viii, 17, 18, 23, 25, 59n, 72n, 90, 136, 157, 158
Geoffrey of Anjou, 164n
Geoffrey of Monmouth, 156
Geoffrey of St Alban's, 31
Gerins, 205, 207
Gilbert Crispin, 30, 184
Gille Michel, 81n, 105, 204, 210
Giso of Wells, 115n
Godiva, 6, 11, 14, 119, 136
Godwin, 8, 39, 41, 51n, 73n, 83, 87n, 119, 134, 138, 204, 211
Golden Legend, viii, 8, 23n, 59n, 86n, 146
Goscelin, 20n, 26, 28, 33, 35, 36, 110, 157n
Gregory of Tours, 24, 55
Gregory the Great, 8, 16, 52, 59n, 110
Guernes, 37, 39, 40

Harald Hardrada, 25, 136, 175
Harold, 73n, 136, 177, 204
Henry I, 25, 36, 164n, 203
Henry I of France, 76n
Henry II, 4, 17, 18, 37, 38, 46, 47, 48, 57, 59n, 64, 156, 163, 170, 203n, 208
Henry III, 57, 91n, 147
Henry of Huntingdon, 8, 18, 22
Herod, 154n
Hildelith, 28, 33, 33n
homosexuality, 8, 24, 64, 66n, 83
Horton Abbey, 26, 34
Hugelin, 80, 203
Hugh Candidus, 22

Hugh of Barking, 37

Ida, Adeliza's niece, 39
Indian myth, 180n
Irish, 106
Irish myth, 180n

Jerome, 32
Jeu Saint Nicolas, 211
Jewish people, 92n
Jocelin of Brakelond, 129
John of Canterbury, 39
John of Salisbury, 5n, 31n, 36
John, Saint, 11, 12, 42, 58n, 83, 146, 204
Joseph (OT), 83
Joseph of Arimathea, 19
Judas, 156
Judith, 41, 83, 207
Judith/Wulfruna, 35

Katherine, Saint, 32, 38, 86n
Kenilworth, 122
King Arthur, 77, 180

Lanfranc, 28n, 41, 158, 179, 185n, 207
Last Supper, 141n
Laurence of Westminster, 48, 55, 57, 79n, 146
Laurent, Françoise, 4n, 5n, 8, 9, 12, 41, 43n, 57, 57n, 70n, 78n, 85n, 91n, 111n, 146n, 152n, 211n
Lawrence, Saint, 32
Lent, 28
Liber Eliensis, 23, 179, 179n, 212n
Lievrich, 5, 51, 119, 204
Lifleda, 35
Lincoln, 129
London, 35, 110
Louis VII, 64

Macrobius, 16, 69n
Magnus of Norway, 91n
Magnus of Orkney, 7

Malchus, Saint, 8
Malory's *Morte Darthur*, 122
Marcabru, 208
Margaret of Scotland, 164n
Marie de France, 28, 39, 46, 147
Marie de Saint-Pol, 51
Marie of Ely, 28, 39
Martin, Saint, 106
Mary Becket, 37, 38, 46
Mary, abbess of Shaftesbury, 27
Marzella, Francesco, 6, 13, 14, 23, 25, 38, 77, 90, 99n, 105, 119, 136, 137n, 138, 141n, 146, 156, 166n, 170, 177n
Matilda the Good, 6, 18, 25, 36, 164n
Matilda, abbess, 27, 37, 156
Matilda, empress, 60n, 164n
Matilda, Stephen's queen, 36
Matthew Paris, 51, 179n
Maud, dressmaker, 187, 205
Maurice, monk, 120n
medieval romances, 53, 83, 179
Mellitus, 33, 103n, 204
Merlin, 142n
Merlin, 179
Michael, Saint, 105
Michal (OT), 106
modesty, 39, 44, 46, 50, 55, 56, 163
Mount Sinai, 45
Muriel of Wilton, 36

Norman Conquest, 20, 32, 33, 35, 145n, 154n, 177
Norman dukes, 17, 24, 76n
Normandy, 8, 65, 72n
Nunnaminster, 31

Of Arthour and of Merlin, 11n
Old Norse, 53n
Orderic Vitalis, 8, 21, 31n
Original Sin, 83
Osbern, 157, 157n, 158, 191n

Osbert, viii, 4, 10, 22, 26, 31, 32, 37, 38, 120, 157, 179, 179n, 187, 191, 194, 196, 205
Osbert, viii, 8, 13, 15n, 18, 23, 28, 33n, 38, 65, 100, 102, 110, 129, 131, 137n, 142n, 146, 157, 163, 168n, 179n, 181n, 203, 211
Osbert's nieces, 39
Osith, Saint, 9
Oswald, 73n
Ovid, 32
Owst, G. R., 41n, 146n, 156n

Paul, Saint, 94n, 187n
Pentecost, 5, 90, 210
personification, 97, 123, 127, 148, 153
Peter, Saint, 5, 11, 42, 45, 83, 94n, 100n, 102, 104n, 203, 204, 210
Philip Augustus, 64
Philip Sidney, 80
Plato, 44
Pool of Siloam, 6
Pope Adrian IV, 7n
Pope Alexander III, 4
Pope Benedict X, 114
Pope Innocent, 172
Pope Leo, 20, 41, 94n, 99n, 102, 102n, 203
Pope Nicholas, 5, 100, 114, 119, 204
Prose Brut, 129n, 132n
Prose *Vie*, 3, 7, 50, 105, 199
proverbs, viii, 49, 60n, 62n, 63n, 72n, 74n, 87n, 88n, 123n, 139n, 147n, 152n
Pseudo-Seneca, 32

Ralph the Norman, 172, 205, 210
Ramsbury, 68n
Ranulf Flambard, 8
Resurrection, 33, 185n
Richard I, 64
Richard of Cirencester, 77n
River Thames, 32

Robert de Boron, 19, 179
Robert, archbishop, 156
Roger of Wendover, 119
Rome, 5, 210

Sebert of Essex, 110
Seven Sleepers, 16, 134, 204
Shaftesbury, 23, 31
Shakespeare's *Macbeth*, 122
Simeon of Durham, 105
Simon of Walsingham, 55
Sir Gawain and the Green Knight, 11
Solomon, 15, 18, 76n, 78n
Spillecorn, 132n
St Alban's, 8
St Paul's, 110
Stephen, 36, 60n
Stephen of Hungary, 72n
Stephen, Saint, 10, 133n
Stigand, 114, 156, 179, 205
Susanna, 83
Swedish king, 72n
Sybil, 44
Syria, 204

Tennyson, 119
Theobald, archbishop, 37
Thomas Becket, 21, 38, 40, 42, 51, 179n
Thomas of Kent, 21
Thorney Island, 110n
Three Kings, 146
Tortgith, 33
Tostig, 25, 136, 175, 204
Transfiguration, 6
Tristan, 41n, 43, 56, 152n
Turgot of Durham, 18

Ulstan, 2, 10, 18, 53n, 179, 185n

Vie de Saint Clement, 24, 43n
Vikings, 34
Virgil, 32
Vision of Leofric, 120

Volsunga Saga, 53n, 180n

Wace's *Brut*, 3, 4, 11
Wace's *Rou*, 18, 138n
Waldef, 21
Walter Daniel, 22
Walter of Hereford, 115n
Warwick, 97n
Westminster, 13, 14, 32, 100, 103n, 147n, 189n
Westminster Abbey, 117n, 119, 153n, 209, 210
White Ship, 8
William I, 17, 18, 35, 60n, 166n, 179
William of Malmesbury, 3n, 4, 9, 18, 21, 22, 23, 25, 28, 31n, 34, 35, 60n, 65, 90n, 110n, 122, 131, 138, 144n, 156n, 157, 157n, 158, 163, 179, 179n
William of Palerne, 11
William Rufus, 8
William the Atheling, 8, 156
Wilton, 31, 33n
Winchester, 68n, 74n
Wlsino the hermit, 102
Worcester, 121n
Wulfhild, Ethelred's daughter, 35
Wulfhilda, 27, 28, 34
Wulfric of Haselbury, 51n
Wulfstan, archbishop, 179, 179n

Young King, 38